When Good Drugs
Go Bad

Dan Malleck

When Good Drugs Go Bad: Opium, Medicine, and the Origins of Canada's Drug Laws

UBCPress · Vancouver · Toronto

23 22 21 20 19 18 17 16 15   5 4 3 2 1

Printed in Canada on FSC-certified ancient-forest-free paper
(100% post-consumer recycled) that is processed chlorine- and acid-free.

Library and Archives Canada Cataloguing in Publication

Malleck, Dan, author
    When good drugs go bad : opium, medicine, and the origins of Canada's
drug laws / Dan Malleck.

Includes bibliographical references and index.
Issued in print and electronic formats.
ISBN 978-0-7748-2919-9 (bound). – ISBN 978-0-7748-2920-5 (pbk)
ISBN 978-0-7748-2921-2 (pdf). – ISBN 978-0-7748-2922-9 (epub)

    1. Narcotic laws – Canada – History. 2. Opium abuse – Law and legislation –
Canada – History. 3. Drugs – Law and legislation – Canada – History. 4. Drug
addiction – Social aspects – Canada – History. 5. Drug addiction – Economic aspects
– Canada – History. 6. Drug control – Canada – History. 7. Medicine – Canada –
History. I. Title.

| KE3720.M34 2015 | 345.71'0277 | C2015-903303-9 |
| KF3890.M34 2015 | | C2015-903304-7 |

Canadä

UBC Press gratefully acknowledges the financial support for our publishing program of the Government of Canada (through the Canada Book Fund), the Canada Council for the Arts, and the British Columbia Arts Council.

This book has been published with the help of a grant from the Canadian Federation for the Humanities and Social Sciences, through the Awards to Scholarly Publications Program, using funds provided by the Social Sciences and Humanities Research Council of Canada.

Page 1 image: Poppy NLM, a012406, courtesy of the National Library of Medicine

UBC Press
The University of British Columbia
2029 West Mall
Vancouver, BC V6T 1Z2
www.ubcpress.ca

For Jack Blocker and Jackie Duffin
Because they got me hooked

Contents

Tables and Figures

Acknowledgments

This book is the product of two distinct phases of research. The core of this project was my doctoral project completed in 1998. The acknowledgments in that document still stand. Yet since completing that work, I have undertaken further new research, and it has led to a new set of obligations.

First, essential to this project were the many archivists and librarians who went out of their way to help me dig up a range of material. To all new researchers: remember that archivists and librarians are your project's best friends. They often know the material better than you, and normally they will do what they can to help you access it. That even applies to the archivists whose job is to manage the various Access to Information restrictions across the country, as onerous as such procedures may be. Even in the jurisdiction (that shall remain unnamed) where the rules were so asinine and bloody minded that I never did see the material I wanted, the archivists tried their best to help me out. Never underestimate the knowledge and power of an archivist or librarian in getting you to the material you need. Since I cannot name everyone who helped me, the following paragraph is my general group hug and thank you.

Thanks, then, to archivists and librarians at the Nova Scotia Provincial Archives; New Brunswick Archives; Library and Archives Canada (who do their best under the current counterproductive political environment); Archives of Ontario; University of Guelph Special Collections and Rare Book Room; Archives of Manitoba; Saskatchewan Archives Board (both Saskatoon and Regina branches); Esplanade Archives in Medicine Hat; Glenbow Archives (Calgary); Archives of Alberta; British Columbia Archives; University of British Columbia Rare Books and Special Collections; and a special thanks to whomever was wise enough to think that it would be a good idea to retain so many provincial government documents in the basement of the University of Toronto's Robarts Library; and to Sherry Smugler, who, with good nature and exceptional accommodation, let me into the stacks to dig through them.

Although publishers may not like me saying so, I also must offer my thanks to those unnamed heroes who digitized so many government documents, newspapers, and other official records. Although digitization tends to favour the popular over the essential, being able to read legislative records from my home made more efficient the research trips to view the essential but obscure records in the archives listed above.

Professional connections, collegial interactions, and informal discussions are fundamental to scholarly knowledge creation. I had stimulating discussions with a range of academic colleagues who helped me shape my ideas, including, in no reasonable order, James Nicholls, James Kneale, Angela McShane, James Mills, Tricia Barton, Alex Mold, Virginia Berridge, Deb Toner, David Herzberg, David Courtwright, Emily Barton, Renee Lafferty, and Cheryl Krasnick Warsh. I'm honoured to be able to call them colleagues and friends.

Ideas need places to sleep and dream, so I thank the friends and colleagues who facilitated my travel, both by boarding me and providing much-needed distraction at times. The following people put me up and put up with me: Steve Gamble and Dee Rothwell (and Annika and Fisher); Melissa Pitts; and Jayelle and Jon.

I cannot say enough good things about the staff at UBC Press. As I explained to them after they converted my first book: they make me look good. Darcy Cullen has done heroic service encouraging an insecure historian that his work is worth reading, and Megan Brand put up with more last-minute changes and general disarray of the poorly organized than should be necessary. Melissa Pitts, director and awesome friend, encouraged and supported me through many visits. Copyeditors and proofreaders made sure these word usements are clarificatorized. It's all just the service of a good press, and UBCP is the best. Even with the skunk smell.

My research assistant Cara Pedersen has been especially helpful in pouring over many digital texts and old-school microfilms. The day we went to Guelph and she got to crack open a 200-year-old recipe book and expressed her thrill that this was "real research" was the day that I knew she was a true history geek and valuable research assistant. She has never proved me wrong.

It seems fitting in a book about drugs, which were often sought for palliatives and distractions, to acknowledge my own distractions and palliatives, and the people who facilitated them. For me this means two groups: those who provided me with good beer, (thank you Merchant Ale House and craft brewers everywhere); and those who got me under the water, where you can't think about the next chapter when you're looking for octopi and nudibranchs, navigating around anemones, hovering over a wreck, or equalizing. Most notably, Jaia, Tess, and Ray provided essential aquatic distraction.

I also offer a deep thanks and sincere apologies to YDM, who, I have learned, was smarter than I thought.

My thanks also to my family. They put up with my absences and let me get on with researching and writing, generally with few complaints (at least not expressed to me).

I am grateful for the financial support of the Social Science and Humanities Research Council, which permitted the extended research trips across the country, to expand and deepen the scope of this project, and hire a great research assistant. SSHRC's granting of the funds immediately before beginning a research leave was impeccable timing; kudos to them.

Parts of several chapters were included in earlier published articles, although not in the exact same form found here. I thank the editors of *Medical History* and the *Canadian Bulletin of Medical History/Bulletin Canadien d'histore de la médecine* for permission to reproduce this material.

This book is dedicated to two people who set me on this intoxicating path. Jack Blocker was my master's supervisor and showed me the world of alcohol regulation and prohibition, which established the foundation for investigating the legal management and contested status of substances more broadly. Jackie Duffin supervised my doctorate and fuelled my interest in the history of medicine. She remains a mentor and exemplar of how to do medical history well, and also how to be an inspiring teacher. I try to channel their examples of scholarly excellence and personal decency every day. I hope they are not disappointed.

All these folks supported, encouraged, or provided necessary distraction from this work, so they can be credited for its completion. With only one named author on this book, I must take responsibility for any errors. Although in the era of crowdsourcing, I really should be able to find someone else to blame.

When Good Drugs
Go Bad

Introduction:
Its Baneful Influences

Opium is awesome. A versatile medicine, it can treat the symptoms of a variety of ailments and ease the pain caused by many others. It is especially useful for dealing with illnesses of urbanization, such as dysentery, cholera, and tuberculosis – conditions that result in the excessive expulsion of bodily fluids. As a substance that dries up pulmonary secretions and slows gastro-intestinal action, it significantly reduces the vomiting, diarrhea, coughing, and other actions related to conditions caused by polluted water, dirty air, and substandard food storage. Moreover, as a pain reliever, it has few substitutes. It is no surprise that the pain killers of today are modern opiates and that they continue to be overprescribed and misused.

Opium is awe-inspiring. Taken alone or combined with alcohol, opium is a hallucinogenic that fuelled much of the intense imagery of early-nineteenth-century Romantic poetry and fiction. Samuel Taylor Coleridge's *Kubla Kahn* is said to have been the result of an opium-inspired dream; *Frankenstein* was written after a hallucinatory trip that Mary Shelley experienced while visiting the chalet of opiated bon vivant Lord Byron. And of course let us not forget the *Confessions of an English Opium Eater*, written by Romantic author Thomas De Quincey. Although ostensibly offered as a cautionary tale, it did not hold back on indulgent reminders of how lush and complex opium dreams could be, and it was criticized, appropriately enough, for *romanticizing* recreational opium consumption. In a literary style that was heavy in intricate imagery, Romanticism was an opiated wonderland.

Opium is awful. De Quincey was not the only sufferer to detail the terrible effects of prolonged exposure to, and numerous attempts to break the habit of using, opium. The nineteenth-century popular press is full of such images, some more celebratory than others. One of the books that inspired this research was Oscar Wilde's *The Picture of Dorian Gray*, which begins with a character smoking an opium-laced cigarette as an image of genteel excess and devolves (spoiler alert) into Dorian haunting the opium dens of London amid scenes of debauchery and decline. By the end of the century, the white person in Chinese opium dens of Chinatowns in London, Vancouver, and San Francisco was a familiar, and frightening, representation of the West in decline and of the threats that it faced from within and beyond its borders. But the awfulness extends well beyond the trope of the white person lured by the exotic excesses of the Chinese man. The addicted middle-class woman, hooked by medical treatment (iatrogenic addiction), although a less prominent image of literary conceit and social danger, was an equally familiar figure in the Victorian world and likely more personally resonant among polite society.

These three sides of opium converged at the beginning of the twentieth century to drive the impetus for policy change that, to this day, has significantly affected the lives of citizens. They combined, intertwined, and constructed discourses constraining the idea of opiate consumption. In turn, embedded within these discourses, was the acknowledgment that such a complex, powerful, and dangerous substance needed careful management. A valuable but dangerous medicine required prescription and distribution by responsible health professionals; a substance of indulgence and fantasy in a society increasingly fixated on self-control, productivity, and abstemiousness required strict containment; and a dangerous habit-forming drug required judicious oversight, government intervention, and rigorous enforcement. In an era when ideas of nation were intertwined with concerns about the character and behaviour of the citizenry, these were powerful forces.

The stories of the development of anti-opium legislation have been told for many Western countries, and the histories of Great Britain and the United States have considerable bearing on what happened in Canada. Historians including Virginia Berridge, Terry Parssinen, Geoffrey Harding, and Louise Foxcroft have traced the social, cultural, and legal development and impact of opium legislation in Britain.[1] There, concerns about domestic opium consumption were combined with discussions of the national disgrace of Britain forcing the opium trade on China and the effects that such self-interested imperialism had on Asia in general.[2] For the United States, David Musto, David Courtwright, Wayne Morgan, Timothy Hickman, and Caroline Acker have chronicled similar stories, showing how the complex development of urban America, the industrial needs of the state, the rising medical and reformist perspectives, and a crisis of modernity drove the creation of restrictive drug policy.[3]

There has been no similarly detailed treatment of the origins of Canada's drug prohibition. Canada's history has often been influenced by the legislative and social movements of its continental neighbour and its imperial motherland. As we will see, these countries had some influence over components of Canada's drug policies, although Canada's path was unique in many ways. With few exceptions, research on Canada's drug laws has concentrated on the impact of drug legislation, not on its creation. As a result, the first federal law, the Opium Act of 1908, which was passed before similar legislation in the United States and Great Britain, has been interpreted not only as the foundation of Canada's drug laws but also, since it came on the heels of anti-Asian riots in Vancouver, as a product of racism instead of part of a long process of changing ideas about what we might today call recreational drug use. The reason for such close association with racism is understandable. As a consequence of the damages caused by those riots, Deputy Minister of Labour William Lyon Mackenzie King was dispatched to Vancouver on a one-man Royal Commission to assess damage and allocate reparations payments. While there, he was encouraged by several influential local residents to investigate and report on what he saw as a troubling opium industry in that city. In his Royal Commission report, he observed that "its baneful influences are too well known to require comment." He followed this report with a separate, detailed discussion of what he saw as the need to suppress opium. Notwithstanding the fact that most of the legislators to whom King's report was written likely had first-hand experience with opium as a useful but habit-forming medical substance, and probably had at least one addicted acquaintance (as did King), historians of Canada's drug laws have generally viewed these "baneful influences" as referring to Chinese opium smoking.[4] Three years later, with this precedent for federal drug prohibition established, the government expanded the legislation into the Opium and Drug Act of 1911, including morphine and cocaine alongside opium in an unholy trinity of dangerous substances. The impetus for this legislation, so King told Parliament, was pressure by police chiefs in Montreal and Vancouver and by several moral-reform agencies, who all insisted that more needed to be done to control the possession of opium, morphine, and cocaine, drugs that continued to be associated with opium dens and Chinatowns.

For the most part, King's report and the 1908 legislation have served as a preface to studies of the impact of the legislation. In arguments showing how the creation of a new class of lawbreakers (i.e., addicts) was an example of the labelling approach to criminology or tension between materialist and functionalist impressions of Canada's drug-policy formation, well-meaning sociologists and criminologists did not see a need to dissect the creation of the laws. Historian Catherine Carstairs's important study of what happened to addicts when subjected to the power of the state, a sensitive and detailed examination of the impact of criminalization and the cultures that it engendered, did not need to explore the complexity of law creation, although her popular article on the "racist origin" of Canada's drug laws reproduced the tantalizing but distorted excesses of the narrow historical view.[5] As a result, most of these histories assert the racism underpinning the legislation and then move forward. The few studies that have touched on the precursors to 1908 have been generally short and similarly focused on the post-1908 period.[6] None of this is intended as a criticism of these scholars. Their interest was in the results of criminalization, their intention was not to study the origins of the legislation, and, to be fair, they did not have histories of the pre-1908 story on which to draw. Even P.J. Giffen, Shirley Endicott, and Sylvia Lambert's insightful *Panic and Indifference,* which provides a detailed critique of the simplifications of earlier histories, is likewise focused more on the consequences of the laws than on their multifactorial origins.[7]

This historiographical gap is problematic not only because it is important to get the history right but also because it has led to distorted statements in policy formation. Attacks on our current drug laws as being "racist," intended as laments of misguided legislation, lack the sophisticated appreciation of the social and cultural context in which legislation was formed.[8] Racism may have framed some discussions, but as Giffen, Endicott, and Lambert note, King heard from a number of prominent Chinese residents of BC who wanted the government to take action on opium use.[9] If one wants to use history to argue that a law should be changed, the history should be presented with its many nuances. Law formation is a complex social process, normally involving the emergence of some understanding about the problem that exists and the way to fix it. Simple allusions to racism do not help us to understand the origins of these laws or to see a way forward if we want to modify them. We should be asking questions like: What was it that made such restriction even possible in an era when government control of trade was a touchy subject and when laissez-faire proclamations continued to have ideological weight? Is it enough to say that the legislation should be discarded because the roots were racist? Of course not. When history is distorted, credibility is diminished.

We live in a complex society, as did our Victorian forebears. It is not enough to conclude that legislators could be swayed by arguments that opium was bad because the Chinese used it. Was King so influential that his little report changed everybody's mind? This is doubtful. Anti-Chinese sentiment, while undeniably a feature of the Victorian Canadian psyche, was not the only realm of understanding in which opium existed. Indeed, the real home of opium in Victorian Canada was the Victorian Canadian home. We need to look no further than the Dominion House of Commons and at no other time than the same session in which the Opium Act was passed into law. A week before debating and passing that legislation, the Canadian Parliament passed the Proprietary or Patent Medicine Act, legislation that placed new restrictions on prepackaged proprietary medicines. The new law, the outcome of years of debate and lobbying by the medical and pharmaceutical professions, required precise labelling of the ingredients of alcohol, opiates, and cocaine. The Proprietary or Patent Medicine Act passed with minimal debate, although more than the first Opium Act. The baneful influences of proprietary medicines were also well known.

Notable in these two pieces of 1908 legislation are the assumptions and absences. In King's report to Parliament, he urged "the enactment of such measures as will render impossible, save in so far as may be necessary for medicinal purposes, the continuance of such an industry within the confines of the Dominion."[10] The legislation's title specified that the prohibition was on the "Importation, Manufacture and Sale of Opium for Other than Medicinal Purposes." In other words, medical professionals retained the power to control the use of opiates. This is what Paul Starr, channelling Max Weber, calls *social authority*, which he describes as "the control of action through the giving of commands" or, in this case, the writing and filling of prescriptions.[11] With this power came the definition of what proper and improper use meant. This, again quoting Starr, was Weber's *cultural authority*, or "the construction of reality through definitions of fact and value."[12] The legislation inscribed the social authority of physicians in controlling access to opiates, and it included them in the broader process of constructing meanings of opium use. This latter process, although suggesting a degree of cultural authority in defining the "fact" of the dangers of certain drugs and suggesting certain "values" associated with their use, was not absolute: the law gave the authority to prescribe and dispense, but it also constrained the actions of physicians by forcing them, and their pharmacist colleagues, to submit to strict processes for distributing narcotics. It still does.

Although they may seem obvious today, with medical authority proclaiming confidently on everything from somatic illness to gambling addiction, the reasons for the medical exemption are worth considering in more depth. After all, the Opium Act tacitly recognized medical definitions as legitimate ones but then constrained medical authority in the Proprietary or Patent Medicine Act. It seems more appropriate to consider the two pieces of legislation to be complementary. Indeed, they were the outcome of social agitation that redefined various channels of authority and constructed a new discourse of proper and improper social behaviour. For example, this session of Parliament also saw the passing of a law that prohibited the sale of cigarettes to minors, an ongoing issue for the temperance movement. Much of this agitation manifested both secular and religious notions of the modern state. Evangelical reformers, known for their agitation for alcohol prohibition more than drug prohibition, as well as Sunday-closing laws, anti-gambling legislation, school reform, and other progressive policies, sought to elevate the nation to a (higher) state of grace. Secular reformers often joined their evangelical colleagues, seeing the role of the state in such areas as public health and social welfare as crucial to the nation's stability and future.

I see this broad discourse of national welfare, whether secular or religious, moral or healthful, as speaking to the idea of *national integrity*. The term holds a convenient double entendre: on the one hand, "integrity" suggests strength and stability, important goals for the young nation; on the other hand, it implies something fundamental or crucial, those aspects of a nation that are *integral* to its success. Perhaps it holds a triple entendre, since "integrity" may describe an individual's character, and the idea of moral strength, or strength of character, informed discussions about the future of the country. As we will see, professionals like physicians manifested this triumphalist discourse when defining their role in the country's future. They argued that the integrity of the profession would help to protect and guide the integrity of the nation. So did temperance reformers, possibly the most vocal of those seeking progressive social change. They advocated the restriction or prohibition of alcohol as a key step toward social elevation, be this elevation part of a postmillennialist construction of the Kingdom of God on Earth or, less aspirational but no less inspirational, part of an improved society for all. The control of access to medications, including the strict definition of proper and improper use of such substances, was but one part of a broader vision for the future of Canada and, really, the Western world.

The idea of "national integrity" raises a second question: What do I mean by "national"? Simply put, "nation" meant different things to different people. Canadians who expressed a sense of the nation deployed an idea that was based on their own sense of the essential characteristics of that nation. This is the notion of "imagined communities" discussed by Benedict Anderson.[13] People had their individual idea of what their community was, and in a large, geographically dispersed nation, the only way to experience this national community was to imagine it. So arguments in which we find allusions to a sense of national integrity may not always agree. They may contradict each other, or at least work at cross-purposes. For example, a moral reformer who thought that all patent medicines containing opiates needed to be restricted because they were debilitating to good, middle-class women might have a heated argument with a pharmaceutical manufacturer who felt that his remedies were helping many people and that constraints on the free market were a national disgrace. The former argued from a sense of nation based on ideas of health and (gendered) vitality, whereas the latter saw a strong nation as one where industry was allowed to be economically vital. We will see many contrasting views of nation, and of how to ensure that its integrity remained intact, throughout the course of this study.

There were common elements of nation along with many nuances. For many influential Canadians, their nation was white, European, and (for English Canadians) Anglo-Saxon, or Anglo-Celtic. So even when the editor of the *Halifax Morning Chronicle* read the results of the Royal Commission on Chinese Immigration and decided that Chinese people were not such bad additions to the national economy, he did not go so far as to consider Chinese people to be suitable Canadians.[14] They were not the people who fitted into the vision of nation held by most white Canadians. But beyond basic ethnic categories, different communities viewed the nation differently. Evangelical Protestants had an idea of national values and culture that included a certain way of behaving and acting in order to build the Kingdom of God on Earth. Major political reformers, including William Lyon Mackenzie King, drew inspiration and motivation from this vision.[15] Others saw the nation differently and elucidated a discourse of nation that drew on their own values and ideas about the best way to construct, physically, economically, and morally, the young nation of Canada.

Such visions informed governance. Government is not simply the operation of a political class on the people, writing laws, and enforcing them. It is a process that begins and ends with value formation. Philip Corrigan and Derek Sayer call this "moral regulation," a "project of normalizing, rendering natural, taken for granted, in a word 'obvious,' what are in fact ontological and epistemological premises of a particular and historical form of social order."[16] In this process, some behaviour is normalized, and other behaviour is rendered *ab*normal. Moral regulation is partly a form of governance, and the state's ability to manage certain challenges to the continuance of the state by encouraging certain forms of behaviour has been described cleverly by Michel Foucault as governmentality – the "conduct of conduct." This is the way that governing bodies view and affect the behaviour of citizens. The structure of this vision of the activities of the people is more simple and mercurial than it may appear. It is what Mitchell Dean has labelled the "field of visibility" of government, which changes depending on the priorities and values of the state regulatory apparatus.[17] I characterize it as akin to a spotlight in the darkness. A field of visibility is the way we understand what is "seen" during the construction and operation of law. Like a spotlight, all within the light's glow is illuminated, possibly even distorted, in sharp relief. But all outside of the beam remains unseen. In the construction of drug laws, the field of visibility shifted several times, as certain behaviours were interpreted differently depending on *who* viewed them.

This "who" is, of course, key. Different social and political groups had different ways of defining and interpreting behaviour. Governing bodies – not just state governments but also regulatory bodies, colleges of medicine or pharmacy, and other social actors, including temperance and religious groups – took on an overseer role, saw social issues illuminated by their own specific spotlights, and asserted an esoteric authority over them. They sought to influence the way that citizens perceived their own physical behaviour. This is an example of Foucault's biopolitics, the notion that government's role includes the regulation of life and thereby shapes our understanding of ourselves as embodied beings, people whose bodies are the conduit through which we act in society. This may seem self-evident, but what is important here is to consider how various forms of governance shaped ideas of proper personal behaviour, how those ideas changed as different authorities' views became prominent, and how those views of self and of others affected the definition of proper and improper use of drugs. For groups like pharmacists and physicians, these definitions were not just about personal consumption of drugs, they were also about proper distribution of them. And all of these ideas were shaped within a national framework.

Although governmentality is normally used to describe the work of states themselves, it can help us to understand the work of the governments of various professions, the licensing bodies. For example, associations that gained the legal right to oversee and license their members, such as colleges of physicians and pharmaceutical associations, deployed a different type of governmentality because the conduct that they were conducting was not uniform. The responsibility of these agencies was to encourage their members to act properly within their scope of practice while also stopping individuals from outside the profession from acting as professionals. Their enabling legislation provided them with the legal right to undertake certain activities that other people could not, so these professional governments had a responsibility to the state to stop nonmembers from doing these things. Consequently, pharmacists spent a lot of time making sure that only licensed pharmacists were dispensing medicines, and physicians made sure that only licensed physicians were providing medical advice. In these activities, we see other aspects of governmentality as discussed by Dean. Not only did it imply a certain way of seeing behaviours (i.e., field of visibility), but it was also involved in the "formation of identities" and deployed certain forms of truth.[18] So the work of professional regulatory bodies involved a certain way of viewing certain behaviours that were related to a certain type of technical prowess, while simultaneously establishing and defending the unique professional identity of the profession. We see these elements reproduced in the discussions by pharmacists and physicians, by their own regulatory bodies, by their confreres across professional lines, and by governments. Since physicians were allowed to dispense medicines and pharmacists were consulted by customers on the best remedy for various symptoms, the overlap and conflict between these two professions, as they attempted to conduct the conduct of their professional brethren and those outside of the profession, often involved tense definitions of proper professional behaviour.

The drive for professionalization did not operate in a cultural vacuum, and the rhetoric connecting the professionalization project to other social concerns was itself contextualized and articulated through other symbolic meanings. In the discussions over the consumption of habit-forming drugs, for example, the late-century debates drew on discussions that had been going on for decades about the problem of the habitual consumption of alcoholic beverages. The temperance movement and medical debates about the impact of alcohol on the body provided a framework with which physicians could build, or at least against which they could test, their ideas about the habitual consumption of other drugs. As we will see, these ideas were intertwined but never really connected. Medical concern about habituation created a cohort of interested practitioners, leading to the development of associations interested in dealing medically with the problems of substance habituation. But the relationship between ideas of drug use and alcohol consumption was never entirely comfortable; drugs were medicines first, but alcohol, although often used medicinally, had a much more expansive social and cultural existence. Consequently, when we look at ideas of drug habituation, we need to examine them in relationship to ideas of the alcohol habit but remember that they were different, notwithstanding current debates about whether alcohol is simply "another drug."[19]

The turn of the century in Canada was a time of transformation – with expanding urbanization, industrialization, and immigration – and therefore a time of hand-wringing over the nation's future in the face of such changes. This book seeks to add to our understanding of this period, while contextualizing the development of drug laws within it. In *The Age of Light, Soap and Water*, Mariana Valverde notes that most historians think that their period of investigation is transitional and important but that her book's period, the 1880s to the 1920s, was especially significant to Canada.[20] I concur in both sentiments. The turn of the century was a time when reform movements, politicians, industrialists, labour unions, and other influential voices, progressive or not, were all spending a tremendous deal of energy, spilling a lot of ink, and pulping a lot of trees to push for significant reforms. Many of these looked to a better future, be it the city on the hill, a new Jerusalem, or just simply keeping the country from sliding headlong into moral disaster. These varieties of perceptions of what Canada should be included eugenic concerns over the physical integrity of the citizenry, racial concerns about outsiders dragging down the character of the nation, progressive concerns about the need for better laws to elevate the poor and disenfranchised, and political concerns about Canada's place in the world.[21] This was, after all, the era during which, at an inaugural meeting of the Canadian Club, Sir Wilfrid Laurier made the oft-misquoted prediction that the twentieth century belonged to Canada: "I think we can claim that it is Canada that shall fill the twentieth century."[22] He was responding to a toast made by one Mr. W.L.M. King, first vice president of the club, who spoke of "the unselfish ability and commanding integrity heretofore shown by Canada."

This book places the emergence of the 1908 legislation in that broader framework of change, and roots it in the discourse of national integrity. It does not view 1908 as the beginning of the story but as a significant moment of transition. It looks at how broad nineteenth-century changes drove twentieth-century policy. These discursive shifts were complex, involving changing perceptions of the body and its processes; medical innovation; the development of a modern, progressive state; the place of the individual body within the body of the state; and, conversely, the place of the state in managing the body of the individual. Necessarily, the book takes a long view, considering events and contexts stretching back at least to the beginning of the nineteenth century in order to build a picture of how things converged in 1908. It follows the course of several streams of change: the emergence of various health professions and the authority that they wielded; the growth of social reform movements, most notably temperance; epistemological shifts in the medical and social perception of the habitual use of mind-altering substances; the development and problematization of new drugs such as cocaine and heroin; international influences, including the opium trade, on the national economy and politics; and the idea that the problems presented by habitual and nonmedical drug use required the various levels of government to take a stronger role in conducting the lives of individuals. Following these streams as they grew, sometimes into raging torrents of rhetoric and hyperbole, we will see how ideas about drugs emerged and changed over the course of the nineteenth century and then converged in the first decade of the twentieth century to form raging rapids of prohibitory legislation – all of this springing from the baneful influences of opium, that awesome, awe-inspiring, and awful substance.

1
Medicating Canada before Regulation

Prior to the last quarter of the nineteenth century, most people living in Canada had access to what may be called a virtually open medical marketplace. They could choose from a variety of types of practitioners to consult when ill and had nearly unregulated access to medications. A druggist or merchant might stock any number of dangerous substances that could be used medically, including opium, strychnine, and arsenic. A number of familiar remedies might also be available, such as Dover's Powder, a cough and fever compound of ipecacuanha and opium that induced sweating and reduced coughs; and paregoric, a mixture of opium, alcohol, and camphor, which was often used as an anti-diarrheal medicine.[1]

However familiar mainstream medications were to everyday people, access to them depended on access to the providers of such products. In a country as broad and rural as Canada, the availability of formally trained health professionals and vendors of exotic remedies was limited. Opium came from the Middle East and Asia. Its harvest was (and remains) time-consuming and people-intensive. In the traditional method of harvesting opium, the poppy head was scored with a small knife, the juice that oozed out of it dried on the bulb, and the resulting black gummy substance was scraped off by hand. This gum was combined into balls, often wrapped in leaves, and dried in warehouses before being transported. Since the best opium poppies grew in remote hilly regions of areas like modern-day Pakistan, India, Afghanistan, and Turkey, the opium had to make a long journey to Canadian markets. Before the middle of the century, professionally trained doctors, although less exotic and less frequently scored by knives, came from outside of the country, too. As a result, many people relied on the tried and true, remedies handed down through generations, advice from local elders, and what literature the literate could access.

The limited access to opiates challenges a key assumption about the place of opium in the Canadian family drug cabinet prior to the advent of restrictive pharmacy legislation. Although it may seem reasonable to assume that, before opiates were placed under the control of pharmacists they were a normal part of everyday life, we should ask how accurate such an assumption is. Many histories discussing drug policy contain an either implicit or explicit observation that opiates and other soon-to-be-restricted drugs were the only options people had for effective self-medication.[2] This idea is based on the assumption that opium was the preferred treatment for coughs, diarrhea, general pain, and other common ailments, and that the regulation of pharmaceuticals further limited treatment choices. Yet this conclusion does not necessarily follow. Even though opiates were generally not restricted before the enactment of pharmacy legislation, their expense, their potency, and the transportation networks needed to get them to the local market may have precluded their general use. When talking about the changing perceptions of opium, then, it is important to understand the place of opiates in everyday home medicine in Canada.[3] We can then understand the context from which emerged the new idea that certain problematic drugs needed to be controlled.

Undoubtedly, nineteenth-century Canadians used opium. Official documents show us that its importation followed average trends for imports from the last quarter of the nineteenth century. The Department of Trade and Navigation's import records, reproduced annually in the *Sessional Papers of the Dominion of Canada,* list the quantity and value of imports of medicinal opium, morphine, and later, smoked opium. Table 1 provides the quantities of opium (combining powdered and crude opium) and morphine that were imported "for home consumption,"[4] along with their value. Prior to 1875, imports of opium were recorded only as "packages," so the table lists only values until 1875, when amounts were included as pounds of import. For basic comparative purposes, Figure 1 charts the quantity and value of imports, with the left y-axis listing pounds of opium and the right y-axis indicating ounces of morphine. Since the value of opium generally did not vary significantly during this period, we can compare the value of opium imports to the value of all imports to Canada (Figure 2).[5] Such a comparison indicates that, generally, the value of opium imports followed roughly those of all imports until the sharp rise in opium imports in the early part of the 1890s, which was followed by a rapid and prolonged decline. From 1908 to 1912, when federal legislation began to restrict the trade and manufacture of opium, imports of opium dropped steadily.

The increase in imports during the 1880s and 1890s contrasts with a relatively steady growth in per capita imports, but it reflects not domestic policy but the international context. The period from the mid-1880s to the mid-1890s roughly coincides with a period of high American duties on smoked opium.[6] Several states placed high taxes on opium at this time, and the refining of opium in the United States was subject to an excise tax of

Table 1

Imports of opium and morphine into Canada, 1867–1912

Year	Opium		Morphine	
	Pounds	Value ($)	Ounces	Value ($)
1867		4,252		
1868		11,317		
1869		4,732		
1870		9,196		
1871		6,873		
1872		5,856		
1873		15,590		
1874		11,737		
1875		37,440		
1876	23,457	113,397		
1877	455	2,170		
1878	17,523	82,011		
1879	29,379	117,306		
1880	17,210	83,372	276	488
1881	22,962	96,027	1,007	2,440
1882	31,752	112,724	825	1,525
1883	29,229	101,359	358	597
1884	63,910	213,692	321	454
1885	85,012	281,860	481	1,027
1886	75,460	249,054	637	694
1887	97,325	299,663	69	64
1888	107,018	319,572	227	328
1889	69,636	196,100	1,290	1,507
1890	129,581	325,903	5,152	6,703
1891	156,841	372,676	3,821	5,264
1892	146,625	384,705	4,288	3,996
1893	155,151	430,366	5,083	4,359
1894	87,050	211,103	2,267	2,587
1895	32,755	85,046	3,986	4,223
1896	53,275	139,418	5,722	5,913
1897	57,285	149,138	1,649	2,061
1898	60,060	163,526	3,552	3,743
1899	65,789	195,153	2,405	2,695
1900	59,573	196,647	1,482	1,898
1901	85,675	391,326	3,702	4,600
1902	73,026	250,490	3,071	3,655
1903	64,742	196,805	10,200	10,680
1904	50,883	195,350	5,414	6,420
1905	45,750	185,791	5,949	6,711
1906	87,200	321,343	5,441	6,431
1907	69,144	270,619	1,523	1,960
1908	92,274	356,468	1,506	2,952
1909	35,626	151,797	133	330
1910	3,947	14,282	1,590	2,902
1911	7,482	24,149	1,250	2,337
1912	4,708	25,422	440	1,142

Source: Annual *Sessional Papers of the Dominion of Canada.* See note 5.

Figure 1

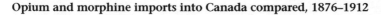

Opium and morphine imports into Canada compared, 1876–1912

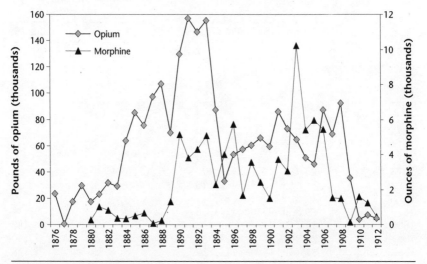

Source: Annual Sessional *Papers of the Dominion of Canada*. See Chapter 1, note 5.

Figure 2

Opium compared to all imports into Canada (in millions of dollars), 1876–1911

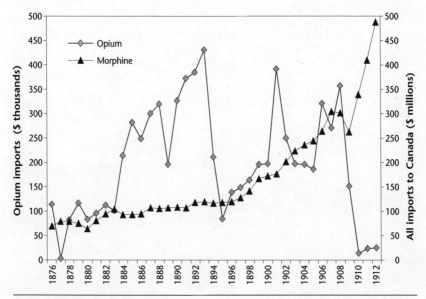

Source: See Chapter 1, note 5.

$10.00 per pound. So this bump indicates the increased domestic production of opium for export, or more likely smuggling, to the United States. These import statistics, however, do not indicate how Canadians used the drugs that stayed in the country. The nascent Canadian pharmaceutical industry was expanding, and many of the imported opiates may have gone into large-scale drug manufacturing, likely for a domestic market. These import statistics provide a broad view of the opium trade, so we need to look to other sources for a sense of how the drugs were used.

One view into the use of drugs, channelled through expert hands, may be provided by pharmacy records. These are often a rich source of information on drug use, albeit providing case studies of local patterns rather than enabling any general conclusions. Extensive records remain from an apothecary in Niagara, Ontario (later Niagara-on-the-Lake), which opened early in the nineteenth century and remained in operation, through several owners and under different names, well into the twentieth century. In the "Niagara Apothecary" files, customer accounts, which record selected customers' purchases, demonstrate both the extent of drug use and cases of potential drug addiction. Customer accounts do not record every transaction made at the business. They are skewed toward the wealthy or those deemed by the proprietor to be trustworthy, and customers were often recorded by family name, infrequently distinguishing for which member of the family the order was intended. So, although we cannot use these records to make any conclusions about the class, age, or gender of habitual drug users, they are illustrative of the prevalence of such substances among some of the people in that region.[7]

Several examples demonstrate the variety of preparations in which opium figured prominently. The account of "Robert" a local butcher shows from 1860 to 1872 the purchase of such diverse medicines as laudanum, paregoric, soothing syrup, tincture of opium, pain killer, cherry pectoral, Winslow's Soothing Syrup, and Browne's Chlorodyne. Most, if not all, of these substances would have been opiate-based. These records also suggest a comparative value in self-medication versus visiting a doctor for a prescription. These drugs were relatively inexpensive; 1 ounce of laudanum, for example, which would thereby contain several doses (unless the patient was addicted to opiates), was a mere 25 cents. A doctor's visit, as Jacalyn Duffin has noted for the same period, usually cost $1.00, exclusive of the actual cost of a prescription.[8] The most expensive item that Robert's family purchased was a bottle of Browne's Chlorodyne, which cost $1.25. They bought this in 1872, two years after the Pharmacy Act limited the sale of certain drugs. There is no indication of whether Robert purchased this product through a doctor's prescription, but it is unlikely: Chlorodyne was a proprietary medicine and therefore unrestricted under the act.[9]

Some self-medication led to addiction, and the Niagara Apothecary records also show signs of this condition among the customer records. A local legal professional in the region began purchasing a solution of morphine in 2-ounce units in 1855. That is a lot of morphine. These purchases continued several times a month until the middle of 1857. This record suggests a certain guardedness over the individual's purchases. Whereas the first few entries list "morphine solution," the remainder, noting the same amount at the same regular intervals, record it only as "solution – as before." Such cryptic notation was unusual for these records; generally, the clerk listed the name of the substance every time. Although such vagueness forbids us from concluding that this customer (or a family member) was a morphine habitué since we cannot be certain that every instance of this "solution" was morphine, the evasive note taking invites speculation that something about the order needed to remain secret.

Other cases of habitual drug use also suggest themselves in the Niagara Apothecary records. Between 1853 and 1875 approximately fifty customers' records indicate repeated and regular purchases of narcotic drugs. The occupations of those customers whose information I could trace in manuscript censuses suggest that these patients ranged in status from the skilled working class to the social elite: masons, shoemakers, carpenters, farmers, clerks, merchants, army officers, ministers, legal professionals, and politicians. One case of a problematic drug habit can be confirmed. A thirty-year-old single woman with an account at the Niagara Apothecary in the early 1870s seems to be the same woman who arrived at the Toronto Asylum later that decade, where she was diagnosed with a mania from opiate use.[10] This woman's account notes that she purchased morphine, Chlorodyne, and laudanum around 1870 and continued to buy laudanum in 2-ounce vials for the next two years.

Since the identifiable occupations of the Niagara Apothecary's customers tend to exclude the poorer in society, the value of the Niagara Apothecary records is limited by the demographics of the customers. As noted earlier, we must be cautious not to presume that the patterns in Niagara are indicative of general drug use or the prevalence of misuse. The Apothecary's records do, nevertheless, show us that people were turning to opiates in various forms for relief of a range of illnesses and that sometimes this use could transmogrify into habituation.

What about the poorer Canadians and those without ready access to the stock of a drug store or sufficient credit to run an account? Reconstructing patterns of drug use among the working class and poor is difficult, but we do have suggestions from home remedies, self-help books, compilations of folk remedies, and several recent studies on self-medication to give us an imperfect but broader view of the medication of the people.[11] Unable to afford a doctor's care, many people would rely on local home remedies to treat themselves or members of their families. Made from common kitchen ingredients or indigenous plants, most home remedies may very well have been the preferred treatment for common conditions. We find them often included on handwritten notes stuck in recipe books, or in scrapbooks of newspaper clippings, or in other almanacs, notebooks, or even family Bibles. Handwritten recipe books, secondary collections of home medicines, and published self-help books suggest that, far from the major source of therapeutics, opiates were a small portion of a broader, non-narcotic therapeutic regimen.

If we look at conditions for which opiates were often found to be especially effective – cough reduction, gastrointestinal illness, and pain relief – we see that opium certainly had no monopoly on palliation. Several researchers have investigated and assembled collections of home remedies, which include a variety of remedies for different common complaints that plagued early Canadians. Many of these researchers, like Marion Robertson of Nova Scotia's Shelburne County, author of *Old Settlers' Remedies,* and Sheila Kerr, author of *Early Prairie Remedies,* offer regional impressions of home medicine.[12] Although they do not indicate any level of rigour in their sampling, their studies do suggest a blending of local horticulture and more exotic ingredients. Robertson, in her regular column for the *Shelburne Coast Guard,* informed readers that, for example, ground ivy could be made into a tea, mixed with honey, and taken to ward off colds and coughs or mixed with egg yolks and made into a soup to treat dysentery.[13] Coughs could also be relieved by the juice of a turnip sweetened with sugar, by "water whitened with oatmeal," or by the "inspissated milky juice of sowthistle ... dandelions or 'lettuces.'"[14] Plasters of mustard, Indian meal, and vinegar, or mustard and egg white, or onions fried in lard also might relieve the phlegm of the chest.[15]

Opium was not entirely absent from such modern edited collections, although it was rare. For instance, boiling poppy heads with different substances, like lemons and brown sugar or marshmallow root, was useful to treat coughs.[16] Opium appears only once in the home medical interventions that Kerr lists, and this occurs in a section that provides recipes for popular proprietary medicines.[17] In other words, in Kerr's retelling of home treatment, opium was marginal. It is impossible to know how frequently such recipes were used, and we can only infer from their inclusion in recipe books that they were seen as potentially helpful. Nevertheless, home-remedy collections often included many recipes for the same condition; it would be inappropriate to attempt to draw any conclusions about the popularity of any specific preparation from these records. The best we can say is that opiates, if used, were part of an array of substances deployed to treat common ailments and that a vast majority of the conditions for which opium may have been recommended also had many other remedies for which the exotic gum of the poppy was not needed.

It is difficult to use these home remedy collections to draw any conclusions about the appearance in the family pharmacopoeia of substances such as opium. We simply do not have a convincing weight of evidence. Many of the popular chroniclers of "olde tyme" medicine relied on verbal recall, which may be heavily biased away from substances like opium that were later restricted and linked with social deviance. Jim Cameron, reflecting on the interviews he undertook when writing *Good for What Ails You*, noted that he did not consciously exclude opium from the recipes in his book. It was just that none of the people he interviewed about their recollections of home remedies ever mentioned it.[18] Still, and with due respect to the memories of Cameron's interviewees, in places where a person could visit a pharmacist or (prior to the late 1860s at least) a general merchant and purchase the basic ingredients of a "modern" medicine cabinet, many people would have had access to various forms of opium.

Nevertheless, these published folk-medicine collections are valuable: they provide a glimpse into an eclectic approach to self-medication and may also reflect a diverse understanding of various physical conditions. We will never know whether some of these remedies, as bizarre or quaint or funny or ill-advised as they may seem to a modern reader, were based on a sophisticated perception of the function of the human body or just on the observation that, well, they worked before, so why not try them again? Indeed, in her discussion of Hildegard of Bingen's medieval text of medical treatments, Victoria Sweet observes that, however common St. Hildegard's eleventh-century treatment may have seemed, and however folksy and simple the explanations may appear, Hildegard's ideas related closely to more scholarly medical philosophies handed down through generations in Hippocratic and Galenic texts (often referred to as Hellenic medicine).[19] Hippocrates developed (and Galen expanded on) a sophisticated medical system based on the idea that health was the result of a balance of the four humors: blood, phlegm, yellow bile, and black bile. Each humor represented two of four basic "qualities" (dry, moist, hot, and cold). So blood, for example, was hot and moist; phlegm was moist and cold. Foods were often associated with these characteristics. A major component of medical treatment involved connecting the humoral imbalance with foods that would correct it.

To counter the recall bias of the editors of quaint home-remedy collections, we have access to many personal recipe books, often written by rural women or men who lived away from major trading centres, in which a range of recipes was recorded. The University of Guelph's Una Abrahamson

Canadian Cookery Collection includes dozens of home-recipe books, many of which include recipes for home remedies. Like most textual material, these documents provide insight into the behaviour of only the literate; at least the people writing them down were literate. Often we do not know from whose mouths the recipes originated. Although some do not have specific dates and others are not geographically specific to Canada, we can see how these remedies encompassed an extensive range of ingredients. Again, considering conditions for which opium was traditionally employed, we see that opium was simply one choice in a complex array of medications and certainly not the most important in the home pharmacopoeia.

There is no standard format for cookbooks and recipe books. Some were compendia of material culled from newspapers and the wisdom of friends and family. Some of these collections divided food and medicine, whereas others interspersed them. In some cases, like treatments for diarrhea, the therapy may have been entirely dietary, so distinguishing food from medicine is tricky, although Hippocrates would not have bothered to differentiate. Moreover, as we have already discussed, the idea behind home remedies was in fact to find convenient treatments for common ailments. The ingredients, therefore, would naturally be easily available, and they usually included common herbs, spices, and plants widely available or easily accessible. For example, in her recipe book dated circa 1811, Hannah Jarvis, wife of prominent Loyalist William Jarvis, included a recipe for whooping cough that required boiling a common field turnip, adding sugar, simmering the mixture, and then administering from one to three teaspoons of it at a time. Bowel complaints might be treated with a pint of the best port wine, cloves, cinnamon, mace, nutmeg, and loaf sugar boiled together for ten minutes and then stirred into two beaten egg yolks.[20] An anonymous recipe book from around 1805 included a cough remedy that contained exotic and local products; honey, sweet almonds, lemons, and half a pint of rum were heated and administered "whenever the cough is troublesome."[21] This was essentially the same as a hot toddy, the mainstay of many home cough remedies to the present. A further example of a cough remedy from a "Housekeeper's Book" is one that consisted of syrup of mulberries, rum, and oil.[22]

Relatively few home remedies included opium. Often it would appear in the form of the aforementioned Dover's Powder or paregoric, both of which appear to have been as common a household item as many spices. So Jarvis included an additional recipe for bowel complaint that required a tablespoon of "oiled butter [and] five grains of Dover's Powder."[23] A.G. Higgionson's recipe book, dated between 1833 and 1876, included a recipe for whooping cough that called for paregoric, Squills (a remedy derived from sea onion), and water.[24] Another anonymous author from later in the century included a cough remedy of water, treacle, paregoric, and a balsam extract.[25] Yet opiates and non-opiated cough remedies coexisted. Immediately after this paregoric-based remedy, the anonymous chronicler included a cough remedy of sweet almonds and white sugar mixed with boiling water.[26]

The recipe books illustrate clearly the broad array of substances and combinations in nineteenth-century household medicine. The household pharmacopoeia was diverse, both in its ingredients and in their geographic origins. Local plants like turnips were found alongside less readily available products like lemons; manufactured but generally ubiquitous ingredients such as rum and sugar were found alongside products like paregoric and Dover's Powder. This diversity suggests both the eclectic mix of remedies and the seasonality of the recipes. Constrained trade routes during the winter, when coughs may have been more prevalent, may have led to other palliatives like balsam, mulberry syrup, honey, and rum, although not in that specific combination. What we cannot tell from these recipes is whether there was any therapeutic justification. In other words, were these remedies the result of a humoral interpretation of the qualities of certain products and the conditions of the body, as Sweet noted in her discussion of Hildegard's recipes, which were drawn from plants in the garden but linked to broader Hellenic ideas of balance and qualities? Or were they simply concoctions that people found to be effective? Clearly, these recipes came from a variety of sources. One recipe was followed by a woman's name, likely crediting her as the source; another, giving measurements in "pennysworth," appears to have come from a British publication. So along with demonstrating how opium was but one component in a broad spectrum of therapeutic substances, these recipes indicate that personal medical treatment was simultaneously local and, as much as it could be, cosmopolitan.

In the later part of the nineteenth century, authors and publishers had begun to augment these personal home-remedy collections by assembling and publishing authoritative compendia of effective remedies. Although many people might have relied on older popular publications like John Wesley's *Primitive Physik* or William Buchan's *Domestic Medicine*, new compilations of more recent recipes using plain language and familiar products were appearing on a rapidly expanding self-help market. In *The Household Guide or Domestic Cyclopedia*, published in Toronto in 1894, B.G. Jefferis and J.L. Nichols followed the general style of many of these homemade recipe books by including general advice for health, cooking recipes, cleaning solutions, and other domestic advice. In this guide, opium's uses and dangers were understood. In a section on disease, "Dr. Abernethy of London" was cited as saying that all disease was a result of "violations of the laws of our being ... most of these being connected to dietetic abuses, with such as are produced by the use of intoxicants, tobacco and opium."[27] In a decade in which the anti-alcohol movement had reached a fevered pitch amid concerns about the effects of alcohol on the body and about the morality of the individual, such proclamations were mainstream ideas. In *The Household Guide*, opiates were also credited with increasing nervousness since "the longer you take opiates the less you will sleep, as they will tend to make you nervous and restless." To deal with this problem, the individual had to "bravely give them up and depend upon alkalies which are mild sedatives."[28] Opium appeared mostly in the relatively safe form of topical remedies like ointments for piles, old sores, and "accidents, bruises, lameness and swelling."[29] Nevertheless, even such a guide recognized the prevalence of opium in everyday treatment. Although by the 1890s pharmaceutical laws had made access to the raw ingredients of opium and morphine much more difficult, *The Household Guide* included a table of "How much medicine to take as a dose," listing common doses in the form of drops and grains.

In *The Household Guide* many of the conditions for which opium was traditionally prescribed were, as we saw in the manuscripts of home recipes, supplanted by more familiar and safer products. Substances that could be used to remedy coughs and colds included dandelion, eggs, gum Arabic, goose grease, horehound, pennyroyal, sage, snakeroot, and wild cherry. Diarrhea could be treated with baking soda, blackberry, camphor, eggs, ginger, oak bark, and "White everlasting," a plant that the book's author described as a "Sure cure for Diarrhea." Pain, meanwhile, was treated variously, depending on the type of pain. So headache, which could easily be treated with opium, required any number of therapeutic regimes, involving both remedies and practices (such as dealing with eye strain, soaking the feet or hands in hot water, or making sure bowels were active). One topical remedy for headache, which the author said was "much to be preferred to powerful drugs," was cayenne pepper mixed with vinegar and spread on a strip of cloth placed on the forehead between the temples.[30] Again, reiterating the strong cautions against medications, the author informed the reader, "I know of no more dangerous practice than to treat headache pain blindly with drugs, unless it be to treat insomnia with sedatives. Both lines of treatment lead to the abuse of anodynes and hypnotics, and as a usual thing result in a continued condition of invalidism."[31] The guide's cautions against opiates and alcohol and its emphasis on home-based remedies and even therapeutics that eschewed any sort of medication, however natural the substance, appealed to many readers; the book went through over twenty editions in a decade.[32]

The publishing boom that led to such household guides may have been the result of the therapeutic skepticism (also called therapeutic nihilism) that characterized mid- to late-nineteenth-century Anglo-American society.[33] This skepticism was a reaction against the excesses of the so-called heroic remedies of the late eighteenth and early nineteenth century. Heroic remedies were excessive therapeutics such as heavy doses of purgatives, which resulted in massive and violent vomiting or defecation, as well as bleeding regimens, which called for draining large amounts of blood from the patient to gain a violent and excessive reaction. By the middle of the century, a reaction against such therapeutics resulted in their general rejection. It was this cultural shift that drove the rise of viable alternative medical professions, such as homeopathy, Thomsonianism, and so-called eclectic medicine, against whose incursions so-called regular medicine began to lobby for occupational closure. Therapeutic skepticism included such perspectives as those elucidated in *The Household Guide's* observation that all illness was the result of excesses and in the cautions against "strong drugs." Mild therapies, gentle treatments, and a wariness of the highly medicating tendencies of regular practitioners characterized the therapeutic skepticism and enriched the self-help home-remedy market. As we will see in Chapter 7, it also fuelled, later in the century, the rapid expansion of secret proprietary medicines, the proprietors of which, while themselves railing against the excesses of the medical profession, were often selling medicines with even more excessive and dangerous ingredients.

Possibly one of the most popular, and most often reprinted, home-remedy books was Alvin Chase's *Dr. Chase's Recipes, or Information for Everybody*. Chase was a merchant and druggist who, he claimed in his introduction, took a degree in medicine and began selling copies of his recipe books. By 1860, he had sold over 13,000 books in the United States and "the Canadas." The subtitle of the book might indicate the more pluralistic bent of Alvin Chase. He was a trained eclectic physician, an adherent of an emerging medical sect that challenged the purported authority of what we might now call "regular physicians." Medical sects such as eclectics, Thomsonians, and homeopaths questioned the claims to authority of allopathic practitioners, those physicians who rooted themselves in the elite trappings of university education and a long, sophisticated philosophical tradition from Hippocrates, through Galen, and onward to the universities of Europe.[34] Eclectics attempted to find the best remedies and approaches to healing from any medical tradition, although they generally shunned the excesses of heroic medicine. Moreover, based in a Jacksonian democratic tradition that eschewed control by elites, eclectics sought to undermine the authority of physicians by freeing medical knowledge from its exclusivist cages. Ironically, while purporting to free the general user from a reliance on the expertise of the general practitioner, Chase assured his readers that the remedies were appropriate and employed his own medical expertise in culling and scrutinizing the remedies. He rarely mentioned his eclectic background, calling himself simply "Dr. Chase." Chase offered his readers a variety of remedies with a broad range of ingredients, noting,

> Many of the articles called for can be gathered from garden, field or woods, and the others will always be found with druggists, and most of the preparations will cost only from *one-half* to as low as *one-sixteenth* as much as to purchase them already made; and the only certainty, now-a-days, of having a *good* article, is to make it yourself.[35]

Most important, Chase reminded cynical readers, who argued that they could get all the recipes they needed from published columns in newspapers, not only that his book was indexed and "handsomely bound" but also that the recipes presented "the advantage of their having passed under the author's carefully *pruning* and *grafting* hand."[36] Chase's book represented a strong alternative strain in popular medicine. It also must have made him and his publisher, who continued to release updated versions of his book long after his death, quite wealthy.

The recipes in Chase's book were eclectic, indeed, and since the book was modified and reprinted over half a century, it is useful to examine its remedies to see whether and how their ingredients changed. Each reprint of the book contained hundreds of recipes for medicines that used local and exotic ingredients. Through the many Canadian editions of the book, the proportion of opiates to recipes grew slightly, but opiates appeared in a relatively low proportion of his remedies. Out of 435 recipes in the first Canadian edition of 1865, for example, 45 (10.3%) contained some form of opium, including Dover's Powder and paregoric. In 1889, the number of recipes increased to 527, with 62 (11.8%) opium preparations. This proportion was higher in 1900 but then declined in 1920. Interestingly, by the end of the nineteenth century, many Canadian provinces and US states had begun to pass restrictive pharmaceutical laws that would have limited individuals' access to many opiates, yet such limitations do not seem to have affected Chase's remedies. Table 2 provides an indication of this change by comparing the use of opium and chloroform to that of alcohol through four iterations of the book. The recipes listing alcohol, however, do not include tinctures like laudanum, which have been placed under "opium" since alcohol is not considered the active ingredient in a tincture — it was the medium in which the active ingredient could be dissolved. In these editions, more than in the home-remedy collections discussed above, opiates vied with other substances to treat common ailments.[37] Chase's remedies for coughs, for example, include several cough lozenges or mixtures employing morphine, opium, or laudanum, alongside a remedy made from "linseed oil, honey and Jamaica rum" and a cough syrup that demanded the following complex procedure:

Table 2

Proportion of opiates to other drugs in Dr. Chase's remedies

	Opium		Alcohol		Chloroform		Recipes
1865	45	(10.3%)	63	(14.5%)	7	(1.6%)	435
1889	62	(11.8%)	69	(13.1%)	18	(3.4%)	527
1900	220	(14.8%)	188	(12.6%)	12	(0.8%)	1,489
1920	45	(13.2%)	58	(17.0%)	7	(2.1%)	341

Source: Alvin Chase, *Dr. Chase's Recipes, or Information for Everybody,* self-published in the years indicated.

[Mix] wahoo, bark of the root, and elecamane root, of each 2 ozs.; spikenard root, and tamarack bark (Unmossed, but the moss may be brushed off), of each 4 ozs.; mandrake root, ½ oz.; bloodroot ¼ oz.; mix alcohol ½ pt. with sufficient water to cover all and let stand for 2 or 3 days; then add more water and boil and pour off, putting on more water and boiling again, straining the two waters and boiling down to 3 pts.; when cool add 3 lbs. of honey, and alcohol 1 gill, with tincture of wine of ipecac 1½ ozs.[38]

Chase recommended equally diverse ingredients and procedures for other complaints, including diarrhea, the recipes for which included those with ingredients like laudanum and opium, as well as others that used roots, barks, and easily available household goods. We can compare the proportion of opiates in Chase's recipes to those in the prescriptions of general physicians. Duffin notes that opium remained one of the most frequently used substances in the practice of James Langstaff throughout his career.[39] The casebooks of Dr. Thomas O. Geddes of Yarmouth, Nova Scotia show a similar high usage of various forms of opiates. In 1880, for example, opiates appeared in over 22.5 percent of Geddes's prescriptions. Fully 10 percent of these were Dover's Powder, which, despite containing opium, remained uncontrolled in Nova Scotia's pharmacy legislation due to its general use and relatively mild effects.[40] (We will look more closely at Geddes's prescribing habits in the next chapter.)

In the records of Dr. William Reinhardt, a physician who practised in several towns in the BC interior, we see an indication of how changes in legislation and the availability of innovative medicines could be reflected in therapeutics. In a small notebook, undated except for advertising indicating that it was printed around 1901, Reinhardt recorded various recipes and therapeutic procedures. He listed over seventy remedies or treatments, of which only two mentioned opium, three mentioned morphine, and five mentioned cocaine. At the same time, Reinhardt made special notes on the efficacy of several new remedies, including Protargol, an early treatment for gonorrhoea with bactericidal properties; adrenaline, which Reinhardt noted could be used to treat conditions such as colds or hay fever, cystitis, internal hemorrhage, and vaginitis; and "phenacetine," one of the first nonopioid analgesics. Phenacetin (sometimes spelled "phanacetin") was introduced in 1878, adrenaline in 1895, and Protargol in 1897.[41] Although these physicians' notes indicate the range of uses and changes in therapeutics over time, their geographic specificity and unclear dates mean that they cannot be taken as definitive proof of a shift in therapeutics. They do, however, show us that opium, inside and outside of professional medical circles, was but one of a number of substances employed in an era of increasingly diverse and changing therapeutics.

Before the advent of restrictive drug laws, Canadians had access to a variety of forms of medical knowledge and a range of treatment options. People without easy access to physicians or to a merchant carrying a comprehensive line of pharmaceuticals could resort to many other means of treating common ailments. Many of these recipes included drugs found in personal and public pharmacopoeias, whereas others drew on widely available substances for their ingredients. Some of these ingredients necessitated access to wild or regionally available vegetation, whereas others required that the aspiring home medic be connected to broader commercial networks. Although people were likely familiar with opiates in common forms like laudanum, Dover's Powder, and paregoric, there is no indication that these were the standard medicines to which people turned for relief of colds, pain, and gastric discomfort. Indeed, the relatively low number of opiates mentioned in *Dr. Chase's Recipes* and *The Household Guide* suggest that, if anything, opium was just one of a number of products to which Canadians had access. The fact that handwritten recipe books and collections of newspaper clippings included an assortment of recipes with a variety of ingredients indicates that, rather than seeking a "one size fits all" approach to home treatment, in which opium was prominent, Canadians resorted to whichever handy remedies might work. Moreover, the soothing property of mixtures like lemon, honey, and rum for colds may have suited the farmer with few resources to buy more powerful remedies or limited access to the major mercantile networks closer to larger communities, although it is difficult to know how much more accessible lemons were than Dover's Powder.

This array of remedies and ingredients is the context in which we must place the development of drug laws and the changes in medical ideas about the danger of certain substances. Attempts to control certain drugs operated within a society that used them only in a limited way. This may have been due to restricted access, to the high price, or indeed to the dangerous properties of these substances when misused. It is difficult to take lethal doses of turnip, but a small amount of opium can kill you. The available folk and home-remedy literature suggests that the main user of medical opiates was the medical profession itself. Chase's validation of his book as a series of recipes approved by a medical doctor (and many of the recipes apparently came from other doctors' contributions) reiterates the necessary relationship between a physician's authority and self-medication. People with limited access to physicians or limited resources to pay them undertook the age-old practice of home treatment, relying on well-known remedies, incorporating information about new mixtures, drawing from indigenous materials along with items that they could access through broader trade networks, and recording these remedies for future reference. In this informal context, opium was a minor part of treatment. This place of opium contrasts to its importance in, even centrality to, the *materia medica* of formally trained physicians. To locate the idea of opiates as a powerful medicine and dangerous poison, therefore, we must consider the discussions of doctors themselves.

2
Opium in Nineteenth-Century Medical Knowledge

Doctors in mid-century Canada saw the general public's unregulated access to powerful drugs like opium, combined with the tradition of self-medicating, to be problematic. Beyond the fact that self-medication would deny the physician his fee, a concern rarely elucidated in medical literature, physicians were worried that dangerous drugs were being used without a doctor's educated supervision. As physicians never tired of reminding each other and anyone listening, medicine was a sophisticated science, based on complex knowledge and deep traditions, and not something that should be undertaken lightly. Moreover, many of the most important substances that they used for medications were powerful, and if misused, they could be deadly. Controlling access to these substances, and ensuring that such potent but valuable medicines were deployed properly, became a major thrust of the Canadian medical leadership in the last half of the nineteenth century. In this activity, doctors employed a variety of understandings of the properties of opiates, and as the century wore on, expressed the belief that the problems of habituation were more than just an annoying side effect of medical treatment. These ideas were part of a broad international dialogue on the properties of medications and the authority of the medical profession, one in which most Canadian physicians participated more often as auditors than as active international voices. Nevertheless, in their medical journals and the work of their medical societies, Canadian physicians integrated international discussions into their understanding of the nature of opium and its use among their own patients and colleagues.

Opiates played an important role not only in the *materia medica* of nineteenth-century medicine but also in physicians' sense of professionalism. Consequently, medical literature was replete with discussions of its correct and improper use. Opium was a valuable medicine but also a dangerous poison, and this dual nature underpinned most discussions of its judicious medical prescription. In the medical textbooks assigned in Canadian medical schools, we can see how ideas about opium as a poison and a medicine empowered physicians to deploy it as an effective treatment of some familiar symptoms even though it was dangerous when misused. Indeed, opium's value to medicine lay precisely in its simultaneously dangerous and efficacious properties. The combined poison/medicine nature of opium meant that it was an effective medicine but only when used properly.

This sense of proper and improper use permeated physicians' discussions of therapeutics and would also become central to arguments about who should have authority over the distribution and control of such substances. Physicians increasingly argued that the safe use of opiates was possible only with the advice of educated professionals; conversely, any medical or non-medical use by someone who was not a medical professional was therefore seen to be dangerous. Moreover, the dangerous nature of opium made its use socially volatile. Doctors were just as concerned that their confreres should be deploying it accurately in their therapies as they were that non-physicians should not be using it. So curbing physician misuse was a fundamental part of the discussions about opiates among doctors since they needed to present themselves as belonging to a learned profession in the business of helping, not hurting, the public. Such a perspective necessarily and not surprisingly influenced broader social perceptions of the problem of easily available, but dangerous, medicine.

Opium the Medicine
In 1869 the *Canadian Pharmaceutical Journal* published an article entitled "What Is Opium?" The author, Dr. F.A. Fluckiger, a chemist from Bern, Germany, observed that, despite persistent investigation, "science is far from having an exact idea of the nature of opium."[1] Drawing on the results of his own experiments and those of other investigators, Fluckiger detailed the chemical complexity of opium. He noted variances and nuances of opium's makeup and explained to his readers how they could test the potency of opiates. Yet, despite its complex language and descriptions of experimental procedures and results, Fluckiger's article provided details to support a well-known fact: opium is a chemically intricate substance. He made no allusion to another, equally perplexing aspect of opium: the social complexity that mirrored, and was a result of, the chemical complexity. In its ability to ease pain, induce sleep, or significantly alter the physical processes of the body, such as reducing intestinal activity and bronchial secretions and increasing perspiration, opium was a valuable medicine of the nineteenth-century pharmacopoeia. These therapeutic qualities also made opium a dangerous poison. When misused, taken in excessive doses, or administered improperly without adequate attention to the details of a patient's illness, opium could kill. Despite the advances of scientific inquiry, "the nature of opium" remained elusive.

Scientific investigations, such as those on which Fluckiger drew, informed and enhanced the knowledge and therefore the authority of medical professionals. In the same way that anatomical knowledge and detailed empirical data empowered doctors to try to establish cultural authority and control over their patients, expanding scientific and chemical experimentation provided doctors, pharmacists, and other members of a broadly defined medical profession with a positivistic and scientifically legitimate means of attempting to explain the actions of drugs. Yet for all of the chemical and pharmacological advances to which doctors had access, opium remained a difficult drug to use accurately. The complexity to which Fluckiger alluded hindered the doctor's ability to predict, with any degree of accuracy, the actions and side effects of a specific dose of a drug and to explain the periodic anomalous and lethal results of drug therapy. When science failed and doctors faced the incongruity between expectations and results, doctors depended on their social credibility and status, derived from nonscientific factors, to legitimize their claims to control over these substances.

Throughout the nineteenth century, medical education sought to inform students of the idiosyncrasies and contextual appropriateness of the application of drugs, most especially those with toxic properties, like opium. Without such knowledge, physicians could not hope to assert their place as authoritative mediators between the natural world and the human condition. Yet scientific knowledge was not only useful inasmuch as it related directly to the treatment of patients; science was also fundamental to the development of medical authority. As S.E.D. Shortt has argued, long before medical science could successfully treat illness beyond, for the most part, basic symptom management, the authoritative language of science helped physicians to establish their profession as one that was socially valuable and therefore deserving of the protection provided by legal professional incorporation.[2] Notwithstanding philosophers who argued that pedantry, or the use of overly esoteric jargon in inappropriate social contexts, was reprehensible, to various learned professions of the nineteenth century, oblique language had social value.[3] Scientific language established the authority of the physicians as experts in the applied science of medicine (even though doctors continued to refer to their practice as an "art") while simultaneously alienating those who could not understand the jargon because they did not have a medical education. So the trappings of science, be they in the complex chemical descriptions provided by chemists such as Fluckiger or in the detailed discussions of the shape and character of various substances provided to students in *materia medica* textbooks, played two roles: directly, they were positivistically informative; and indirectly, they were socially elevatory.

The range of subjects covered in Canadian medical schools expanded seemingly exponentially from the middle to the end of the century. Subjects were added, broadening the scope and sophistication of medical education and knowledge, an undertaking fuelled, no doubt, by an expanding market of medical textbooks. Two key areas of instruction, in which students were taught the properties of medicines, were *Materia Medica* (often renamed "Pharmacology" or "Pharmacology and Therapeutics") and the Practice of Medicine. *Materia Medica* was the study of the properties of medicines themselves and involved speculation on the physiological mechanism behind their effects. *Materia Medica* textbooks provided detailed descriptions not only of the origins of the substances but also and more crucially of the main physiological actions and therapeutic uses of the substances. The Practice of Medicine was in many ways the mirror image of *Materia Medica*. These texts described specific conditions and gave practical instruction on treatment, detailing a variety of therapeutic approaches to different manifestations of the illnesses. A close examination of the textbooks for both of these subjects demonstrates the value and variability of opium and its key derivatives, morphine and codeine.

An overview of the medical textbooks recommended in the course calendars for Canadian medical schools reveals two key features. First, as the century came to an end, the list of recommended textbooks, like the number of subjects taught, expanded considerably. So by 1902, Trinity Medical College included twenty titles on its list of recommended textbooks for therapeutics; McGill recommended four. Second, since students were not expected to purchase or read all of these textbooks, we can assume that the information provided in any one of them was considered appropriately authoritative for the purposes of medical education. The listing in the Trinity calendar was of books "suitable for the Examinations of all the Universities and of the Medical Council."[4] For this reason, the following examination focuses on textbooks that were most often recommended in the surviving calendars of Canadian medical schools.[5]

Just as *Grey's Anatomy* continued to be valued long after the death of the author, a number of textbooks became standard authorities in Canadian medical schools beyond the lifespan of their authors. The most persistently used, and oft-cited, authors on *Materia Medica* were Jonathan Pereira and Horatio C. Wood. Pereira's *Elements of Materia Medica,* first published in two volumes in 1842, was the central text in *Materia Medica* courses at several medical schools. It was reprinted and restructured a number of times, with the final edition, an abridged version, *Pereira's Manual of Materia Medica,* being published in 1874, twenty-one years after the author's death. *"Pereira's Elements"* as it was known, remained a standard text in some Canadian medical schools at least until 1890. Wood's *Therapeutics: Its Principles and Practice* (1874), went through at least fourteen editions, with the last one, edited and expanded by his son Horatio Charles Wood Jr., being published in 1908.[6] This textbook continued to be recommended in Canadian medical schools until at least 1902. Several textbooks were also standard for courses in the Practice of Medicine. Notably, the textbook *A Treatise on the Practice of Medicine* by George Bacon Wood, which was first published in 1847 and went through seven editions, was recommended in Canadian medical schools until at least 1880, a year after the author's death. Part of a Wood medical dynasty, George was arguably the most influential of the medical Woods, being a principal author of the *United States Pharmacopeoia* (1831).[7] His other influential textbook, *A Treatise on Therapeutics, and Pharmacology or Materia Medica* (1857), was also recommended reading at Canadian medical schools. This profusion of Woods may have caused some confusion when a professor advised a student to "consult Wood." Finally, immediately on the 1892 publication of William Osler's *The Principles and Practice of Medicine,* the book became recommended in all medical schools for which we have records. To these four medical textbooks, I will add selections from other often-referenced works.

For the mid-nineteenth-century physician, opium was clearly the drug of choice. In Pereira's *materia medica* textbook, for example, opium was ubiquitous and essential. Weighing in at nearly 2,000 pages in two volumes, Pereira's *Elements of Materia Medica* contained detailed discussion of most drugs available to the nineteenth-century practitioner, if he ever got through it. Pereira provided details on drugs, including their origins, physical properties, methods of evaluating purity, physical effects on animals and humans, and major therapeutic applications. In the section on opium, Pereira was unequivocal:

> Opium is undoubtedly the most important and valuable remedy of the whole Materia Medica. We have for other medicines, one or more substitutes; but for opium we have none, – at least in the large majority of cases in which its peculiar and beneficial influence is required. Its good effects are not, as is the case with some valuable medicines, remote and contingent, but they are immediate, direct, and obvious; and its operation is not attended with pain or discomfort.[8]

Here Pereira is considering not only opium's utility in treatment but also its speedy action as a valuable remedy. As we will see later, such characteristics of a medicine were important in a medical profession that sought to establish its therapeutic perspective as the single, authoritative approach to healing.

Indeed, for Pereira, opium's physiological effect made it applicable in treating many different physical conditions. In the 1842 edition of *Elements,* he listed each type of condition for which opium has been known to be useful and often engaged in a detailed discussion of the specific conditions for which various writers have found it to be of some therapeutic benefit. Beyond those cases where opium's specific properties were directly related to disease symptoms, Pereira explained opium's benefit as a general panacea: "We exhibit it ... to mitigate pain, to allay spasm, to promote sleep, to relieve nervous restlessness, to produce perspiration, and to check profuse mucous discharges ... but experience has proved its value in relieving some diseases in which not one of these indications can be at all times distinctly traced."[9] Pereira presented the strengths and weaknesses of opium in seven physical systems, claiming opium to be effective in treating nearly every major form of illness to which a human could be susceptible:

Cerebro-Spinal system
Digestive system
Vascular system
Respiratory system
Urinary system
Sexual system [of men]
[Sexual system] Of women
On the cutaneous system
Topical Effects.[10]

It was a sophisticated discussion, and to medical writers, careful attention to diverse physical indications was required in order to undertake an accurate diagnosis and therapeutic regimen.

The notion of opium's usefulness was derived not only from its visible effect on the body but also from how this effect suited conceptions of disease. Traditional Galenic medicine, on which much Western medicine was based, viewed disease as being a result of the imbalance of the four humours of the body: blood, phlegm, yellow bile, and black bile. Opium's quality of reducing bodily secretions aided the physician to balance the latter three fluids. Moreover, humoral therapy related the humours to four qualities of the body: dry, moist, cold, and warm. Remedies were deployed based on their own qualities and how they affected characteristics in disease. So opium's sudorific, or sweat-inducing, characteristic was useful when the skin was overly dry and warm because sweating, of course, made skin moist and cooled the body down. Opium was also often combined with calomel, a mercurial preparation that, although itself also toxic, caused salivation, a sort of internal sweating. Such combinations allowed physicians to create distinct effects that fitted extant ideas of medical treatment. This philosophy of pathophysiology, challenged in the latter third of the century by the germ theory of disease, rested on the belief that bodily disease was internal, the result of a systemic imbalance with subsequent morbid manifestations. So both as a straightforward anodyne and in its qualities that related to more subtle and sophisticated interpretations of bodily function and dysfunction, opium was fundamental to medical treatment.

Although many considered opium to be the most important remedy in the *materia medica,* its value was often as a component in a complex course of treatment. For example, in George Bacon Wood's description of the treatment of pneumonia, opium was part of a supportive regimen that came after a course of bleeding and purging, common therapeutic treatments for many gastrointestinal and pulmonary illnesses that were rooted in humoral theories and driven by heroic approaches. The specific combination of substances, the proportion of opium to other drugs in the preparation, and the frequency of the dosage all depended on the specific symptoms and "the susceptibility of the patient."[11] So for the least complicated form of pneumonia, Wood recommended what might be considered a typical humoral-based, heroic regimen. Bleeding would be followed by thorough evacuation of the bowels "by an active cathartic, as calomel and jalap, the compound cathartic pill, infusion of senna with Epsom salt, &c."[12] Then the patient would be given small doses of tartar emetic, a purgative that may have been used as an expectorant.[13] Only two or three days after commencing this treatment regimen, "when the force of the circulation has been sufficiently subdued by the lancet," a mixture of opium, ipecacuanha, and calomel would provide rest and ease the cough while "direct[ing] action to the skin." With the latter, Wood meant that it would increase sweating, a characteristic effect of opium. Wood may have also intended this remedy to help heal skin lesions caused by the various methods of bleeding: leeches, cupping, and lancet.[14] The treatment of other forms of pneumonia – "lobular or infantile," "bilious," "typhoid," and "chronic" – involved similar heroic therapies, with opiates serving in a secondary role to alleviate cough, aid sleep, and dull pain.[15]

Used frequently to alleviate pain, ease gastric distress, reduce pulmonary secretions, and help patients to sleep, opium was especially predominant in conditions that were characterized by diarrhea, vomiting, or excessive coughing. Although not an expectorant, opium does act to reduce the irritation of accumulated phlegm in the chest. So, as with the treatments for pneumonia listed by George Bacon Wood, opium was useful after much of the phlegm had been reduced by other means. Meanwhile, many of the illnesses of the urban environment, be they caused or exacerbated by air or water pollution, could be treated by opiates. Dysentery, cholera, tuberculosis, and other chronic bronchial afflictions manifested major symptoms that opium was especially useful in easing. Yet opium was again part of a broader system of medicine that needed the oversight of a thoughtful practitioner. Wood's treatment for intermittent fever, for example, began with the assertion that sometimes it should just be allowed to run its course, the patient being supported with hot liquids and warm blankets. Opium was his second recommendation, and first drug prescription, said to be useful "when there is much pain or nervous disorder."[16] For cholera morbus, which was characterized by vomiting and purging, Wood recommended administering opium after flushing the stomach. The "moderate action" of opium would ease irritation after the direct purging removed any "irritating cause."[17] In epidemic cholera, a much more violent and lethal purging illness, opium was one of many potential remedies; as Wood wrote, "the plans of treatment are almost as numerous as the combinations of which remedies are susceptible; and, judging from the reports upon a great scale, there seems to have been little difference in the results." The death rates were the same, regardless of the cures attempted. The cholera epidemics in the middle of the nineteenth century resulted in desperate combinations of normally effective remedies. Chief among those recommended by Wood, however, were opium and calomel, to be taken in small and frequently repeated doses.[18] Similar approaches were taken to treating most gastrointestinal conditions.

As noted above, opium is a complex substance made up of several dozen components that have unique properties. The first, most prevalent, and arguably most important component isolated from it was morphine. "Morphia," named for the Greek god of dreams, was isolated by German chemist Friedrich Sertürner in 1805, although it was not in general use until several decades later. Indeed, in 1832, essayist William G. Smith observed that "neither morphia, nor any of its salts, have yet come into very general use in the practice of physicians, at least [in North America]." Smith suggested two reasons for this phenomenon. First, he argued that the price of morphine was too high; second, he cited "an adherence to the old established maxim, never to abandon an article whose virtues are known and universally acknowledged, for one not yet proved, and but just introduced."[19] Morphine soon came into more widespread use. As John Bell, a Canadian medical student in 1863, recorded in his *materia medica* lecture notes, "We use the alkaloids of morphia &c.; opium being used only for laudanum and Dover's Powder."[20] Opium's anodyne qualities remained important, but other substances began to join opium in reducing pain.

When Wood's and Pereira's textbooks were first published, then, opium was generally used in its raw, gum form, or else a dried and powdered version would be rolled into pills or dissolved in alcohol or other liquids as a tincture. When these authors discussed morphine, it was as an aside, a substance with promise in treatment but not yet fully understood. This changed quickly, however, as additional experimentation and isolation of other alkaloids provided the possibility of more sophisticated chemical interventions.

These new substances – derived from opium and other raw drugs, such as strychnine (isolated from nux vomica in 1818) and salicin (isolated from willow bark in 1828) – allowed more therapeutic precision but could also cause confusion.[21] With opium's chemical complexity, the uses and potencies of the alkaloids were the subject of considerable debate during the middle of the nineteenth century. Throughout much of the nineteenth century, many physicians tended to equate morphine with opium since both seemed to have practically the same effects. To many, the only significant difference between the two lay in the dosage. British physician and educator Robert Christison, in his often-cited textbook *A Dispensatory, or Commentary on the Pharmacopoeias of Great Britain* (1842), explained that "there is scarcely any special purpose served by opium, for which this salt [morphine] may not be advantageously substituted, except in the cases of rare occurrence where it is necessary to compel deep sleep, and the constitution of the individual is known to agree with opium itself."[22] Dr. J. Moore Nelligan agreed, noting in 1849, "Notwithstanding the observations of many, that morphia is free from the stimulating effects of opium, and that it acts purely as an anodyne sedative, it would appear that it possesses essentially ... the actions of the drug [opium] itself."[23] Both writers also observed that morphine was not as popular as opium among physicians. Royal physician Sir Henry Holland discussed the effects of "Opium, in one or other of its forms" at length but rarely distinguished opium from its components.[24] He attributed the isolation of morphine to the resurgence of the use of opium in medicine. He also advised his readers to prefer morphine over opium because morphine's effects "are more explicit, more secure, and freer from injury or inconvenience, than those of any other opiate," a sentiment that suggests the physician's authority was thought to benefit from prescribing morphine, just as were the patient's chances of recovery.[25]

It took several decades for physicians to exercise precision in the therapeutic distinctions between opium and morphine. When medical student John Bell observed that "morphia &c" were preferred over opium, he was demonstrating the awareness that opium had variable potencies and that the precision of a dose of morphine was far superior and more manageable than the uncertainty of opiates. But he did not subsequently describe whether and how morphine differed in its physiological effects. Nor, at times, did his textbooks. Pereira, whose textbook was the sole *materia medica* text at Queen's College in Kingston when Bell was a student there, noted that "the precise relation which the effects of this alkaloid and its salts bear to those of opium, is a point on which the profession is by no means agreed ... The effects of morphia ... are in several respects different from those of opium, but they appear to want uniformity."[26] Decades after Pereira had written his text, some of that uncertainty was reduced, but slippages still persisted. In his 1874 textbook on therapeutics and *materia medica*, Horatio C. Wood recognized accurately the proportions of morphine in opium but at crucial times still blurred the distinctions. He explained that the several forms of morphine "differ in their therapeutic value from opium chiefly in that they act with less power as sudorifics and in checking secretions in the bowels, and consequently constipating."[27] Yet in some crucial ways, he was less than precise when distinguishing between the two drugs.[28] For example, when discussing opium poisoning, which will be examined in more detail later in this chapter, Wood wrote, "In regard to the amount of opium which will cause death, the smallest fatal dose on record is half a grain of morphia in the adult ... [and according to another report] four grains of crude opium placed in the ear have caused death; also four grains by the mouth in more than one case."[29] Such imprecise slippages between crude opium and its much more potent alkaloid could prove dangerous in medical treatment since morphine was, at its highest concentration, over ten times as strong as similar amounts of opium. As we will see later, such apparent lack of precision could have deadly effects.

Studies of medical practice confirm the centrality of opium in the nineteenth century. In her study of James Langstaff's medical practice in Richmond Hill, Ontario, Jacalyn Duffin found that opium remained one of the most frequently used substances in the doctor's bag. She also notes that Langstaff was quick to adopt new innovations (like the microscope) into his practice. Yet in her study we do not see a distinction between morphine and opium, suggesting either that Langstaff did not use morphine or that, in his casebooks, he did not make a distinction. In contrast, the casebooks of Dr. Thomas O. Geddes, a physician in Nova Scotia who practised from the 1820s to the 1880s, show that Geddes used morphine in increasing frequency throughout the years of his practice.[30]

A sample of Geddes's casebooks, taken at roughly five-year intervals, shows how morphine remained dominant in his practice from 1859 to 1880 (see Table 3). It also suggests tentative relationships between the different opium-based substances in Geddes's practice. Geddes prescribed opiates in about 25 percent of all cases he attended. A correlation coefficient of 0.8828 between opium and morphine suggests that Geddes was using the two

Table 3

Opiates in Dr. Geddes's prescriptions (%), 1859–80

	Dover's Powder	Morphine	Opium	Tincture of opium	Use in all prescriptions
1859	5.68	11.08	2.22	6.23	25.21
1864	7.07	10.19	1.63	4.89	23.78
1869	8.63	10.75	2.35	3.53	25.26
1874	7.35	8.61	1.37	4.44	21.77
1880	10.05	7.00	1.26	4.31	22.62

Source: Casebook of Dr. Thomas Geddes, Nova Scotia Archives.

substances at roughly the same rate. A strong inverse relationship between Dover's Powder and tincture of opium, on the other hand, suggests that when he used one, he was not using the other. This suggests that Geddes considered Dover's and laudanum to be reasonable substitutions for each other. Statistical analyses aside, what is most notable is that Geddes used opiates in 25 percent of his prescriptions. A second notable feature is that, in the last years of his practice, Geddes seems to have actively reduced his use of morphine, although whether he replaced it with Dover's Powder, the use of which increased, is uncertain, and unlikely. They generally had very different applications.

Opium the Poison

Just as opium was seen to be fundamental to medical practice, it was recognized to be a dangerous poison. An understanding of the dangers inherent to treatment with opium existed simultaneously with discussions of the drug's therapeutic value. As we will see below, normally "poisoning" referred to the acute overdose that could result in death. Doctors were equally aware of the concerns over developing an opium habit – often referred to as "chronic poisoning" – through repeated administration or through allowing patients to administer the medicine on their own. The issues of acute poisoning and chronic poisoning held danger for the authoritative status of the physician as much as for the health of the patient. At the same time, stories about doctors' struggles to save the lives of the victims of acute opium poisoning, detailed in textbooks and reported in medical journals and the popular press, could serve to increase doctors' chances to heal their patients and bolster the credibility of their profession.

For physicians, acute poisoning was a much more serious concern than was chronic poisoning, and much ink was spilled addressing it. In the era before any serious control on the sale of poisonous substances, it was essential for a physician to be able to treat toxic doses of drugs, be they intentionally or unintentionally administered. Moreover, the ability to identify cases of poisoning was an important part of a physician's public responsibility. Called as medical witnesses in poisoning trials, physicians presented their opinions of the nature of poisons for legal purposes. Indeed, from the beginning of medical education in Canada, medical jurisprudence was included as a field of study. In these classes and from the textbooks, students would learn how to identify causes of death through poisoning, both in the physical appearance of a victim and through chemical testing during a postmortem exam. One key work was Alfred S. Taylor's *On Poisons in Relation to Medical Jurisprudence and Medicine,* first published in 1848 and reissued often over the next few decades. A lecturer on medical jurisprudence and chemistry at Guy's Hospital in London, England, whose textbooks on *materia medica* and jurisprudence were essential references for Canadian medical students, Taylor provided cases and examples of the nature of poisons to aid in clarifying legal definitions and precedents. "The Crime of poisoning has been of late so fearlessly on the increase," ran the preamble, "that it seems essential for the proper administration of justice, and for the security of society, to collect and arrange ... those important medical facts in relation to death by poison."[31] Prior to detailing the action of most known poisons, Taylor considered how the law should define the word itself. His definitions submerged the substance beneath a series of categories based on the physiological conditions of the subject's body and the authority and context of the substance's administration. While navigating the rocky terrain of semantic and legal conditions, Taylor observed that a substance was not a poison when the deleterious effects resulting from its use "[do] not depend upon the nature of the substance taken, but upon the system at the time at which it [the poison] is swallowed."[32] Although a true poison would always affect the system negatively, Taylor reminded his medical colleagues that this medical distinction would not suffice for legal purposes. The law was concerned more with the intent to do harm than with the nature of the substance itself. Taylor explained that "whether a particular substance be or be not a poison is a question of fact left for the decision of a jury from the medical evidence given in the case."[33] Scientific knowledge had to yield to legal determinations.

Opium, Taylor noted, was one of the most ubiquitous poisons. He cited English death statistics from 1837 and 1838 that blamed opium for more deaths by poisoning than any other substance. Opium deaths were most often suicide and accidental infant poisonings.[34] Whereas other writers asserted that opiates were valuable medicines when administered by physicians, Taylor also illustrated the corollary: opium was often a poison when administered by the untrained parent or nurse.[35] Incidents of opiate administration to children concerned physicians. An 1827 article in the *Quebec Medical Journal/Journal de Médecine de Quebec* reported the outcome of a coroner's inquest into the death of two infants who had received 7 drops of laudanum.[36] Reminding his readers of the acceptable dosages of laudanum, the editor noted that "practitioners seldom order a greater quantity than a drop for a dose, and generally only half a drop."[37] So in 1870, commenting on the trial of several city pharmacists for selling laudanum contrary to the poison law (see Chapter 3), a correspondent of the *Toronto Globe* insisted that "laudanum is not the deadly poison which would usually be selected to procure the death of an adult enemy. It is *the* deadly poison of the murderer of infants and of the suicide. It is *the* deadly poison of accidental deaths."[38]

In 1847, the Montreal General Hospital was the site of one such accidental death, the results of which suggested a need for the increased control of drugs by doctors. Alexander Campbell, who was being treated for an inflammation of the leg, received an overdose of laudanum when he asked a fellow patient, William Halloran, for a drink of port wine from one of three bottles near his bed. Halloran, who had "sore eyes" (usually a term applied to conjunctivitis), handed Campbell the bottle that the latter had indicated. Campbell almost immediately realized that he had drunk laudanum instead of wine. Despite doctors' attempts to keep him alive, Campbell died seven hours later. The subsequent coroner's inquest needed to determine why Campbell had access to the laudanum, who was responsible for administering it, and whether Campbell had committed suicide by misinforming Halloran of the bottle's contents. The inquiry focused partly on the responsibility of the ward nurse, Susan Oliver, and on the propriety of Halloran's behaviour. Medical witnesses vouched for Oliver's credibility and stated that the practice of patients "assisting other patients when the nurse is absent" was common. The coroner's jury determined that Campbell was the victim of a fatal mistake and that no one was directly to blame. It also asserted that the hospital needed to refine its method of administering and storing potentially dangerous medicines. The boundaries of the authority of administration needed clearer definition to avoid a recurrence of such a tragedy.[39] That the jury closely scrutinized the activities of the nurse, but generally only discussed the actions of the doctors when they described their attempts to save Campbell's life, suggests an acceptance of the credibility of the physicians' actions. The outcome of the inquest, furthermore, provided a justification for increased control by properly trained and respectable medical professionals.

Poisoning by self-administration of opium was not an infrequent occurrence, and in medical journals doctors often outlined their treatments to inform their colleagues. Several articles in mid-century medical journals demonstrated the variety of cases of poisoning that a doctor might face, as well as how experience reinforced doctors' belief that they should have control over the use of poisonous drugs. In 1846, Dr. George R. Grasett, a Toronto physician, reported a case of poisoning by opium to the Toronto Medico-Chirurgical Society. He prefaced his report by stating, "I am quite aware that cases of this nature not infrequently occur."[40] Both cases that Grasett reported were suicide attempts, one having "its origins in pecuniary losses" and the other "being induced by the previous commission of a crime." Ten years later, the *Medical Chronicle* published "Notes on Three Cases of Poisoning," by Dr. A. Grant, an attending physician at the General Protestant Hospital in Ottawa. Like Grasett, Grant also recognized that opium was "one of the agents most frequently used as a means of destroying life."[41] The first of the three poisoning cases that he related was a woman's attempt at suicide with two ounces of laudanum.

The treatment for acute opiate poisoning was well established in the medical textbooks, so Grasett's approach in the aforementioned case was quite literally by the book.[42] First, he attempted to induce vomiting by administering about half a drachm of sulphate of zinc. The patient "was then dragged around the room, more like a corpse than a living being." After about fifteen minutes, Grasett administered another half a drachm of sulphate of zinc because the first dose had not induced the desired purging. Generally, the physician would attempt to pump the stomach, but in this unfortunate case, "a very important part of the tube" was missing. The doctor poured warm water into the stomach and induced vomiting to "irrigate" the stomach, and the attendants kept the young man in "constant motion." The patient slowly regained lucidity and begged the doctor to be permitted to sleep. Since the doctor was worried that the patient would lapse back into an opium coma and not recover, he refused to allow the patient to rest quite yet. He continued the intense treatment, keeping the patient in motion and awake, and he made the young man swallow a good deal of strong coffee. Several hours later, after a vigorous and diligent attention by the physician and the young man's friends who assisted the doctor, they allowed the patient to sleep. He recovered. Apart from modifications in the types or doses of the substances administered, this combination of physical and chemical intervention was typical of mid-century treatment of opium poisoning.[43]

With cases of poisoning by opium, doctors confronted the inexact and subjective nature of their therapeutics, and this subjectivity occasionally resulted in attacks from colleagues. In 1845, Dr. S.C. Sewell reported a case of poisoning by laudanum to the *British American Journal of Medical and Physical Science*, which prompted a medical colleague to challenge Sewell's treatment with vigour. Sewell's patient, seeking to treat his colic, mistakenly took 10 drachms of laudanum instead of tincture of rhubarb. When Sewell arrived, the patient was still "awake and conscious" and seemed agitated. Sewell's immediate action was similar to that of Grasett: administer an emetic and pump the patient's stomach. Sewell and a colleague, Dr. Scott, also administered 2 ounces of vinegar every half hour. As the patient became increasingly lethargic, the doctors ordered two men to walk the patient between them all night. The treatment was successful, and the next day the man began to recover.[44]

Two months later Dr. John S. Stewart of Kingston challenged Sewell's observations and procedures. Stewart argued that several experts claimed vinegar was contra-indicated in opium poisoning; he argued that Sewell's assertion that the patient had felt little effect from the opium over five hours was not supported by the presenting signs of pinpoint pupils and agitated demeanour. Stewart contradicted Sewell's observation that little of the laudanum had been digested and surmised that perhaps he had been misinformed by the patient about the quantity of laudanum ingested. Sewell had noted that colic generally caused "great tolerance of opium" and that since the mucous membrane of the stomach was irritated, the digestion of the opium had been slowed. Stewart saw "no necessity for referring the tolerance of the poison to two of the supposed causes," the irritated mucous membrane and the state of digestion. He impugned Sewell's ability to observe and deduct with the assertion that "reasoning on false premises, and jumping to rash conclusions should be avoided where medical facts are to be ascertained."[45] If Sewell replied to Stewart's critique, the journal did not print it.

These descriptions of poisoning cases illustrate the variety of ways that understandings of opium influenced the physician's authority. Grasett, Grant, and Sewell all faced patients whose access to and misuse of opiates led to possibly fatal results. Their rapid action and ultimate success would reinforce their medical authority. Grasett's ability to treat the patient without the proper stomach pump may have further bolstered his reputation as a skilled practitioner, as well as providing readers with a way of dealing with a problem that they may face themselves in their practice. Consciousness of reputation may have also driven Stewart's attack on Sewell's therapeutics. Sewell's medical degree gave him the authority to practise medicine, and his successful treatment of his patient lent credibility to his ability; his actions would have been valid in the eyes of his patient and in the opinion of Dr. Scott, on whom he called for assistance. Yet to Stewart, Sewell's observations and suggestions had little constructive value to other physicians because his approach was contradicted by accepted authorities on poisons, including Christison and Pereira. This unorthodox stance, in Stewart's eyes, undermined Sewell's credibility.

Intraprofessional Conflict and the Poison/Medicine

Doctors' success in treating patients whose self-administration of opiates led to poisoning may have bolstered their claims to authority, but doctors' failures, magnified by intraprofessional tensions, weakened those claims. Although many of the internecine debates remained in the pages of medical journals and the minutes of medical societies, occasionally medical knowledge, science, and authority entered the scrutiny of the public. During the summer of 1855, the deaths of two men in Toronto brought the issues of medical credibility, honour, character, and pragmatic questions about the nature of investing authority in medical bodies into public scrutiny. Claims to authority over the use of drugs, arguments about the accuracy of medical knowledge, and the imprecise, subjective nature of doctors' legal testimony combined in the outcomes of the deaths of Job Broom and John Blackie.

In mid-July, James Dickson, a student at John Rolph's Toronto School of Medicine, mistakenly administered an overdose of morphine while treating a man named Job Broom for dysentery. During a long day and night, Dickson and Rolph's colleague Dr. William Aikins worked to keep Broom awake, lest he fall into a coma and die from the overdose. They slapped, shook, shouted at, and threw towels soaked in scalding water at the patient to keep him conscious. Broom survived the night but died five days later. When the family called for a coroner's inquest, Dickson became caught in a conflict between the Toronto School and the rival Trinity Medical College. As Jacalyn Duffin has noted, this conflict was rooted in animosities between the two schools.[46] At the inquest, evidence seemed to exonerate or condemn Dickson according to the pedagogical and political allegiance of the witness. A perfunctory postmortem, carried out by adherents of Trinity, determined that Broom "likely" died of both the overdose and the shock to the system caused by the attempts to revive him. Rolph and his colleagues countered that Broom could not have died from an overdose five days after he had awakened; they suggested that the cause of death was dysentery. Outside observers condemned the inadequate postmortem examination and tended to side with Rolph.[47] Despite such support, Dickson was found guilty of manslaughter, only to be exonerated at the fall court of assize.[48] The jury (and the press) admonished Rolph and Aikins for allowing medical students to practise on the poor.

Two weeks later, the tables turned when a field labourer named John Blackie died while under the care of Dr. Cornelius Philbrick. Philbrick was one of the physicians who had performed the postmortem on Broom and had condemned the actions of Dickson, Aikins, and Rolph. Blackie had reportedly suffered an extreme attack of delirium tremens after drinking cold water while working in the fields under the hot sun. Philbrick's treatment included large doses of morphine. At the subsequent coroner's inquest, the medical evidence was much more detailed than that given at the Broom inquiry. Issues emerged regarding medical credibility and authority, physiological uncertainty, and the proper administration of opium. The jury concluded that Blackie had died from delirium tremens, brought about by a drink of cold water, and that Philbrick was not to blame.

Taken together, the Broom and Blackie cases illustrated the subjectivity of the idea of opium's "judicious use" and challenged any conceit of objective medical science. The outcome of the treatments was the same – both patients died – yet the authority of the administrator and the propriety of his therapeutics determined the legal credibility of his behaviour. Dickson's authority was debatable, but his diagnosis seems to have been credible. Philbrick's authority was assured, yet his diagnosis was heavily debated. This legal and social scrutiny reflected the attitudes to which doctors were subject, as well as medical professionals' subjective use of supposedly objective scientific "facts" to bolster their social and political authority. What follows is a brief discussion of the complex relationship between credibility and medical knowledge in these cases and how they combined to affect conceptions of the nature of opium.

During the Broom inquest, the credibility of Dickson, Aikins, and Rolph in their treatment of Broom was connected to their means of reviving the victim of poisoning. As the Grasett, Grant, and Sewell articles illustrate, the methods used by the members of the Toronto School of Medicine generally followed accepted practice. Despite these medical precedents, the jury and the public seem to have been upset at the treatment of Broom and at the physical state of the man's corpse. The apparent physical abuse, explicitly detailed by several of the witnesses at the inquest, seems to have violated a line of demarcation between acceptable and unacceptable medical treatment. Neither legal nor medical justifications could alleviate public concern over such apparent disrespectful "mistreatment." Conversely, the means of diagnosing Broom's cause of death was through an extremely limited autopsy of Broom's body, yet the Trinity professors' testimony held more weight. The plausibility of the Trinity professors' testimony was based more on their social credibility, compared with the weakening of Rolph's and Aikins's medical authority, than on conclusive, objective science.

In the Blackie inquest, more emphasis was placed on the scientific explanations, but ultimately the credibility of the administrator prevailed. As Duffin observes, "Teachers of both medical schools had boned up on their pharmacology for *this* inquest."[49] The key determinant of Philbrick's authority was his demonstrated understanding of the physiological changes wrought on the body by the chronic use of alcohol. Blackie was a habitual drunkard, who had rarely been seen sober, although he was hardly ever so drunk as to be unable to work. His immediate affliction seemed to be delirium tremens, a somatic condition identifiable through observation and associated with either prolonged drinking or the abrupt cessation of drinking.[50] This condition became a key aspect of the trial because the coroner was "prejudice[d] against all alcohol-consuming creatures."[51] Yet the shaking of the limbs, hallucinations, and general derangement typical of delirium tremens were not exclusive to that condition. Rolph suggested that Blackie had probably been suffering from meningitis, whereas several of Philbrick's colleagues argued that Blackie's body displayed the symptoms of apoplexy. Some doctors questioned the judiciousness of the large doses of morphine. Rolph noted that whether or not his diagnosis of meningitis was correct, he would not have administered such a large dose of morphia. He also suggested that Philbrick's behaviour was irresponsible, whether or not the patient had been suffering from delirium tremens:

> More persons have been killed in delirium tremens by over doses of opium than ever have been cured; the mortality from inordinate doses of opium is very great ... it is plain to me that when Dr. Philbrick called on Monday

morning and caused the patient to be roused ... he must have thought the patient was under the influence of morphia.[52]

Rolph testified that according to Christison, 7 grains of morphia are equivalent to about 42 grains of opium, or 1¾ ounces of laudanum.[53] Aikins concurred with his colleague, arguing that the dose that Philbrick gave was "a fatal dose and not a proper one for delirium tremens or any other disease, *unless* the patient has been long habituated to the use of opium in very large quantities."[54] However, contemporary medical writing suggests that Rolph and Aikins's testimony on the treatment of delirium tremens was incorrect. Many nineteenth-century commentators argued that opium in large doses was crucial in the treatment of delirium tremens.[55]

Qualifying his assertion with reference to the opium habit, Aikins reflected concerns about the uncertainty presented by the inebriate's deranged constitution. Physicians often generalized when discussing the physiology of the habitual user of alcohol or narcotics. In the Blackie inquest, several physicians believed that a drunkard could easily handle a large amount of opium, just as an "opium eater" would do. Testifying on Philbrick's behalf, a Dr. Russell noted that "there are some diseases which render a patient tolerant of opium, delirium tremens for instance."[56] Dr. Widmer reinforced the notion that the system of the habitual user of opium or alcohol was deranged. He explained that he had always been cautious with morphine, but

> I once gave a huge poisonous dose of laudanum to a respectable person in this city – in the course of an hour, I gave an ounce of laudanum in two doses – the patient went to sleep, slept all night, and recovered perfectly ... That patient had not been in the habit of taking laudanum, but he had been in the habit of taking large quantities of [alcohol].[57]

According to this perspective, a healthy body would die after a large dose of morphia, but a deranged body needed a shock to help rebalance the system. Blackie, a drunkard who required sleep to alleviate his delirium, needed a large dose of morphia to achieve this end. Philbrick was therefore justified in administering enough morphia to, as he described it, "kill four persons in perfect health."

Other doctors challenged this justification. Echoing Pereira's advice to "confess our ignorance" about the effects of opiates on the body, a Dr. Nicol observed that "it is impossible to say what would be the proportion of doses of morphia administered to a habitual drinker labouring under delirium tremens, and to a person not so affected an almost unlimited amount could be given to some patients in delirium tremens, especially the tremens produced by opium eating."[58] Nicol argued for an approach to physiology that recognized different actions of drugs on different physical states. This variability repeatedly challenged physicians. In the positivistic search for hard and fast rules regarding the effects of therapeutic measures on the body, the variability of somatic reactions was the physician's albatross. In the face of conflicting medical testimony, eight of the fourteen members of the jury determined that Philbrick had not acted improperly and that Blackie's body and habits had caused his death.

The outcomes of these two inquests was a tarnished reputation for doctors, public scrutiny of the internecine conflicts within the medical "fraternity," and a demonstration of the socially determined nature of medical scientific knowledge. In both inquests, the juries – groups of laymen not medically trained – rendered their decisions based on whether the evidence accorded with generally held physiological perceptions, the character of the individuals involved, and what the jury perceived as acceptable medical treatment. Newspaper commentaries attacked doctors for their undignified behaviour and suggested that the city was safer only because everyone now knew the low quality of medical practice.[59] Doctors' authority rested on public perceptions of their character, a reality that the two inquests made strikingly clear.[60] The variability of the actions of opiates, the uncertainty of the condition of the body in specific diseased states, and a divided medical profession weakened the authority of doctors. That Philbrick was exonerated whereas Dickson was condemned suggests that the dual nature of opium as a poison and a medicine was socially determined; the judicious use of opiates related to the public acceptance of the individual's actions.

Chronic Poisoning

Chronic opium poisoning, caused by the development of a habit through repeated dosing of opiates and other substances, was less prevalent than acute poisoning in medical discussions for much of the century. Textbook discussions that mentioned the development of an iatrogenic opium habit tended to present it as an inconvenient problem that doctors should try to avoid. Medical journals similarly observed it as a complicating factor in the treatment of other conditions. Until the final years of the century, writers of general medical textbooks rarely spent time discussing how to treat it, although the cautions against inadvertently creating an opium habit through careless therapeutics became more shrill.

In his 1842 version of *Elements*, Jonathan Pereira discussed the opium habit mostly as a reflection on Chinese opium smoking and as a problem in Asia and the Middle East, not in Western countries. He spent some time deliberating on how destructive this habit might be, concluding that its dangers were connected more to the economic class of the smoker than to the physiological effects of the drug itself: "The practice is most destructive to those who live in poverty and distress, and who carry it to excess, yet it does not appear that the Chinese, in easy circumstances, and who have the comforts of life about them, are materially affected, in respect to longevity, by the private addiction to this vice."[61] When he turned to opium eating in Europe, Pereira referred his readers to the recent writings of Thomas De Quincey and Samuel Taylor Coleridge. He then reproduced travellers' accounts of witnessing the effects of opium eating in Asia, emphasizing that these examples of addiction in the "orient" often had iatrogenic origins. Yet despite recognizing the iatrogenic origins and physical problems of chronic opium poisoning, Pereira observed that there was some doubt as to the "alleged injurious effects of opium-eating on the health."[62] Still, for Pereira, opium eating appeared to be an exceptional habit, an outlier behaviour mostly undertaken by foreigners, not something that required medical attention unless it interfered with the treatment of other conditions.

For mid-century writers, the issue of habit was related mostly to concern about its relationship to therapy and about how it complicated the physician's ability to treat properly. Because habitual users of some substances developed a tolerance, figuring out what constistuted an effective dose was problematic. This circumstance, we should note, was the underlying justification that Philbrick made for his treatment of Blackie with dangerous doses of morphine. Pereira noted that "instances of the use of enormous doses of opium, with comparatively slight effects, will be found in every work on pharmacology."[63] The likelihood that chronic opium eating would mess up effective medical treatment was a concern for the welfare of the patient and for the image of the physician.

The most significant danger was in treating chronic illnesses with opium, thereby creating a repeated administration for anodyne purposes. Discussing treatments of neuralgia, George Bacon Wood combined the benefits and dangers of opium in one passage: "The most efficient [treatment] beyond all comparison is opium in one or another of its forms ... The great danger in the use of opium is that the patient may contract a pernicious habit which he may afterwards be unable or unwilling to break, when there may be no longer occasion for the medicine."[64] He made a similar caution in the treatment of diseases like those of the digestive system, rheumatism, and gout.[65] For the latter, he listed a range of opiate therapies but preferred mixing it with colchicum wine because it was less pleasant and reduced the tendency of repeated use. Austin Flint, whose *Treatise on the Principles and Practice of Medicine* was a recommended text in Canadian medical schools from the 1860s to the 1890s, echoed Wood a decade later. On the treatment of chronic bronchitis, opium "is to be prescribed with circumspection ... lest the habit of using it be formed."[66] Flint cautioned against using opium too enthusiastically in all chronic conditions. For example, in chronic gastralgia, a condition of chronic pain in the stomach area, opium was recommended to relieve pain. But as with chronic bronchitis, "as in other painful affections which are apt to be persisting, the liability to the formation of a habit of using opium is to be considered."[67] Flint, as with many of the textbook authors before the end of the century, did not provide any recommendations for treating the opium habit itself. It was merely a troublesome side effect of medical treatment. Even in the final edition of the book published a decade after Flint's death, treatment of the opium habit was not mentioned.

Opium administration for chronic and somatic conditions was problematic, but its administration for mental illnesses was even more troublesome. In the first edition of his highly influential *Principles and Practice of Medicine* of 1891, William Osler noted that some neurasthenic patients "drift into a condition of chronic invalidism or become slaves to morphia or chloral [hydrate]." He recommended nonmedical treatments, preferring convalescence and travel over chemical intervention. Fifteen years later, he expressed his concerns more directly: "I have been repeatedly shocked by the loose, careless way" that physicians administered opiates for "simple headache or a mild neuralgia."[68] Similarly, in his *Insanity and Its Treatment* of 1871, G. Fielding Blandford wrote, "I believe there is no drug, the use of which more often becomes abuse, than that of opium in the treatment of insanity ... do not be led away by the fatal facility with which you can administer it by subcutaneous injection. Inject it in the case of a melancholic patient, if you like, but in this furious delirium you must abstain from the administration in all its forms."[69] For Blandford, the physician must be abstinent because a manic patient would not be.

Along with simply not using opiates in treating some conditions, another recommended way to avoid a development of the opium habit was not to tell patients what they were receiving. Arguing in *Nervous and Mental Diseases* (1900) that opium "is a sort of specific for melancholia," A. Church and F. Peterson reminded readers that, "needless to say ... the opium treatment should not be made known to the patient, and is carried out with more safety, as regards the formation of a habit, when the patient is in an institution."[70] Such active deception of patients would protect them from the potential of developing an iatrogenic addiction and simultaneously protect the authority of the physician, whose judicious application of his knowledge and use of opiates could be tarnished by the development of a habit.

To Treat with a Better Knife – the Hypodermic Syringe[71]

Underpinning the discussions about the problems with creating the opium habit was the issue of the physician's control over the patient. Control was fundamental to a physician's power, so not informing a patient about the remedy given was a way of mitigating potential dangers. This idea of control, expressed by Church and Peterson, and the need to manage a potentially troublesome patient in order to avoid any damaging side effects, informed discussions of the use of the hypodermic syringe for administering opiates, specifically morphine. In Osler's jeremiad against physicians administering opiates for a simple headache, his concern was the injection of morphine with the hypodermic syringe and the "loose and careless" way that the physicians made such items available for their patients' use.

Technology like the hypodermic needle permitted the physician to manage the patient more precisely, distancing the autonomous individual from the medical intervention. N.D. Jewson has characterized the increased technical- and laboratory-based development of medical knowledge as "the disappearance of the sick man" because the characteristics, status, and individuality of the sick person ceased to be important in the development of atomized medical knowledge.[72] A similar argument can be made about the changes in medical treatment throughout the century. Although physicians continued, of course, to face the full person when treating them, any resistance or wilful actions of the individual could be mitigated. Surgery under more precise anaesthetics allowed for total control of a limp body. Diagnostic tools that allowed the physician to "see" into the body without the medium of the patient's subjective interpretation, such as the stethoscope, sphygmograph, and other devices, allowed more objective interpretation of the body's operations. John Harley Warner has demonstrated how therapeutic descriptions shifted about mid-century from emphasizing "natural" bodily functions (those that were natural for the individual's characteristics) to "normal" functions, an assessment based on standardized notions of a body's proper operation – pulse rate, blood pressure, and so on.[73] Diagnostic technology removed individual idiosyncrasies from a role in diagnoses, the shift to the lab distanced knowledge creation from actual individuals, and the hypodermic syringe allowed more precise delivery of drugs, without the pesky problem of interference by an autonomous patient.

Just as the stethoscope fundamentally altered a physician's diagnostic capabilities, so the hypodermic syringe revolutionized therapeutics. The syringe (the simple tube and plunger) has been used since classical times, but the hypodermic needle (the hollow needle attached to the syringe) was an innovation of the nineteenth century. Use of hypodermic medication developed slowly from the 1830s to the 1850s.[74] Wielding a syringe, the doctor could administer medicine without the participation of the patient and notwithstanding the body's physical rejection of the substance. So the doctor did not require the patient to swallow, and the drug would not be discharged through vomiting (or defecation in the case of suppositories). The individual became a passive – although not disinterested – player in the medical drama. The hypodermic syringe, therefore, gave doctors control over the administration of drugs that they viewed as essential to their ability to treat the patient.

The hypodermic injection of morphine quickly became a popular form of medication, and its spread may be considered uncontrolled. When René T.H. Laennec introduced the stethoscope, he trained his students to use what they heard in order to inform their understanding of the body.[75] Unfortunately, no similar course of study seemed to be considered for the hypodermic needle; many doctors used it in apparent reckless abandon. As one writer noted of the hypodermic syringe in 1871, "Physicians of the present day carry in a pocket-case more active elements of prompt medication than used to be packed in a good-sized pair of saddle bags."[76] Here the issue of power and control are central: the syringe enabled the prompt action that Warner noted was key to a doctor's ability to secure power. Also the ability to administer drugs without the participation of the patient is a powerful one. These sentiments emerged in the numerous discussions of the benefits and dangers of hypodermic medicine printed in Canadian medical periodicals in the middle of the century and (eventually) in medical textbooks. These discussions suggest how doctors quickly came to recognize that hypodermic morphine could be a panacea for many illnesses. Considering this potent therapeutic tool, some felt that the habitual use of morphine through hypodermic injection was nothing more than an inconvenient side effect, potentially beneficial, and neither serious nor difficult to treat. As long as doctors retained their control over the patient, morphine injection was exclusively beneficial.

Many historians of opium addiction have seen in the rapid expansion of the hypodermic injection of morphine a key turning point in the development of ideas about the problems of addiction.[77] It is not surprising that this was the case. Hypodermic injection, like morphine itself, was a medical innovation designed to make medical treatment more efficacious. These were both advanced technologies that expanded medical authority and, ideally, improved the lives of patients. Therefore, the misuse of such technologies was reprehensible. It was some kind of corruption of a positive, progressive development, leading to regressive and destructive ends. Nevertheless, it was decades before the hypodermic syringe itself was controlled. As we will see in the next chapter, controlling access to substances was a difficult enough process; stopping people from buying hypodermic syringes was not even mentioned in the debates.

By the beginning of the twentieth century, then, even though opium remained central to medical treatment, its place in the therapeutic spectrum had begun to change. The humoral explanation of illness – evident, for example, in the view that opium's sudorific, or sweat-inducing, quality was useful in cases where skin was "dry and warm" – was in decline. Heroic therapies such as we saw with George Bacon Wood's excessive bleeding regimens had been replaced with more subtle chemical interventions. Pharmaceutical advances, such as the isolation of active components of many formerly raw substances, resulted in a broader range of treatments that could be more specifically targeted at individual physical symptoms. Finally, and not insignificantly, technological changes in the delivery of medicine into the body, specifically with the development of the hypodermic syringe, allowed physicians to have greater control of the illness condition by being able to control more directly the delivery of medicine into the body.

Hypodermic medicine, powerful doses of opiates, and complex prescriptions based on a sophisticated conception of the functioning of the body all gave authority to physicians' claims to be protectors of the public's health – but with some limitations. These medical technologies also presented danger. Doctors themselves at times could not control their own use of powerful medical technologies like the hypodermic needle, and they debated among themselves how to effectively treat patients and avoid harming them further. The reputation of physicians, both as members of a profession and as individual healers, was at stake, as was the health of their patients. Since opium was so fundamental to medical treatment, and therefore to the reputation of the medical professional, it stands to reason that physicians would be intensely concerned with the ability of the everyday person to access the drug. As a poison, opium presented a dire threat to people; as a medicine, its effective use could be guaranteed only through administration by the educated and respectable physician.

Yet access to drugs was not the only issue: physicians needed to ensure that the people who were compounding their prescriptions were capable and responsible professionals. When doctors contemplated the best way to judiciously and effectively treat people, they – not surprisingly – looked at the individuals who were responsible for distributing and compounding these powerful medicines. Since the medical profession's reputation depended on access to therapeutically valuable drugs and accurately compounded remedies, physicians needed the services of capable and responsible dispensers and compounders of medicines. The process of defining proper and improper use, and suitable and unsuitable access to drugs, however, involved often disparate ideas about professional authority and occupational integrity, which were all made more significant by the potency of the substances in question.

3
Canada's First Drug Laws

Until the last half of the nineteenth century, the sale of medicines, poisonous and otherwise, was essentially unregulated in British North America. Most of the pre-Confederation jurisdictions had some kind of law proscribing the unfettered sale of poisons, but these laws were concerned with substances used maliciously or for suicides, and they were poorly enforced and generally considered ineffective. For example, both Canada East and Canada West had Strychnine Acts that placed minimal requirements on the sale of "arsenic, corrosive sublimate, strychnine, or other ... deadly poison[s]." The Canada West legislation required the hopeful purchaser of poisons to produce for the vendor "a certificate or note from ... a Physician, Surgeon, or some Priest or Minister of religion," which attested to the customer's good moral character.[1] By imbuing in several types of professionals the authority to assess the moral capability of the person who sought to buy poisons, the legislation reiterated a regime of control that was rooted in traditional notions of morality, credibility, and social order. Yet such static delineations of who could be considered an authority in the distribution of dangerous substances were far from uncontested. When it came to the sale of poisonous substances that were also used as medicines, one group was noticeably absent: the pharmacists.

In Toronto in November 1870, the problems with weak poison laws became clear in a trial that shook the local pharmacy community. John Gale and George Mason began a project to test the integrity of the city's druggists.[2] Gale would enter a drug store and attempt to purchase laudanum. He offered various reasons for the purchase but never provided any type of "certificate or form" as the Ontario Strychnine Act required. Twenty-five of the druggists sold Gale the drug; some of them confided that they were contravening the law, whereas others demanded a detailed explanation of the ailment for which Gale needed the substance. This type of investigation was not new to Mason, who had earned the nickname "Whiskey" Mason for his efforts to entrap liquor vendors into breaking the law. His notoriety may be the reason he had Gale make the purchases. According to the liquor-licensing law, the prosecutor would receive half the fine levied in any such conviction.[3] This was also the case under the Strychnine Act.[4] Mason and Gale were set for a substantial payday since a fine for violating the Strychnine Act could be up to $40.00. So, with their evidence in hand, Mason and Gale initiated court proceedings.

Arguments at the subsequent trial demonstrated the ambiguities of the term "poison" and the need to define who had authority to delineate which substances should be controlled. During the trial, doctors and druggists formed temporary alliances to assert the capacity of medicine to authoritatively define a drug's potential danger. The defence argued that a "deadly" poison, which the Strychine Act did not clearly define, was one that caused death immediately. Witnesses for the defence included physicians, university professors, and pharmacists, all of whom argued that laudanum was not a deadly poison and, in fact, "is kept in almost every house as a medicine."[5] The *Toronto Globe* supported the pharmacists by asserting that a too-strict definition of the law would be inconvenient for the public. The editor argued that, although laudanum was indeed "often resorted to by suicides, [it] is not deadly in small quantities, such as are needed, say, to ease a toothache or to check diarrhea, and it is a resort at all hours when the application to the minister or surgeon would be very difficult or inconvenient."[6] The prosecution challenged these assertions. When cross-examining the pharmacists, the lawyers for the Crown asked, if laudanum was not a "deadly" poison, then why had they been so careful to scrutinize the purchaser's motives?[7] According to the prosecutors, since the pharmacists recognized the dangers of laudanum, they must have believed it was poisonous, despite what the expert testimony argued. The magistrate agreed, deciding against the druggists and fining each $25.00 and costs. It was a temporary defeat since the convictions were overturned four months later.[8] The legal confusion of the Strychnine Act was about to end.

It was probably cold comfort to the twenty-five pharmacists now $25.00 poorer that the law was about to change. Between the middle of the nineteenth century and the beginning of the twentieth, the legal status of pharmacists in the distribution of dangerous substances changed. Pharmacists and their allies argued for, and eventually achieved legislation, which recognized pharmacy as a profession that was legally empowered to establish criteria for licensure, regulate its members' activities, and prosecute anyone who transgressed the parameters of the law. Each provincial pharmacy act legally incorporated a professional body, be it the pharmaceutical association, society, or college of pharmacy, and empowered them to determine who was and was not able to practise pharmacy – that is, to compound and sell medicines on the orders of a physician. The legislation also changed the mercantile landscape, since it was the first time in Canada that the right to distribute a specific group of products had been placed in the hands of one group of vendors. These provincial pharmacy acts, in effect, created a monopoly over the sale of drugs, a trade monopoly in a political and economic system where monopoly was anathema.

Yet these laws, often called "incorporation acts" or "enabling legislation," went further. Since they were designed to regulate an occupation whose primary role was the compounding and selling of medicines, the pharmacy acts also included a list of substances that would hereafter be restricted to sales by doctors and druggists. This list was often called a "poison schedule." All of these provincial laws identified the physician's prescription as the main means by which individuals could obtain these newly controlled substances. Some allowed druggists to make their own judgments of character, permitting licensed pharmacists to sell at least some of the controlled substances to individuals who were "familiar" to the pharmacists or who were introduced by someone familiar to the pharmacists.[9] All pharmacy bills empowered the pharmaceutical associations to identify substances that should be added to the poison schedule; all required the agreement of the governor-in-council to make this change happen. All provincial pharmacy laws exempted physicians from the restrictions of the legislation.

These were Canada's first drug laws. By constructing a new system of management over the distribution and sale of drugs, by identifying authoritative actors whose role included restricting access to dangerous drugs, and by empowering one educated professional group to define new dangerous drugs and to be directly concerned with the enforcement of the legislation, the pharmacy laws of the provinces and territories of Canada ushered in, however piecemeal, drug control in Canada. Much of the agitation to create some kind of authoritative management of the pharmacy profession and the sale of drugs began in pre-Confederation Quebec, but Ontario was the first province to pass a pharmacy law, basing its 1871 act, which had first been proposed in 1869, on the British Pharmacy Act of 1868. Soon afterward, Quebec, Nova Scotia, and Manitoba followed suit, each with similarly structured legislation. By the end of the century, all Dominion provinces and territories except for Prince Edward Island had pharmacy laws on the books. P.E.I. passed its law in 1905 (see Table 4).

Canada was not alone in the drive for pharmaceutical professionalization as a means of controlling access to dangerous drugs. Great Britain, the United States, Mexico, and Australia, for example, all saw the potential of a regulated pharmaceutical profession as a means of controlling access to problematic substances. The British legislation on which the Ontario Pharmacy Act of 1871 was modelled, built on half a century of attempts to restrict and control the sale of medicine and dangerous drugs.[10] Britain's Pharmacy Act included a bifurcated poison schedule that listed the drugs to be controlled by professional oversight. In the United Sates several states had passed pharmacy laws early in the nineteenth century, but however effective they may have been, by 1868 all but one of the states' laws had become ineffective or had been actually repealed.[11] The laissez-faire approach of the US economic system, combined with the remnants of Jacksonian democracy, which rejected aristocratic dominance, made passing laws that seemed monopolistic and elitist politically tricky. By the end of the century, the American Pharmaceutical Association was recommending a model law to state legislatures.[12] This renewed drive toward pharmacy legislation in the states and territories near the turn of the century was also aimed at controlling drugs like opium, along with new upstart drugs such as cocaine, a process to be discussed in later chapters.[13] Similarly, in Mexico attempts to control the spread of non-medical drug use started with pharmacy legislation, although these efforts were national rather than state-wide and took place in the early part of the twentieth century.[14] Australia's legislation was first passed at the state level, with Victoria and New South Wales both instituting poisons acts in 1876 that restricted the sale of poisons to doctors, druggists, and licensed vendors in rural areas.[15] Canadian pharmaceutical legislation, then, was part of a broader move to place drugs under professional control rather than absolute prohibition. The prohibition part came later.

The creation of provincial pharmacy legislation involved a negotiation between different voices and claims to authority, played out in a legislative arena. The symbiotic relationship between physicians and pharmacists was fundamental to the creation of these laws, but this professional relationship was always tenuous and strained. Both hoped to see some kind of restriction over the distribution of dangerous drugs, but they had different ideas about the best way to achieve it. Although doctors and druggists agreed that pharmacists were the best vendors suited to compounding and selling drugs, they became hung up on several key questions, not the least of which was determining who was best suited to evaluate a pharmacist's competency. Early on, as they were expanding their own professional scope, physicians argued that they were best suited to examine and license pharmacists since, for their prescriptions to be effective, they would need competent compounders of medicines. Pharmacists countered that they were best able to regulate themselves since chemistry was a complex science, physicians did not receive the sort of training necessary to be able to evaluate a pharmacist's abilities, and such interference was an affront to any self-respecting learned profession. However, it was not merely about skill and chemical or pharmacological knowledge. Effective pharmacists needed these things, to be sure, but they also required the moral capacity to control access to substances that were increasingly being seen as dangerous. As with the Mason and Gale trial, in these discussions we see manifested the uneasy relationship between physicians and pharmacists, the territorial disputes over both esoteric knowledge and social power, how these issues related to the authority of various professions to manage the health of the people, and a conflicting notion of the role of the professional in a market-driven society. In this sense, the prescription was a "boundary object," something that linked these two professions but "served to mark their different roles and relative power."[16]

We must be careful not to draw the professional lines too sharply. Even within their ranks, pharmacists and physicians did not always agree. In the 1860s physicians were attempting to unite a disparate profession and achieve occupational closure in the Province of Canada, a story that has been told well elsewhere.[17] Physicians from medical sects that included the allopathic (often called regular medicine), homeopathic, eclectic, and Thomsonian all disagreed both on their philosophies of healing and on which substances were viable medications. Pharmacy too was not a homogeneous profession. Divisions often arose between wholesale and retail drug houses, between elite urban pharmacists who could get by on compounding and vending drugs nearly exclusively and rural druggists who needed to operate full retail general stores, and between small retail druggists and the growing multi-department stores (called "departmental stores"), which included pharmacies as a department and many of which offered mail-order services to remote customers. Simultaneously, representatives of pharmacy presented arguments of economic justice, social stability, professional rights, and national integrity, all in an effort to protect their profession and expand their authority.

The debates around the professionalization of pharmacy involved complex discussions about the role of various professions in maintaining and protecting the health of the people. Although some have argued that it was really all a financial issue, the idea of the professional as an honourable, morally responsible individual whose interest was to protect the good of the people rather than base economic motivations informed many of the discussions of the professionalization of pharmacy and the control of access to drugs. Pharmacy laws were not, then, pushed just for economic gain; they were part of a broader pursuit of social stability. In this view, the professional transcended the nasty business of trade and was above the temptations of the marketplace.[18] Yet this was more myth than reality. When the professions had to mix it up in the free market, all sorts of high ideals and rhetoric faced serious challenges from the fiscal reality of running a business.

The pharmacy acts were part of an expansive governance of the population that combined internal controls of the profession with external control over the broader community. The pharmacy laws' purpose, driven by the perceived threat of easy access to dangerous poisons, was to govern access to medicines that could be misused and to make sure that only the proper type of person was controlling that access. Setting and defending professional boundaries, deciding what type of behaviour by one profession violated the authority of another, and asserting the right of one professional body to investigate and prosecute transgressions to the laws were elements of the professional governmentality discussed in the Introduction. In effect, this construction of a new system of governance of drugs created new knowledge producers and over time led to an expansion not only of the type of drugs that would be controlled but also of the very definition of a "dangerous" drug and what that meant to society. Creating, reinforcing, and managing these relationships between professional authority and individual behaviour as it related to medicines were parts of a biopolitical process: the governance of life. Moreover, the laws and regulations that affected what constituted the proper and improper use of medications created a sense of power and authority in which a citizen who misused a "controlled" substance – either for nonmedical self-indulgence or for malicious purposes, including murder or suicide – operated outside of an established norm of behaviour. Provincial pharmacy laws, then, were fundamental to reshaping the relationship between the citizen and the substance.

Finally, a word on terminology. Through the middle of the nineteenth century, the terms "apothecary," "pharmacist," "chemist," and "druggist" were often used interchangeably, but they have different etymologies. Apothecaries have a deeper history, and until the nineteenth century, apothecaries in Britain acted as medical practitioners and vendors of medicines.[19] Druggists were usually simply traders in drugs. Pharmacists and chemists, meanwhile, presented more scientific foundations for their work. By the middle of the nineteenth century, however, in Canada the terms "apothecary," "pharmacist," "druggist," and "chemist" were generally synonymous, with "apothecary" rapidly becoming archaic, while many chemists were forming their own professional identity as analytical chemists, divorced from the compounding and vending of drugs. It can be confusing, and consequently I intersperse "pharmacist" and "druggist" for the sake of variety, and use "apothecary" and "chemist" only when the sources do so.

Pharmacy Education and Licensure in the Province of Canada

In the early part of the century, the stated reason for regulating "apothecaries" in the Province of Canada was to ensure that physicians had reliable sources of medicines that were compounded by well-trained and respectable professionals and always judiciously dispensed with an eye to the protection of the public. As with the British Apothecaries Act of 1815, one of the earliest attempts to oversee the education and licensure of apothecaries came by way of the physicians' efforts to regulate themselves. During the 1840s physicians in Lower Canada were pressing the legislature for the broader powers associated with professional incorporation.[20] They argued that doctors should control most facets of medical treatment, including the licensing and education of pharmacy. In Lower Canada this expectation was not a tremendous stretch. From 1788, there had been legal provisions for the registration of the vendors of medicines, who needed to obtain a licence from the province's governor, who would appoint an appropriate examiner, although the law set no specific educational requirements.[21]

In 1842, Archibald Hall, a prominent Montreal physician, addressed his "Letters on Medical Education" to the members of the legislature. Hall observed that the current state of medical education in Canada was unsatisfactory. He proposed a detailed and ambitious bill that would encompass the occupations of physician, surgeon, "Man-Midwife," and apothecary. Hall's proposal placed apothecaries in a distinctly subservient but necessary place within the spectrum of health services. Even the title of his bill, an "Act to Regulate the Study and Practice of Physic, Surgery and Midwifery," excluded apothecaries, a slippage that suggests Hall's view of the secondary place of apothecaries in the medical hierarchy. Yet he did recognize the importance of pharmaceutical education. His bill required each aspiring apothecary to serve a three-year apprenticeship with a physician or apothecary and to attend classes in chemistry, pharmacy, and *materia medica*. Prior to receiving a licence, each apprentice had to sit an examination in these three subjects before a medical board. Anticipating future pharmacy bills, Hall also included several clauses that outlined the conditions under which poisons "such as corrosive sublimate, arsenic, laudanum and the like" should be stored and sold.[22]

Hall's suggestions were reflected in the medical and poison legislation that he and his confrères presented to Parliament over the next few years. In both 1845 and 1846, Lower Canada physicians presented an "Act Respecting the Medical Profession and the Sale of Drugs." This bill detailed the responsibilities of the proposed College of Physicians and Surgeons to examine and license physicians, surgeons, midwives, and apothecaries. Dr. A. Von Iffland proposed that the doctors should include a section governing the education of apothecaries and druggists, "as might ensure to the public as well as to the medical profession, men of good education and thoroughly versed in chemistry and pharmacy."[23] Briefly united to oppose this initiative, several apothecaries protested to Von Iffland, explaining that they were preparing to petition the legislature for their own act of incorporation. The doctors acquiesced, and the legislation that passed in 1847 mentioned pharmacists only to reaffirm the provisions of the Quebec Act of 1788. A decade later, Von Iffland complained that the pharmacists had "abandoned the measure then contemplated for their self-improvement, preferring to remain as individuals or associated traders, and subject ... to no other responsibility than that of tradesmen."[24] He concluded that it was time, in 1857, for the College of Physicians and Surgeons to take action, "as may guard against the evils of ignorance."[25] Von Iffland's attack was factually inaccurate; in 1849 the pharmacists had presented legislation that attempted to create a college of pharmacy, but this legislation did not pass.[26] Nevertheless, they had not presented legislation to the government since then.

To physicians, the lack of professional oversight of the druggists left the public's health in danger by the unscrupulous nature of the competitive marketplace. Von Iffland observed that the College of Physicians had recently examined and licensed two pharmacists. It would be "an act of gross injustice to them," he stated, "were they to be placed in the same position for public consideration and patronage, as others who are not so qualified by the College."[27] He recognized the pressures of the market on an occupation that was predominantly about trade in commodities rather than exclusively about the command of philosophical concepts and esoteric knowledge.[28] In 1860, Hall agreed that the dangers posed by the pressures of the marketplace were specifically the reason that the public should demand properly qualified apothecaries. The pharmacists' knowledge of drugs was important, but equally important was that their "character should be a guarantee of the purity and genuineness of the materials which they are using."[29] Hall further argued that the sale of poisons needed tighter regulation. Economic necessity, Hall claimed, may cause an apothecary to use cheaper or adulterated substances when making up prescriptions or to sell poisons to anyone who demanded them, with no regard to the use for which the purchaser intended the substance.

Eventually, the doctors achieved some control over pharmaceutical education in Lower Canada. From 1858 to 1860, the Lower Canada physicians repeatedly presented bills in the legislature specifically designed to "regulate the education of Apothecaries, Chemists and Druggists, and the Sale of Poisons." In 1863 a bill was presented that would require anyone who wished "to sell or distribute medicine by retail in Lower Canada" to be licensed by the provincial Medical Board. This did not pass second reading. Then, in 1864, the legislature amended the Medical Act of 1847 – the legislation from which the clause giving physicians oversight of apothecary education had been removed – placing the responsibility for licensing pharmacists under the auspices of the College of Physicians and Surgeons. The following year, the college amended its bylaws to detail the specific educational requirements for pharmacists.[30]

Nevertheless, the lobbying by pharmacists (and by physicians) continued. Pharmacists in Ontario had been actively working to achieve incorporation for several years prior to Confederation. After a few stalled attempts, their efforts led to the first provincial pharmacy act in Canada in 1871. Although Quebec's pharmacists now had to undergo the scrutiny of the College of Physicians and Surgeons, pharmacists continued to lobby for the creation of their own college and the professional autonomy that went with it, which they achieved in 1875. The push for pharmacy laws in Canadian provinces and territories was drawn out over the first four decades of Canada's existence. Pharmacists achieved their legislative independence in Ontario, Quebec, Nova Scotia, and Manitoba in the 1870s, in New Brunswick in 1884,

Table 4

Years of first post-Confederation provincial and territorial pharmacy legislation

Province	Year
Alberta	1892, 1910
British Columbia	1891
Manitoba	1878
New Brunswick	1884
Nova Scotia	1876
Ontario	1871
Prince Edward Island	1905
Quebec	1875
Saskatchewan	1892, 1911

in British Columbia and the Northwest Territories in the 1890s, and in Prince Edward Island in 1905 (See Table 4). When Alberta and Saskatchewan became provinces in 1905, the North-West Territories Pharmaceutical Association continued in existence until it determined whether it was pragmatic to split the association and divide the assets among the two provinces. Consequently, pharmaceutical legislation was passed in 1910 in Alberta and 1911 in Saskatchewan. In these legislative efforts, the key issue was to ensure that the right type of person was selling dangerous drugs. What was left to be determined was how to define both the "right" type of person and what types of substances would be considered dangerous.

Arguments for pharmacy legislation combined the need for a skilled individual familiar with the technical aspects of compounding medicines, the need for an educated individual who understood the fundamentals of pharmacology, and the need for a responsible individual who possessed the right "character" to be considered a guardian of the public's health. Von Iffland's 1846 measure stressed that the doctors had to ensure that pharmacists were "of good education *and* thoroughly well versed in chemistry and pharmacy."[31] Similarly, in 1860, Hall stated that the education of pharmacists should include "a thorough classical education," along with attendance at lectures in chemistry and *materia medica*.[32] In their work on the professions of Upper Canada, R.D. Gidney and W.P.J. Millar have discussed how "good education" meant a classical education and related not only to imparting knowledge but also to development of character. In Von Iffland's statement, the moral character of the individual was a key aspect of pharmaceutical education since, he implied, whereas many people could learn chemistry and pharmacy, only men of "good education" could adequately take on the responsibilities of a pharmacist. The provisions for education that the College of Physicians in Canada East passed in 1865 made a classical education a prerequisite for studying medicine, surgery, midwifery, or pharmacy.[33]

These requirements for a classical education reflect the broader issue of the honourable nature of certain occupations and professions, assured by the moral character of the individual. Commenting on similar requirements demanded of applicants to colleges of physicians and surgeons, Ronald Hamowy contends that this sort of prerequisite was unnecessary and indicative of the self-serving, class-based interest among physicians to restrict access to the profession. By setting up a number of ad hoc barriers to licensing, he argues, doctors could keep the number of physicians low and increase their own economic and social position in society through the simple mechanism of supply and demand.[34] Gidney and Millar disagree with Hamowy's perspective. They argue that doctors and other professionals viewed classical education as indicative of the moral capacity necessary for an individual to adequately carry out a professional calling that had special legislated status precisely because they were performing an essential public service. For the physicians who demanded that aspiring pharmacists have a classical education, the requirement was meant to ensure that the *right* *type* of people were in control of the distribution of drugs.[35]

Yet the emphasis on the character of the pharmacists also had a practical purpose. Since compounding medicines required detailed technical aptitude, ensuring the good character of the druggists would guarantee that the profession was made up of competent and responsible people. During the 1871 debates on pharmacy laws in Ontario, the *Toronto Globe* argued that no act of incorporation could prevent some of the mistakes caused by basic human failings since "the most intelligent men, with every certificate of competence, may fall into unsteady habits and make some mistakes when more or less intoxicated."[36] The *Halifax Citizen* echoed this concern in 1874 when the province's doctors presented a bill to control the actions of pharmacists. The *Citizen* opposed the bill since it would examine only the dispenser's knowledge, without considering character. "He may be constitutionally careless and slovenly, or he may be a man of unsteady or dissipated habits."[37]

Pharmacists did not deny the importance of proper character to their profession; but they disagreed with physicians about the best way to ensure it. Doctors argued that a proper classical education was essential to making moral pharmacists, whereas pharmacists and their supporters contended that a better way to ensure the best character of the pharmacist in the community was to grant pharmacists self-regulating powers. The difference in opinions was a key point of contention during the discussions of a Quebec pharmacy bill in 1869. In a conference with representatives of the province's doctors, members of the Montreal Chemist's Association discussed the different perspectives of the two groups. The doctors claimed that they needed to retain "their present position with increased powers," that the pharmacists were not numerous enough to form a college, and that in any case the legislation to incorporate a college should not precede "a grand educational scheme." The pharmacists explained that "there are means of education at present in existence, but there is absolutely no authority to prevent incompetent persons entering the trade." The Montreal chemists were surprised by the extent of physicians' resistance to the legislation. Yet the doctors, by their own arguments, supported the aim of the druggists. "One [physician] asserted that [the pharmacists of Quebec City] were not deserving of the confidence of the public, and that he could not trust one of them to make up a prescription. Our instant reply was that ... nearly all [of these pharmacists] held the licence of the College of Physicians to pursue their calling."[38] In October 1869, John Dougall, the editor of the *Montreal Witness*, a notorious spokesperson for liberal and evangelical reform causes, and a strong supporter of the efforts of the pharmacists to resist the avarice of what he saw to be an elitist medical profession, insisted that pharmacists should be allowed to regulate themselves, "without the aegis' of medical boards," and to educate their pupils free from "the evil influences which surround the medical schools."[39]

Dougall's suggestion that medical schools were "evil," and of dubious character, hints at another conflict related to the concern over the improper use of poison: who, really, was at fault? Physicians often characterized pharmacists as incompetent, but pharmacists and their supporters responded in kind, with charges that doctors were just as liable as anyone else to make mistakes and be tempted by the lure of financial gain. In 1874, the Nova Scotia Medical Society presented its bill "for restricting the sale of poisons &c., by druggists in the province of Nova Scotia." The title suggests that the legislation targeted the activities of pharmacists as requiring vigilant supervision. The bill met stiff resistance in the legislature and the popular press. The *Halifax Citizen* noted that some sort of regulation was necessary but characterized the Nova Scotia Medical Society as too "grasping" to be trusted to have the best interests of the public at heart.[40] A correspondent to the *Halifax Reporter and Times,* calling himself "Medicus," argued more passionately that the bill was a conspiracy by the doctors, who were "afraid of the superior intelligence and attainments of those engaged in the Drug and Prescription business."[41] Medicus characterized physicians as interested only in personal gain. He argued that the public needed protection not from pharmacists but from "the grabbing and grasping rapacity of the medical profession generally ... Most of them like to, and do, demand and take a good fat fee *whenever* and wherever it can be got."[42] In the *Witness* of 27 October 1869 Dougall made similar charges. Since doctors billed patients per visit, and often per prescription, Dougall reasoned, it was in the doctor's interest to extend the length of time for treatment, to keep the nature of disease a mystery, and to prescribe more drugs than necessary. He likened doctors' business practices to those of trades whose position provided them with the opportunity to mislead the public for pecuniary gain. "A shoe-maker who made boots that would not wear out, would soon be gazetted for lack of custom," argued Dougall, "the doctor who should make all his patients well, would be a like sufferer."[43] However, whereas "boots are things people understand a little ... diseases are things no one understands, – not even the doctors, – and so it is the doctors' interest that your case becomes as difficult and interesting a one as possible. It is much to their credit when this interest does not bias them, but they would be saints indeed if it never did, unconsciously at least."[44]

Thrusting the doctors' interests into the capitalist market, Dougall questioned the relationship and interdependence of physicians and pharmacists. He observed that until recently in England, doctors were paid only for writing prescriptions, an outcome of the Apothecaries Act of 1815: "This was good for apothecaries, and terrible for patients; and it is still suspected that doctors have an interest in the amount of drugs consumed." He suggested that a better means of remunerating doctors would be to set up a system in which families paid doctors an annual salary whether or not the physician had to treat any illness.[45] The writings of people like John Dougall, Medicus, and the editor of the *Halifax Citizen* denied that physicians possessed any special rights or qualities that raised them above the baseness of capitalist competition.[46]

Pharmacists and their supporters often accompanied their attacks on doctors' integrity with assertions about the honour of the apothecaries themselves. Medicus insisted that the pharmacists would never defraud the public as doctors were apt to do. "[Pharmacists'] standing as a class in society is too high for that, for they fully realize the responsibility resting upon them in the sale of poisons."[47] The *Toronto Globe*'s editor argued likewise, saying that "the educated druggist is one of the most careful of traders. A high sense of responsibility governs his proceedings, whether dispensing or retailing his goods."[48] Writing on the Gale and Mason incident, pharmacist "J.B.D.," in a letter to the *Globe*, attested to the integrity of all pharmacists in the careful dispensing of poisons. "There is no druggist in the Dominion," he asserted, "who would knowingly and willingly contravene the law as it now exists." Yet J.B.D. himself proceeded to demonstrate how a caring pharmacist, concerned for the health and comfort of his patrons, would in fact contravene the law with impunity, albeit under specific conditions and with noble intent:

Even now, while I am writing, occurs an instance of the inefficiency of the law as it now stands. A lady had just entered the shop and request[ed] a remedy for toothaches, with which she is at the time sorely tormented. I immediately (knowing her well) offer her a mixture – properly labelled – of chloroform, camphor, laudanum, &c. which I have reason to believe will at once give her relief ... At the same time, I know I am breaking one of the laws of the country ... and am rendering myself liable to the infliction of a penalty. But what is to be done?[49]

J.B.D.'s gendered imagery – the compassionate male professional risking his licence to assist the needful woman – helped him to bolster his assertion that pharmacists were righteous and honourable men, whose capable and efficient service to the public was hindered by burdensome laws. The solution to this problem, he asserted, was clear: incorporate the pharmacists, and they would regulate themselves.

In many of the poisoning cases that caught the attention of the public, neither doctors nor druggists were exclusively at fault. As Mason and Gale (and J.B.D.) demonstrated, pharmacists often broke the law by dispensing dangerous drugs. Notorious cases of murder by poison publicized the dangers of this practice. The case of James Deacon of Clarendon County, Ontario, who poisoned his wife with strychnine in 1870, caught the attention of the public. He had purchased half an ounce of the drug from a local grocer, and the poison had been "as easy to purchase as so much tobacco."[50] Poisoning also often occurred through the mistakes of druggists. In 1865, a man in Quebec City died after taking a tonic compounded by a local apothecary. The druggist mistakenly included a dose of aconite, or wolfsbane, which is a powerful poison.[51] Still, in other cases doctors were at fault. During the 1874 debates in Nova Scotia, the member who had introduced the pharmacy bill – which pharmacists disparaged – cited an incident of poisoning by a drug mistakenly sold in the place of Epsom salts to justify the need to regulate pharmacists' actions. The *Halifax Citizen* pointed out that a physician had sold the drug, not a pharmacist; the proposed law would have affected dispensing by pharmacists, not physicians, and would not have prevented similar accidents.

Not only did pharmacists argue that doctors were equally culpable in cases of poisoning; they also emphasized that druggists themselves needed protection against ignorant vendors of medicine. Unscrupulous traders damaged the reputation of honourable members of the profession by selling medicine to anyone, regardless of the intent or identity of the purchaser. Here we see governmentality in action. During the second reading of Ontario's first pharmacy bill in 1869, Dr. William McGill, who presented the bill, claimed that "there were a number of persons acting as chemists who caused by their carelessness and blunders more evil than was generally known."[52] McGill insisted that "the respectable educated chemists felt that they required protection from such men."[53] The incorporated pharmaceutical association would help pharmacists to protect themselves from unscrupulous or careless individuals in their own ranks, like the grocer who sold James Deacon the strychnine. As we will see, the relationship between pharmacists and other retail vendors remained a serious point of contention long after pharmacy acts became the norm.

Despite the conflicting views of how to assure pharmaceutical integrity and the health of the people with respect to access to poisons and medicines, doctors generally endorsed the professional aspirations of pharmacists. In 1870, the *Canada Lancet* supported the pharmacists in the Gale and Mason case by condemning the magistrate's decision.[54] The bill to incorporate pharmacists in Ontario was presented by Dr. McGill, a physician, and had the support of other doctors in the legislature. Likewise in Nova Scotia, one of the most vocal supporters of the pharmacists' bill in the Legislative Council was a Dr. Parker, who illustrated his speech with his own positive experiences with a dutiful and educated pharmacist, who caught Parker's (rare) prescribing errors.[55] Yet the relationship that physicians envisioned was distinctly hierarchical. The Nova Scotia Pharmacy Act of 1876 was championed by doctors and placed much of the blame for the misuse of poisons on the province's pharmacists. Archibald Hall's letters to the legislature and his writings in medical journals had also demonstrated this perspective. In the *British American Journal* of 1860, he argued that the legislation to regulate the education of apothecaries sponsored by Lower Canada doctors was not an attempt to enforce "an especially obnoxious measure" on the apothecaries. "The interests of the [medical] Profession are too closely interwoven with those of the Apothecaries to permit of a serious antagonism."[56] His protests notwithstanding, consider his language: the doctors were the only "Profession" in this statement.

Further complicating the attempts to construct either profession as immune to the lure of the market, economic arrangements between individual pharmacists and doctors suggested that, notwithstanding high-minded rhetoric, being licensed by a professional college delivered neither pharmacists nor physicians from temptation. One example of this supposed economic motivation that frustrated a number of the key pharmacy voices was the "percentage system." In 1869, a pharmacist wrote to the *Montreal Star* complaining about the agreement between some city doctors and druggists by which the pharmacist would give a doctor a percentage of the cost of a prescription – sometimes a third of the price – if the doctor sent his patient to that pharmacist. The correspondent, calling himself "Justice," explained that he was often asked by customers to prescribe for them, but according to the law, he sends them to a doctor for advice. "And what return do you think I get for doing so?" he roared, "in nine cases out of ten, my customer is prescribed for by the doctor, *and sent to some other store to get his prescription dispensed.*" Justice asked why he "has any incentive to keep within the law ... when a doctor knowingly influences his patient, to leave the drug store where he may have dealt with satisfaction for years, in order to send him elsewhere, and that, for no other reason but because he has an underhand arrangement." What surprised Justice the most was that the practice was carried out by men "who hold positions as professors of medical colleges."[57] In the *Canadian Pharmaceutical Journal,* Edward Shuttleworth called the practice "undignified ... unfair ... and dishonest" and agreed that "if ... the druggist is so effectually cut off, by medical law, from any profits he might derive from prescribing, we think the charge of 'undignified' professional business may well lie at the door of the physicians."[58] Shuttleworth did not blame only the physicians. He recognized that both doctors and druggists participated in this unfair business. A correspondent to the same journal agreed, saying that "the public may be hoodwinked for a time by a designing physician and a dishonest apothecary."[59] The results, Shuttleworth explained, would hurt only the public since the percentage system would cause a proliferation of "cheap drugs, incompetent assistants, and high prices ... We hold that no honest trade can admit of a reduction of 33 per cent in its profit ... the public cannot long remain blind to such a flimsy artifice, and the sooner the veil is raised, the better for honest men."[60] Agreeing with the argument that the practice was unfair to "honest" apothecaries and to the public, another correspondent argued that the solution was to incorporate provincial pharmaceutical societies so that they could regulate their own and ferret out deviant vendors.[61]

The pharmacists and their allies also argued that the percentage system weakened the integrity of the profession and safety of the public because it threatened to undermine pharmacists' hopes of training competent assistants. They explained that not only did the system force druggists to pay their clerks less, but it also forced apothecaries to make their clerks work longer hours and neglect their education. This issue was the impetus for another round of debates on the percentage system in late October 1869. A bill was presented in the Ontario legislature to restrict the hours of operation by apothecaries in the province. The restriction would have allowed clerks to attend lectures, something pharmacists saw as essential to building a well-educated profession that looked to its future. Since clerks were often the main contact with customers, a properly educated and informed clerk was important to a competently run pharmacy. The bill had divided the province's pharmacists, some agreeing with the provisions and others arguing that the legislation interfered with their rights to operate their businesses when they desired. Dougall of the *Witness* suspected a conspiracy: "It is whispered that some proprietors are scarcely their own master in the matter, that certain medical men claim a share of the profits of dispensing, and that they expect, as 'sleeping partners,' to have access to those dispensaries under their particular patronage at all hours. Has the 'percentage system' anything to do with this?"[62]

Dougall viewed such collusion as dangerous to the public and immoral. He argued that the druggists who wished to close their shops early in order to permit their clerks to improve themselves should do so and allow "the public to judge." Dougall's proffered solution suggested that ultimately the druggists and doctors were subject to the judgment and actions of the market; laissez-faire capitalism would regulate away unethical practices. Whereas both physicians and pharmacists believed that professional bodies were best able to protect the public from the unscrupulous, Dougall argued that the well-informed public had the integrity to decide who was more deserving of patronage.

The principal reply from some doctors did not deny the existence of the percentage system but rather argued that it ensured the safety of the public. The Montreal-based *Canada Medical Journal* pronounced the practice to be beneficial for all involved. According to the editor, the pharmacists started the "custom" in response to market pressures. As the numbers of drugstores increased in Montreal, proprietors tried to induce people to bring in their prescriptions, not to gain profits from prescriptions but to increase sales of other items. Owing to competition among druggists, the practice became "almost universal." The editor proceeded to argue that, even though the market pressures drove the combination, the financial arrangement was beneficial to the public specifically because of the dependent position in which it placed druggists. "The practice of sending his prescriptions to one shop enables the Physician to exercise a degree of control over the compounder, as to the quality of the drugs, &c., which are supplied." He also argued that the oversight of the physician would induce the pharmacists to "avoid mistakes and employ more skilful assistants." As to the charge that the financial arrangement induced doctors to prescribe more drugs than necessary, the editor explained that only a foolish patient would "take physic" from someone whom the patient suspected of being influenced by a financial motive.[63] In this view, the professional physician's honour was unimpeachable.

The *Canada Medical Journal*'s defence drew on the key points of tension between the doctors and the druggists. The doctor's role was to protect the people, and with respect to dangerous drugs, the best way the doctor could act as guardian of the public's health was by regulating the behaviour of the pharmacist. The argument implied that pharmacists were less able to avoid temptation, more liable to corruption, and in need of assistance to elevate themselves above market pressures. This perspective incited the wrath of several pharmacists, who vented their spleens in the pages of the sympathetic *Montreal Witness*. One correspondent claimed that just in proportion as the legitimate profits of the druggist are cut down, so will the quality of the articles and the quality of the salary of his assistants be cut down also ... if the writer [of the *Journal* article] is so exceedingly mean as to take his pay out of the ordinary profits of the druggist; and not out of the extraordinary profits put on to cover the percentage system, then he must be a mean man indeed.[64]

Another writer challenged the journal's claim that doctors were too honourable to be tempted to order more drugs than necessary. While working in England, the writer had observed that doctors often prescribed more medicine than necessary: "Instead of ordering an honest six or eight ounce mixture, a dozen draughts are very likely ordered, which will cost at least three times the amount, and I need not say that the druggist's share of the spoil is a very small one."[65]

Clearly, the pharmacists and physicians saw the market, and their place within it, as crucial to ensuring the health and safety of the people; what remained was how to bridge this gap. It may never have been resolved since even today some pharmacists and physicians continue to gripe about each other's incursions into their professional scope of practice. Nevertheless, in the process of legislation building, easing these tensions was important. Pharmacists saw collegial and active associations of pharmacists to be the solution. For example, John Kerry, one of the founders of the Montreal Chemists Association, recognized the pressures of trade and observed that a professional association would help to alleviate the dangers of competition. Kerry noted that

though some part of their time is occupied in the practice of what is a professional calling, the larger portion [of their time] ... must be given to trading on its narrowest sense, and the [Montreal Chemists] association, by promoting the study of the sciences which bear upon their occupation, was not only calculated to elevate their minds, but to implant and cultivate a brotherly interest in their fellow members.[66]

The "brotherly interest" would eliminate competition. Although their income depended on day-to-day commodity trade, pharmacists' perceived role as independent and educated guardians of the public health would be improved by the creation of some form of pharmaceutical association. To assure their independence, the druggists had to deal with the percentage system. At the next annual meeting of the Montreal Chemists Association, a Mr. Gardiner presented a resolution to search for alternatives to "the system adopted for many years by most of the leading medical men of this city, of insisting upon their prescriptions being taken to one druggist in particular,

thereby practically ignoring all others equally competent to dispense them."
Gardiner moved that the association form a committee "to devise the best
means to remedy this evil."[67] The percentage system remained a point of
contention until well into the next century.

Assertions over the need to preserve and build the professional integrity
of pharmacists, expressed in the debates over the percentage system and in
the need for incorporation generally, reveal a contradiction that suggests
pharmacists' aspirations were about more than just the protection of the
public's health. After all, although supporters like John Dougall and Medicus
of Halifax argued that physicians, safely incorporated as a profession, were
not above the temptations of the market, pharmacists like Kerry and Gardiner
insisted that the creation of a pharmacy association would in fact enable
the pharmacists to rise above the sort of temptations to which the medical
profession was not immune. The contradiction suggests that protecting the
public was secondary to a desire to protect the pecuniary interests of bona
fide members of the pharmaceutical fraternity. There is some evidence, then,
that although the rhetoric was about honour and respectability, the need
to protect the pharmacist's financial integrity was at least as important.

Pharmacists' claims to require professional organization to help raise
themselves above the temptations of the capitalist marketplace did not
convince many opponents of the incorporation acts. The effect of professional aspirations on the integrity of the free market was at the heart of
critiques of pharmaceutical professionalization. The editor of the *Montreal
Evening Star,* Hugh Graham, questioned the motives of the pharmacists.
He noted that although the apothecaries claimed that their incorporation
would help to protect the public, "those two human weaknesses, love of
gain and misuse of authority, are too equally distributed to make it safe to
trust altogether their [pharmacists'] purity."[68] Graham reasoned that if the
existing state of education was adequate, a new college was unnecessary
since the medical college was equally capable of licensing pharmacists.
However, if the existing state of education was bad, and the new college
was intended to remedy a bad situation, why did the pharmacists include
a clause exempting practising pharmacists from examination?[69] Graham
decided that, if the legislation was passed, "the safety of the public is no
better served" than it was before. The *Montreal Witness* came to the defence
of the pharmacists, reasoning that pharmacy "is a calling requiring great
manipulative skill ... [and] those who exercise it are likely to be the best
judges of the competency of candidates for licenses."[70] Likewise, in Ontario
opponents were in favour of restrictions on the sale of poisons but saw the
proposed pharmacy act as creating a trade monopoly, as opposition leader
Edward Blake noted, that would be much like the "ancient guilds of the
middle ages."[71] The *Toronto Telegraph* objected to this contention, arguing
that by a system of licensing and registration, "the public will be properly

protected,"[72] but opponents were not convinced. Critics in the legislature managed to modify the bill in order to weaken its impact on trade. The revisions made by the Committee of the Whole demonstrate the strength of the anti-monopoly sentiment in the legislature. Provisions restricting the "sale" or "trade" of medicines, except for the most dangerous poisons, were deleted, leaving the bill to regulate principally the action of compounding medicine. Compounding required specific esoteric knowledge of pharmaceutical properties, whereas selling was only an issue of trade.[73]

Yet it was the very nature of pharmacists as traders that exacerbated tensions *within* the ranks of pharmacy. Many rural pharmacists were concerned that the pharmacy laws favoured vendors in urban areas to the detriment of the health and access to medicines of people in remote areas. Concerns in Nova Scotia about how the incorporation of a pharmaceutical society would affect trade focused not on whether druggists would have a monopoly over other merchants but on how the city druggists in Halifax and Dartmouth were trying to control and restrict the actions of medicine vendors (and, in fact, of pharmacists) in rural areas. In 1875, and again in 1876, members from rural ridings persistently argued that the bill should be amended to make its conditions apply only to Halifax and Dartmouth. In the country, the trade would remain unrestricted. This clause was the subject of considerable debate, with arguments touching both on the issue of the convenience to the people in remote areas and on the hostility that rural dwellers felt toward the perceived dictates of urban professionals.[74] The 1875 bill did not pass, and when in 1876 an almost identical bill was brought forward, the first proposed amendment, by Mr. Whitman of Annapolis, would have changed the bill from incorporating a "Nova Scotia" pharmaceutical society to incorporating a society in "the city of Halifax and the town of Dartmouth."[75] After more heated debate, this proposal did not pass, and later that year the pharmacists saw the creation of the Nova Scotia Pharmaceutical Society.

The rural-urban tension was an issue across the country. The Quebec legislation was the project of the Montreal Chemists Association, but this group was not alone in its support for the bill. Petitions of support came to the legislature from pharmacists in "Montreal, Three Rivers, Sherbrooke and Coaticook."[76] Yet some commentators still had their suspicions. In 1869, the *Montreal Evening Star* argued that the proposed pharmacy act "is designed to deprive general dealers and grocers of the right to sell those simple medicines in common use which trade has always been, particularly in the country parts, a portion of their business."[77] As Johanne Collin and Denis Béliveau note, many pharmacists from outside Montreal believed that it was simply an attempt by "des pharmaciens montréalais" to control the trade and that they had little interest in "l'avancement du caractère scientifique de la pharmacie."[78] When the Quebec Pharmaceutical Association was incorporated in 1870, it was as a *voluntary* organization that was interested in expanding the knowledge and abilities of its membership. The legislation specifically exempted rural merchants from requiring membership. Pharmacists continued to be licensed by the College of Physicians until the Quebec Pharmacy Act passed in 1875. In Ontario the issue of remote locations manifested itself in the legislative debates of 1871. A Mr. Perry argued that "in many places in the country, it would not pay to establish a drug store and consequently drugs had to be sold by the common storekeepers. Under this [Pharmacy] Act a farmer who might happen to have a tooth-ache would have to go perhaps twenty miles before he could find a man licensed to sell him a few drops of laudanum."[79] However, the Ontario Pharmacy Act of 1871 did not distinguish between rural and urban pharmacies.

Only in British Columbia, two decades after Ontario's legislation was enacted, did the rural-urban tension manifest itself in actual occupational-closure legislation. In the 1891 "Act to Establish a Pharmaceutical Association in the Province of British Columbia" the provisions against using the various titles of the pharmacist and the conditions on the sale of poisons applied only to vendors "within the limits of an incorporated city or town, or one mile thereof."[80] An 1895 amendment to that act added a clause on how to deal with unlicensed vendors when a city or town became incorporated. Interestingly, in the pharmacy legislation of the Northwest Territories, a geographic area much larger than British Columbia and with a population more broadly dispersed and at least as difficult to access as its western neighbour, no similar distinction was made between rural and urban areas. The issue of access to medicines was immaterial to Edward Shuttleworth, the editor of the *Canadian Pharmaceutical Journal*, who saw it as something ameliorated by the availability of physicians with the right to sell drugs. In 1877, when musing on the need for a Dominion pharmacy act, Shuttleworth observed that, although some people might argue that "legislation suitable for towns is not equally well fitted for the back settlements of the country," he rejected this assertion. He noted specifically that in those areas, physicians dispense their own, and "the public are protected."[81] Despite this dismissal of a fundamental aspect of Canadian life, in all provinces and territories legislators' perceptions of the relationship between the city and the country affected the nature of the pharmaceutical legislation and the sale of poisons.

The Pharmacy Acts and the Control of Poisons

Differences between provincial debates notwithstanding, the pharmaceutical legislation was normally framed as legislation to ensure public safety by protecting individuals both from inadvertent overdoses and from intentional ones, either suicidal or homicidal. In all provinces and territories, a key part of the legislation was the list of specific substances that would be placed under the control of pharmacists. Some legislation also provided methods of accounting for those poisons. Yet each law had differences that are worth considering; each jurisdiction structured differently the authority of the pharmaceutical profession in defining dangerous drugs. All provincial acts specifically exempted licensed physicians and surgeons from the statutory prohibition on the sale of drugs; wholesale manufacturers were also exempt. Finally, all included a process of amending the list of poisons, some of which required consultation with a legally recognized medical authority.

Prior to the passing of pharmacy acts, when the distribution of poisons was subject to regulation it was imposed on a narrow band of substances, and the authority over that distribution was assigned to recognized officials. Most provinces had poison laws that restricted the distribution of a small number of dangerous substances, such as Ontario's Strychnine Act, which Gale and Mason tested in 1870. The Strychnine Acts of both Ontario and Quebec were holdovers from pre-Confederation times (both originally passed in 1849) and Ontario's act was the only legislation in the province that oversaw the activities of the vendors of a select number of dangerous drugs.[82] Nova Scotia, New Brunswick, British Columbia, and the Northwest Territories also had poison legislation that predated pharmacy laws, relating to substances such as pesticides and rat poisons that needed special labelling.[83] But these laws concerned the general vending of specific substances or their use as a pesticide, not the practice of compounding medical preparations and recording the names of their purchasers. One of the main justifications for poison restrictions was to ensure that substances used for poisoning wild animals were accessible to farmers, although some jurisdictions, such as Manitoba and the Northwest Territories, had begun to prohibit the practice of randomly putting out poisoned bait by the 1880s.[84] Although we cannot be certain, in British Columbia it may be that the logic behind applying the provisions of the 1891 Pharmacy Act only to municipalities was that the province's Poison Act of 1881, which restricted the four pesticides listed in Table 5, meant that poisons were already suitably controlled in the rural areas.

Within many of the pharmacy acts themselves, pharmacists were bestowed with more authoritative power than previous vendors had received. Although the criteria for being licensed were subtly different in each province and

Table 5

List of substances in the BC Poison Act of 1881

Arsenic and its preparations
Prussic acid
Strychnine and all poisonous vegetable alkaloids and their salts
Corrosive sublimate

territory, and additional amendments or wholesale rewriting of the legislation might change these criteria, the benefits of gaining a licence sounded substantial. Being members of the pharmaceutical profession, pharmacists had the exclusive right to trade in poisons as long as they followed proper procedures. Only physicians and surgeons were exempted from the provisions of the act. In Ontario, Quebec, Manitoba, the Northwest Territories, and British Columbia, pharmacists were trusted to sell poisons only to people with whom they were familiar or to whom they had been introduced by an

Table 6

Poison schedule of the Ontario Pharmacy Act of 1871

Part I	Part II
Acid, Hydrocyanic (Prussic)	Acid Oxalic
Aconite and compounds thereof	Beans Calabar
Antimony, Tartrate of	Belladonna, and the compounds thereof
Arsenic, and the compounds thereof	Cantharides
Atropine	Chloral Hydrat [*sic*]
Conia, and the compounds thereof	Chloroform and Ether
Corrosive Sublimate	Conium, and the preparations thereof
Digitaline	Croton Oil and Seeds
Ergot	Cyanide of Potassium
Hemp Indian	Elaterium
Morphia, and its salts and solutions	Euphorbium
Oil Cedar	Goulard Extract
Strychnine, and Nux Vomica	Hellebore
Savine, and preparations of	Hyosciamus and preparations
Veratria	Iodine
	Opium, with its preparations. Including Laudanum, etc. but not paregoric
	Pink Root
	Podophyllin
	Potassium, Bromide of
	Potassium, Iodide of
	Santo nine
	Scammony
	St. Ignatius Beans
	Stramonium and preparations
	Valerian
	Verdigris
	Zinc, Sulphate of

acquaintance. These sales would be recorded in poison registers. The laws in Nova Scotia, New Brunswick, and Prince Edward Island did not initially contain such restrictions. This provision alluded to a sense of moral authority imbued in the pharmacist but without actually explicitly stating that the pharmacist had the moral authority to determine who could and could not purchase poisons. What, for example, constituted "familiarity"?

Since controlling the access to poison/medicine was the central point of pharmacy legislation, each act included provisions specifying both how poisons should be handled and which substances should be considered poisonous within the meaning of the law. Apart from Quebec, many provinces' and territories' poison schedules included mostly the same items. Quebec's was significantly shorter. Moreover, half of the pharmacy acts contained bifurcated poison schedules, whereas the others had one undivided schedule; the divided schedules related to additional forms of control over the distribution of dangerous substances, as I will discuss in subsequent paragraphs. The original poison schedules for Ontario, Quebec, and Nova Scotia are listed in Tables 6, 7, and 8 since they illustrate the three main forms of poison schedules: bifurcated, nonbifurcated, and the abbreviated schedule unique to Quebec.

Poison schedules constructed two main forms of knowledge with respect to the distribution of dangerous substances. In all provinces where the legislation had a contiguous (nonbifurcated) poison schedule, except in Quebec, the schedule indicated poisons that needed to be obtained normally through a licensed pharmacist (all legislation exempted physicians, wholesale druggists, and manufacturers from these restrictions). These substances were

Table 7

Poison schedule of the Quebec Pharmacy Act of 1875

Schedule A

Arsenic and its preparations
Prussic Acid
Emetic Tartar
Cyanide of Potassium and all Metallic Cyanides
Aconite and its preparations
Opium and its preparations, except Paregoric and Syrup of Poppies
Essential Oil of Almonds unless deprived of Prussic Acid
Corrosive Sublimate
Cantharides
Savin and its Oil
Ergot of Rye and its preparations
Strychnine and all poisonous vegetable Alkaloids and their Salts

Table 8

Poison schedule of the Nova Scotia Pharmacy Act of 1876

Schedule A

Acids: carbolic, muriatic, nitric, oxalic, hydrocyanic or prussic	Euphorbium
Aconite and its preparations	Goulard's extract of lead
Aconitia	Henbane and its preparations
Antimony, tartarized or tartar emetic	Hellebore, black, white and green, and their preparations
Arsenic, and its compounds and preparations	Indian hemp and its preparations
Atropia and its salts	Iodine and its preparations
Belladonna, and its preparations	Mercury, all poisonous compounds of, including corrosive sublimate, red and white precipitates, and iodides of mercury
Cantharides and its tincture	
Chloroform	
Chloral-hydrate and croton chloral-hydrate	Morphia and its salts and preparations
Chloride of Zinc	Nux Vomica and its preparations
Conium and its preparations	Opium and its preparations, except paregoric
Conia	
Colchicum and its preparations	Pink root
Creosote	Phosphorus
Croton Seeds and their oil	Podophyllin
Cyanide of Potassium and all other cyanides	Savin and its preparations
	Santonine
Digitalis and its preparations	Scammony
Digitaline	St. Ignatius's beans
Elaterium	Stramonium and its preparations
Ergot and its preparations	Strychnia and its salts and preparations
Essential Oils of bitter almonds, cedar, rue, savin and tansy	Veratria and all poisonous vegetable alkaloids and their salts
Ether	

considered "poisonous," but apart from restricting where the product could be purchased, the laws had no additional restrictions. Bifurcated poison schedules labelled all substances listed on the schedule as "poisons" but also identified specific substances that needed to be placed under an additional level of scrutiny and control. In Ontario, for example, Part 1 listed more dangerous poisons, including morphine, strychnine, and arsenic, and pharmacists needed to follow specific labelling and bottling instructions and to record the sale. Part 2 listed "poisons within the meaning of this Act" but which were not specifically controlled by labelling, bottling, recording of sales, or familiarity with the purchaser. In other words, Part 2 was a list of substances over which pharmacists had near-exclusive control. Having divided the poison schedule between two types of poisons, the Ontario Pharmacy Act did not outline any means of controlling the poisons in Part 2. It left that consideration to the discretion of the individual pharmacist. Nevertheless, soon after the bill passed third reading, *Canadian Pharmaceutical Journal* editor Edward Shuttleworth explained that he was convinced that there was no danger to the public. He based his conviction on the honour and capability of pharmacists: "The matter is doubtless in safe hands."[85]

The poison provision in the Quebec Pharmacy Act of 1875 was unique among provincial pharmaceutical laws. It established similar labelling and recording requirements for poisons listed on a shorter poison schedule, but it did not have the additional list of substances that, although considered poisons and under the control of pharmacists, did not need to be labelled. In other words, Quebec's legislation was initially less restrictive on the types of substances that needed to be distributed through a pharmacy. Since, as noted earlier, during the attempts to pass the legislation numerous opponents voiced concern about access to certain drugs outside of the major cities, the unique poison provisions in Quebec's legislation may be a result of those concerns without making a clear rural-urban split. Quebec broadened its poison schedule in the 1880s and 1890s.

The provincial pharmacy legislation recognized in law pharmacists' authority to define poisons and established clear forms of surveillance by and on pharmacists with respect to the distribution of dangerous substances. The laws included the provision for identifying on the label the vendor of the poison, thus drawing a line of responsibility for the substance back to the pharmacy. Legislation with bifurcated schedules also drew a line of responsibility outward from the pharmacy. These laws required the pharmacists to record in a separate book the name, address, substance, and date purchased. This process of recording information enmeshed the pharmacy and the customer in a web of accountability and surveillance. It allowed deviation from the law to be identified and, one would imagine, controlled. A customer who misused a poison would be traced, as would a pharmacist who sold it. By creating processes for clearly identifying dangerous drugs, the bifurcated poison schedule was intended to limit the sort of accidental poisonings that appeared frequently in newspapers and were the subject of cautionary tales in pharmacy journals.

Indeed, when this additional cautionary process was missing, some pharmacists saw the legislation as flawed. Ontario's law followed closely the British Pharmacy Act of 1868, including a bifurcated poison schedule and requirements for textured bottles and distinctly coloured labels. Clearly, Edward Shuttleworth, a key player in the development of this legislation, saw his province's law as the standard bearer of pharmaceutical safety and responsibility. He thus looked with approval on Quebec's labelling provisions when its Pharmacy Act was passed in 1875.[86] But when Nova Scotia passed its law in 1876 with a single poison schedule and no provisions for labelling poisons and recording their sales, Shuttleworth was not impressed:

> There are no restrictions as to the purchaser, nor need sales of poisons be recorded. This appears to us to be an important omission. The registration of sales of poison incurs a very trifling amount of trouble on the part of the druggist and not only throw[s] many obstacles in the way of those who desire to purchase poisons for illegal purposes, but often furnishes most important assistance in carrying out the ends of justice.

He then proceeded, with too-common central-Canadian chauvinism, to observe that many of the items listed on Nova Scotia's poison schedule did not need to be so restricted.[87] Eight years later, the New Brunswick Pharmacy Act of 1884 was almost exactly the same, also having no provisions for labelling and recording the sale of poisons; accordingly, Shuttleworth's comments were almost entirely the same as his comments on the 1876 legislation.[88] The New Brunswick legislation was changed seven years after the first act was passed; the Nova Scotia provision was changed thirty years later.[89]

It is difficult to determine the reasons some provinces divided their schedules and some did not. It was not an example of policy learning or legislative evolution, during which the dire results of less restrictive laws informed new legislation and created more restrictive ones, since three of the first five pharmacy laws (those of Quebec, Nova Scotia, and New Brunswick) had a contiguous schedule, whereas the first (Ontario's) and the fourth (Manitoba's) had a bifurcated one. Indeed, the only delineation seems to be geographic: all legislation passed in provinces east of Ontario had a single schedule; legislation passed in Ontario and to the west contained divided schedules. Yet it may not have been an accident of geography: many pharmacists who populated the early pharmaceutical societies west of Ontario were trained in or came from that province or Great Britain; it is possible that they, like Shuttleworth, saw a bifurcated schedule to be the ideal.[90]

Along with determining how poisons should be handled, and who should handle them, all pharmacy acts had provisions for adding items to the poison schedule, and in these provisions we find varying authorities to distribute epistemological power. In most provinces, the decision on which substances should be added was left to the executive council of the provincial (or territorial) pharmaceutical society, association, or college. All such additions had to be submitted to the government and approved by the governor-in-council. Some suggested that only a pharmacy council could make changes. For example, the New Brunswick Pharmacy Act of 1884 specified that the poison schedule could be augmented "by authority of the Governor in Council, upon the recommendation of the Pharmaceutical Council," wording repeated twenty years later in Prince Edward Island's legislation.[91] Others, meanwhile, appeared to leave the source of suggestions for change more open. For example, in British Columbia "the [Pharmaceutical Association's] Council shall submit [proposed additions] for the approval of the Lieutenant-Governor in Council."[92] In this wording, it was possible for other agencies to recommend changes to the legislation, whereas in New Brunswick the governor could act only on the recommendation of the council. This ambiguity notwithstanding, in these provinces the decision to identify certain substances as poisons involved the pharmacists and the government, whereas in Nova Scotia, New Brunswick, and Quebec, physicians were legally included in the process of defining dangerous drugs. The Quebec Pharmacy Act of 1875 required the pharmacists to seek "the approval of the board of governors of the College of Physicians and Surgeons" to add poisons to the schedule.[93] The Nova Scotia Pharmacy Act of 1876 required all new poisons identified by the council to receive "the concurrence of the chairman of the Provincial Medial Board,"[94] and the New Brunswick law was similarly worded.

All pharmacy acts in the provinces and territories held essentially the same key components, but there is evidence that some earlier debates informed later legislation. For example, when the BC Pharmacy Act came into force in 1891, it included the unusual provision that the prescription was the property of the patient. This addressed a question that pharmacists, physicians, and the general public had been debating for decades. And it was not an insignificant issue to the economics of the practitioners. If the prescription was seen to be the property of the patient (or customer), by all rights the patient could take it to many different pharmacists to have it filled. If it was the property of the physician, it represented the knowledge and, if you pardon the anachronism, the intellectual property of the physician. If it was considered the property of the pharmacists, a pharmacist could use the prescription to make up a generic medicine that he or she could sell to other patients displaying similar symptoms. The BC legislation, unlike other pharmaceutical laws in Canada, resolved the debate by stating that "any person who presents a prescription to any qualified druggist to be filled shall be entitled to have such prescription returned to him by such druggist."[95] The solution was not to the satisfaction of many of the professionals involved in deliberating the intricate politics of the prescription.

Another key issue that remained a point of contention was the jurisdictional wrangling between pharmacists and physicians. Given the rhetoric of people like John Dougall of the *Montreal Witness,* which presented physicians as no less self-interested than pharmacists, it should not be surprising that the relationship between doctors and druggists remained tense when it came to statutory enactments. While paying lip service to the interdependence of the two professions, pharmacists wanted a clear jurisdictional separation. One of the sticking points for all pharmacy societies in Canadian provinces remained the fact that physicians were exempt from the requirements of the various pharmacy legislations. Physicians argued that they should be allowed to compound medicine when necessary and should not be required to send their patients to a pharmacy; nor should they have to submit to the examination and licensure of a different regulatory organization. This debate could be the cause of some rhetorical acrobatics. For example, in 1878, while the Ontario College of Pharmacy was attempting (unsuccessfully) to amend its Act in order to require physicians to be registered with the College of Pharmacists, the *Canadian Pharmaceutical Journal's* editor, Shuttleworth, in a heroic display of mixed metaphors, noted that jurisdictional disputes had resulted in "the ill feeling which has been engendered and kept alive between medicine and its handmaid ... civil wars are the most cruel and family quarrels the most bitter."[96]

Through the last part of the nineteenth century, pharmaceutical associations, having achieved legislative occupational closure, attempted to address the physicians' loophole and were repeatedly thwarted by a strong and convincing medical lobby. For example, in 1883 the Pharmaceutical Association of Manitoba, having been incorporated five years earlier, petitioned the government to pass an amendment dealing with some of the weaknesses in the original legislation. Amongst other changes, the Association asked that physicians "who engage in the business of pharmaceutical chemists [be obliged] to register as such and pay the fees required by the by-laws of the council of this association."[97] This provision was dropped in committee, and the exemption for physicians remained intact. Likewise, the Ontario College of Pharmacy failed in its attempt to have the physicians' exemption rescinded in the Ontario Pharmacy Act of 1884. As the explanation in the *Canadian Pharmaceutical Journal* noted, "Physicians have always had the right to keep and sell poisons, and it is plain that they do not now intend to relinquish it. Our readers may accept the fact that everything was done that could have been done, and they must take the result as gracefully as possible."[98]

Of course, the territorialism went both ways. Physicians were wary of pharmacists who appeared to be practising medicine. Several provincial court cases attempted to hammer out the distinction between practising

medicine and simply recommending a product. In Quebec in 1884, physicians brought suit against a pharmacist, Theobold Chive, for both practising medicine and assuming the title of doctor, two things specifically
prohibited in the Quebec Medical Act. For the former charge, the pharmacist had recommended remedies based on the information provided
by two customers. One had said he had an inflamed bladder, and the other
had said he needed a tonic. The judge determined that neither of these were
cases of practising medicine: "The defendant is proved to be a licensed
druggist, and he had a right to recommend his wares, and receive the price
of them, which is all he did." In the latter charge, the pharmacist sold
remedies that included the words "Dr. Chive." This was a little more complex, but the bottle labels noted that the said "Dr. Chive" was an intern
at a hospital in Rouen. The magistrate decided that whether or not this
was the same "Chive," the defendant was not passing himself off as a doctor.[99] In 1889, a detective hired by the Ontario College of Physicians and
Surgeons brought a suit against a pharmacist in Belleville, claiming that he
had practised medicine. As with the Quebec case, the magistrate decided
in favour of the defendant, arguing that

> if the Medical Act actually interferes with the druggist's right to prescribe
> for a cold, toothache or disordered stomach, or any of the minor ills which
> poor mortality has fallen heir to, from the drugs on the shelves[,] it becomes
> a very serious matter both to [the] druggist and the public at large. If the
> druggist has no right to reply to the often asked question "I have a cold or
> sore throat, what do you recommend?" under pain of [a] $25 fine ... it seems
> to me the Medical Act has gone much further in the way of protection of
> the faculty than is consistent with good sence [sic] or public policy.[100]

These jurisdictional disputes continued to be points of tension between
medical and pharmaceutical professions, and some argue that they continue today.

By the end of the 1890s, most provinces and territories had passed legislation that both incorporated a pharmaceutical regulatory body and identified, with the advice of physicians and pharmacists, the medications that
needed to be restricted for the good of the people. This legislation allowed
the unpleasant idea of monopoly, seen by many as antithetical to the free
market and democracy, to be encoded in law. The pharmacy monopoly was
for the safety of the public. Thereafter, those who sold dangerous drugs
outside of the environment managed by the responsible pharmacist or the
authoritative physician were deviating from established norms. The pharmacy acts with their appended poison schedules established the idea that

some substances were dangerous and needed to be distributed with caution by duly qualified and properly accredited professionals. The idea that certain authoritative bodies were more suited to managing the activities of others was not new, but the pharmacy laws were part of a process that expanded the cohort of responsible professions. Now doctors and druggists had the authority to determine how individuals should manage their own bodily integrity. Such authority could protect the people and was therefore presented as being for the good of the country. After this time, when drugs were distributed outside the aegis of pharmacy or medicine, the vendors were deemed suspicious at the least; more often they were considered to be criminals, shady outsiders whose actions would endanger the health of the people and therefore the health of the nation.

By creating a self-regulating body with the authority to investigate transgressions of the law and to make authoritative declarations about the dangers or healthfulness of certain substances, provincial pharmacy legislation established a new self-interested regime of control. The result was a sort of epistemological colonialism. Incorporated by the governments and empowered to define the scope of their practice, these pharmacy associations policed the trade and attempted to assert control over an increasingly broad range of issues related to the sale of drugs. This legislated authority and responsibility to protect the public were reiterated repeatedly in the actions of the regulatory bodies that had the most interest in the legislation. Just as physicians sought to prosecute people, including pharmacists, who were allegedly practising medicine without due registration, pharmaceutical licensing bodies acted swiftly and repeatedly to ferret out activities that crossed passionately defended professional borders. These activities, often appearing in court and detailed in local newspapers, reiterated the seriousness of the pharmacist's work and the danger imbedded in the substances listed on poison schedules. This was a form of governance that aimed to conduct the conduct of those within the profession in order to strengthen its social status, and the conduct of those outside of the profession who were trying to act like insiders. In the views of the pharmacists, professional governance had a higher purpose than simply personal gain. The poison schedules, and the pharmacists who judiciously controlled access to dangerous drugs, protected the people from danger. The pharmacists' legislated authority to define dangerous substances, and the oft-required consultation with physicians, was a biopolitical practice creating layers of governance that shaped understandings of proper and improper behaviour of the citizen as an embodied individual.

Not only did these professional pharmaceutical bodies seek out and prosecute transgressors of the law, but they also had the authority to expand the scope of their profession's activities. This situation could lead to some strange bedfellows. For example, in June 1873 an Ontario druggist charged that the College of Pharmacy was using the services of the pharmacists' nemesis, George "Whiskey" Mason, to investigate grocers who sold drugs without a licence. The registrar of the college denied the accusation, although, given Mason's track record, it would not have been such a bad idea.[101]

4
Chinese Opium Smoking and Threats to the Nation

Although residents of British North America may have been aware of opium as a poison and a medicine, the substance did operate on a third level: opium as an exotic indulgence and a danger from faraway places. The smoking of opium, normally associated with Chinese people, and the various interpretations of its meaning increasingly became issues of concern to Canadians throughout the nineteenth century. In the decades before Confederation, stories and descriptions of Chinese opium smoking were often filtered through reports of mission work in China. Viewed through such a lens, opium smoking could be considered a personal moral failing, an indication of the moral weakness of the "heathen," or simply a pastime that paralleled drinking. Or it could be considered all three. Then, after the mid-century "Opium Wars," during which the British military forced China to accept imports of Indian-grown opium, opium smoking was linked to a further moral failing, that of the British Empire, which was pushing the degrading product on an unwilling population. So by the time residents of British Columbia were beginning to look askance at the leisure pursuits of Chinese "sojourners" in that region, opium smoking was already embedded with multiple meanings, and none of them was positive.

A close examination of discussions of opium smoking in the nineteenth century reveals that in its smoked form opium was normally considered something distinct from non-smoked opium, even as, later in the century, ideas of opiate habituation converged, and commentators began to see dependency on non-smoked opium as a social problem. Prior to the rising concern over the presence of Chinese labourers in British Columbia, opium smoking was a decidedly foreign vice, and a source of pity and wariness towards Chinese people, often expressed by evangelical missionaries. As more Chinese people arrived in North America, discussions aimed at addressing Chinese labour issues and the "Chinese evil" included the spectre of opium smoking as one of the dangers Chinese people were thought to pose to the young province and young country. By the end of the century, opium smoking and images like the diabolical opium den and the dissolute Chinese opium smoker were tropes of indulgence, debasement, and cultural danger. These were threats to national integrity, and distinct from, but at least as problematic as, more "Western" behaviours such as alcohol drinking and opium eating.

To Western eyes, opium smoking was an exotic activity, with the practice as undertaken in Asia requiring a different apparatus and process than tobacco smoking. The pipe was a longer device than a tobacco pipe, with a mouthpiece at one end and a cup at the other. The cup was not packed with material the way that a tobacco pipe was used. Instead, a bead of opium gum was held over the pipe, usually on a thin metal needle, and lit with a candle or taper so that the fumes could be inhaled by the smoker. For this reason, smoking opium usually required two people, the smoker and the person who lit the opium. Thus it would be easy to interpret the assistance of the lucid attendant as an attempt to corrupt the lulling smoker.

The relationship between China and Britain, and especially the Western perceptions of the relationship between Chinese people and opium, has a complex and fraught history. The general story has been that the British forced opium on China to expand trade and that the Chinese government was an unwilling victim of this narcotic colonialism.[1] Consequently, images of Chinese people smoking opium and the debasing effect of this pernicious habit were framed as the outcome of rapacious imperialism. This view drove a process of national self-shaming by organizations like the Society for the Suppression of the Opium Trade, which became the main voice of criticism labelling the opium trade an immoral imposition on an innocent people.[2] These were dominant discourses related to Chinese opium smoking in the nineteenth century. Yet as Frank Dikötter, Lars Laamann, and Zhou Xun have argued, historical interpretations of opium in China have been based on several "myths" of opium. They argue that historians have too readily accepted the thesis of gunboat trade diplomacy and the resulting narrative of the innocent victim. Instead, Dikötter, Laamann, and Xun argue that opium was not nearly as problematic as these histrionic perspectives assert, and we can see that by restoring agency to the Chinese people, opium was a valued commodity, existed in a complex cultural space, and was not so debilitating as the moralistic interpretations of the opium wars assert.[3] This is an important perspective, yet in this case we should not let the truth get in the way of a good story. Because it was not the actual situation on the ground that motivated reformers and affected perceptions of Chinese opium smoking in Chinatowns around the world; those metaphors and the rhetoric of imperialist aggression and chemical moral degradation infected and affected Westerners' observations of this particular leisure pursuit of Chinese sojourners. The myths, not the realities, imposed meaning on a behaviour that may have been more complex and benign than reformers may have thought.

These myths began to take shape well before the opium wars. Although Canadians did not begin to send their own contingents of missionaries to far-flung regions like Asia and Africa until much later in the century, Canadians were being informed of the pernicious habit of Chinese opium smoking well before Confederation.[4] Publications as diverse as the *Canadian Baptist Magazine and Missionary Register,* the *Catholic,* and the literary journal the *Colonial Pearl* ("devoted to polite literature, science and religion") reproduced stories from missionaries providing to impressions of opium smoking. For example, in 1838 the *Canadian Baptist Magazine'*s abstract of reports by the American Board of Commissioners of Foreign Missions described Chinese people as "eager to make money, and inveterately fond of gambling, opium, smoking and other pernicious indulgences."[5] It is unclear whether the comma after "opium" was included by the magazine's editor due to a lack of familiarity with smoking as a way of consuming opium, but soon other journals were not so confused. A year later, the *Colonial Pearl* published an article entitled "Effects of Opium" that contained passages extracted from a pamphlet ostensibly written by a British merchant, "an eye-witness of the deplorable effects of opium-smoking."[6] And in 1843, the *Catholic* reproduced, with some sectarian satisfaction, a story of Protestant missionaries' failures in Asia. Under the heading of "apostates," the journal noted that many converts ended up leaving the fold, one of whom "has now fell [*sic*] into the deadly habit of opium smoking."[7]

Such new and exotic behaviour needed to be situated in the cosmology of the readership for it to have meaning. As Charles Rosenberg has written with respect to epidemics, "perception implies explanation."[8] Recognizing a new disease, a set of symptoms and bodily conditions distinct from other sets of symptoms, involved some way of fitting that new disease into an extant worldview. The same happened when Canadians were introduced to opium smoking, even though it was not a disease per se. For example, the article in the *Colonial Pearl* compared the effects of opium smoking and alcohol consumption, noting that "the intoxicating property, or rather properties, of opium, differ in their nature from the intoxicating property of alcohol." Not only were these properties different but, more significant, "in some ways the effects of the intoxication are also different." The author then put the actions in medical terms. Both alcohol and opium "stimulate the nervous system to an unnatural degree" and should be used only when bodily illness required such stimulation, a reference to the waning but still powerful influence of Brunonian therapeutics, which saw all diseases as results of over- or understimulation of the body's systems.[9] In addition, however, the stimulus could be dangerous, so the illness had to be such that "a stimulus of this nature [would be] subservient to the restoration of other vital functions."[10] As we saw with medical discussions of medicinal opium later in the century, the idea that the dangerous properties could be offset when bodily illness redirected or modulated these properties also existed in the physiological interpretation of smoking opium. Just as physicians saw a dualistic danger in medicinal opium, so too did the early observers of Chinese opium smoking. Alcohol and opium were similar, said the anonymous author of the *Pearl* article, but "one point of difference between ... the intoxication of ardent sprits and that of opium ... [is] the tenfold force with which every argument against the former applies to the latter. There is no slavery on earth to name with the bondage into which opium casts its victim."[11]

Although such comparisons might have helped British North American audiences to appreciate the dangers that Chinese people faced from smoking opium, there was little agreement, at least initially, on how much concern this behaviour should engender. Indeed, as noted in Chapter 2, in his first edition of *The Elements of Materia Medica,* published in 1842, Jonathan Pereira argued that opium smoking "is most destructive to those who live in poverty and distress and who carry it to excess" but that "the Chinese in easy circumstances" do not appear to suffer physically in any measurable degree.[12] This uncertainty would continue throughout the century. In 1874, in the Montreal-based magazine the *Favourite,* an article discussing the social lives of Chinese people in China included a discussion of the luxuries in which Chinese people indulged. Similar to Pereira's reflections a generation earlier, the article discussed opium smoking as "the worst species of debauchery" but qualified this statement by observing that "these are the consequences of the abuse of the practice; when used in moderation, it is said to be comparatively innoxious."[13] Two decades later, the *Canadian Journal of Commerce,* when discussing the implications of all forms of opium consumption for the insurance industry, concluded that opium smoking was "the vice of the very few" and that "the use of opium (even habitually) in hot climates is no less deleterious than is the temperate use of alcoholic or fermented liquors in colder zones."[14]

Comparisons of opium's effects with the dangers of alcohol were especially potent in the late 1830s and early 1840s for two reasons. First, this was the period that saw the initial broad-based push toward restricting alcohol consumption in North America. The earliest "temperance" organizations in Canada began to appear in the 1820s, and by the late 1830s, despite the usefulness of taverns in social life, the first wave of temperance movements had become a small but well-organized social phenomenon.[15] Early temperance movements did not see all alcohol consumption as problematic. As the article in the *Colonial Pearl* indicates, spirits were the substance of concern in the West, not wine and beer. In 1855, the Western distinction between wine as a substance of moderate consumption by elites and the drunkenness of ardent spirits was used to characterize opium smoking. A letter to the *Gospel Tribune* signed "An Old Resident in China" insisted that "Opium smoking is not a parallel to wine drinking" since the Chinese themselves see opium smoking as "a ruinous vice," not just a harmless indulgence. Instead, opium smoking was more suitably paralleled with the drunkenness of the Western world.[16]

The other reason that comparisons between opium and alcohol were especially powerful at this time was that, while British North Americans were wrestling with the issue of drink, the British government was forcing opium on the Chinese. In 1839, Chinese authorities attempted to enforce an edict prohibiting the sale of opium in the country by halting shipments of opium from India, the main supplier. The British were not impressed, and the resulting conflict, often called the First Opium War (1839-42), resulted in a humiliating defeat for the Chinese, a slew of uneven regulations that favoured trade by British and other Western powers, and further provisions that undermined the sovereignty of the Qing Dynasty. The war initiated what some have called the Century of Humiliation for China. The Second Opium War (1856–60) was more broadly imperialistic, involving French, American, and Russian forces imposing additional uneven trade conditions on the Chinese government. Not incidentally, one of the conditions of the peace was to open China to more missionaries.[17]

Britain's success in the First Opium War was not necessarily a cause for celebration. It was, after all, a war to force a country to accept trade in a problematic substance simply for the enrichment of another. Future prime minister William Gladstone, at the time a newly elected member of the British Parliament, mused that if there had ever been "a war more unjust in its origin, a war more calculated to cover this country with permanent disgrace, I do not know."[18] Missionaries were similarly concerned. The "Old Resident" told the *Gospel Tribune* that "it rests with the British nation to say whether they will incur the guilt of completing the ruin of the whole of China, or urge the East India Company to seek a more honorable revenue ... China is rushing to poverty and ruin, and we as a Christian nation are chiefly instrumental in effecting this."[19] The concerns about how the imposition of opium on the Chinese people reflected on the apparently more civilized British people would, as we will see, add strength to anti-opium efforts at the end of the century.

The British imperialism and Western influence affected China much more than just in terms of forcing open the opium trade. Partially spurred by the defeat of the Ch'ing Dynasty at the hands of the British in the First Opium War and drawing his philosophy from translations of the Bible and other Christian literature, Hong Xiuquan led a revolt against the monarchy in the early 1850s, establishing the Taiping Heavenly Kingdom in the southeast of China.[20] Christian missionaries commented positively about the actions of what Andrew Porter calls a "quasi-Christian movement." The *Church Times* reported with ecstatic surprise that "the rebels are really a body of Christians! That is to say, they have renounced idolatry, worship Jehovah and Jesus, and believe in the Trinity!" It also published a version of the Ten Commandments, noting that "in the seventh commandment opium-smoking is forbidden, as leading to the breach of that command."[21] The *Presbyterian*, also excited about "the remarkable events now transpiring in the interior of the vast empire of China," provided information from the London Missionary Society that included a fuller account of the ardent opposition of the rebels to any form of opium smoking. Two months later, the *Presbyterian* published a letter from a Dr. Medhurst, likely pioneering missionary Walter Henry Medhurst, that described the fervour with which Taiping adherents rejected opium. While giving a sermon at one of the London society's Shanghai missionary chapels, Medhurst was addressed by "a follower of Tae-ping-wang" who

> went on to inveigh against the prevailing vices of his countrymen, particularly opium-smoking – "that filthy drug[,]" he exclaimed[,] "which only defiles those who use it, making their houses stink forever in hell unless they abandon it. But you must be quick," he adds, "for Tae-ping-wang is coming, and we will not allow the least infringement of his rules[:] no opium, no tobacco, no snuff, no wine, and no vicious indulges of any kind." He touched also upon the expenses of opium-smoking, which drained their pockets, and kept them poor in the midst of wealth: whilst we, who never touch the drug, are not put to such expense, our master provides us with food and clothing, which is all we want.[22]

Yet the correspondents from the London Missionary Society were cautious about the rebellion. The *Presbyterian* warned its readers "not to be induced, by the avowed adoption of the Christian faith by the insurgents, to draw inferences, which subsequent events may fail to justify; more especially since the better element, that characterizes the movement, is evidently mixed up with much that is heterogeneous and immoral."[23] It provided no additional information on this point, preferring to expand on the parallels with Christianity.

This cautious enthusiasm was, like the uprising itself, short-lived. The Taiping Rebellion was over by the beginning of the 1860s, and the quasi-Christian movement had little long-term hold over the people it sought to "liberate." Nevertheless, with the opening of more Chinese ports after the Second Opium War, and the ability of Christian churches to expand their missionaries' reach, more Western missionaries sent home more reports of the problems of opium smoking. The difference now was that opium smoking could represent not merely a Chinese indulgence and indicator of heathen weakness but also an indictor of arrogant and some would say immoral Western powers who forced the demoralizing substance on the weaker race. If the quasi-Christian philosophy of the Taiping rebels suggested to missionaries that their efforts were having some effect, the rebels' interest in ridding their compatriots of the scourge of opium reinforced the missionaries' zeal to address the opium trade.

Although opium smoking was considered by outsiders to be a terrible scourge, its existence also had powerful benefits at home for missionaries' work abroad. It illustrated, from early in the century, their conviction that the "heathen Chinee" was in dire need of saving, thereby justifying the missionaries' endeavours. The opium smoker was constructed in many missionary reports both as a victim of debauchery and as an example of the power of the Christian god. The narrative structure of these stories followed patterns similar to those of the redemption parables of the evangelical temperance movement: a good person becomes debauched and through the intercession of Christ is saved. Sometimes the conversion was simple. In 1855, in an article entitled "Increasing Success," the *Gospel Tribune* reported that "the power that 'raised up Jesus our Lord from the dead'" was working in China. It continued,

> Perhaps some of the most remarkable resurrections ... have been in the case of those who have been well-nigh physically dead, as well as morally destroyed, by the sin of opium smoking. I have, within these few days, seen several of them, and the effect upon their bodily health has been such that it is difficult to recognize them after a few months of abstinence from their former vicious indulgence.

The triumphant writer noted that such salvation could reverse decades of debauchery: "In some cases, men who have smoked opium for ten, twenty, and even thirty years, have relinquished the habit from the convictions of the Spirit of God."[24] This was a common theme in missionary reports related to opium smoking. The *Home and Foreign Record* reported that two missionaries on the Island of Formosa (Taiwan) had been having remarkable success ridding residents of many of their vices: "some have burned their idols publicly; others have given up their opium smoking, and many have relinquished lucrative professions for the sake of the Gospel."[25]

Missionaries reported such successes in the face of indigenous pressures. In 1843, the *Catholic* had noted that Protestant missionaries' conversion work would result in the natives being alienated from their communities; with the issue of opium smoking, the local pressure not to give up opium was substantial. The journal *Earnest Christianity* recounted the tale of the convert "Old Father Ling," whose "heathen friends" told him that he could not give up opium smoking after forty years because it would kill him. "His reply was, 'I belong to Jesus. I have promised to give up every sin. I would rather die trying to conquer this sin than live an opium smoker.'"[26] This particular conversion seemed easy, but as with every Christian effort to resist sin, more often the process could be difficult, and constant vigilance was necessary. In 1890, the *Maritime Presbyterian Journal* printed a story that started out to be inspiring but ended in despair. A young man who was an opium smoker resolved to quit the habit after attending a missionary's "inquiry class." He struggled daily: "One day he would smash his pipe to pieces, and the next day he would buy another." After a long struggle, the man succeeded in escaping opium's grasp, but then his health began to fail. His friends pleaded with him to return to smoking opium for the sake of his health, but he refused, to the satisfaction of the missionaries. Then one day he failed to show up at the mission. After a few days, the missionaries found him back in the den. The resulting confrontation was an invective against Christianity and Jesus: "He turned upon us with wild eyes and awful imprecations, cursing us and the very God that we hoped he had learned to love." The story ends with a plea to action: "Those who have themselves gone through desperate struggles against some besetting sin, yet one not so strong as the opium habit, will not be able to think lightly of the British policy to which such death struggles are directly due."[27]

These stories gave missionary reports a tone of triumphal success, made more poignant with reminders of the urgency and difficulty of this work. The victories over opium reiterated the power of Jesus to strengthen the resolve of the penitent, and they justified the work of the missionary. This thread appeared often, as when a smoker, having been told that "Christ could give him the power to break off the evil habit of opium smoking," seems to have quit easily: "The power was given to him. His opium pipe was smashed in two and from that time he took no more."[28] Here the very act of helping missionaries get to China so they could do their work might be enough to produce good results.

The second thread was less positive, recounting a more desperate and fraught struggle intended to inspire good evangelicals to broader social and even political action. Here the forces of Christ and the poor debauched opium smoker faced not only the physical ravages of opium but also the pressure of the heathen community and, regrettably for the Western Christian missionary, the forces of commerce and imperialism, which had imposed smoking on the poor Chinese population. Kathleen Lodwick argues that the stories of failure might have a third purpose: that of explaining away the limited success of the missionary work.[29] Nevertheless, missionaries were nothing if not determined, so barriers to their success would require action to remove such impediments and let the Word of God flow and be effective.

Smoking Sojourners

Opium smoking, like the Chinese people themselves, was not confined to the country of China; by the 1860s and 1870s, the practice of smoking opium was found in many cities around the world. The narrative of Charles Dickens's unfinished novel, *The Mystery of Edwin Drood,* revolved around opium dens of London's East End (an area populated by many Chinese people); a generation later, Oscar Wilde's Dorian Gray was found ruining his picture in similar places. In 1868, the Canadian journal *True Witness and Catholic Chronicle* commented on the immorality of London, noting that "all the world's felonry seems to contribute to the tumefaction" of London. Here the journal connected "Chinese opium smoking houses in one quarter, and gangs of Russian bank note forgers in another ... French and Italian burglars here, and swarms of foreign profligates there."[30] In the 1870s, discussions of Chinese opium smoking demonstrated general acceptance of its status both as an exotic deviance and as an indication of moral failure, while locating it, always, in areas where many stars burned in what John Burnham has called the "vice constellation."[31]

By the 1870s, speculations about the impact of Chinese people in North America had become increasingly negative. In 1874, the (secular) *Canadian Monthly and National Review* published an article entitled "Celestial America" by J.D. Edgar. Writing it as an extended exposé of the life of "John Chinaman" in North America, Edgar observed many of the idiosyncrasies of the Chinese expatriate, including the Chinese man's most notorious pastime, opium smoking. Edgar linked the existence of opium dens to the liberty of the West. Although "various repressive measures" had occasionally been taken to stop the practice of opium smoking in China, it could continue unchecked in "free countries" like the United States and Canada. They "furnish John with an opportunity to indulge his cherished vice, only limited by his capacity to enjoy, and his coin to pay for it." Edgar offered a stark cultural contrast between ideas of "Oriental luxury" and the place where Chinese people in North America were found smoking opium, describing the opium den's "squalor and an entire absence of any attempt at elegance."[32]

Such descriptions, removed from the missionary framework, allowed writers to indulge in literary flights of fantasy into the exotic spaces of their own country. Dickens's opium dens may have been inspirations, but writers like Edgar expanded the genre with purple prose and a lascivious eye. In 1878, the *Canadian Illustrated News* presented one such journalistic indulgence, pairing a sketch of a Chinese opium den with a description of the writer's journey into darkness:

> From the theatre to the opium den is but a short step in China Town. How do we get there, and where is it? No one of us can tell, further than this – that we follow our guide blindly through a network of passages, narrow

alleys, with the rough cobblestone pavement under our feet, and alleys that have no pavement but the refuse filth of China Town; that we grope and feel our way after the glimmering star of his little candle-end, and, turning a corner, come suddenly upon a dimly lighted window, breast-high from the ground; that he pushes open a low, battered door, and straightway following the motion of his hand, we are standing in the Chinaman's paradise.[33]

The author then presented the stereotype of the opium den that appears throughout most literature on the topic. As Edgar had done, the *Canadian Illustrated News*'s journalist described a dark, shadowy place full of dazed denizens lying on wooden shelves, oblivious to the world around them. The images related to the standard impressions of lazy and self-indulgent opium smokers. The habit led to lassitude and dissipation. Continued use made them sickly and prone to criminality in order to sustain their habit, while forcing them to live in squalor before dying an untimely death.

In this construction, the opium den held a moral danger that was distinct from the drinking space, regardless of whether one could associate the effects of alcohol with smoked opium. Whereas the tavern was a place of a boisterous, if often violent, masculine sociability that was familiar and Western in its character, the opium den was a quiet, shadowy place that was full of uncomfortably shady characters who lurked in dark corners. Oblivious to the world around them, languid, lounging opium smokers sought to do harm to themselves, and to curious individuals who ventured inside.

Yet the mythical opium den existed in spite of numerous arguments that contradicted the basic foundation on which it was premised: the inherent destructiveness of opium smoking. In 1879, both the *Canadian Illustrated News* and the *Manitoba Daily Free Press* reported an account made by a British consul to Chefoo (now Yantai) that described in detail the effect of opium and his assessment of it.[34] Having found himself chronically ill, this consul "felt justified in trying upon myself the experiment of immoderate opium-smoking." He provided as his "results" a list of what he experienced while under the influence and when trying to quit and then offered his reflections on how his experience fitted into other ideas about opium smoking. To the chagrin of the growing anti-opium forces, this consul's observations were much more moderationist than a moral panic might merit. In comparing it to alcohol drinking, he saw opium smoking to be less dangerous. For example, although "the temptation to excess" was greater in opium smoking than in alcohol consumption, the process of smoking it was complex and opium smoking was generally a solitary vice, so "a man cannot ... be surprised into an excess of opium as he can be into an excess of alcohol." Moreover, opium was not adulterated as alcohol could be, so "no artificial craving is created by poison, such as potato spirit, strychnine and sulphuric acid, with which the drink of our poor is drugged." He agreed that it was "possible" that continued use might impair the moral faculties and blunt the moral sensibilities and "probable" that excessive smoking impaired fertility, but he also knew habitual users who had large families. He recognized that many families "are reduced from comfort to penury" and that poor opium users might resort to crime in order to pay for their habit, but he also noted that the same may be said "of any other habit of self-indulgence." He cautioned that not as many opium smokers suffered ill health from smoking opium as people imagined, and he added that, in fact, the assumption that a sickly opium smoker's condition was caused by smoking ignored the fact that many people who were sickly turned to opium for some relief. Moreover, he noted, "thousands of hard-working people are indebted to opium smoking for the continuance of lives agreeable to themselves and useful to society." In his final point, the consul agreed that breaking the opium habit was more difficult than breaking the alcohol habit, but he maintained that this difference did not justify the complete vilification of opium smoking: "The argument that those who use a commodity as a medicine and harmless luxury should not be deprived of it because weaker brethren abuse it is stronger in the case of opium than in that of alcohol. No one is maddened by smoking opium to crimes of violence."[35]

By the end of the 1870s, then, the opium den and opium smoking operated on at least two levels. On the one hand, opium smoking was a foreign indulgence, undertaken in shadowy places by shady characters who may have been out to destroy the moral integrity of curious, unsuspecting, individuals. The substance was by now considered far worse than alcohol, creating a much deeper physical and moral debasement and resulting in a kind of slavery that was far more difficult to escape even than slavery to the bottle. These were the persistent tropes of opium smoking that operated throughout Canadian and indeed Western culture, the tropes that allowed Dickens and Wilde to send their characters into opium dens, indicating moral danger and debauchery. Yet at the same time, discussions of opium smoking were also imbued with the moderationist tone often adopted by those who, not viewing such indulgence through the missionary perspective or through the salacious view of the journalist seeking sensationalism, tried to present "the facts" rather than the myths. Indeed, in 1895 the British Royal Commission on Opium offered many moderate statements about the trade and the habit in Asia, which Victoria's *Daily Colonist* argued "will no doubt surprise many who read it and shock nearly as many others."[36] In 1901, Rudyard Kipling added to the moderationist perspective when he argued from his first-hand experience that opium smoking's benefits had been overlooked and that opium was normally not taken in extreme quantities.[37] These various myth-debunking perspectives were generally ineffective in reducing the negative associations with opium, notwithstanding the fact that, as Dikötter, Laamann, and Xun's work suggests, these perspectives probably characterized more accurately the nature of opium consumption in China than did the alarmist stories of debasement spread in the religious and secular Western press.[38] As we turn to considering Canadians' views of Chinese people in Canada, we see that these two contrasting perceptions of opium smoking battled for supremacy in the national psyche. And at the end of the century, the baneful influences of opium smoking increasingly intersected with other troublesome indulgences and unnatural habits to become threats to the vitality of the nation.

Chinese People and Opium Smoking in North America
It was through this prism, refracting opium smoking into multifaceted moral and physical dangers, that Canadians viewed the appearance of Chinese opium smokers in North America. By the 1880s these stories were received in Canada under notably different circumstances than the tales of Chinese opium smokers in the early and middle of the century. The West Coast gold rushes of the 1850s saw an increased immigration of Chinese labourers to the country. Many of them stayed after the gold rushes, taking up often menial, low-paid jobs in the mines. When British Columbia joined Confederation, there were reportedly 3,096 Chinese people in the province, amounting to 14.6 percent of the population.[39] These numbers are tenuous because the Chinese were seen as sojourners who came to the region for a few years to make money and then left, either heading to the United States or back to China. This temporary status was actually a cause of concern for people in British Columbia, which used the idea of the "sojourner" as a way to condemn Chinese labourers for not being willing to spend their wages in the country.

The British Columbia government's early attempts to restrict Chinese immigration quickly conflicted with Dominion and imperial priorities. In its 1883–84 session, the BC legislature passed an ordinance to restrict Chinese immigration into the province.[40] The next year, the Dominion government disallowed the legislation on the basis that provinces did not have the authority to restrict immigration. In response, the BC legislature struck a Select Committee on Chinese Restriction, which resolved that the legislature "extremely regret[s] the disallowance of the Act for the prevention of the immigration of Chinese."[41] It requested that Ottawa pass Chinese-exclusion legislation of its own, possibly modelled on legislation that had been passed in some western states south of the border. The 1885 resolution listed a series of issues with Chinese labourers in the province, including concerns that "the Chinese are alien in sentiment and habits," that "they are slaves or coolies of the Chinese race" (in other words, the lowest class of Chinese people), and notably, that "their presence exerts a baneful influence on restricting the immigration of white labour" due not only to competition but also to the fact that white people, such as servants, did not want to work with Chinese. Beyond economic arguments, the resolution was about cultural infestation. "The use of opium has extended throughout the Province to the demoralization of the native [Aboriginal] races, and the Chinese encourage the use of this drug amongst others of our own rising population."[42] The legislature argued that the best course of action was to restrict Chinese immigration in order "to prevent our Province from being completely overrun by Chinese."[43]

This series of legislative resolutions was the outcome of several decades of what may be considered, at best, an uneasy relationship between Chinese and non-Chinese residents of Canada's West Coast and, at worst, a situation of outright conflict. Chinese labourers arrived during the gold rush years of the late 1850s and early 1860s. Initially, there were few problems since there was a tremendous labour shortage and Chinese people tended often to do the jobs that other workers did not wish to do. But their unfamiliar customs and behaviour always made Chinese people stand out. As both Patricia Roy and Peter Ward have argued, it was in the area of the economics of labour relationships that the race conflict had its most intense manifestations.[44] In times of economic boom, when more workers were needed than were available, racial tensions were generally low; but when the economy went through a lull – for example, as the gold fields were closed and white labourers found themselves destitute – tensions rose. Ward sees the conflict as fundamentally about white elitism and entrenched racism, whereas Roy argues that it was much more specifically about the economics of the time and about the political advantage that could be gained, both by the labour movement and by politicians in general, with anti-Chinese rhetoric.

Given that the 1908 law has been framed as mostly a reaction to Chinese opium smoking, it might make sense to assume that this activity was a major issue in anti-Chinese discussions. Yet, despite the inclusion of opium smoking in the BC legislature's 1885 list of reasons to exclude Chinese immigration, the habit was a relatively minor issue to many Sinophobic BC residents. In its 1884 justification for the provincial legislation prohibiting Chinese immigration – the legislation that the Dominion government nixed – the BC legislature did not specifically mention Chinese opium smoking as a problem, although there was also a bill making its way through the legislature to "prohibit the use of Opium, except in certain cases." This legislation did not go to a second reading.[45] In an 1879 House of Commons Select Committee on Chinese Immigration, which was chaired by Amor de Cosmos, someone who could hardly be considered sympathetic to the Chinese in British Columbia, opium smoking was mentioned rarely, and when it was, its significance was marginal. The committee interviewed several prominent BC residents, mostly members of the Dominion Parliament or other people in positions of authority. One of the few mentions of opium occurred when a witness was discussing why people were repulsed by the odour of a Chinese dwelling, where the mixture of Chinese cooking, tobacco, and opium was unpleasant to unfamiliar noses. The other two mentions of opium were prompted by committee members themselves. De Cosmos asked F.J. Barnard, who maintained that the Chinese were a sober people, "Do they not use a good deal of opium?" Barnard admitted that they did use a good deal of opium, but despite his opposition to the Chinese in British Columbia, he insisted that it was not problematic: "It has a soothing effect upon them ... They are perfectly quiet and still until the feeling passes off."[46] When Mr. Brooks asked the same question of Mr. Dewdney, who was decidedly more sympathetic to Chinese immigration than was Barnard, their exchange suggested the inconsequential nature of opium smoking:

Q. What sort of stimulants do they indulge in? –
[A.] They have some sort of sweet mixtures, which they import from China
   – some sweet wines. Some of them will drink our ordinary spirits, but
   not in large quantities.
Q. Do they use opium? –
[A.] Some of them do.

By Mr. Trow:

Q. Are they temperate as a rule? –
[A.] As far as I know they are.
Q. More so than the whites? –
[A.] Oh, much more so.[47]

To these witnesses, opium smoking by Chinese people in British Columbia was simply not a significant issue. They smoked it, just as white people drank liquor, but unlike whites, the Chinese generally did not get boisterous when under the influence of their chosen intoxicant.

This distinction would have resonated with the commissioners. By the 1870s the effect of working-class liquor consumption was the topic of increasing social concern. The temperance movement was gaining strength, manifesting itself in national and international bodies such as the Woman's Christian Temperance Union (first Canadian branch founded in 1874) and the Dominion Alliance for the Total Suppression of the Liquor Traffic (founded in 1876). Although much of the temperance movement's work was aimed at protecting the social fabric of the community from the negative effects of the saloon, the consumption of alcohol in remote locations among groups of working men, such as lumberjacks and miners, was also seen as problematic. Even the Knights of Labor – a working-class organization that, in the West, was especially virulently Sinophobic – encouraged sobriety among its members as a mark of respectability, not to mention a way of increasing household income.[48] So identifying Chinese workers as generally more sober than their better-paid white counterparts would be a major issue but could be taken as a positive or negative characteristic. To employers, it might suggest that Chinese workers were more compliant and docile than white workers – although, to be fair, employers could also see a concern with an influx of Asian foreigners to Canada, notwithstanding their immediate economic benefits. To white workers, Chinese docility and sobriety were a threat. As both Roy and Ward note, the idea that the Chinese were sober workers may have added to the anti-Chinese sentiment: white workers would be threatened by this efficiency, and in times of economic downturns, the fear of the Chinese workers would be intensified by this knowledge that they would work for less and were considered more efficient.[49] Of course, this efficiency was rarely used as a justification to expel or refuse to hire Chinese labourers; to do so would be to argue that white workers were inefficient.

In its report to Parliament, the Select Committee of 1879 noted that to make more sophisticated conclusions than its brief investigation provided would require taking the committee's work to British Columbia itself. This did not happen initially, and between 1879 and 1884, when Parliament ordered the Royal Commission on Chinese Immigration to undertake an extensive examination of the impact of Chinese people on the economic and moral well-being of BC residents, considerable demographic change affected both the perception of Chinese people in the province and the ideas about their impact.

Although it is clear that the Chinese population in British Columbia grew considerably at the beginning of the 1880s, any attempt at quantification must be decidedly tentative. Immigration agent John Jessop noted in 1886 that there were no reliable statistics: "the only basis of calculation as to the number of immigrants arriving in British Columbia that may be made use of is that of Custom House returns from steamer and ships' manifests."[50] When the federal Department of Agriculture began to ask for annual immigration reports, it received uneven statistics. In 1883, J.W. Trutch, a customs officer, reported to the minister of agriculture that 6,200 whites and 7,727 Chinese people had arrived in Victoria in 1882 and that 1,065 Chinese had proceeded to the United States.[51] A year later, newly hired agent Jessop estimated that roughly 9,000 people had immigrated: 6,000 whites and 3,000 Chinese. He repeated this estimation in 1884. In 1885, his numbers became more precise: 16,047 whites and only 4,097 Chinese people.[52] So although the real number of Chinese immigrants was increasing, it was proportionately much lower than the number of whites. The next year, however, Jessop reported something very different: "The influx of Chinese, consequent upon the imposition of a special tax and the completion of the Canadian Pacific

Railway and Esquimalt and Nanaimo Railway[,] had practically ceased."[53] This change was partially a result of the investigation by the Royal Commission on Chinese Immigration, which, although leading to the imposition of a head tax on Chinese labourers, was more sympathetic to their presence and less tolerant of myths about troublesome behaviours like opium smoking than such an outcome might suggest.

Opium's marginal status in the evidence of the 1879 Select Committee is in marked contrast to the way that opium appeared five years later in the evidence taken by the Royal Commission on Chinese Immigration. Convened to determine the efficacy and form of some kind of Chinese exclusion legislation, the commission's perspective seems to have been skewed from the beginning. Although its chair, J.A. Chapleau, the federal secretary of state, might be considered to have approached this issue with limited bias, the second member, Mr. Justice J.H. Gray of the Supreme Court of British Columbia, was not so inclined. As Ward notes, Gray "came to the investigations with well-fixed preconceptions." He saw the object of the commission to be to gather evidence in order to prove that restricting Chinese immigration was good for the province and the country.[54] It may be due to those strong opinions that Chapleau and Gray penned separate reports that were bound with selected evidence in the commission's final report to Parliament.

Since it was charged with considering the advisability of excluding Chinese sojourners, it should not be surprising that the commission began by investigating the perceptions of Chinese sojourners in the United States, where the Chinese Exclusion Act had been in place since 1882. Presented in the commission report's appendix as abstracted, rather than verbatim, evidence, the testimony of witnesses from San Francisco contained repeated indictments of the character of the Chinese labourers. Take, for example, the words of William Vinton, a tailor from San José, just outside of San Francisco, which had a Chinatown district of about 1,000 people that occupied one block near the centre of town:

In this one block, from information from a missionary, there are twenty-eight places of prostitution, the number of prostitutes being about 143. There are thirty-eight gambling dens, besides a number of opium rooms. There are also two lottery drawings daily. At Chinatown there are about 400 who never do a days work; they live by trading, stealing and gambling, the two latter largely predominating ... Among them there is a secret order of thieves, who have a Joss-house specially devoted to them, and they certainly deserve credit for one thing, and that is, they have got the cleanest Joss-house, and the most elegantly ornamented that I have ever seen. As to their habits of cleanliness, words fail to describe it. It has to be seen to be understood.

The short descriptions in the margins of the report are indicative of the point made in this evidence: "143 prostitutes ... character ... dirt." Vinton continued to link the Chinese residents of San Jose to increased crime, illegal lotteries, and of course, the decline of white immigration into town because the Chinese degraded the labour market.[55]

This testimony is typical of the discursive construction of the Chinese labourer on the West Coast. To such witnesses, the Chinese people represented all of the degradation, vice, and immorality that good citizens wanted to see chased from their land. This view was a clear example of the demonization of the nonwhite "other," who was, contrary to the impressions of the missionaries in China, an immediate threat to the well-being of Canadians. As David Roediger has shown for post-emancipation cities in the United States, the construction of a racial "other," who embodied all of the negative characteristics that white workers feared in themselves, was part of the shifting language of race in the reconstruction period. White workers, threatened by this new competition (in this case, from former slaves), projected onto black workers all of the lascivious, drunken, disorderly characteristics that they wanted to discursively distance from their own characters. Thus constructed, this mythical embodiment of vice would stand as a degraded contrast to the upstanding, sober, diligent, virtuous white worker.[56] Just as this process took place in the post-emancipation United States, so too did it emerge around the same time on the West Coast. But here the Chinese labourers, described as filthy, degraded, whoring, thieving gamblers, stood in contrast to the upstanding white, Anglo-Saxon worker.

This process of "othering" the Chinese labourers, however, reveals the important place of opium within this construction: opium was generally an indication of degradation but not itself something degrading. Opium smoking was not the immoral behaviour; rather, it led to immorality. Opium smokers were lazy, listless, and lascivious. Their tendency to consume something that had such negative outcomes was just another indication of their degraded state. Physically degraded Chinese opium smokers were a problem to white society because they lured unsuspecting or thrill-seeking white boys and girls to their demise. Opium smoking was a social concern because it led to other, more dire impediments to the future of society. Given its associations with the vice constellation, opium smoking was a problem because of the danger of moral and social decline – for example, due to sexual immorality, gambling, and laziness.

Many of the stories told to the Royal Commission reflected that sensationalism, yet this was often in spite of evidence calling it into question. Just as the Chefoo consul's moderationist perspective challenged earlier impressions of opium smoking, the commissioners heard voices of moderation that contradicted the perception that the evil of the Chinese opium den would swallow them all. One of the most unique was Emily Wharton, a twenty-year-old opium smoker who had been smoking for four years while living in Victoria after developing the habit in San Francisco. Wharton's testimony is striking because, although it described some of the standard tropes of the opium den's lure, it also challenged many of the myths. Wharton claimed to have begun smoking opium because of "trouble." By the time she spoke to the commission, she was hooked. She explained that she smoked "because I must: I could not live without it. I smoke ... mainly to escape the horrors which would ensue did I not smoke." Yet Wharton's testimony was not entirely damning of the habit. She was troubled by the representations of utter debasement of the opium smoker. When asked whether she had read *Confessions of an English Opium Eater,* she said that she had but that it was neither the reason she had begun smoking nor accurate: "De Quincy's [sic] book is a pack of lies." Moreover, she argued that smoking opium was better than drinking alcohol: "People who smoke opium do not kick up rows; they injure no one but themselves and I do not think they injure themselves very much." Wharton testified that after reviving from opium's "somnolence and complete rest," she woke up and could get on with being productive. And when asked whether she was a "fast woman," she said yes but cautioned the commission against believing that "all the women who come here to smoke are of that character. In San Francisco I have known some of the first people to visit opium houses, and many respectable people do the same here." Moreover, she insisted that the Chinese men whom she had met in the dens had always treated her well. When asked whether she had been well educated, Wharton said yes but added, "that is neither here nor there now." She concluded her testimony with a final connection with drink: if the government licensed opium smoking as it did the saloon, "one need not have to come into such holes as this to smoke."[57]

It is difficult to know how observers responded to Wharton's testimony. Her evidence was included verbatim in Gray's report as part of a selection of examples of the various aspects of the Chinese question, so her words were presented presumably without modification. Yet even if readers noticed her dismissal of the myths of the opium den, it is likely that they also recognized that she represented one of the major fears about the opium den: its ability to lure in and destroy erstwhile respectable young women. Indeed, in his report Gray specifically discussed opium in a section tellingly entitled "Opium Smoking and Prostitution." He began by setting out a simple line of inquiry, infused with a concern about the integrity of the nation: "What we have at present to determine is whether the Chinese are the cause of these evils in the country for if not, punishing them will not only not remove the evil, but would be an act of injustice, discreditable to a free and self-governing country."[58] He proceeded to provide a brief description of the origins and history of opium, recognizing its uses in medicine. He noted (erroneously) that the habit-forming substances morphine and chloral hydrate were derivatives of opium (chloral hydrate is not), that using them was more dangerous than smoking opium, and that they, too, had led white women in other places into degradation.

Gray's report is also remarkable for the discursive connections he made within his discussion. Just as he linked opium smoking and prostitution, he connected "secret societies – want of truth – filthy habits [and] – disease and leprosy" by using these issues as headings to subsections.[59] Such subheadings could lead one to biased conclusions because in reading a large volume of evidence, it was likely that many people would skim for the main ideas. Moreover, the terms appear to emphasize structural challenges to the existing social order; perhaps in his judge's gaze, Gray saw them as distinct from opium smoking and from what he argued were marginal incidents of prostitution. As a Supreme Court justice, Gray clearly wanted to get beyond what he considered superfluous cultural issues and focus on the crux: the effect of the Chinese on labour. So after dealing with these various moral issues, which he saw as "more or less aside of the main issue," he concluded that, indeed, Chinese labour did have a degrading effect on white labour.

Most remarkable about Gray's reflections on opium smoking is that they stand in marked contrast to other chapters on the character of the Chinese. Although he began with the intention of proving how bad the Chinese were to the country, his report was much more equivocal than such initial biases might have indicated. He still concluded that legislation to restrict Chinese immigration was desirable, but just as he concluded that Chinese labour was not as bad as he had initially presumed, he rejected the stereotype that opium smoking was an indication of more extreme degradation and heightened danger to women than were any habits or vices of the Anglo-Saxon race: "In every city; in every part of the world, there will possibly be found persons of the lowest and most degraded habits who frequent opium dens, but they are almost always persons who have fallen so low from previous debauchery and vice; that there is no lower depth to which they can descend."[60] Indeed, this is a section that resonated beyond the commission itself. In its report on the results of the commission, the *Halifax Morning Chronicle* picked up on a few key notes from Gray's report, two of which were that "opium smoking is not such an evil as has been represented, and [that] there are only seventy Chinese prostitutes in all British Columbia."[61] Based on this report, the *Chronicle* wholeheartedly endorsed increasing Chinese immigration to provide labourers who could work Canada's "millions of vacant acres."[62]

Although it is impossible to argue that the Royal Commission affected Canadians' perception of Chinese opium smoking – such commissions usually reflect opinion rather than form it – the 1880s seem to be a benchmark in the level of discussion of opium smoking in the Canadian press. Indeed, the commission's report came about just as other social movements against the opium trade and against opium smoking were gaining speed. As Katherine Lodwick notes, the anti-opium crusade within the missionary movement was heating up by the last quarter of the nineteenth century. Growing Canadian missionary endeavours meant that more missionaries were returning to Canada with stories about the opium problem in China.[63] Moreover, the international manifestation of the Woman's Christian Temperance Union, the World's WCTU (founded in 1883) added the elimination of the opium trade to its global temperance crusade.[64] And within Canada, opium smoking was becoming even more firmly fixed in the popular imagination as a trope for lassitude and indulgence, which could lure in unsuspecting Canadian young people and rot from within the integrity and heart of the nation. The Royal Commission had touched on some of the key issues that became cornerstones of the anti-opium crusade. In the final decades of the nineteenth century, ideas about the dangers of opium smoking, especially as represented by the vices of the opium den, were considered insidious and immediate threats to national integrity.

The opium den would destroy the shining youth of the nation. No matter how much she insisted that opium smoking itself was not the cause of her downfall, Emily Wharton, an educated young woman, was nevertheless a "fast" woman in an opium den. The images of the destruction of promising youth, especially educated elites, appeared repeatedly in the media. The *Manitoba Daily Free Press* reprinted a story from the *San Francisco Chronicle* of "a gentleman" who learned that his son had become an opium addict from his son's friend, who had himself "been a victim of the opium-smoking habit." The article, which was also reproduced in the *True Witness and Catholic Chronicle* concluded that "this is one of the most malignant phases of the Chinese evil, and one that has its most awful meaning for the better classes of society."[65] The *Canadian Presbyterian* attached the blame directly to the "large immigration of Chinese to this continent," which "aroused" the "curiosity" of the white man. "Many were induced to try the experiment of opium smoking. The bewildering sensations overcame their reason, conscience and common sense ... like driftwood in the maelstrom they were dragged down beyond hope of escape." It continued to warn of the broad social danger that opium smoking and the opium dens presented: "The well-born are to be found side by side with the veriest social pariah. Members of the best families, young men and women, fall beneath what proves to them an irresistible fascination."[66] Using a punchy one-liner to titillate and shock its readership, the *Free Press* printed a single-sentence article encapsulating the problem: "There are a dozen opium smoking dens in Virginia City, Nev., and young girls patronize them."[67] As the pace of these images intensified and became closer to home, the *Toronto Globe,* a newspaper with sympathies for the temperance movement, invited caution. It noted that rumours of ladies frequenting opium dens "are too often put forth by writers who are utterly ignorant of what constitutes a lady, even in the merest conventional sense." The idea that "ladies" would frequent such low places was simply beyond belief:

> It exceeds the wildest bounds of probability that any woman recognized by respectable society has ever been seen indulging in the delights of an opium den or drinking at a bar, no matter how private ... it is worse than brutal ... to malign an entire sex for the sake of mystifying ignorant people and selling a few hundred extra papers.[68]

Either this caution was ignored or the moral status of the individual before entering the opium den was immaterial to the media. Indeed, two years after commenting on the sensationalism of these stories, the *Globe* itself recounted a story of two "young society men" in Bloomington, Illinois, who were found unconscious after smoking opium. One was the son of a former mayor, and the other was "a writer and poet of no mean ability." Both "will probably die."[69] The *Free Press* saw the danger as growing and immediate. In November 1888, it reported on "a pretty Canadian girl," the "happy innocent" daughter of a well-to-do family from Toronto, who had graduated "from a leading female seminary" but was found dead in an opium den in Chicago.[70] A year later, it noted that opium smoking had become prevalent in Winnipeg, as evidenced by the arrest of "a young white girl" in "one of the Chinese opium joints."[71] Such stories were repeated in newspapers and magazines throughout the country.

By the end of the century, the opium den had become an established trope of insidious immorality, a place of creeping, secretive dissolution where, in contrast to the very public and boisterous saloon, foreign interlopers undermined the morality and integrity of the white race by destroying the young men and women who were lured there. The imagery was shocking and sensationalist. White women were depicted lying with white or Asian men and smoking a substance that lulled them into the sort of lassitude that caused them to let down their guard and allow any number of violations to their virtue. Whether or not they entered the den as "easy" women, they would soon become so labelled. Educated young men were depicted being destroyed in these backroom hovels, an uncivilized heathen environment in the heart of North American cities. The opium den's influence was a persistent and expanding danger, a social pathogen whose epidemiology could be traced in the pages of the newspaper. Opium dens on the West Coast were depicted moving eastward into Canadian cities. Canadian girls in American cities were depicted dying in these dens of iniquity.

Indeed, the opium den and opium smoker had entered popular consciousness to such a degree that they functioned as their own metaphors for vice in other forms, often in contrast to less dire problems or as representative of further social decline. The *Manitoba Daily Free Press* reproduced a story from the *New York Mercury* of a Chinese man's wedding to a German woman. The wedding took place in his laundry, and in an adjoining room, "a few of the guests were smoking opium." Near the altar was a table with "a complete opium lay-out, including a pipe, a few pounds of smoking opium, a peanut oil lamp and an instrument for lifting the opium out of the cooking vessel."[72] The incongruity of the mixed-race marriage was reiterated by the alienness and immorality of those who attended and, one must suppose, endorsed the union. Opium dens were common settings of stories of moral failure and redemption. The literary journal the *Week* reviewed a book entitled *The Lovely Wang*, a satire about a "Charming young girl" in China who had to buy her lover back with forty pieces of silver from "the old crone" who kept the nearby opium den.[73] Would it have been lost on Christian Canadians that the crone's price was higher than that of Judas Iscariot himself? Not only a place of dangers, the opium den was becoming known simply as a place of sleepy lethargy. The writer of an article criticizing the teaching of literature in college observed that he had never "breathed an atmosphere more somniferous out of a Chinese 'opium joint'" than that which he had found in the lecture he attended.[74] The World's Fair in Chicago was reported to have "a correct representation of a Chinese opium joint," with a Western actor, E.W. Wood, "acting as Gee Chung of San Francisco. He will show the matter and mode of living, and will expose their use of opium in every particular."[75] Ten years later, an exhibition for Citizenship Day included a freak show and a megaphone artist entreating the patrons to "see the opium den in full operation" while "a dopy looking individual shows visitors how to 'hit the pipe.'"[76] The irony that an activity, associated with members of an ethnic group who were actively denied citizenship, had been turned into a sensationalized sideshow display may have been lost on the audience of Citizenship Day. Or perhaps the display reiterated the superiority of the Canadian or British citizen over the lesser races of the East.

As the new century began, then, the opium den and opium smoking had taken their place in both the language of deviance, and accounts of criminality, immorality, and insidious threats to the nation. Numerous sensational stories in the newspapers included crimes that either took place in opium dens or were somehow associated with opium smoking. Not the least among them, in June 1893 ten senior government officials in Puget Sound, British Columbia, were arrested for smuggling Chinese people and opium into the United States. "The immense profit in the business seems to have corrupted many officials."[77] More often, however, the association with criminality was more subtle. When someone attempted to blow up the court house at Steveston, British Columbia, the reports blamed "some fiendish Chinaman" who, with his compatriots, had been converting the small town "into a

Monte Carlo with opium den attachments" every night.[78] The *Victoria Daily Colonist* attributed the act to "A Diabolical Chinaman."[79] An article entitled "Chinese Gaming in Toronto" told of a raid on "the premises of ... a Chinese laundryman and grocer," where six arrests were made. Although the arrests were for gambling, the report noted that "the basement was fitted up elaborately for gambling and opium smoking."[80] A 1908 cold-blooded murder in Montreal's Chinatown took place in an opium den, and although the murder appears to have had nothing to do with opium smoking, the *Lethbridge Herald* entitled the article, in large type, "A Tragedy in an Opium Den."[81] In 1908, "four colored men" were charged with stealing heavy overcoats. Although it had nothing to do with the crime, two of the men were reported to have been running an opium den.[82]

The Opium Trade and the Guilt of Association

Although such images of the opium den and opium smoking served to remind Canadians of the immediate threat both to law and order and, more generally, to the safety and future of the country, this was not the only threat to national integrity represented by opium smoking and the dens in which it took place. Canada's relationship with Britain, the imperial power that had forced the opium trade on the unwilling Chinese people, meant that in the minds of many anti-opium advocates, Canada's reputation was sullied by association. By the end of the century, the anti-opium movement was combining the missionary zeal of its evangelical members with repeated reminders that the opium trade had been forced on China by the British. A report from Burma noted, "[The fact] that opium smoking is spreading at an alarming rate under our rule does not admit of doubt." And the chief commissioner of "British Burmah" noted that opium smoking had resulted in "a change which was gradually coming over the Burmese national character."[83] The literary journal the *Week* recognized that, because Chinese people carried opium smoking wherever they went, "the whole world over which they wander is thus made to suffer for the fell necessities of Anglo-Indian finance."[84] Missionaries were especially vocal. Rev. H. Lloyd described his encounter with a young man of a good Chinese family who bore all the physical evidence of the opium smoker: "His cheeks were sunken and his whole appearance was that of a man who had smoked opium for many years." Lloyd was remorseful and, true to his evangelical calling, reminded his readers of their responsibility: "I felt that as an Englishman I was, in some respects, responsible for the terrible harm we are doing in China by sending the opium to this people."[85] In 1888, the *Missionary Review of the World* provided a detailed account of the World's Missionary Conference, at which the opium trade was a major concern. Rev. J. Hudson Taylor, founder of the China Inland Mission, "arraigned the opium traffic as the sum of all wrongs and villainies, and affirmed that when the first British ships bore to the land that fatal drug, an injury was inflicted that in one day works still more harm than the gospel can offset in a year."[86] Later at the conference, the opium traffic joined the liquor traffic and "licensing sin" (prostitution) in "a trinity of monstrous evils" that the conference denounced. Speakers clamoured that "on the matter of the opium trade the Christian conscience of Great Britain has of late gone to sleep."[87]

For missionaries, the connection between British imposition of the opium trade and their evangelical work was additionally problematic because Chinese people often associated Western missionaries with the arrival of opium in their country. One missionary told "a sad story" of an encounter with three old women who were smoking opium in their house. When one of them "caught the name of Jesus," she stood up and said, "Do not mention that name again. I hate Jesus; I will not hear another word: you foreigners bring opium in one hand, and Jesus in the other ... I do not want your opium or your Jesus."[88] A subsequent story in the same issue of *Canadian Independent* argued that "the Christian Church must face the fact that she has no greater hindrance to her own work [in China] than the habit of the opium victim ... The Christian missionary sees in all opium dens a product of so-called civilization," which the writer characterized as "a greater obstruction to his work than the superstitious practices of heathen idolatry."[89] A missionary teacher to India, Miss Ackerman, was dumbstruck by a high-class Brahmin who clearly presented the essence of Western hypocrisy and the way that Britain forced opium on dark-skinned people:

> Here in India the poppy is cultivated; opium is manufactured by the government; every ball of opium that goes out from factories bears the stamp and seal of the British crown. When I was in England I went to a chemist, and I said to him, "I want some opium." He said, "where is your prescription?" "I have no prescription." "You must get it, you must go to a physician and get a prescription before we can sell you any opium." I went to a physician and the prescription was written out, and the opium was placed in my hands, and it was marked "poison." Now ... can you tell why it is that to England's white-skinned subjects it is sold as poison, and to its dark-skinned subjects it is sold as food?[90]

To the Canadian missionaries who saw it as their job to bring the word of God to the heathen, the actions of their own government were undermining these civilizing efforts. The spread of opium, and the government's complicity in that trade, was a disgrace to the nation and as much a threat to the morality of that nation as the consumption of opium in Canada.

As the twentieth century began, opium smoking had become a clear threat to the health of the nation and in fact to its own soul. Invective against the

Chinese in Canada, founded on concerns about the damage that the Chinese labourers were doing to the growth of the white population, enabled Sinophobes to paint various culturally specific activities as gambling and opium smoking as dire threats to the character of the provinces and the country. Just as the Chinese supposedly undermined the economic health of Canada by undercutting wages, not spending their earnings in Canada, and monopolizing certain occupations like household service and market gardening, so too did their chosen intoxicants present a threat to the physical and moral health of Canadians. Through voices as diverse as labour activists who were hostile to all things Chinese and missionaries who sought to rid the Chinese of their heathen culture and strange, immoral customs, Canadians learned that opium smoking meant the demoralization of self and of nation.

The growing concern about the infiltration of Canadian life by Chinese opium smoking was a powerful metaphor for the concern about national decline, but it was not the only concern presented by opium. At the same time that people in British Columbia were expressing their misgivings about Chinese workers and reiterating the Chinese man's alienness by pointing to the opium pipe, physicians were discussing the problem of the habitual use of opiates, normally medically prescribed, by respectable Canadian patients. So whereas fears about opium smoking seeped from concern over an opium den in the backroom of a Chinese restaurant or the strange smells wafting from a city's Chinatown, and hung like a cloud over the international alarm about the imposition of opium on China, the emerging fears about an opium habit that was unrelated to the long pipe and shadowy den charted a parallel course. Emerging medical concerns over the habitual use of opium began as an intraprofessional discussion about the problems of iatrogenic habituation and about how they might reflect negatively on physicians themselves, but this discussion then expanded to embrace the physicians' self-perception as guardians of the national health. And the discursive links and dangers overlapped. The growing concern over the impact of opium smoking, which was undertaken in secret, lured the innocent, and demoralized all in its path, joined concerns over other insidious, secretive activities that threatened to undermine the integrity of the nation. Throughout all of these practices, the problem was both the substance and the behaviour that it engendered. "Addiction," a term rooted in notions of slavery and loss of freedom, was the big threat. From that, all other debasement flowed.

5
Medicine, Addiction, and Ideas of Nation

While concerns about Chinese opium smoking were connecting the local to the international, enmeshing Canadians in a discursive net that linked their imagined nation to a threat from "over there," physicians, reformers, and other commentators were attempting to understand the habitual consumption of non-smoked, often medically prescribed opium, something that decidedly took place "back here." Interpretation of this behaviour as it affected both the individual and society was subjective enough to permit wide discussion and continued debate, engaging Canadian physicians in an ongoing international dialogue. It did not simplify matters that biological science was changing rapidly throughout the century. Increasingly sophisticated scientific instrumentation, new theories of disease causation, and confidence that science could (eventually) answer perplexing social questions all meant that the debates about habituation (or dependency or chronic poisoning or addiction) were intricate, disparate, and inconclusive.

This should not be surprising. Not only is addiction a complex physiological process, but it is also a complex idea. It can connect to a variety of values and ideals and to explanatory discourses that range from biological science to political theory to theology. Originating in a term indicating obligation (or at its extreme, slavery), "addiction" had multiple meanings by the middle of the nineteenth century that were connected to the various types of addicts and types of substances to which one could be addicted. One could "be addicted" to something or, later, could "addict oneself."[1] Ideas about addiction are both informed by and in turn inform social, political, moral, and cultural norms. A person may begin taking a psychoactive substance for any number of reasons, broadly defined as medical, social, cultural, or even political. A person who has become habituated to the consumption of various psychoactive substances presents a moral, cultural, and biological dilemma. Is the act of repeatedly consuming a substance indicative of physical incapacity? A moral failing? An expression of defiance? The answers are context-dependent. One person's inability to resist temptation or one person's interest in participating in certain (counter)cultural activities is another person's idea of irresponsible deviance. In addition, the physical condition of a seemingly irresistible substance dependency is subjected to different interpretations depending on the conceptual prism through which it is viewed. Is a physical addiction the result of "brain disease," "moral paralysis," or a dysfunction of dopamine receptors, as more contemporary biology suggests (which brings us back to brain disease)? It all depends on whom you ask, where you ask them, and when the conversation takes place.

Discussions of the changing meanings of addiction have placed concerns about the perceived growth of addiction in a number of contexts. The "discovery of addiction" has been linked to industrialization, where drunken or hung-over workers would upset the workplace discipline of bourgeois industrialists.[2] Although not dealing specifically with drugs, ideas about the alcohol habit created a template that shaped some commentators' ideas of habitual substance consumption more broadly. Different medical interpretations of the physical cause of addiction have been seen as the result of rapidly changing medical science.[3] Others have noted that the assumptions of science remained hybrids of moral and physical interpretations of the functions of body and mind.[4] So cultural influences, such as fears over addiction and especially the opium-smoking of Chinese people, allowed physicians in the United States to build their professional authority in the face of a crisis of modernity.[5] Concerns over addiction to opium and to other drugs could also combine with nationalism and led to policies that were driven by national self-perceptions and international influences.[6] At the same time, just as national cultural self-identity affected policies, so too could the cultures of research and interprofessional politics affect the way that scientists and policymakers viewed addiction.[7] Such varied research demonstrates the range of historical interpretations of how scientists, physicians, and social commentators framed addiction. These diverse and often contradictory interpretations are, of course, all valid. Nation, morality, science, and culture have all affected ideas about addiction, and their influences are intertwined.

Although ideas about addiction were driven by a variety of factors, the most significant historical change in the way the ideas were discussed was the shift of focus from the moral being to the physical one, the somatic interpretation of mental, as well as physical, dysfunction. With these ideas in hand, physicians could offer new-sounding treatments that merely reframed old methods in somatic terms and scientific jargon. The emerging ideas about addiction, especially the problems with iatrogenic addiction, influenced physicians' notions of both their professional authority over the body of the individual and their role as protectors of the physical health of the nation. Since addiction was increasingly recognized as a threat to the bodily health of many elite citizens, and thus a threat to the integrity of the nation, the judicious treatment of addiction and the strict control over access to opiates could be important nation-building, or nation-strengthening, activities. In Canadian medical literature, international discussion about alcohol and drug habituation combined with domestic experiences of physicians to provide a perspective that, although not necessarily uniquely Canadian, certainly put the issue into a national context, which in turn informed broader discussions of what addiction meant.

Opium and Alcohol Habits Compared

Habitual consumption of opium was not new in the nineteenth century, but it was not nearly as problematic as habitual alcohol consumption. As noted in Chapter 2, physicians described the opium habit, usually iatrogenically induced, as "chronic poisoning." For the most part, it was problematic only inasmuch as it interfered with the physician's ability to provide an accurate dosage of therapeutic opium to habituated patients or when insurance companies refused to insure opium habitués. In contrast, physicians considered the alcohol habit to be a serious physical concern. For example, whereas physicians and the insurance industry debated about the impact of the opium habit on longevity, chronic alcohol consumption was indisputably a worrisome condition and normally a barrier to coverage.[8] Moreover, both Thomas Trotter and Benjamin Rush, Anglo-American physicians who reconceptualized the alcohol habit as a medical problem, compared the alcohol habit to the habitual use of opium in their pivotal works.[9] Both argued that opium and alcohol operated differently on the physical system, using simple observation of the process of intoxication by alcohol and by opium to demonstrate this difference. Both saw the opium habit in a more positive light than alcohol addiction, and both saw opium as useful in treating the condition that would, a generation later, be named "alcoholism" by Swedish physician Magnus Huss.[10]

In his *An Essay, Medical, Philosophical, and Chemical, on Drunkenness, and Its Effects on the Human Body*, Trotter made a clear distinction between habitual consumption of alcohol and that of substances including opium.[11] Trotter cast his net widely to capture many of the psychotropic substances then known in Western society. He noted that alcohol had been included in the class of narcotics that included "opium, bangue, cicuta, belladonna, hyosciamus, nicotiana, lauro-serasus."[12] Yet these substances were not as problematic as alcohol, even though they could bring on the sort of "delirium, stupor, and other phenomena of ebriety ... universal debility, emaciation, loss of intellect, palsy, dropsy, dyspepsia, hepatic disease, and all others which flow from the indulgence of spirituous liquors."[13] He justified distinguishing between alcohol and these other substances simply because, whereas the latter "produce nearly the same phenomena, and their habitual use almost the same diseases," their use was not nearly so common as alcohol. So a detailed discussion of the problems with their overconsumption was not necessary.[14]

In Rush's *An Inquiry into the Effects of Ardent Spirits on the Human Body*, a relatively short jeremiad that blended moralistic and physical arguments against the consumption of strong alcohol, opium appeared both as a dangerous substance and as a palliative.[15] The *Inquiry* set much of the discursive foundation for the arguments of the North American temperance movement over the next century, and for this reason it is useful to see that even at the end of the eighteenth century, opium was recognized as dangerous but discursively distinct from alcohol, which was deemed much more problematic. Rush used the fact that opium was often chosen for suicide to argue that the persistent consumption of alcohol was a form of gradual suicide, noting that a drinker is "perpetuating gradually, by the use of ardent spirits, what he has effected suddenly by opium."[16] Yet even though Rush saw opium as a key tool for "the suicide," he did not hesitate to recommend that both wine and opium "are far less injurious to the body and mind than spirits." Indeed, the habits created from wine drinking or opium consumption were, Rush argued, "easily broken, after time and repentance have removed the evils they were taken to relieve."[17] He considered these conditions so marginal to the topic at hand that all he saw as necessary were "time and repentance," neither of which, one might presume, would require a physician's intervention. This religious language also illustrates a distinct difference between much of the literature arguing against the habitual consumption of alcohol (and at times other substances) produced in the United States and that produced in the United Kingdom: the American literature, even that generated by physicians, was often much more imbued with the language of evangelical Protestantism. Repentance was not normally required for a medical solution to be effected; but it was essential for the salvation of the soul.

Notwithstanding historians' debates over the claims of who first defined alcohol habituation as a disease, both Trotter's and Rush's work set the stage for an increasingly intense discussion of the social problems of drunkenness. One of the works referenced often by authors of medical textbooks discussing substance habituation was Robert MacNish's *Anatomy of Drunkenness* (1828). MacNish, a Scottish physician who, like Trotter a generation earlier, wrote his doctoral dissertation on drunkenness, cast the definition of "drunkenness" well beyond that caused by alcohol. His work, however, was not dedicated exclusively to the habitual use of substances: much of the essay considered therapeutic and diagnostic issues, including the "physiology of drunkenness," "pathology of drunkenness," "sleep of drunkards," and "method of curing the fit of drunkenness." Although alcohol consumption was the main issue in his essay, MacNish also included "drunkenness" from opium. For example, in the chapter on the "method of curing the fit of drunkenness," MacNish included a section on how to deal with a drunkenness caused by opium. Here "drunkenness" had a strictly physiological meaning: it was used to describe acute poisoning rather than the chronic habituation about which many writers would spill so much ink as the century wore on. Moreover, MacNish presented a much more balanced appreciation of the issue of drunkenness. Unlike Rush, with his fervent redemptionist language, MacNish recognized that some people simply would not stop drinking. For them, he included a chapter entitled "Advice to Determined Drunkards," where he explained that "if a man is resolved to continue a drunkard, it may here be proper to mention in what manner he can do so with least risk to himself." The advice included such useful gems as not to drink spirits on an empty stomach, to "shun raw spirits," and never to mix your wines, sentiments that may, indeed, stand the test of time.[18]

MacNish also offered points of comparison between opium and alcohol, and here we see, as with Trotter, not only a recognition that the two substances bore similarities but also the different manner in which the medical community viewed them. He noted that opium "resembles the other agents of intoxication" because "the fondness for it increases with use" until "it becomes nearly essential for bodily comfort and peace of mind."[19] Moreover, the development of a habit such as that seen in the case of opium "exists as a general rule with regard to all stimulants and narcotics."[20] Yet, for MacNish, as well as for Trotter and to a lesser degree Rush, although some of the characteristics of the opium habit were similar to those of the habit in ardent spirits, the substances needed to be treated differently. Drunkenness itself, MacNish observed, was "modified by the inebriating agent." So "ebriety from ardent spirits differs in some particulars from that brought on by opium or malt liquors, such as porter or ale."[21] The key substance of social opprobrium remained strong spirits, and in direct comparison, other substances were simply not as problematic.

These discussions were taking place around the same time as the publication of Thomas De Quincey's *Confessions*, so it is difficult to determine whether that tantalizing tale of woe affected early-nineteenth-century medical writers' ideas about the opium habit. Both Virginia Berridge and Geoffrey Harding argue that De Quincey's *Confessions* did not influence discussions about opium consumption in the first part of the century, but Berridge notes that the work became important in ideas about addiction as the century came to a close.[22] Yet De Quincey's ideas were certainly known. As we saw in Chapter 2, De Quincey's writings were so familiar to readers that, for those who wanted an account of some of the issues related to opium eating, Jonathan Pereira needed only refer to the writings of "Mr. De Quincey and of the late Mr. S.T. Coleridge" in his *Elements of Materia Medica* (1842).[23] Such a cursory reference indicates the marginal status of the habit as a medical issue. Indeed, normally when discussing an issue that seemed properly medical, textbook authors such as Pereira would reference other physicians' work, not the sensationalized tales penned by Romantic authors. As we will see, the lines between opium and alcohol, the type of substance used and the way that it was used, and most fundamentally, the user's social class and at times race affected interpretations of its meaning and significance to the progression or regression of society.

Although opium and alcohol were not normally considered similar, they were considered to be linked socially: the use of one substance often led to the use of the other. William G. Smith observed in 1832 that women resorted to opium as a substitute for gin and brandy.[24] In 1849, a legislative committee of Upper Canada, while considering a bill to regulate the sale of alcohol, noted the connection between alcohol and opium but rejected its significance. The chair, A. Gugy, recognized that some people felt that liquor restriction might result in more people "resort[ing] for excitement to opium or to some other drug."[25] Gugy said that this trend would not occur since opium was a private indulgence, whereas liquor was more social and public. Nevertheless, the linkage between alcohol and drug abuse was clear. An alternative to Gugy's point had been made in Britain by Edwin Chadwick in 1834. Chadwick reported to the Select Committee on Inquiry into Drunkenness that "if alcohol sales were restricted, people might be driven to some other form of enjoyment," mentioning specifically the opium habit as one of several "gross and noxious forms of excitement."[26] Chadwick's perspective was reiterated forty years later when, in 1878, an anonymous writer in the *Canadian Monthly* charged that the temperance movement was causing an increase in the number of addicts to "opium, hashich, hydrate of chloral, and other such still more noxious substances" by making alcohol more difficult to purchase. He cited as proof his own experiences as an opium eater.[27] A case of opium poisoning reported in the *Canada Medical Journal* in 1869 also alluded to the connection between alcohol and opium. A man was found unconscious in his office after taking over an ounce of laudanum while in a drunken stupor. Although the writer, George Ross, made no direct connection between the two drugs, he did not consider the incident to be an attempted suicide but rather a progressive form of indulgence.[28] When considering the social effects of prohibitory laws, Joseph Parrish explained at the first meeting of the American Association for the Cure of Inebriety that drugs in the form of "bitters, cordials, syrups, essences and tinctures ... are not only used as intoxicating drinks where there is prohibition, but when there is not these compounds are sold at the public bars alongside of whisky, brandy and gin."[29]

This connection of vices was not merely a substitution of one intoxicant for another; it also related to a broader range of unsavoury behaviours that were indicative of a profligate lifestyle. These activities formed what John Burnham has labelled the "vice constellation" – which encompassed behaviours often found to be culturally related, including drinking, sexual promiscuity, gambling, and drug taking – and they informed physicians' interpretations of drug use through much of the century.[30] De Quincey and Coleridge may have been notorious for their status as opium eaters whose indulgence was little more than a personal problem, but as we have seen, the habitual use of opium, alcohol, or other substances was often considered to be a variation of a similar indulgence. Moreover, given that the alcohol habit was becoming the subject of intense discussion and a series of popular social-reform movements, the language of the alcohol-temperance movement influenced other debates. Consequently, many physicians interpreted drug addiction through the lens of this broader idea of debauchery.

Take, for example, the story of a New York morphine addict in Ottawa. In 1867, Dr. D. McGillivray, a physician at the Ottawa Protestant Hospital, visited a thirty-seven-year-old barrister from New York identified only as Mr. M.D.B., who was complaining of delirium tremens. Mr. M.D.B confessed to the doctor that he was a habitual user of alcohol and morphine. Two years earlier his doctor had prescribed laudanum to ease the pain of a leg injury. Over time the habit grew; owing to the excessive amounts of laudanum he would need to maintain his habit, Mr. M.D.B turned to morphine, which satisfied the addiction in smaller doses. McGillivray treated the delirium tremens but continued to observe Mr. M.D.B. with fascination. The barrister was intent on displaying his ability to withstand morphine's toxic effects. He took a one-drachm bottle of the drug – enough, McGillivray noted, to kill twenty people – mixed it in a tumbler with whiskey, drank it, and went off to enjoy the theatre. McGillivray was surprised and concerned at such excess, and he cautioned his patient "against the results sooner or later to follow such enormous doses of poison and such flagrant abuse of his constitution." The man's response was simple: "I am used to it and there is no danger." Several days later, Mr. M.D.B. returned to New York.[31]

The doctor's report of the case may never have been printed if his experience with this patient had ended there. However, after four months, the barrister returned to McGillivray's office, "feeble and exhausted, worn and emaciated, apparently fast sinking a victim to his evil habits[,] of the dangers attending which he was now fully convinced." He began to try to resist his cravings. "With perfect consciousness that he was destroying himself and with every desire to struggle against the insatiable cravings of his diseased appetite[,] he found it utterly impossible to offer the slightest opposition to them." Unable to control his addiction, Mr. M.D.B. continued to weaken until "death closed his sad career."[32]

McGillivray's article presents a vivid example of the transitional phase in the medical ideas about habitual substance use. In the 1860s, physicians had not yet formulated a disease theory of addiction, yet they did encounter habitual drug use. Mr. M.D.B.'s condition fitted precisely the notion of "chronic poisoning." It was a problem but not a severe one, and it may often have been disregarded by physicians because it was so difficult to fix. McGillivray's reference to Mr. M.D.B.'s "diseased appetite" indicates that he viewed the condition as akin to what David Musto called a "vice-disease, easily acquired, progressively damaging, and difficult to cure," resulting from a weakness of the will.[33] Although Mr. M.D.B. did recognize the need to resist after he had begun rapidly to decline, McGillivray was more interested in the patient's initial unwillingness to stop such dangerous behaviour. The concept of vice-disease related to a moralistic interpretation of recreational substance use, a practice connected to, but distinct from, habitual alcohol consumption. Although he was healthy in appearance, Mr. M.D.B. was "an inveterate smoker, and a hard drinker, almost incessantly revelling in debauchery and profligacy." McGillivray interpreted these excessive habits as having led to increased use of morphine since "the more whiskey he drank the more morphia he was required to take." Although dubious, this causation does indicate how the physician viewed the relationship between morphine and alcohol. Liquor, the focus of a great deal of social opprobrium, was the destroyer; morphine, a valuable medicine, was merely the agent of that destruction, not the initial cause. Mr. M.D.B. presented what doctors labelled an "addictive personality," a person whose character tended particularly toward excessive habits.[34] All of these elements, the association between alcohol and morphine, the diseased appetite, and the relationship with the broader vice constellation, illustrate how McGillivray set his interpretation of Mr. M.D.B.'s condition within the established framework of a combined medical and temperance discourse.

So opium habituation was familiar to physicians; what was less certain was what it meant to medicine. McGillivray's story was a cautionary tale, instructive not in how to treat this condition but in what physicians should try to avoid. But merely avoiding being the cause of iatrogenic addiction would not help physicians to undertake their main professional task: healing the afflicted. Treating the habitual use of opiates and other substances, whether or not they were connected to alcohol, was rapidly becoming something that physicians needed to be able to do – most especially because, unlike Mr. M.D.B, many of the opium addicts met by physicians tended not to be debauched libertines and prodigal sons but middle-class patients, who were often young or middle-aged women, the type of people who could be considered innocent victims whose addiction came about through no fault of their own. Indeed, their condition was the fault of the very physician on whose successful treatment the patient, and the credibility of the profession, relied.

The perceived problems of habitual opium use had been well articulated in the medical literature by the 1870s. As we saw in Chapter 2, chronic opium poisoning took on a more dire meaning when morphine was isolated and especially when its hypodermic injection became both wildly popular and quickly overused. Both Wayne Morgan and David Courtwright argue that the use of morphine injection by soldiers in the years after the US civil war gave rise to a new concern over its habituation, although David Musto has challenged earlier assertions to this effect.[35] Moreover, physicians like British physician Clifford Allbutt were beginning to discuss the potential problems of morphine habituation as something worse than opium eating, while simultaneously other physicians continued to extol the virtues of hypodermic morphine and to hand out hypodermic needles to their patients.[36]

Many historians point to one book in particular as giving a name, a medical interpretation, and a new urgency to the problem of morphine habituation. German physician Eduard Levinstein published *Die Morphiumsucht* in 1877, and it was quickly translated into English and published in 1878 as *The Morbid Craving for Morphine*.[37] Levinstein offered a contrast with earlier interpretations of the meaning of morphine habituation, challenging terms such as "Morphinismus, Morphia-delirium, and Morphia-evil"[38] as being unable to "sufficiently answer to the character of the disease as delineated by me." "Morphinismus" referred to poisoning, but many cases of routine use – for example, by those in prolonged medical treatment – did not, Levinstein argued, result in the habit after the medicine was removed. He rejected "Morphia-evil" and especially "Morphia-mania" because they suggested some kind of diseased state of mind. He argued that, since many people who were habituated to morphine did not display any signs of mental illness or an alteration of their character, it was clearly a somatic condition: "Morbid craving for morphia means the uncontrollable desire of a person to use morphia as a stimulant and tonic, and the diseased state of the system caused by the injudicious use of the said remedy."[39] Whether or not Levinstein was the first to pay careful attention to the problems of morphine addiction, the enthusiasm with which physicians adopted his perspective is entirely understandable. Levinstein was wresting substance habituation out of the realm of the moral and religious by placing it squarely in the hands of those individuals who professed expertise in somatic illness.

Some Canadian medical journals were quick to take an interest in this ground-breaking research. Levinstein's work was noticed in Canada a year before *Die Morphiumsucht* appeared. In 1876, both the French-language *L'Union Medicale* and the English-language *Canada Lancet* published summaries of several of Levinstein's journal articles. The *Canada Lancet*, in a brief paragraph discussing Levinstein's observations, emphasized the associations between the delirium tremens caused by alcohol and those by morphine use. *L'Union Medicale*, in a detailed abstract of Levinstein's work reproduced from several French journals, provided several facets of the condition, drawing the distinction between "morphinisme" and "alcoholism" just as Levinstein distinguished *"Morphiumsucht"* from *"Trunksucht."*[40] It followed this article with a second abstract on the abuse of the subcutaneous injection of morphine, observed by a Vienna-based physician, Dr. Weinlechner.[41] Yet the interest in the research did result in some conceptual confusion. For example, the *Canada Lancet's* article equated *"Morphiumsucht"* with "Morphiomania" and *"Trunksucht"* with "Dipsomania." These differences are noteworthy because, as Levinstein noted in his book, not all cases of the morbid craving for morphia were manias. In the realm of addictions, just as with the taxonomy of other diseases, how the condition was interpreted affected how it was treated.

Levinstein was at the forefront of a change in the way that physicians viewed drug habituation. In the last quarter of the century, addiction specialists began to make sharper distinctions between the physical and moral results of alcohol and opium addiction. These distinctions, although couched in medical terminology, recognized an implicit link between moral and physical conditions. In his expanded version of *Inebriety or Narcomania* (1894), Norman Kerr, president of the British Society for the Study of Inebriety, compared opium and alcohol addiction as being both somatic and moral-mental phenomena. Alcohol indulgence could be either social or solitary, whereas opium was exclusively consumed alone. "Alcohol infuriates," whereas opium generally soothes the habitué. Opium raised the temperature, whereas alcohol lowered it. "Carefully conducted scientific experiments" suggested that alcohol affected animals but that opium generally did not. Alcoholics were more untruthful than opium addicts, and exercising moderation was more difficult for opium users than for alcoholics. Under the subtitle of "perversion of the affections," Kerr presented a gendered moral interpretation of the differences between the opium and alcohol habits. "Opium transforms the manly, high-toned, pleasant companion into an effeminate, drivelling, querulous bore. Alcohol changes the neat, active, attractive and devoted helpmeet into a dirty, idle, repulsive and selfish brute."[42] This distinction is curious since many writers associated opium with women and alcohol with men. Perhaps Kerr was trying to draw on a gender-specific worst-case scenario.[43] Since the long-term use of opium "is seen in a rather nervous disquietude and excitability," opium was connected to speculation and gambling, whereas alcohol "is apt to provoke the animal passions and incite to lust."[44] Physically, alcohol presented a much more severe pathological transformation than did opium, although opium presented a "more irreclaimable and incurable diseased condition." Both substance negatively affected the reproductive system.

The ideas of commentators on alcohol and opium use demonstrate that in both their immediate physical effects and long-term dangers, opium and alcohol could be simultaneously similar and different, notwithstanding the distinctions that Rush and Trotter had drawn earlier in the century. What made a difference was the way that class affected the perception of substance use. Simply put, the elevation of the higher or nobler aspects of humanity, presented by opium's hypnotic effects, contrasted with the debasement caused by alcohol. Opium was especially a problem because of the way that it could affect the elite in society, whereas alcohol was seen as socially problematic mostly when consumed by the poor. However, the moral dangers of opium habituation were equally as troubling as the moral dangers of alcohol consumption. As addiction research became more formalized, doctors like Kerr tried to draw distinctions based on scientific categories but fell back on moralistic observations. Since both alcohol and opium were part of the *materia medica,* what needed to be understood was what, exactly, caused habituation and how best to alleviate the dangers of these substances. Such a project would enhance doctors' ability to use these medicines effectively and safely and might also aid them in providing viable medical treatment.

"The Enemy Within": Defining and Locating Addiction

Commentators on the opium habit rarely offered a concrete definition of the condition itself. In his 1875 essay "Opium Poisoning," Joseph Parrish considered the variety of effects of opium on various individuals to be the result of "an abnormal predisposition to organic disease of some kind ... That this predisposition resides primarily in the germinal cell, there can be no doubt." Note how Parrish located addiction in the biological body and adeptly used the language of microbiology and cellular pathology as the new touchstones of medical authority. "As every element of the physiological structure exists in the germ before the time of its maturity ... so the tendency to disease, exists in the same germ, and is as certain to be developed ... as the embryo itself is certain to develop into a human being."[45] Addiction was part of a "variety of tendency to disease" but was still undefined. In the 1890s, Norman Kerr offered a similarly elastic definition. He spoke of "narcomania ... a mania for narcotism of any kind, an inexpressibly intense involuntary morbid crave [*sic*] for the temporary anaesthetic relief promised by every form of narcotic."[46] In *The Disease of Inebriety* (1893), authored by members of the American Association for the Study and Cure of Inebriety (AASCI) but often attributed to its long-running secretary, T.D. Crothers, the definition of opium neurosis paralleled Kerr's ideas: "a central neurotic change, brought about by the long persisting perversion of function and impairment of central nervous nutrition, from its persisting presence in the nutrient pabulum of the circulation."[47] The vagueness of these terms enabled investigators to link them to any number of factors based on race, ethnicity, class, gender, or even profession. "Germinal cell," "nervous nutrition," "nutrient pabulum": these renowned commentators used cutting-edge scientific terminology that was essentially meaningless, except inasmuch as it linked the authors' ideas to the increasingly opaque and simultaneously authoritative jargon of science.

The idea of opium habituation as a chronic form of poisoning located it in a specific place within medical cosmology and also within the law. Since habitual consumption was a form of poisoning, it was possible that extant poison legislation could control the trade in habit-forming poisons. In 1880, the editor of the *Canada Medical and Surgical Journal* drew his readers' attention to this potential when he reprinted an item from the *British Medical Journal*. A correspondent suggested that all narcotics should be labelled "poison" so that the extant poison laws could prevent inadvertent "abuse of narcotics."[48] Clearly, for this correspondent, in any narcotic, notwithstanding its actual physical effects, lay potential danger. Although there is no indication that his views were mainstream in 1880, when the article was published, it was a harbinger of what was to come. This view, which broadened the field of responsibility of physicians by expanding the definition of "dangerous" imbedded in drugs, would ultimately lead to the idea that a much wider range of drugs should be limited by legislation and controlled by professionals. As we will see in later chapters, this form of justification also occurred in the drive to restrict addictive drugs in Canada at the end of the nineteenth century.

If "chronic poisoning" may have described the long-term consumption of a poison, it did not explain the causes of drug habits. Causation, which could lead to a treatment grounded in physiological science, was essential to extending medical authority over the habitué. Understanding the physical reasons for drug habituation was therefore a point of intense debate among doctors. Some writers skirted the issue; they preferred to describe the effects of drug habits and appealed to the reader to treat these substances with caution. Others, like Francis Anstie, alluded to an inherent weakness in the individual addict. Using a distinctly subjective means of investigating – personal experience – he speculated that only specific constitutions were particularly susceptible to the positive effects of recreational opiates: "In the great majority of European constitutions, opium produces nothing resembling mental excitement; the effect on myself, for instance, of a large dose, is mere depression and misery. But with most Orientals and with some Europeans whose constitutions or whose habits of life are peculiar, a condition is produced ... which is very remarkable." These individuals "appear much exhilarated in spirits, and their minds work with much freedom."[49] Not only did Anstie deny that opium had a universally uplifting effect, but he also suggested that those who found opium alluring were somehow outside of the "normal."

Yet, although articulated in the last part of the nineteenth century, these debates were rolling over familiar territory, the combined medical-moral discourse that had been claimed by the temperance movement for decades.

It would be no surprise, then, that the arguments of the temperance movement were embedded in the late-century medical ideas about addiction,
notwithstanding the language of science. Writers like Edward Hitchcock
alluded to the idea that physicians would later label "diathesis" in his *Essay
on Alcoholic and Narcotic Substances,* published by the American Temperance
Association in 1830. He argued that there was indeed a predisposition to
inebriety, but rather than suggesting that certain people were susceptible,
he suggested that anyone may be so predisposed.[50] This conception of
an internal depravity that needed to be suppressed by wilful action was a
fundamental Christian tenet. A Baptist minister from New York summarized the nature of human depravity in an article reprinted in the *Montreal
Transcript* in 1847. Rev. Mr. Cushman wrote, "We have ... an enemy within.
To do good requires self-denying effort – to do evil is easy."[51] This idea of the
depraved human condition, susceptible to all sorts of temptation, remained
one of the dominant interpretations of addiction into the twentieth century.
Toronto physician James Bovell, in his *A Plea for Inebriate Asylums* (1862),
argued that some people suffered from "imperfect development of their
moral qualities" and therefore needed to be educated and enlightened. The
role of the state was "to conserve the morals of the people, for the end of
all good government is the morals of the people."[52] However, even the state
and the benign control of a well-meaning medical professional were secondary to the real source of self-improvement since "no mere human efforts
can possibly reclaim fallen human nature." Redemption came through com-
munion with God.[53]

As the century wore on, science increasingly replaced religion as the
definitive language of authority. Science sought conclusive answers to
materialistic questions, whereas religion admitted the realm of the unknown:
the will of God.[54] The language became more esoteric and inaccessible to
the public, but the ideas underlying this medical scientific language continued to rest on a moralistic foundation. Doctors asserted their authority
over the physical well-being of the population by reifying moral and spiritual
concepts.[55] As physicians' voices became more authoritative, and the emphasis on medical language similarly gained credence, the blatant moral language faded.

In 1870, the medical consideration of alcohol inebriety and substance
habituation in general took a decidedly institutional turn, a process that
began to cement the scientific nature of investigations into addiction. The
AASCI met for the first time as the American Association for the Cure of
Inebriates (it renamed itself at the second annual meeting) in the parlour
of the Young Men's Christian Association in New York, a location that suggests a link between religion and inebriety science at the time, although it
may just have been a convenient meeting place.[56] Under the presidency of
Dr. Willard Parker and the secretaryship of Dr. Joseph Parrish, the association

brought together interested physicians and inebriate specialists at a "scientific gathering." In his opening address, Parker noted that at the beginning of the century, insanity had not been considered a medical problem but a "visitation of God's displeasure," whereas by 1870 it had become a treatable condition. Parker hoped that the association would be able to demonstrate that the same was true for inebriety: habitual substance use would cease to be an issue of morality and become an issue of medical science. He concluded by stressing a constructive motive for the association: "It must be the steady aim of this body to impart scientific truth, and thus enlighten the mind of the public, inducing it to move in its power, and demand protection against a disease, infinitely more destructive than cholera, yellow fever, small pox, or typhus."[57] The association asserted that "intemperance is a disease ... It is curable in the same sense that other diseases are."[58] Although centred on alcohol inebriety, the AASCI included other addictive substances in its field of visibility. One of the invited attendees was Alonzo Calkins, whose book *Opium and the Opium Appetite* (1871) had a subtitle linking opium to all of the well-known psychoactive substances of the day: "alcoholic beverages, cannabis indica, tobacco and coca, and tea and coffee."[59] At the concluding session, Dr. D.L. Mason "called attention to the fact that the opium disease required attention from this body."

In some of the discussions of the AASCI and its British cousin, the Society for the Study of Inebriety (SSI, founded in 1883 as the Society for the Study and Cure of Inebriety), medical investigators attempted to distance themselves from religious ideas.[60] Samuel Parrish discussed both intemperance generally and opium addiction specifically in papers he presented to the AASCI. Parrish criticized the moralists and reformers who viewed drinking as the first step on a downward path that ended in physical debasement. He argued that intemperance was most often the result, not the cause, of personal weakness. He drew out his argument in detail, before recognizing intemperance as a "pravity" rather than "depravity" of the will:

> Depravity of will signifies a state of natural debasement, without any cause ... Pravity of will signifies a departure from a right purpose, and implies a *cause* for such departure; hence it is a disordered, enslaved will; the cause of which, may be in a limited or inharmonious organization, or it may result from the ignorant or reckless indulgence of modes of life.[61]

By insisting on a "departure from a right purpose," Parrish allowed the possibility of a cure. What the physician needed to do was to determine the cause of the departure. Parrish here reflected earlier temperance physicians like Bovell when he allowed for a diversity of causes – spanning moral and physical. He placed the onus to find the cure, however, on proper scientific investigation.

The primary defect that both moral and medical reformers hoped to address was the impaired will. The majority of AASCI members considered the damaged will to be the result of a distinctly physical disorder rather than moral tendency.[62] Parrish turned the moralists' causation on its head, charging that nonmedical reformers were "unaccustomed to investigate the philosophy of physical cases."[63] Instead of drunkenness leading to impairment and debasement, "we have primarily a defective condition of body or mind, and an impaired will, among its earliest evidences; then an appetite, and lastly, drunkenness with all its resulting ends."[64] Parrish did admit that there were cases in which the individual chose to drink from "a deliberate perversity or recklessness of will," but he conceded that those cases were outside of the purview of human law or medical treatment. It was then, he proclaimed, a matter between the "human consciousness and its Divine Author." Having removed the anomalous wilful drunk from the equation, Parrish determined that he and his colleagues had to treat intemperance as a disease.[65] Only the physician could successfully identify and treat the ailment that caused uncontrolled drinking.

When he turned to considering opiate use specifically, Parrish refined his perspective to account for conditions that he observed in the habitual use of the drug. In 1875, he presented his "Opium Poisoning" to the AASCI, in which he asserted that "there exists an abnormal predisposition to organic disease of some kind in most individuals."[66] This predisposition meant that for some people, opium could have a stimulant effect, whereas for others it was a narcotic.[67] By asserting this dual nature of opium, Parrish was able to account for the variety of observed effects of opiates on different systems, a variety that had perplexed investigators like Francis Anstie. The multiplicity of somatic reactions suggests what John Harley Warner explained as a denial of disease-specific therapeutics, the recognition of which was essential to the elevation of the medical profession.[68] Parrish called opium "a fascinating drug, in its influence upon both mind and body, with persons who have not an opposing idiosyncrasy." This fascination, whether it was with the stimulant or narcotic effect of opium, was a "variety of tendency to disease."[69] In his initial statements about opiate addiction, then, Parrish elaborated a developing conception of addiction as a condition of some constitutionally abnormal type of person. Although he asserted that he did not believe alcohol and opium habits to be "identical in constitutional origin," by suggesting a medical explanation for the conditions under which opiate and alcohol addiction could develop, Parrish made a key contribution to a medical discourse of addiction founded simultaneously on moral and scientific grounds.[70] Yet, despite the scientific rhetoric, the conception remained essentially unchanged from the earlier moralistic precursors: addiction was the result of an unexplained (pre)condition of the individual. The difference lay both in the scientific jargon and in the expectation of an eventual remedy or treatment. A medical condition could be treated by humans; a moral condition, at some point, had to rely on divine intervention.

This emerging disease theory of addiction had its adherents in Canadian medical circles.[71] Stephen Lett, the pre-eminent addiction specialist in Canada, argued in an address to the American Medical Association in 1891 that "it is all important [that] the physician should eliminate from the mind the *vice* theory, and consider the case in the light of a *disease* ... requiring skill, patience, and sympathy to successfully combat."[72] Lett's confidence that scientific labelling would permit successful treatment did not always see results in practice, as Cheryl Krasnick Warsh has demonstrated.[73] The disease theory did not entail a distinct therapeutic program but rather permitted a range of interpretations. In 1896, members of the Montreal Medico-Chirurgical Society discussed their adherence to the disease theory of inebriety as it related to alcohol use. Dr. O.C. Edwards presented a paper on treating alcohol inebriety with "the hypodermic administration of chloride of gold." This specific remedy mirrored the "cure" marketed by Leslie Keeley, whom many regular physicians condemned as a quack.[74] Edwards and others argued that the gold cure was not quackery in the hands of a skilled and conscientious doctor.[75] At the society's meeting, several doctors vehemently disagreed with Edwards's treatment, while agreeing that inebriety was a disease. They presented different explanations of how the disease operated on the body. Dr. T.J.W. Burgess called it an inherited unstable nervous organization; Dr. James Stewart insisted that inebriety disease was "due to paralysed control"; and Dr. J.B. McConnell stated simply that the inebriate was "neurotic."[76] These explanations demonstrated the fluidity of the disease theory of addiction. Moreover, they all presented explanations for the somatic basis of inebriety that merely attached contemporary medical language to an observed behavioural condition. They offered no interpretations significantly different from the earlier idea that inebriety resulted from a weak will and immoral behaviour. Christian temperance asserted that one's improper actions could result in damnation and social decline, whereas scientific, medical inebriety studies argued that one's actions could lead to disease and social decline. Both relied on the conception of a fundamentally flawed individual; the physicians, however, argued that some were more likely to become diseased than others.

Diathesis and the Potential to Heal

This tendency toward certain pathological conditions that led to mental disorders was often labelled a "diathesis." In addiction research, the existence of a diathesis – a predisposition or primary derangement of the system, which led to the use of some addictive substances – was a key factor in the development of the disease theory. Researchers saw the diathesis as answering questions regarding both the agency of the addict and what physical or moral conditions could lead to addiction. Yet what the diathesis provided was a flexible etiological trope with which almost all behavioural anomalies could be defined as simultaneously physiological and moral in origin. The *Oxford English Dictionary*'s definition remains extremely broad: "a permanent (hereditary or acquired) condition of the body which renders it liable to certain special diseases or affections; a constitutional predisposition or tendency."[77] W.F. Bynum explains that the concept of diathesis "was a useful but extremely elastic and ultimately unfalsifiable idea" and that this adaptability gave it tremendous explanatory power.[78] French physician August Morel deployed the term in developing a theory of degeneracy that incorporated intoxication from opiates and alcohol as potential causes of decline. Morel argued that a degenerated human nervous system operated at a subnormal level and that "the nervous functions of the afflicted person declined from the high moral levels of normalcy to abnormal, instinctive, and animalistic."[79] Morel's corollary applied the idea of diathesis to this form of degeneracy. American alienist George Millar Beard's neurasthenia thesis presented physicians with another potential piece to the addiction puzzle. Beard argued that humans had only a limited supply of nervous energy, which could be taxed by stress. The theory led to the supposition that modern life and mental activity tended to put a strain on the reserves of nervous energy.[80] The result of a weakened mental state was a search for stimulus, and the result of stimulus was a debased human nature. Inebriety through opiates or alcohol, therefore, led to mental and moral decline.

When applied specifically to addiction, the diathesis gave urgency to the need to deal with opiate addiction since elites were becoming addicted to opiates precisely due to the nervous organization that made them elite. In the literature advertising his "Opium Cure," H.J. Brown noted, "Opium is a *corrosion and paralysis* of all the noblest forms of life."[81] Brown's rhetoric may have been partially self-motivated, since he was marketing an opium cure. But this viewpoint was not unique. Indeed, to sell his product, he needed to speak the language of his target market, a language that was infused in the medical literature. Many writers noted that self-control was the principal loss of the opium addict, and this concern reflected an upper-class fear of decline. Stephen Lett included an account in the *Canada Lancet* of a man who was "absolutely owned" by morphine after a first, and relatively minor, dose of the drug.[82] An anonymous writer in the *Canadian Monthly*, who charged the temperance movement with driving him to opium addiction, recounted his experience with drug dependence as a cautionary tale against "opium slavery" for upper-class readers.[83] He set himself apart from the image of the libertine who took drugs for pleasure since he did not become addicted through "vicious disposition towards the use of opium" but through self-medication. Dr. J.B. Mattison, a Brooklyn addiction specialist and occasional contributor to Canadian medical journals, noted the insufficiency of the term "opium habit" since it implied that the opiate was "quite under individual control," which was not the case.[84] Samuel Parrish concurred in this opinion. Personal restraint and integrity disappeared when the individual became "enslaved to the drug." The result was a dramatic decline in social mores, and addicts "no longer conceal the fact [of their enslavement] from the public, but indulge with the same *abandon* of self, and the same disregard of public sentiment, that distinguishes the confirmed alcoholic sot."[85] The message Parrish sent was dire: although opium may have been the habit of the more refined classes, indulgence lowered elites to the state of the shameless drunk on the street. Such a merging of alcohol temperance with anti-opium sentiments, uncomplicated by physiological explanations, provided a clear image of the dangers of opiate indulgence.

Although the idea of a diathesis could fuel fears of upper-class decline through nervous exhaustion and a search for stimulation, it could also explain debasement through hereditary taint.[86] T.D. Crothers, editor of the AASCI's *Quarterly Journal of Inebriety* and a central figure in the turn-of-the-century inebriety movement, asserted in 1902 that over 60 percent of inebriates "have inherited a predisposition to seek [alcohol and drugs] for some relief" from the stress of modern life.[87] This diathesis fitted into a Darwinist conception of society and constructed those whose predisposition to addiction overwhelmed their ability to resist their urges as social "others" in need of reform.

Both the AASCI and the SSI emphasized the idea of inherited diathesis as the predominant cause of addiction. The existence of a diathesis became almost assumed when discussing cases; its fluidity also permitted observed anomalies in addictive behaviour. After detailing the idea of the evolution of brain and nerve defects, attributed to "environment, nutrition, growth and development," the AASCI asked, in its collected volume *The Disease of Inebriety* (1893), "Why should an increasing number of persons take opium continuously for the transient relief it gives? Why should the effects of this drug become so pleasing as to demand its increased use, irrespective of all consequences? The only explanation is the presence of a neurotic diathesis, either inherited or acquired."[88] Conversely, although opium was used in many treatments, the AASCI opined that "all these and similar cases do not become opium takers ... owing to the absence of some diathesis inherited or acquired."[89] Only those persons with an inherited or acquired diathesis would become addicts; the AASCI dismissed the potential for a nonphysical cause of addiction. Although appearing to reject the moralistic approach to addiction, what the AASCI did was attach pliable medical jargon – diathesis – to an unexplained psychosomatic phenomenon, which earlier writers had attributed to a weak morality, impaired will, or the "addictive personality" of the late Mr. M.D.B.

The malleability of diathesis permitted multiple uses and some confusion. Norman Kerr, ardent supporter of the disease theory of addiction and the central voice in the SSI until his death in 1899, refused to attach the term "diathesis" to all causes of addiction. The distinction was semantic rather than philosophical. Kerr mentioned the term "diathesis" only when discussing heredity; he may have considered diathesis to describe an inherited condition, but he did not believe that opiate addiction was always inherited. Opiate addiction, he said, "cannot lay claim to so great indebtedness to heredity ... or so marked pathological disturbance as an antecedent or coincident condition; but it is in a vast number of cases an undoubted disease, a functional neurosis."[90] Kerr's ideas may have been shaped by the inability of investigators to find distinct physical lesions related to opium addiction.[91] His reference to "carefully conducted scientific experiments" reveals the limits of physiological investigation. He used these experiments to demonstrate that opium acted differently on animals than did alcohol, but he could not reach a conclusion about the physiological mechanisms that opium affected. Kerr and others paralleled limited "scientific" investigations with detailed clinical observation of the various forms of addiction, according to racial and gendered taxonomy.[92] Subsequently, Kerr conceded that a functional change, rather than physical lesion, was at the heart of the behavioural and somatic deterioration wrought by opiate addiction. The results, however, were the classic slippery slope to depravity, reiterated in both temperance tracts and medical investigations throughout the century. He listed the effects of opium addiction in a declining list of depravity: "functional derangement, impairment of the nutritive process, nerve exhaustion, slovenliness, aimless laziness, a dried, wrinkled cadaverous skin, general wasting and emaciation, and a bent form, are prominent links in the lethal chain."[93]

The disease theory of inebriety did not go unchallenged by addiction reformers. Robert Harris, of the Franklin Reformatory in Philadelphia, rejected it. At his institution, they treated drunkenness "as a habit, sin and crime." Although the appetite for alcohol may have been inherited, Harris explained, "the *passion* for it, can only be obtained by indulgence."[94] His perspective echoed the arguments of other temperance reformers, whom Parrish characterized in his 1870 paper as lacking the scientific appreciation of the process of addiction.[95] These writers were not always the non-scientific ignorant moralists that Parrish characterized them to be. In the *Canada Lancet* in 1892, New York City physician Charles Dana challenged the tendency of investigators to find disease where no distinct pathological or somatic etiology could be determined. Dana insisted that too little was known about the source of addiction for it to be properly considered a disease. He also linked drunkenness with other forms of socially proscribed behaviour: "In a certain sense ... criminals, sensualists, libertines, drunkards are all the victims of a disease, *ie*, of a constitution and personality which are abnormal. But ... we still consider disease to be a disorder of the body and its organs; vice to be a disorder of the character, for which the individual must be held responsible."[96] Alluding to the vices in John Burnham's "vice constellation" and redefining them as forms of functional disease, Dana reasserted the agency of the addict but insisted on medical treatment of this condition.[97]

Henry Howard's Somaticism and Social Progress

The diathesis gained traction at a time when researchers were redefining behavioural anomalies with opaque technical language that affirmed medicine's authority in addressing deviant behaviour. It was part of a broader shift toward asserting a distinct somatic origin for behavioural problems. In Canada the somatic focus in mental illness was championed by Dr. Henry Howard, superintendent of the Longue Pointe Asylum in Quebec. Howard insisted that all mental disease was the result of physical lesions in the mental apparatus, and he used the term *"materia cogitans"* to describe the physical location of all mental phenomena. The brain was not the only place of mental activity since studies suggested that the nerves and the spinal column affected mental processes.[98] In an article on "Man's Moral Responsibility," read to the Montreal Medico-Chirurgical Society in 1875, Howard explained the delineation between will, soul, mind, and morality. The will was the action of the immortal and immutable soul on the body, but the individual's morality was determined by his or her physical makeup. "The mental and physical organization, being one mind and body, constitute one animate man, inseparable and indivisible; both are the act of procreation."[99] Ten years later, his materialist conception of disease was more forceful:

> If you enquire of me, what is the mind in the abstract? I answer you, I don't know; I only know it is a phenomenon of matter. What is force? A phenomenon of matter. What is sensation? A phenomenon of matter. What is consciousness? A phenomenon of matter. What is moticity? A phenomenon of matter. What is intellect? A phenomenon of matter. What is instinct? A phenomenon of matter. What is automatism? A phenomenon of matter. What is reflex action? A phenomenon of matter. What is conduct? A phenomenon of matter.[100]

This materialism permitted Howard to see all illness, be it mental, moral, or physical, as based either in early development or in pathological change. "There are very many circumstances over which we had, or have, no control – that lessen our moral responsibility. None of us had a choice of parentage, the time or place of birth, our early education and surroundings."[101]

Howard's passionate somaticism led him to redefine "morality" as dependent on proper physical function and justify an expanded role for medicine in ensuring social progress. A badly conducted muscle was "an immoral muscle; it does not, because it cannot, obey the will." Likewise, the individual's conduct is the result of the physical organization of the *materia cogitans:* "If its functions be normal, the man's conduct will be normal, and he will consequently be a moral man, living in obedience to nature's laws, and delighting in his knowledge of them. If its functions be abnormal, his conduct will be abnormal; he will be a fool, and consequently an immoral criminal." He argued that all treatment of mental illness must be "scientific morality ... [which] consists in knowing the physical cause for physical effect, and this we never will know perfectly till [*sic*] physical science is made the basis of medical knowledge."[102] Such somatic expertise would aid social progress because "every man is intellectually and morally what he is, in virtue of the functions of his physical or structural organization." Strictly somatic medicine could in turn help "the man of law" understand social deviance and the actions of the criminal.[103]

Although Howard did not discuss addiction in any great length, he did suggest how intoxicants might affect the mind and thereby how it might be treated. His argument reflected his debt to Beard's concept of neurasthenia. The higher nerve centres, which control higher reasoning and separate humans from animals, are of a lower (i.e., more fragile) organization and therefore more susceptible to being damaged. "It is well known what a glass of brandy, a dose of opium or a whiff of ether or chloroform will do with these nerve centres; fortunately, the lower centres, because higher organized, are not so sensitive to these drugs, or there would be more deaths from inebriety, and, consequently, less fools and maniacs."[104] Addiction, then, could be either a pathological or a teratological condition of the higher nerve centres. In other words, to be entirely circular in reasoning, it could be diathetical in origin. If possible, treatment of damage to such higher faculties required the same "moral" scientific treatment that other nervous diseases required.

Howard's materialistic conception of disease was part of a broader trend toward locating all behavioural deviances, including addiction, in a poor or damaged physical organization. Although expressed in Latin- or Greek-based jargon, and repeatedly labelled "scientific," this conception of disease merely embodied the unexplainable action – or inaction – of the will. Howard did not deny the metaphysical, and in all of his articles he reminded his readers that he believed in God. Instead, he insisted that by systematic scientific investigation of the body, doctors could find all they needed to know to treat their patients. This substitution of science for religion was part of a broader decline of religion as an explanatory discourse, during which the elements of mystery and stewardship of nature, previously the purview of the ministry, became the domain of a secular scientific community.[105] Although this trend was not restricted to addiction, it was a defining force that gave credence to the emerging addiction profession.[106] Yet, as we have seen, the elements of a moral assessment of this physical process remained. Along with issues of class and gender, this moral framework often affected treatment.

The Science of Treatment

By the turn of the century, physicians could draw on two main approaches to the treatment of addiction. Eduard Levinstein preferred the stoic German approach of an abrupt cessation of morphine. He argued that to do otherwise was like "cutting off a dog's tail one piece at a time."[107] The physician supported the patient as he or she suffered withdrawal symptoms. The alternative to Levinstein's heroic approach was gradual withdrawal, ideally also under the care of a physician. J.B. Mattison, a noted addiction specialist from Brooklyn, New York, claimed this approach as his own, humbly calling it the "Mattison Method" in a book of that name, published in 1902. Yet gradual withdrawal was an approach that had been systematized at least since Allbutt discussed it with his colleagues in the 1860s, and De Quincey's own story was about his personal attempts to gradually wean himself off his laudanum. All Mattison did was offer a detailed process and specific medicines to support the system. Whether or not they overtly adopted Mattison's method, physicians were convinced that their expertise was essential during detoxification.

Both approaches, which different Canadian physicians endorsed, linked the doctor's scientific authority to exert control over the patient with the moral authority to do so. Not only were the doctor's intervention and oversight necessary to ensure the sufficient medical care of the patient, but the physician would also guard against transgression. Levinstein insisted that the patient be locked in a room for several days and watched but rarely interfered with by a vigilant nurse. Preferably, this nurse would be female since a male attendant would be "more accessible to bribing."[108] In 1887, the *Canada Medical and Surgical Journal* argued that addiction treatment required the physician to recognize the inherent untrustworthiness of the addict: "Seclusions and careful watching are in most cases essential, and if communication with the outside world be not entirely cut off, there is very great danger of deception. The devices resorted to are almost incredible, and, as a rule, not the slightest reliance can be placed on the patients' statements."[109] The problem was the suspension of the will. Edward Mann, writing in the *Montreal Medical Journal* in 1894, explained that "such a patient often manifests an utter disregard of truthfulness, honesty and sincerity and after a long time shows a seeming inability to exert the will in any other direction or for any other purpose than the gratification of his morbid appetite."[110]

This opinion of the addict was not without its powerful critics. Mattison himself argued in the *Canada Lancet* that "the habitual use of opium, in many cases, does exert a baneful influence on the moral nature ... but we also know that in the ranks of these unfortunates are those who would scorn to deceive, and whose statements are as worthy of credence as those upon whom has not fallen this blight."[111] Mattison was the superintendent of a private home in Brooklyn. Stephen Lett, also running a private asylum, disagreed. By the turn of the century, Lett was enjoying recognition as the premier addiction specialist in Canada, and he used his influence to present his perspective on the priorities of therapeutics of drug addiction. He challenged William Osler's view that "persons addicted to morphia are inveterate liars and [that] no reliance whatever can be placed upon their statements," which he called, "to say the least, unnecessarily strong." Lett explained that "the condition of the unfortunate habitué ... whose confidence in the good faith and kindliness of his doctor is not established, who surrenders all his drugs at once would be much like a traveller who hands over his weapons and trusts to the merits and goodness of the bandit." Lett's therapeutics would establish the authority of the physician over the addict, for the sake of returning the addict's self-control. To do this well, however, required "a proper man and a proper place." Not surprisingly, given his interest as the medical superintendent at (and a shareholder in) the private Homewood Retreat in Guelph, Ontario, Lett argued for the importance of the kindly but vigilant treatment of the addict far from "harmful and damaging surroundings" in "a haven of rest and safety."[112]

Lett and Levinstein took contrasting approaches to addiction treatment. Levinstein's work was printed in the *Canada Lancet* in 1877, and a similar method from an anonymous "German physician" – likely Levinstein – appeared in the *Canada Medical and Surgical Journal* the following year.[113] His treatment had Canadian supporters. Dr. James Stewart of McGill University argued that, although dangerous, the sudden removal of opium may be necessary. "Success is seldom obtained unless the measure is resorted to," he explained in 1886, concluding that cocaine could serve to allay the depression and support the system through the initial shock of detoxification.[114] That same year, the *Canada Lancet* abstracted a work by Dr. Morandon de Montyel, who tempered the abrupt cessation model. It was a valuable procedure, he explained, unless "contraindicated by the vital forces of the patient or concomitant pathological phenomena."[115] Stewart's and Montyel's therapeutics were fundamentally the same since Stewart would employ cocaine to provide an artificial boost to the flagging physical power that concerned Montyel. More prominent were the physicians who condemned abrupt withdrawal. Lett was first among this group in Canada, and his view was joined – and possibly informed – by the opinions of notable Anglo-American addiction specialists. Lett, Mattison, and Mann all adhered to a disease theory of addiction but insisted on asylum treatment and constant vigilance over the addict by trained addiction specialists.

Doctors Assert Their Authority

Sorting out the complexities of addiction and recommending viable treatments were parts of a broader process in medicine of establishing and strengthening the role of physicians in guiding the future of society. United in formal organizations and engaged in persistent investigations of the physical origin of the moral being, doctors pressed for their elevated leadership role in society in general, and the concern over addiction informed this broader agenda. Linking habit to physical processes and developing scientifically informed treatments helped physicians to assert the importance of addiction treatment to the nation's future. To be sure, physicians had occupied many positions of social prominence for decades; what the doctors wanted was not just personal elevation but also social and cultural acceptance of their perspective. They argued that when the public accepted the medical viewpoint as authoritative, doctors might be more effective in protecting the health and integrity of the nation. Reinforcing these assertions were a reflection on the recent past as a primitive medical period that had been eradicated by progress and an expectation of a near future in which many forms of physical debility (and moral deviance) would disappear. This idea of doctors as stewards of national integrity would help to drive the legislation restricting drugs and to define nonmedical drug use as wrong.

To addiction physicians, medical research would ensure a physically strong citizen. Henry Howard's insistence that progress in somatic medicine would enable lawyers to understand deviance reflected the ideas of the inebriate specialists about the role of medicine in advancing society. Canadian addiction specialist Stephen Lett linked the importance of medical science and medical authority in acting to deal with addiction when he stated in 1891 that only by recognizing the nature of addiction as a disease could physicians look toward a definite, scientific cure.[116] Doctors' social role, combined with their command of medical science, was needed to influence legislation and curtail dangerous social practices. Writing in the *Canada Lancet* at the end of the century, Dr. Edward Mann reinforced the primacy of science to replace morality when he argued that doctors needed to study inebriety "as physiologists and pathologists, and not as moralists or reformers." He proceeded to list more specifically the physical and physiological phenomena that doctors needed to consider, which emphasized the interconnection between the mind and the body. "The laws governing the organism ... must be recognized and applied in the consideration of the subject of intemperance, and in explaining the unnatural phenomena [sic] of the inebriate."[117]

The physician's role of protecting and healing the body of the individual citizen would extend to the body politic, affecting both legislation and the public perception of addiction. In 1875, Samuel Parrish predicted that opium addiction would soon join alcoholism in requiring legislative action to prevent it. In the AASCI, he called on his professional colleagues to take an active role in educating society for this change.[118] Concerning the need to educate the public about the poisonous nature of alcoholic beverages and about their "ravages upon the various organs of the body ... their power to weaken the will and moral sense," J.W. Grosvenor of Buffalo, New York, wrote in the *Canada Lancet* that doctors should take the lead. "The people," he explained, "will listen more attentively to such teachings, from the medical profession than from any other sources."[119] Here the scientific intersected with moral authority: how else could doctors demonstrate the effect not only on the bodily organs but also on the "will and moral sense"? In 1898, when Dr. Alvin Rosebrugh presented the Executive Committee of the Ontario Prisoners' Aid Association with a plan to reform the province's drunkards, the *Canada Lancet* editorialized that physicians should "use their very great influence upon the communities in which they live" to raise public opinions in favour of the bill.[120] This "great influence" was moralistic as well as scientific in nature.

This conception of medical science as saving the nation provided a broad impetus for doctors to claim further social and cultural authority. Considering themselves to be the guardians of physical health, which now meant the entire being, moral and physical, physicians extended their role to vigilantly protecting moral and mental vitality. Dr. John Stewart, the president of the Canadian Medical Association in 1905, connected the physician's role more closely to the moral development of the individual and the nation when he said, "We should accustom ourselves to remember that the body with which we deal is of value only as the tenant and instrument of an indwelling spirit, and that the health of the body is our care simply because its ill-health may hamper the action of the intellectual and moral energy within it."[121] Stewart's purpose was utilitarian; he saw that the only way truly to ensure the health of the body was by attending to the vitality and correct operation of the mental and moral being as well as the somatic. "We cannot treat our patient to advantage if we regard only his physical condition, and neglect consideration of his mental equipment and moral proclivities."[122] In an article in the *Western Canada Medical Journal* in 1907, British physician Alfred T. Schofield illustrated the connections between mind, body, and morality when he wrote that "the wise physician must grasp the underlying unity of the spiritual and material, and recognize that [just as diseases] of the body ... influence diseases of the soul, so does the mind influence states and diseases of the body."[123] Professional authority and scientific advancements had enabled physicians by the turn of the century to extend their hopes for authority and control to the entire being. And the goal remained to elevate the Christian nation. Commenting on the need to treat addiction, the editors of the *Canada Lancet* had noted in 1891 that "when we [cure the morphine habit] without entailing a bondage ... the millennium will be nearer than now."[124] Using scientific knowledge and social power to deal with addiction would elevate the nation both physically and spiritually.

Asserting their authority over the individual body, doctors expected their benign control to extend to the body of the nation. In his presidential address to the Canadian Medical Association in 1886, Dr. T.K. Holmes quoted "Froude" (probably British historian James Anthony Froude), who asserted that "a sound nation is a nation that is composed of sound human beings, healthy in body, strong of limb, true in word and deed, brave, temperate, sober, chaste; to whom morals are of more importance than wealth."[125] A generation later, the editors of the *Western Canada Medical Journal* concurred, noting that "the best asset that any nation can have ... is health."[126] Stewart extended the physician's social role to aid in the development of a strong and healthy "national character ... The medical profession may have a large influence in moulding the spirit of a nation."[127] In this perspective, he created a cyclical argument that reinforced his profession's social importance. Public health laws would help to strengthen and develop the national character, but sufficient laws could be created only by a society of noble character. The physician's role, then, was to guide the public in order to ensure its integrity and strength of character. Stewart further argued that the biggest threat to the individual was an ignorance of medical and physical processes. He concluded that it was proper and important that one's level of education should determine the degree of one's individual freedom.[128] Physicians, educated in the physical mechanisms of the body, were better positioned to guide and protect the nation. Public health and welfare, and therefore the national character, would best be served in the hands of properly educated, duly recognized, and professionally united physicians. Their authority would ensure the liberty and integrity of the nation.

By the end of the century, the doctor's authority over the issue of substance habituation was being accepted beyond the often insular discussions in medical journals. For example, members of the Woman's Christian Temperance Union (WCTU) actively appealed to physicians in their work against both alcohol and narcotic consumption.[129] Their concern was both to remind doctors not to prescribe problematic drugs if at all possible and to ask doctors to educate their patients about the dangers of drug use. The WCTU employed a variety of tactics, such as encouraging members to visit their local physicians, sending letters to medical societies, and entertaining medical students, to reiterate their message of the importance of limiting the prescription of problematic drugs.[130] The Ontario WCTU requested that members of the Ontario Medical Council "pledge themselves against prescribing narcotics, except when positively necessary," but the union received no reply.[131] The WCTU alluded to the ability of doctors to get out the anti-drug message given their important social position. In 1892, the Dominion WCTU's Resolution Committee stated, "Whereas throughout Canada the use of opium in its various forms, simply as an intoxicant, is spreading with wonderful rapidity, therefore be it resolved .... that the druggists and doctors be requested to warn their patients in regard to the nature of opium and other narcotics when used as a medicine."[132] The following year, the committee replaced the word "requested" with "urged," and the same passage reappeared for a number of years.

Yet this appreciation of medical authority on these matters was neither absolute nor entirely positive. The WCTU was well aware of the iatrogenesis of drug addiction and, in its rhetoric, suggested that the doctors (and pharmacists) may not be so deserving of the authority that they had asserted would elevate the nation. In an article on "The Opium Habit" published in the *Woman's Journal* in 1892, a correspondent calling herself Saloma noted that many physicians "prescribe it for the slightest disorder," which often led to addiction. Moreover, she noted that although a scrupulous druggist might "have moral courage" and refuse to sell to "one they are convinced is on the highway to sure doom," the addict merely needed to go up the street to find one who would not be so discriminating. Moreover, Saloma reminded her readers, doctors were known to be highly susceptible themselves to addiction. "One town has a doctor, also a druggist, once a most popular, prosperous man. At present he is a common vagrant and has been sent to jail for two months. He was addicted to the opium habit."[133] Such shocking tales were, if nothing else, embarrassing to doctors and demonstrated the limits to their claims of authority in such complex matters as addiction.

By attempting to wrest definitions and discourses surrounding addiction from the hands of moralists and reformers, physicians asserted the primacy of science in being able to diagnose, treat, and possibly cure addiction. This elevation of science occurred despite any significant advances in the understanding of the physiology of addiction. By reifying addiction and locating it within the body, physicians insisted that society should see its hopes for a cure in the progress of medicine (and associated disciplines). Likewise, they explained their repeated failures as resulting from the fact that addiction was the result of an enigmatic (but scientifically defined, and with a fancy Greek name) somatic condition, the diathesis. The changes in the explanations of the pathology of addiction both contributed to and were the result of an increase in doctors' power, but these changes merely replaced the moral basis for the addict's outsider status with a medical and scientific one. Mr. M.D.B.'s diseased appetite became an addictive diathesis. The seemingly incurable addict who wilfully neglected the body remained, but now the imperative to strengthen the will was a medical problem. The elevation of scientific truth and of the doctor's aspirations to define fact and value helped physicians to establish value-laden facts about addiction. Their authority to explain addiction grew even as the values they set forth remained ensconced in what Geoffrey Harding calls a "moral pathology."[134] Since the medical conception of addiction reiterated an earlier moral definition of habituation, the addict continued to occupy a paradoxical position in the late-Victorian medical mindset as both a vice-ridden deviant and a diseased victim.

6
Madness and Addiction in the Asylums of English Canada

Although addiction specialists and elite practitioners were beginning to view addiction as an issue of concern by the last quarter of the nineteenth century, it is more difficult to determine when the drug habit was being identified as a significant medical problem in everyday life by everyday people. Prior to the significant epistemological and organizational developments of the 1870s, discussed in Chapter 5, doctors fitted patients who habitually used drugs into earlier diagnostic categories based on preconceived ideas of dysfunction. When Dr. McGillivray associated Mr. M.D.B.'s morphine habit with his drinking, he was connecting these tendencies with familiar "ways of knowing" such behaviour.[1] The barrister's actions were the result of a profligate lifestyle; his whiskey drinking and fast life explained his morphine addiction. Indeed, identifying when changes in the everyday understanding of drug habits took place is difficult using available documentary sources. Records of physicians such as James Langstaff or Thomas Geddes rarely included detailed discussions of the physician's perception of the patient's condition, for example, and rarely do we find detailed personal accounts of the drug using tendencies of individuals. So finding reliable examples of how drug addiction and its treatment changed in Canada requires some leaps of faith.

One leap takes us into the asylum. The records of lunatic asylums provide a limited but often detailed account of medical staffs' perception of individuals who had taken excessive amounts of medicines and whose resulting behaviour had been identified as problematic. Since most provinces in Canada required physicians to assess a patient prior to sending them to state-run asylums, the relationship between drug addiction and the medical gaze, albeit within the framework of institutionalized care, emerges. Using surviving asylum admission records and the less frequently available but often well-detailed asylum case files, we can see how the general physicians who were referring patients and the asylum physicians who were admitting and treating them viewed the behavioural changes wrought by drug use – if not addiction itself – within a broader framework of the institutionalization of mental-illness care. Admission records from the middle of the nineteenth century to the beginning of the twentieth permit us to explore the appearance of the addict in the public lunatic asylum in most of English-speaking Canada, specifically Saint John, New Brunswick; Charlottetown, Prince Edward Island; Halifax, Nova Scotia; Victoria and New Westminster, British Columbia; and Toronto, Kingston, and London, Ontario.[2]

The late-century lunatic asylum was viewed in some ways as a triumph of scientific medicine in treating the ills of the modern state. Various state institutions – hospitals, jails, homes for various socially marginalized groups, and asylums – were attempts to create or restore a degree of social stability. In the case of asylums, physicians argued that scientific medicine would protect the mental and physical integrity of the nation by housing and treating the mad among us.[3] Asylum admission processes, usually outlined by provincial legislation, required the agreement of experts, normally magistrates and physicians, that an individual should be sent for care and treatment in an asylum. Yet, as James Moran has argued, there was a notable disagreement between those physicians referring patients and those receiving them into the asylum.[4] Diverse social and economic factors often underpinned reasons for committal, but asylum physicians, who were dealing with often overcrowded facilities, were concerned with curability within an institutional structure that often undermined its own purposes. Nevertheless, when we consider an emerging condition like addiction, the process of admission reveals much about the perception of this condition among a diverse profession. It also suggests, and here we need to be cautious not to overreach the evidence, how and when everyday Canadians viewed addiction to be a problem. How did physicians who were not consciously looking for addiction interpret the condition of the habitual drug user? Did they accept the emerging disease of addiction as a unique entity, or did they view it within the framework of traditional mental illness conceptions? Moreover, why did members of the public, when seeking treatment for their friends and relatives or (less frequently) for themselves, determine that habitual drug use required institutionalized state intervention?

The admission and case files of asylums in Canada, then, provide a useful window into the emerging ideas about addiction in mid-nineteenth to early-twentieth-century Canadian society. By the end of the nineteenth century, drug addiction was being perceived both by the general population and by the medical profession as a problem that required state intervention and institutionalized care. To asylum doctors at the beginning of the period under study, habitual drug use was a secondary characteristic of a more extensive, but traditional, form of mental derangement. In the early part of the twentieth century, however, this diagnostic convention changed. Asylum doctors (often called "alienists," a term that predated "psychiatrist") began to describe addiction as a specific form of mental disease. Along with the medical perceptions of drug use, the asylum records reveal social reasons for sending the addicts to asylums. Many families sent addicted relatives to the asylum only after the addiction resulted in further socially destructive or offensive behaviour.[5] Changing classifications of habitual drug use operated within a broader discourse of mental illness and national development to influence ideas about the potential social problems of drug use. By considering the way that ideas about drugs in therapy changed in the decades before the creation of prohibitory legislation, we can suggest how broader social movements affected medical practice.

Two of the main goals of this chapter are to examine whether ideas about habitual drug use as discussed by addiction specialists appeared among the perspectives detailed in insane asylum records and how the concepts of addiction and insanity were linked. It should not be surprising that, whereas addiction specialists argued about the relationship between the drug habit and mental illness – asking, for example, was it a mental illness, how did it affect the mind, and was there a lesion? – general texts examining mental illness did not normally say much about drug addiction. Indeed, most of the major textbook authors studying mental illness tended to mention the drug habit, if at all, as an appendix to a discussion of "alcoholic insanity." And even this was a highly debatable concept. Not all alcoholism was alcoholic insanity; similarly, not all habitual drug use, which by the end of the century was less frequently called "chronic poisoning," was considered to be a form of mental illness.

To avoid a long discussion on the place of the opium habit in broader mental conceptions, I will confine my analysis to what may be considered the more or less typical placement of the opium habit on the mental-illness spectrum. One of the most influential writers on mental illness, British alienist Henry Maudsley, discussed mental illness as a functional derangement and saw opium as doing specific cellular damage. In *Physiology and Pathology of Mind* (1867), he wrote that "many poisons besides alcohol [and here he included opium] stimulate and ultimately derange the function of the supreme cerebral cells." Maudsley created a progression – or digression – of effects, in which hallucinations were but steps on the path to madness: "More or less delirium, hallucinations, and insanity are the result of their continued abuse."[6] In his influential 1884 textbook *Insanity and Its Treatment,* a set of practical lectures rather than a discussion of the physiology of madness, G. Fielding Blandford was of two minds on the issue. On the one hand, he disagreed with Maudsley: "That opium produces curious phenomena and trains of ideas out of the control of the will must, I think, be admitted by all. I cannot say, however, that in my experience it has been often found to produce insanity." He explained that the symptoms were the result of "a poisoning going on at the time" but that if the opium was withdrawn, the strange symptoms vanished. He likened the effect of opium to that of breathing nitrous acid gas and stated that removing the cause removed the symptoms. "We do not find," he concluded, "that opium eating or smoking swells the population of the lunatic asylums of this [England] or other countries." And finally, weighing in on the question of opium versus alcohol, he noted that "there is an immense difference between the results of the continual use of opium and alcohol."[7] On the other hand, later in the same book, Blandford discussed "insanity, the result of alcohol, opium or haschish," noting that it was preventable but that when dealing with such cases, "we have to deal with acquired habits," which complicated the picture.[8] To be fair to Blandford, it is worth noting that in the 1892 edition of the book, he clarified that "not every drunkard is insane ... any more than a confirmed gambler or opium-eater."[9] Although baffling, Blandford's contradictory perception of the opium habit is also illustrative of the way that physicians at the time viewed and attempted to address the opium habit. That is, they were not always looking for it, they did not always consider it to be madness, but when they found it, they also had to deal with the treatment of habituation before addressing varying degrees of mental alienation.

Asylum Admissions and Categories of Diagnosis

Such perceptions of opium addiction were often squeezed into the specific bureaucratic structure of asylum admission documents, so before turning to the admission of people who used drugs, it is important to discuss briefly the asylum admission process. This was an administrative interaction between general practitioners, the public, and asylum physicians that was constructed and mediated by government authorities. The provincial governments entrusted the care of the insane to a medical superintendent and his staff, but the decisions to send the patient to the asylum came from several directions. Looking at asylum admissions in Ontario and Quebec, James Moran has noted that although each province's processes were unique, there were many similarities.[10] This statement can be extended to the other provinces of the Dominion. Ideally, a patient would arrive at the asylum after family and local officials had agreed on the need for asylum care. Usually, the officials included at least one physician, along with magistrates or other local authorities. In Ontario, for example, by the 1870s three physicians' references were required; elsewhere, usually two would suffice. Patients could also come from jails or other institutions, and in areas like the remote mining and railway camps of British Columbia, officials were usually company officials. In such cases, the family was often not involved, although normally friends might show some interest in the patient's welfare and sometimes come to the asylum to take the person home or into their personal care.

By the last quarter of the century, the admission documentation, like the admission procedures, was standardized. The admission form contained a variety of questions to help the admitting physician and the asylum staff to classify the patient and, if the asylum layout permitted the separation of patients, to assign the patient to the proper ward. Information gathered in these forms included habits of life, sometimes specifically indicating whether the patient was "temperate" a term which did not always indicate whether or not the individual drank alcohol. For example, a patient who arrived in Halifax was "not temperate – [but] does not drink to excess – uses tobacco," and another was "not addicted to drunkenness but not temperate."[11] Other key information included the referring official's opinion of what might have caused the condition. Normally, the documentation required the official to speculate on two causes of the patient's debility: a long-term or older condition, what was called a "predisposing" cause in some jurisdictions and "remote" cause in others; and a more immediate reason for the current attack of madness, called an "exciting" or "recent" cause. Additional information could vary; for example, the forms for admission to the Halifax Hospital for the Insane, established through legislation, requested such details as "age at first attack," "duration of existing attack," "whether suicidal," "what delusions," and "whether dangerous to others."[12] These data were normally also required on other admission forms in asylums across the country. Such documentation could provide a wealth of subjective information. (Or could provide very little information since most forms were incomplete.)

A doctor's examination and referral often paved the way to the asylum gate. The development of the system of admissions, and the several flaws of the system, have been the topic of other works and do not need to be examined here in any depth.[13] For our purposes, it is important to recognize that the records of the initial visit to the asylum were not just the impressions of the asylum personnel. The admitting officers generally recorded the information provided on the referral letters, along with other information provided by family, friends, or even the police officers who brought the patient to the asylum. In some records, all that has survived is this information from the admission files, whereas in others, subsequent case notes provide reports of the patient's progress or lack thereof. Asylum physicians often took this admission information with a grain of salt. For example, the superintendent of the BC Asylum, G.H. Manchester, noted in his 1903 report that "the causes alleged by the relatives, when they allege any at all, are often absurd, either through ignorance or wilful deception, and are not always accepted by us."[14] Although the information sent by referring physicians may seem more technically competent and less "ignorant," it was also suspect. As Moran has noted, there was considerable tension between referring physicians (i.e., those in the community) and admitting physicians (i.e., those in the asylum).[15] Likely attempting to resolve this tension, T. Millman, second assistant physician at the London Asylum, explained in an 1880 article in the *Canada Lancet* that doctors needed to observe proper diagnostic procedures in order to aid the asylum personnel in their treatment.[16] The process was important since this documentation provided the asylum staff with an initial impression of the patient's case up to the time of his or her arrival and was considered crucial to providing adequate treatment.

Even though the legislated admission process limited the medical superintendent's control over who entered the asylum, some evidence suggests that he could shape the demographics of his institution in accordance with personal or governmental policy aims. In the 1850s, owing to overcrowding at the Toronto Asylum, for example, the government gave Joseph Workman permission to deny entry to patients whose condition he did not consider urgent. This policy could allow Workman to refuse those he did not believe to be insane based on his personal criteria.[17] Other asylum superintendents were not so fortunate. The superintendent of New Brunswick's Saint John Asylum, John Waddell, who was a dedicated temperance advocate, repeatedly noted his outrage at the government's decision, in the early 1850s, to permit police who picked up drunks on the street to take them to the asylum. This procedure contradicted medical authority and defined drunkenness as a form of insanity that deserved state intervention. Waddell followed the rules of his superiors, but he was not happy about it. Similarly, several entries from the early years of the Toronto Asylum note repeated visits by individuals suffering delirium tremens – the trembling, hallucinations, and mania associated with a habitual drinker's withdrawal from alcohol.[18] Some of these patients' visits lasted only a few hours.[19] Yet delirium tremens was not necessarily an admissible form of mental disorder. In 1850, when admitting a patient suffering from delirium tremens, a Toronto Asylum official wrote across the admission form, "Delirium Tremens – ought not to have been admitted."[20] Whether this reflected a policy decision or a revised definition of insanity by asylum personnel is unclear. Yet after that note, admissions of patients with delirium tremens practically ceased.

Asylum physicians drew on knowledge of physical processes and practical experience to interpret the diagnoses of patients who arrived at their institutions. Asylum records demonstrate how the physicians viewed conditions through potentially static diagnostic paradigms that precluded the incorporation of different forms of derangement. As Howard J. Shaffer notes, clinicians generally find only what they are looking for, rarely new conditions.[21] Here medical knowledge confined the aim of asylum physicians' field of visibility, so to explain behaviour they often sought conditions that seemed to fit a specific etiology, and they used their expertise to challenge the diagnoses of general practitioners. These revised diagnoses incorporated moral or behavioural conditions and may also have been the result of personal agendas. For example, Waddell's temperance perspective may have coloured his diagnoses since he often looked for alcoholism to explain behaviour that appeared to be that of a drunkard. In the 1860s, the Saint John Asylum did not routinely assess a patient's "habits of life," so when Waddell indicated whether or not a patient was temperate, the inclusion was significant. For a man who arrived at the asylum in February 1863, Waddell observed that there had been "no report of his being in liquor," although the symptoms suggested otherwise.[22] Another man, who had tried to kill himself with an overdose of laudanum, was "a temperate man," an observation implying that the attempt at suicide would often indicate the patient was a drunk.[23] More perplexing for Waddell was Michael Q., brought to the asylum by police and acting rowdy, not unlike "someone who had partaken of a stimulant, but [the police] could not detect the alcoholic breath."[24]

Waddell was not alone; other physicians' comments suggest similar diagnostic presuppositions, often challenging the information provided in referral forms. While an assistant physician in the London Asylum, Stephen Lett noted of one patient's admission forms, "Causes said to be unknown but I (S.L.) fancy drink."[25] When trying to determine whether another patient's condition was hereditary, Lett commented, "Friends say not hereditary, but I (S.L.) think this doubtful."[26] Masturbation was another convenient diagnostic category. One patient at London was "in good bodily health; looks like a masturbator."[27] At the Toronto Asylum, the admitting physicians occasionally rejected the exciting causes suggested by referring doctors and inferred the "solitary vice" instead. One patient's insanity was "said to be [the] death of his mother, but masturbation more likely," and another's doctor suggested that the cause was sunstroke, but the admitting physician observed, "more probably masturbation."[28] In British Columbia, the appearance of a Chinese lunatic at the turn of the century usually included speculation about whether he had used opium. One Chinese patient who arrived on 28 January 1898 was described as having habits of life that were "not known, probably an opium smoker." Despite the uncertainty, both the remote and recent causes were listed as "opium."[29]

This tendency to seek causes where none may have existed, and to marginalize the observations of referring physicians and others who were more familiar with the individual patient, reflected a significant aspect of asylum medicine. More than just demonstrating the subjectivity of asylum diagnostics, it implied a belief in the authority of the asylum medical personnel in the nascent field of psychiatry and challenged a fundamental aspect of the referral system. While reinforcing a hierarchy of psychological knowledge, at the top of which sat the asylum medical staff, it also challenged the authority of the broader medical profession. Doctors often argued that the specific nature of disease was unique to each patient and therefore required individualistic treatment. This argument was also fundamental to their defence against patent medicine vendors and self-help schemes, and it bolstered their bid to gain broader professional powers. Yet asylum physicians' tendencies to extrapolate certain conditions from symptoms where they may not have existed challenged the spirit of that more nuanced medical knowledge. Disregard for letters of referral also made asylum physicians liable to overlook key aspects of the patient's condition. Taking patients from an often broad geographic area, medical superintendents rarely had prior knowledge of the individuals who arrived at the asylum gates. Asylum medicine became a process of dividing people into pre-existing categories.

The subjectivity of diagnostics suggests the potential that drug use or addiction could remain unidentified or that, when identified, its significance was marginalized. Prior to the turn of the century, although drug habits occasionally appeared at the asylum, rarely was drug addiction considered a form of mental disease. This is not surprising. Affecting both behaviour and physical appearance, addiction could fade before more common diagnostic precedents of asylum medicine. As we have seen in previous chapters, addicts could appear emaciated and drawn; some exhibited mania and were violent, whereas others were melancholy, desultory, and suicidal. Such conditions were not exclusive to addiction. Compounding the problem of diagnostics was the potential that addicts might not disclose their condition. The Ontario provincial inspector observed in 1886 that any list of causes of insanity would be flawed because, among other reasons, the family or the individual may not wish to divulge embarrassing information, such as "if the patient has been addicted to any particular vice or excess."[30] Long before investigators attached a social opprobrium to drug addiction, Thomas De Quincey preferred to keep his addiction secret and published his first version of *Confessions of an English Opium Eater* anonymously.[31] Moreover, insurance companies were concerned about the drug habit not only because of its debatable effect on longevity but also because habitués were considered inveterate liars. This recognition of the secrecy of drug users was not confined to the users themselves or the medical profession. The comments of the chair of the 1849 legislative committee investigating liquor laws in Upper Canada, discussed in Chapter 5, recognized the idea that drug use was a solitary indulgence.[32]

The solitude of the drug user fitted a pattern of behaviour that concerned asylum physicians: the improper and introspective focus of mental energy. As Michael J. Clarke has discussed, a key aspect of theories of mental alienation from as early as 1800 was the belief that conditions like morbid introspection – focusing too persistently on a single activity or idea – were central causes and forms of insanity.[33] Moral treatment, which attempted to redirect the patient's attention to a variety of "healthy" pursuits, attacked this single-mindedness. Clarke mentioned specifically masturbation as a form of particularly aberrant behaviour (to the Victorian physicians) that contributed to, and was indicative of, deeper mental derangement. (We saw examples of this in cases mentioned above where masturbation was implied in the patient's history.) The drug user's tendency toward secret or solitary activity paralleled the behaviour of a masturbator. The thematic similarity between masturbation and addiction as causes of insanity should not be overlooked as merely coincidental since both behaviours in those deemed insane reflected a dominant theme in nineteenth-century psychiatry: the concern over morbid introspection. The behavioural similarities between masturbation and drug addiction led us to speculate that addiction was another one of those single-minded pursuits that doctors felt could not possibly have been healthy. Nonmedical drug use was, unlike drinking, self-indulgent and inspired introspection, and (as with drinking) it had no practical purpose. It also spent vital force and misdirected time and energy in a developing industrial civilization forged by a work ethic that eschewed self-indulgence and wastefulness.[34] Drug addiction, therefore, bore aspects of behaviour that fitted into Victorian psychiatric diagnostics, yet the addiction itself did not need to be identified for a drug user to be a candidate for asylum treatment.

An examination of the annual reports of asylum superintendents demonstrates two significant characteristics about the relationship between habitual drug use and insanity. First, the perceptions varied widely by province. This variation may have been a result of the leadership of the asylum superintendent himself, provincial legislation, demographics, or all three. For example, as I will discuss later, the relatively large number of Chinese people in British Columbia placed opium smoking within the diagnostic view of medical personnel relatively early. In Nova Scotia, meanwhile, the availability of an asylum for inebriates nearby may have affected the admission process. In thirty-five years, the use of opiates was considered a cause of insanity only once, described in this case as the "abuse of morphine."[35] The proximity to the inebriety asylum may have affected the admission of drunks as well. Whereas in British Columbia alcohol was considered a cause of insanity in 10 percent of cases, it was cited less frequently in Halifax, being linked to insanity in just under 4 percent of cases.[36] Second, even including British Columbia's addicted Chinese lunatics, for much of the time under examination, habitual drug use was simply not within the field of visibility of the medical observers. In an ironic geo-ideational distribution, Nova Scotia's example is one end of a fairly limited spectrum, with British Columbia on the other end. In New Brunswick, between 1875 and 1903, for example, narcotics or opium as a cause of insanity appeared ten times, in three men and seven women.[37] In contrast, twelve men were apparently driven mad by tobacco. Even in British Columbia, the numbers were low. Between 1883 and 1893, among 357 admissions, 8 men were described as having madness caused by "intemperance in opium"; these were likely Chinese residents.[38] After the turn of the century, the manifestations were more diverse but also quite low. As Table 9 shows, out of nearly 1,000 admissions to the BC Asylum between 1901 and 1907, only 11 cases of insanity were attributed in some way to drugs. We have more details from the Ontario asylums, where both exciting and predisposing causes were provided in annual reports. As Table 10 demonstrates, drug use was rarely cited from 1885 to 1908, but by the turn of the century, it did appear more frequently. Yet apart from the anomalous explosion of female drug users in 1904, it continued to occur far less often than did alcohol, which was routinely either a predisposing or, more frequently, an exciting cause of insanity.

Although the reported causes suggest that drug habits were rarely connected directly to the onset of insanity, the case files indicate more debility from drug use than was indicated in official reports to the legislature. Many descriptions of patients arriving at the asylums allude to the possibility that the patient used drugs, but before the last decades of the century, physicians rarely considered habitual drug use as a cause of insanity. We need to be careful here: it is inappropriate to attempt to rediagnose a patient using the scant records that have remained behind. Without proper training and a face-to-face encounter with the patient, our perspective would be at best a clumsy amateur's tertiary diagnosis and of limited value. Instead, what we can do is see how drugs appeared in the patient records, how this appearance was interpreted by the personnel of the time, and whether and when the patient's condition was redefined in relation to habitual drug use.

When drugs did appear in patients' records, they were linked to an earlier conception of the relationship between mind and body. As Charles Rosenberg has shown, the idea of psychosomatic illness had an entirely different meaning in mid-nineteenth-century medical treatment: physicians often attributed physical disease to mental or moral dissolution, and mental derangement could similarly be the result of distinct physical causes.[39] In most asylums, the superintendents encountered some patients whose insanity was apparently the result of physical shocks, like being dunked in or showered by cold water or the shock of excessive medication. Michael M., an Irish farmer, arrived at the Toronto Asylum in June 1847 with a condition that was "thought to be from taking med. which did not agree with him." He stayed there for the rest of his life.[40] Likewise, physicians attributed the derangement of Delilah H., a twenty-six-year-old domestic who arrived at Toronto in 1864, to "med'n used for bronchitis."[41] When mining engineer John H. arrived in Halifax in 1873, it was after he "took chloral [hydrate] which caused excitement."[42]

Table 9

Causes of insanity in the BC Asylum, 1901–7

Cause of insanity	Men	Women	Total
Abuse of drugs and old age	1	0	1
Abuse of drugs and alcohol	0	2	2
Abuse of opium	4	1	5
Abuse of morphine	1	2	3
Total admissions	741	247	988

Source: "Annual Report on the Hospital for the Insane, New Westminster," *Sessional Papers of the Province of British Columbia* (1901–7).

Table 10

Substance use as cause of insanity in Ontario asylums, 1885–1908

	Drink				Drugs				Total admissions	
	Predisposing		Exciting		Predisposing		Exciting			
Year	M	F	M	F	M	F	M	F	M	F
1885	4	3	12	7					271	237
1886		1	10	6					269	203
1887	4	1	7						203	251
1888			14						224	212
1889	9		21	2		2	1	2	359	312
1890	4		13	1					294	265
1891	4	1	6	6					321	376
1893	2	1	19	3					461	436
1894	3		12	2					401	419
1895	6		13	4					407	374
1896	11	1	22	2					532	516
1897	4		20	1			1	1	436	414
1898	8		18	9	1		3	1	545	444
1899	11	1	21	3				1	379	445
1899	8		24	2					407	386
1900	6		21	5					397	396
1901									405	392
1902	13	1	24	12			2	8	410	606
1903	16	2	25	10			2	8	434	455
1904	31	4	42	8	1	20		25	458	500
1905	25	4	62	5					511	538
1906	52	14	44	18		2			519	568
1907	29	5	42	4					566	528
1908	74	12	27	3	5	4	2	2	525	497

Source: Reports of the Provincial Lunatic Asylums of Toronto, Kingston, and London. Note there were no causes listed in the 1892 Report. In 1899 the legislature sat twice, and there were, therefore, two reports.

Yet given their range of experience, combined with personal biases, referring and asylum physicians could understate or miss aspects of the individual's condition that were later found to be significant. Drug use was one
such condition. In the Saint John Asylum, Waddell also often attributed
behavioural change that may have resulted from drug use to other, more
orthodox diagnoses. Joseph S., who had been treated by Dr. Thomas Geddes
of Yarmouth for rheumatic affliction in the thigh and hip, seems to have
been a victim of classic iatrogenic addiction. The treatment of the leg was
unsuccessful and resulted in a maintenance supply of hypodermic morphine
to deal with the pain: "About 8 months ago he first showed symptoms of
imbecility which increased to a form of hypocondriasis. [The patient] was
formerly lively [and] cheerful, is now sad and despondent, and the tendency
is to injure himself by taking morphine."[43] Joseph's case demonstrates the
potential for viewing an addiction as a different form of mental disorder. The
physical manifestation of prolonged opiate dependency could appear as a
form of depression or imbecility. The "potential to injure" could be read
several ways. Was the patient attempting suicide or just using an amount
of morphine that could be fatal to one who had not developed a tolerance?
Or was this Waddell's perception of the meaning of "chronic poisoning"?
Finally, a desire for repeated doses of medicine like morphine could fit a
loose definition of hypochondria. That Joseph was an addict seems highly
likely; that his addiction was not identified suggests physicians' difficulty
in recognizing addiction when they were not yet looking for it.

The only case in which Waddell recognized the opium habit was that of
William M., who had become addicted to opium while in the East Indies.
Here again, Waddell – and the referring physicians – initially diagnosed the
condition with more common categories of concern, despite a history of
opium use. William arrived at the asylum as a "suicidal drunkard," and
Waddell's description of the case identified the process of the patient's opium
addiction. He "had previously been to the East Indies as Capt[ain] of a ship,
and it is supposed that he contracted there the inordinate use of opium."
Once he returned to Canada, he lost his supply of opium and spent the
winter in a state of delirium. "He had so far [ceased] ... his opium in May
that he crossed the Atlantic as a mate in a ship of his father intending to go
East again, but having returned to his old habits again in Liverpool, he was
[urged] ... by the Capt. of [the] ship to return home."[44] William's story
reflected the discourses surrounding the opium habit in Western cultures.
The exposure to the dens in Asia, slow decline into opium, the pain of release,
the return to old habits, and the moral and physical decay that resulted (he
arrived at the asylum "dissipated and dark") were images from contemporary
alarmist narratives describing the dangers of opium.[45] However, even with
this suggestive history, William did not arrive at the asylum until he appeared

to display suicidal tendencies. It was the danger of suicide, not the drug use, that necessitated asylum treatment. Although the above cases suggest that drug addiction was a major cause of the behavioural changes that led to these asylum admissions, our observations must remain speculative since the physicians themselves downplayed the addictions in favour of more traditional forms of mental derangement.

An addiction would more frequently be identified only after a patient entered the institution. Four examples illustrate the ways that drug use could appear in the etiology of the patient's insanity and indicate the process of epistemological shifting. A minister who arrived at the Halifax asylum in 1862 had been treated with morphine to quiet him down for a few weeks previously. On the admission form, under the category of "habits," the referring physician had written "not addicted to opium or intemperance." Someone, likely asylum staff, later added "much" after "not," making it read "not much addicted," which suggested that there was an addiction but that it was mild. The cause of his insanity was suggested to be "over working his mental powers."[46] Catherine A. conceded on her arrival at Toronto in September 1884 that she habitually took the impressive amount of 30 grains of morphine, yet her referring doctors had not mentioned this condition.[47] Although they recognized the extreme quantity of Catherine's opiate consumption, the asylum physicians were not certain that the drug use was the primary cause of Catherine's debility. The "morphia [was] stopped on admission which *might* clear insan[ity]," wrote the admitting physician.[48] Here, too, the direct relationship between insanity and the drug habit had not been established. The exciting cause of her condition was listed as "mental trouble upon loss of property."[49] Neither physician who referred John M. to the Toronto Asylum in 1895 mentioned the existence of a drug habit, but John admitted on his arrival that "he had abused the use of chloral [hydrate] and other drugs."[50] He was a model patient, "always acted quiet and gentlemanly," and appears to have recovered rapidly. He left the asylum two months after his admission.[51] In contrast, Melinda T. arrived at the BC Asylum in 1901 listed as "a total abstainer from alcoholics [sic][,] good housekeeper, conduct blameless." Her condition was listed as resulting from the death of her eight-year-old son two years earlier, but written above this entry in a separate pen was "real cause was abuse of morphia," and the name of her disease was entered as "Morphinism."[52]

In these cases, the main cause of the patients' aberrant behaviour may have been drug addiction; however, whenever these doctors noted that the patients used drugs habitually, they considered the addictions secondary to more traditional categories of mental alienation, normally melancholia and mania. Their reliance on traditional categories was bolstered by the fact that the patients were not sent to the asylum until they demonstrated behaviour that challenged social norms. The patients were suicidal or homicidal or had at least threatened violence, and these conditions suggest the social role of the asylum as a place to correct deviant behaviour. Addressing the overt behaviour of the patient was central to asylum therapeutics. Sometimes superficial symptoms were all that asylum physicians addressed. Likewise, when treating patients who may have been habitual drug users, the doctors sought specific behavioural aberrations that challenged social norms; until addiction became one of these forms of deviance, it was a secondary condition of insanity.

The identification of drug use as a primary factor in insanity was a gradual process that unfolded at different times in asylums across the country. For some patients who arrived at the asylum, drug use did appear in their psychological profiles, yet their physicians were uncertain whether drug addiction itself constituted insanity. A physician sent Thomasina M. to the Toronto Asylum in 1875, noting that hers "is more probably a state bordering on insanity, than active insanity [and] is apparently caused by the habitual and excessive use of opium." Thomasina confirmed her use of 3 to 4 ounces of laudanum each day, but her doctor could not decide whether this was insanity.[53] Charles O., who arrived at the London Asylum in 1871, had been "under treatment by private practitioners who have by all appearances given him large doses of morphine or some other preparation of opium." Yet the referring physician was unable to determine whether addiction was actually insanity and questioned "very much this being a case of brain disease; I fancy the great trouble was the use of too much opium ... to procure sleep."[54] For these cases, addiction was a problem, but it was not insanity. In 1878, a Roman Catholic priest arrived at the Halifax Asylum with habits listed as "intemperate and uses opium to excess." The admitting physician noted that the priest was sent "as a means of breaking him of the habit. No insanity that I can see."[55] This conclusion may indicate that in the official statistics, such cases, as rare as they were, would be classified under "no insanity," which indicates the place of drug habits in the asylum cosmology but is frustrating for historians desperately seeking statistics. For this asylum physician, even a dual addiction to alcohol and drugs did not constitute insanity. In contrast was the case of Fred A., a twenty-six-year-old male druggist who arrived at the Halifax Asylum in 1887. His habits were listed as "not temperate, uses opium," and the causation was debatable. Although the admitting physicians noted that he had a history of the excessive use of alcohol and opium, his disease was labelled "primary dementia," and additional manifestations of his condition included "failure at business, mental depression and attempts at suicide." As a reminder to us that we need to be careful not to attempt to second-guess asylum assessments, Fred's condition appears indeed to have been something more than drug-induced:

he stayed for nine years and was eventually sent to the Halifax Poor Asylum, a local workhouse.[56]

Despite the difference in conditions and results, all the above cases are of patients whose drug use was not considered to be their form of mental derangement; at most, it was a contributing factor to their insanity. As the Ontario provincial inspector noted, the usefulness of any list of causes of insanity was restricted by the fact that the cause was often unclear. The Toronto Asylum's superintendent, Daniel Clark, also argued this point in his 1898 report, noting the difficulty in linking insanity directly to alcohol or (less frequently) to drug habituation. Usually, he said, drug use that appeared at the asylum was an indication of a deeper problem.[57] This etiological construction began to change near the end of the century. More patients arriving at asylums across the country had conditions that were clearly caused by the habitual use of opiates or, less frequently, other drugs.

Cases of addiction in the admission records of the asylums suggest how drug use entered the lexicon of asylum diagnostics through traditional channels. It was either a cause or a result of more familiar forms of insanity, such as melancholia and mania, and later became itself a form of mental alienation. In the first years of the twentieth century, earlier categories broke down as psychologists sought new answers to the persistent problem of diagnosis of insanity. In 1908, for example, the Government of Ontario legislated a new system for categorizing insanity based on German alienist Emil Kraepelin's new and innovative taxonomy.[58] The categories began with "Psychoses Associated with Toxaemia," which included the subcategories of "morphinism, cocainism, and several forms of dementia associated with alcoholism."[59] Yet these classifications, which reflected a complex new way of conceptualizing insanity and which incorporated drug addiction, could not eliminate the subjectivity of the asylum physician's diagnoses. Moreover, as Cheryl Krasnick Warsh has noted, "The shortcomings of Kraepelin's work was that the innovation ended at classification."[60] New classifications did not lead to either new treatments or a decline in the subjectivity of asylum diagnostics. Patients were simply placed in more jargon-heavy categories and essentially treated the same as before.

Prior to this official shift, physicians had begun to reconsider their classification system, a process that increasingly recognized drug addiction as itself a form of mental derangement. Table 10 illustrates the "forms of mental derangement" for which drug use appeared either as an exciting or, less frequently, as a predisposing cause in patients entering the Toronto and Kingston Asylums. Since, as demonstrated earlier, drug use in the nineteenth century could often be misinterpreted or miscategorized, we cannot conclude that incidents of drug use increased, yet the growing frequency of drug use as the cause, and of addiction as a form, of insanity illustrates a changing recognition of the potential of drugs to significantly alter behaviour. Therefore, these statistics suggest a terminological incorporation of drug use and addiction within the classification of causes and forms of insanity in the first decade of the twentieth century. Habitual drug use was now a mental illness that observers, be they family, friends, doctors, or other officials, believed required institutional care.

This terminological shift did more than recognize the drug habit as a form of insanity. Just as alcohol use and masturbation were causes of insanity that doctors expected to find when confronting certain behavioural anomalies, some evidence suggests that drug use became a similarly presupposed cause of insanity. This change took place about the same time that habitual drug use was formally included as a form of mental derangement in Kraepelin's new taxonomy. In Kingston, in 1907, the admitting physician began to note the absence of drug use in manic and demented patients who arrived at the asylum. A farmer suffering from "acute mania" had habits described as "industrious, temperate, no drugs," a housewife with chronic dementia was "active intemperate no drugs," and another with delusional mania was "active not addicted to alcohol or drugs."[61] When we compare the referral forms, where details of the cases were provided by the patients' referring physicians, with the admission registers, where the asylums' admitting physicians transcribed the information on these forms (and supplemented it with their own observations), we see a further tendency to regard drug use as a cause or form of insanity. A grocer who entered the paid wards at the Toronto Asylum in August 1899, for example, was melancholy from the death of several children and business losses. His doctors noted that these tragedies had driven him to take "drugs, chloral and laudanum," but they considered the predisposing cause of his derangement to be the loss of his children and the exciting cause to be financial difficulties. The admitting physician dismissed this diagnosis and listed the cause as "alcohol, laudanum & chloral." The man's condition, however, was probably more than just an addiction since he remained for over two years.[62]

This determination that drug use was a distinct cause of insanity may have served to blur other conditions. Just as we must be careful when trying to identify addicted patients who were not described as addicts, we must consider carefully any attempt to reconsider a diagnosis that included drug use. Several cases for which drug use was recorded as a cause but not a form of mental derangement demonstrate that we must be cautious in our interpretation of any case. Given the identifiable effects of the drugs I am exploring, we would expect a patient whose condition was caused exclusively by addiction to require only a few months' stay to recover from the addiction and withdrawal symptoms; yet, as we have seen, this pattern was not always typical. A woman at the London Asylum, for example, had taken drugs for a tumour and the pain that resulted from it. The tumour disappeared, but she continued to take opium. She remained at the asylum for a year and a half.[63] A medical missionary who arrived at Kingston, Ontario with both predisposing and exciting causes listed as "morphine habit," but with no listed "form of mental disease," remained at the asylum for over five years before leaving "improved."[64] A Victoria printer arrived in the BC Asylum in 1896 with the supposed cause of insanity to be "heredity." The admission records noted that he had used opium for ten years. When discharged three months later, he was labelled "recovered?"[65] The asylum physicians learned a lesson. When he returned in 1900, his remote and recent cause of insanity was listed as "opium smoking."[66] That notwithstanding, his illness was called melancholia, and he remained in the asylum for years.

Although opium addiction was not an expected diagnosis for most patients in asylums across the country, Chinese patients in British Columbia were an exception. Given the popular associations between Chinese people and opium smoking, it should not be surprising that many of the cases of Chinese people who arrived at the BC Asylum included a mention of opium smoking as a cause of insanity. In the twelve years between 1896 and 1908, sixteen Chinese men were admitted with conditions that the admitting physicians linked to opium. By contrast, fifteen of the hundreds of non-Chinese patients admitted had some kind of drug use listed in their profiles. Yet the percentage of people of Chinese background who were in the asylum never rose above 14 percent in that time, whereas whites usually made up over 85 percent of the population, the remainder consisting of a few Native Canadians and the occasional Japanese person or patient identified as "coloured." So a disproportionate number of Chinese people were admitted with conditions that were linked (how accurately cannot be determined) to opium smoking.

Keeping in mind that it is fallacious to second-guess the conclusions of the superintendents, it is worth noting how this habit was discursively connected to other forms of debasement or to moral judgments of the Chinese person in general. S. Yong, a Chinese man who arrived in October 1900, was described as living outside a camp and stealing food from other Chinese men, who did not want him around. Having no clear indication of the form of insanity, its causes, or his habits in life, the admitting physician recorded only, "wants opium." There is no indication that Yong was insane, but he did remain for years.[67] Similarly, a man who arrived a few months later also did not have his condition linked to a form of insanity, but his habits of life were linked to Chinese stereotypes: "dirty opium smoker and idler." The superintendent noted a year later, "I got the opportunity of sending this man away to China & I seized upon it."[68] A year after this "dirty opium smoker" arrived, another Chinese man's insanity was attributed to "lack of proper food and opium habit," although it is unclear whether the idea of "proper food" was a judgment on Asian culinary choices or actual nutritional deprivation. Similar to the others, even though the opium may have been seen as a cause of the insanity, it is unlikely that it was the only problem. This person remained seven years before dying, and he was described as delusional for all this time.[69] Similarly, when W. Quong showed up in August 1903, his habits were described as "smokes opium, not industrious." He was listless and poorly nourished but craved opium, which he was given in a small dosage, just enough to satisfy; within three weeks, he was "completely broken from his opium habit." Yet Quong was suicidal, and his condition was diagnosed as dementia praecox. He remained until 1909, when he was returned to China.[70]

These examples demonstrate vividly the subjectivity of the diagnostic process since entrenched cultural assumptions coloured evaluation of what conditions were important to note. Since any apparent insanity caused directly by the habitual use of opium would ease on cessation of habit, it is likely that in all of these cases, the mental illness was more profound than just the opium habit. But the discursive connection between being filthy, being malnourished, and being an opium smoker indicates how socio-economic forms of deprivation were linked to a specific, racialized form of opium consumption and how all were considered forms of degeneracy that could cause insanity. As we saw in Chapter 4, the lazy, listless, slovenly Chinese opium smoker was a dominant trope in Western views of Chinese habitués. Moreover, the fact that in these cases no attempt was made to place a label on the form of madness may suggest a lack of interest in the patient, but it also may indicate that the Western medical personnel had trouble diagnosing individuals who were so culturally different from themselves.

Shifting diagnostic classifications in the admission records may serve to hide a process that was taking place before habitual drug use itself became a reason for admission to the asylum. Some medical personnel began to view drugs as the only cause of some patients' distress rather than as an exciting or predisposing one, and their impressions subsequently blurred the lines between things that caused madness and the "form" that the mental disease took. By the turn of the century, for patients whose condition appeared to be caused by alcohol, the BC Asylum routinely labelled the mental illness "toxic insanity" or less frequently "alcoholic insanity." At times, the condition was called "toxic insanity (alcoholic)," which suggests, as did the medical literature of the day, that other forms were possible. C.E. Doherty, the medical superintendent of the BC Asylum, wrote in his first report to the provincial government that some of the asylum patients were victims of "toxic causes, drugs and alcohol." Yet the casebooks and admission registers suggest that "toxic insanity" was normally attached only to people whose madness seemed a result of the overconsumption of alcohol. The attribution of some form of insanity to toxic causes is significant because "toxicity" was a more sophisticated label placed on poisoning. Here we see that chronic poisoning had been transformed into an actual medical condition.

Possibly due to its past life as an annoying condition demonstrating a simple personal indulgence that interfered with physicians' treatment methods, toxic insanity was a contentious diagnosis. Reflecting the organicity arguments of Henry Howard discussed in Chapter 5, the Toronto Asylum's superintendent, Daniel Clark, refused to consider any form of addiction to be insanity without some kind of physical mechanism. In *Mental Diseases* (1895), Clark argued that "the delirium or mania induced by ... toxic agents such as alcohol, opium and its salts, cocaine, hydrate chloral and such like, are not insane conditions." He disagreed with authors who called such states "toxic insanity ... alcoholic insanity, morphinic insanity, haschish insanity, etheric insanity, chloralic insanity, cocainic insanity, and oxy-carbonic insanity." Clark insisted that drug use was a form of insanity only when a permanent derangement of the brain followed the disuse of the substance.[71] However, in letters to the family and colleagues of patients whose insanity was caused by drug use, but who were not classified specifically as suffering from addiction or the drug habit as a "form of mental disorder," Clark's discussion suggests that his may have been a semantic delineation. In these letters, Clark explained his treatment of each patient's condition. Often Clark and his staff interpreted and treated the patient's condition as though drugs were the only cause of the disorder, the insanity caused by drugs being viewed as potentially temporary.[72] This interpretation contradicted the position that Clark took in *Mental Diseases*. There he appears to have accepted drug addiction as a viable form of mental derangement prior to more formal recognition of this etiological shift. At the turn of the century, Clark's therapeutic perspective straddled two periods, one when drug use was a cause of more extensive mental problems and another when addiction itself became a form of insanity.

Diagnostic Deviance and the Madness of Edward C.
Clark's interpretation of addiction was shaped by the conditions in which he worked and may not reflect the perspective of all medical superintendents at the time. Having the benefit of a "superior ward" for wealthy insane patients, Clark may have looked on mental affliction caused by drug addiction more sympathetically, or even with more awareness of the concerns manifested in the medical literature about upper-class addiction. Hence he may have been more willing to link addiction and insanity directly. Other

physicians, less familiar with addiction or less sympathetic to the drug habitué, may have interpreted addiction differently. We are rarely fortunate enough to have a case in which two medical superintendents assessed the same patient. However, in 1896, a patient arrived at the London Asylum and then was transferred to the Toronto Asylum. His condition became the subject of considerable scrutiny by both Richard M. Bucke and Daniel Clark, as well as by the provincial inspector, R. Christie. The case of Edward C. provides a valuable opportunity to compare directly how substance use operated in the subjective terminological realm of asylum diagnostics.

When Edward, a resident of London, Ontario, and a confirmed liquor, cocaine, and opium user arrived at the London Asylum, it was after being treated for liquor and cocaine addiction at the Keeley Institute in Dwight, Illinois, and then a series of misadventures in Georgia. He had hallucinated that people were trying to kill him, he had threatened the life of his wife, and he had attempted suicide in an Atlanta police lockup. When his family took him to the London Asylum after retrieving him from Atlanta, he was described as "intemperate, has used cocaine, alcohol and opium. Imagines that his family have all turned against him ... Hesitating speech and tremors. Excitable. Incoherent and talks about great wealth and fortunes he is making. Excitable."[73]

Prior to departing on his exploits in the United States, Edward had incurred a number of debts and had misused funds from his father's estate. These activities took place while Edward was "laid up" from drinking and possibly from other drug use. Apparently as a result of these debts, the Toronto General Trusts Company sued Edward's family to retain control of the estate of Edward's father. The exact conditions around this case are not clear, although it seems likely that Edward's brother, Andrew Jr., appealed to the company to get the money that was intended for dependent relatives, but for which Edward (the eldest) was responsible, into safer hands. To facilitate this court case, the family barrister, Mr. Gamble, requested a psychiatric evaluation of his client. Bucke examined the patient, collected a mass of paperwork describing his various exploits, and determined that Edward was "an insane person and a dangerous lunatic." Bucke drew mostly on accounts of Edward's "moral" behaviour:

> He has been careless and reckless in his life and in his business, has drank spirits almost continuously in sufficient quantity to keep him a large part of the time in a dazed state, and has spent money so much in excess of his income as to deprive his family ... of the ordinary comforts of life ... The people who have stood by him for years ... who have assisted to support his family, who have supplied him with money ... he looks upon with indifference or as his enemies ... seems indeed to be destitute of any feeling of obligation or gratitude.[74]

Bucke concluded that Edward was "a moral imbecile," who "cannot recover from his debility, and [it is] very doubtful if [he] will ever [recover] from his delusions."

Edward's barrister then asked Daniel Clark to examine the patient. Clark's observations drew on the same documentary evidence as did Bucke's, combined with personal interviews, but he concluded that Edward was not insane. Bucke had considered the aberrant moral behaviour, whereas Clark had looked at the gaps between these fits of insanity:

> Assuming all that has been stated ... to be true, it is evident that intermittently he was subject to hallucinations and delusions. It is, however, noticeable that also intermittently he was rational and in his right mind and did at these times intelligent work ... It is evident then that there was no fixed or permanent brain disease at this period, else would his delusional state have been continuous and incapacitated him from earning a salary in responsible positions.[75]

Clark did not deny that "no man in his right mind" would display such conduct and have such hallucinations. He also drew attention to "the fact that he not only drank liquor heavily but was also a victim of cocaine, which he acknowledges, and experience teaches us that the excessive use of these deleterious poisons not only causes delirium, but also often excites to hallucinations of sight and hearing as well as delusions of persecution."[76] Nevertheless, Clark was adamant that "these intermittent periods of undue excitement cannot be rightly called insanity." He likened Edward's insistence that the delusions in Georgia had been real to dreams, which "impress us with an intensity almost equal to real actions and waking mental impressions."[77] Contrary to Bucke, Clark suggested that Edward should be released on probation to see whether the patient had recovered. This probation began in January 1897. In March, Edward was formally discharged.[78]

Both Canadian alienists' opinions are consistent with their published perspectives on the nature of the human mind and the effects of drugs on it. As noted above, Clark argued in *Mental Diseases* that the mental derangement caused by substance use was not itself insanity. He argued that the only time delirium caused by substance use should be properly labelled insanity was when "a permanent mental disease follows the use of and *abstinence from* these drugs."[79] Edward's condition was temporary. That Edward was lucid and rational on cessation of the substance use suggested that no mental disease was present. Bucke's writings focused less on the biological or organic nature of insanity and more on broader questions of the moral nature of the individual and the human race. Although not exploring the case of Edward C. specifically, both S.E.D. Shortt and Rainer Baehre have explained that in his work Bucke consistently made a case for the developing moral superiority of humanity, validating this perspective with organic theories of moral growth.[80] In *Cosmic Consciousness* (1901), his most celebrated work, Bucke argued that humanity was reaching a moral transcendence that few had yet achieved. So Edward, an individual whose wilful indulgence led to violence, abuse, and rejection of the sympathies of others, was, to Bucke, an irredeemable individual and potentially an example of what Shortt calls "atavism ... regression to a more primitive state."[81] Edward's refusal to accept the illusory nature of his hallucinations and his history of aberrant behaviour suggested to Bucke one who was morally regressing, instead of developing.

Both arguments related to broader issues of social progress and the role of addiction as deviance within the larger social context. Clark's arguments drew on generally accepted ideas about the effects of drugs on the behaviour of the individual but offered an optimistic assessment of the prospects of treating addiction. Addicted to drink, cocaine, and (in some accounts) opium, Edward personified the social panic over the substance abuser.[82] He was a wealthy man who had indulged too frequently. He fell into bad habits and then became delusional and unable to keep his job. His addiction led to temporary insanity, which in turn caused havoc to the family and potential danger to society. For Clark, to see the potential for restoration of the individual's faculties was to offer hope to those seeking a treatment for society's growing "problem" of substance use. Bucke, meanwhile, provided no solution but perpetual incarceration and pessimism. His interpretation of progress meant that when a wealthy individual squandered his property and abused his relatives and peers, this behaviour demonstrated a threat to the positivistic, progressivist perspective that Bucke embraced. For the superintendent of the London Asylum, irredeemable insanity was the only way to explain such behaviour.

The Elite Drug User and Social Decline

Edward's case provides both a glimpse of the different ways addiction can be interpreted by experts, and how it illustrates the connection between addiction and disruptive social behaviour. The issue of opiate (and later cocaine) use and its debilitating effects on the moral and physical character of the individual was especially of concern since it affected social elites. As we saw in Chapter 4, the perceived danger of the Chinese opium den hinged on the fear that this foreign, debilitating habit would infect the children of the upper classes. Yet as the records of asylums indicate, luring elites to addiction was not the purview only of the opium den. Iatrogenic addiction was a condition most familiar to the better-off citizenry, whose doctors prescribed opiates or who self-prescribed. Not only could rich white people purchase opium-laden proprietary medicines without a prescription, but the fact that many pharmacy laws allowed pharmacists to sell opium to people who were familiar to the druggist meant that, for many whose character seemed unimpeachable, opium remained readily available. It should not be a surprise, then, that so many of the habitual opium users in the asylum records were drawn from social elites, either professionals or their family members. Given that the asylum was a place to reinstill social order on the citizen's body, it should also not be a surprise that elite families sent their addicted relatives to the asylum when that addiction resulted in social disorder. We have seen this in several cases already, and explored it in depth with Edward C., so let us turn to a few additional cases to see how the threat to social order, and the impact of addiction on family life, could result in people turning to formal medical institutions, and the purview of the state, to deal with addiction.

Asylum admission records primarily track medical (and sometimes legal) definitions of mental illness, but the people sending the patient to the asylum often had different reasons. Addiction specialists and asylum physicians focused on mental and behavioural conditions that would help them to understand and treat the patient's condition. The families of addicts, on whose initiative most addicts were sent to the asylum, looked at aberrant behaviour as justification for committal. The weakened will could be of particular concern to the families of the addicts: a weakened will and profligate lifestyle could lead to family disgrace or even to economic ruin, as was vividly clear in the case of Edward C. Not only did the asylum generally admit wealthier patients, but these patients also arrived after causing considerable family upheaval. The stable family was a Victorian ideal; the health and background of the families of addicts who were admitted to the asylum were significant to the asylum personnel.[83] The addicts who arrived at the asylum ended up there because they threatened either the physical health of family members or the moral integrity of the family. These familial conditions suggest that the asylum was an endpoint in a broader struggle with personal addiction, and they expose the social forces that contributed to the extended problematization, medicalization, and institutionalization of drug addiction.

The identified drug users in the admission registers of the Toronto Asylum reinforce the stereotype of the late-nineteenth-century addict outside of British Columbia as a wealthy, middle-class individual and reiterate patterns that we have seen in other asylums. Both the wealthy woman who may have been discontented with her expected role in life and the restless male relative who found no satisfaction in following the family business could find in drug use a temporary escape.[84] Yet, unless Canadians were particularly abstemious, few addicts ended up at the asylum. Those who did enter asylums not only appear to have been addicted to substance use but, like Edward, also displayed behaviour that was socially disruptive or upsetting to the family or friends who decided to send the individual to the asylum. Just as alcohol use was constructed by the middle class as an antisocial behaviour that ran contrary to the values of industry, moderation, and the work ethic, so too did families often look on relatives' addiction as equally contrary to such values. In the following series of cases, I explore how addiction that manifested itself in disruptive behaviour that violated preconceived notions of propriety and station in life – determined by social factors, most notably gender but also class – was a key issue in the decision to send an individual to the asylum. I end the discussion by considering how the perception of the demographics of addiction simultaneously informed and was the result of a class-based moral concern about the dangers of drug addiction.

The drug user whose behaviour challenged the social value of industriousness is typified in the experience of William B., a forty-year-old manufacturer, who arrived at the Toronto Asylum in July 1894. William's "form of mental disorder" listed on his admission records was mania, but his referring physicians could not detect any sign of that condition when they interviewed him. Both relied heavily on family testimony that William was paranoid, occasionally violent, and overly extravagant. Furthermore, "he neglects his business ... [and] under the impression of great wealth he spends his money with irrational extravagance." The only suggestion of any problem came from William's own admission to one of the doctors that he used morphine. William remained at the asylum for three months and did not return.[85]

An alternative to the manic patient was the melancholy one. Juliana B. entered the Toronto Asylum at least twice in two years, suffering from melancholia. At Juliana's first admission, morphine was the predisposing cause of her derangement, and grief was the exciting cause. She had also taken chloral hydrate, opium, and bromides. The drug use may have been considered a predisposing cause because, according to the records of the first visit, Juliana had stopped dipping into her personal pharmacopoeia between twelve and eighteen months earlier. However, the form of mental disorder was unclear. The individual who had filled in the admission form wrote, "melancholia," but that was later crossed out with a question mark after it.[86] The role of drug use in the etiology of Juliana's disorder was also not clear to the admitting physicians. On the second admission, the physicians noted that Juliana had "formerly used chloral and opium," that the insanity manifested itself in being "very fretful, wants drugs," and that she was "taking drugs &c." Drug use may have been a major part of Juliana's behavioural change, but she was sent to the asylum only after she began displaying protracted symptoms of grief. Her case suggests a pattern that Cheryl Krasnick Warsh has observed with respect to older women who were being sent to Homewood. Social redundancy, a state that particularly affected women, such as widowed mothers living with adult children and unwed daughters or sisters living with relatives, often drove families that were unwilling or unable to take care of widowed or invalid members to admit people who otherwise would be cared for at home.[87]

An addicted family member whose behaviour was socially aberrant could wreak havoc on the family to an extent that even the asylum may not have been able to remedy. The case of Theresa E. provides an example of the potential family upheaval of late-nineteenth-century addiction. Theresa was an intelligent, educated, trilingual, twenty-five-year-old divorced mother of one from Niagara, Ontario. She "craves for alcohol, morphia and cocaine," behaviour that led to further social deviation. At one point, Theresa "was drunk and found in a bar with a lot of soldiers who were trying to lead her away." The key reason for the incarceration, however, was that "her mother cannot manage her at all[,] she abuses her mother at times ... Mother says patient came home Friday night in an intoxicated condition[,] raved all night and had to be carried up stairs, she was completely exhausted with Alcohol and narcotics." Theresa's mother, Mrs. R., was an attentive, concerned, and "anchious [sic] mother," as she described herself, and sent magazines and money for her daughter's well-being in the asylum.[88] She simply did not know how to control her daughter.

After a few months, Theresa appeared to recover, and Clark asked her family to take her home. Apparently, they refused to do so. In July, soon after her mother died, Theresa received a letter from a man who was probably her brother-in-law: "Mother ... is gone[,] it is you that kill her[,] you broke her hart [sic] ... I hope God will forgive you and you have made poor mother poor, she had not one cent when she died and everybody knows that you have kill [sic] mother[.] We never wont [sic] to see you again in this world."[89] Clark wrote back acknowledging that the family did not want to have anything to do with Theresa, but he explained that he could not keep her at the asylum any longer. He noted that Theresa was willing to go to New York, but she needed money for the train. If the family did not send money, Clark would be forced to release her in Toronto, and she would most certainly end up back in Niagara.[90] Her sister sent $18.00 and vented to Clark about the terrible state in which Theresa had left the family: "She is not to be trusted with monny [sic] so look after this monny[.] Please as I have had hard work to get this to geather [sic] it is just offull [sic] what that woman has had she has made mother poor and broke her hart [sic]."[91] Theresa did go to New York, but three years later she sent a letter to Dr. Clark saying, "I am without a home and it seems nearly impossible for me to make an honest living out in the world and I thought maybe you might be able to give me something to do in the institution or near by."[92] Clark's reply was concise: "I have no situation that you could properly fill. I am sorry for your condition."[93]

Like the assessment of Edward, that of Theresa provides a useful glimpse at the social interpretation of addiction and at the conditions under which it could fall within the state's purview. Theresa's family sought state intervention only when the woman's conduct was too much for her family to handle alone. Once removed from her old life and placed under the surveillance of the asylum, Theresa recovered quite rapidly. Clark did not feel that Theresa required state oversight once her addiction and its attendant behavioural excesses had ceased. The reaction of Theresa's family to her impending release and the woman's subsequent appeal to Clark for financial help suggest the dependency of the addict while in the care of the state. Theresa's letter did not discuss what other events had affected her life. We cannot determine whether Theresa was unable to find work because she had succumbed again to her drug use or whether she was a victim of the plight of an unmarried, middle-class woman who had been cut off from familial support.

Edward and Theresa also give us a glimpse into the class-based interpretation of addiction. Both came from wealthy families. Although Theresa's stay at Toronto apparently left her mother poor, she was staying in the $6.00 ward, which suggests that she or her family were wealthy enough to afford that level of comfort and personalized treatment. The emotional and economic havoc that Theresa wreaked on her family is indicative of the moral panic that fuelled social concern over drug addiction. Her substance use was believed to have led to Theresa's sexual impropriety in public, and the family's attempts to have her contained and treated drained familial resources. The result was economic and emotional disaster. Edward's addictions had also placed an economic burden on his family members. However, when they were able to limit his ability to do further damage by having the Toronto General Trusts Company retain control over the estate of Edward's father (apparently to the advantage of the rest of Edward's family), they were willing to accept Clark's diagnosis that Edward was sane and take him home.

The asylum could provide an outlet for wealthier families to protect themselves from the economic and moral ravages of an addiction that became too disruptive to be relegated to private treatment outside of the view of the state. The role of the asylum in protecting people from damaging social deviance may have affected the state's formal policies toward the treatment of cases that came under the purview of the asylum. As mentioned above, in 1908 the Ontario government recognized behavioural changes caused by morphine and cocaine use as distinct mental illnesses, worthy of treatment in public asylums. It may be no coincidence that this change took place in the same year that agitation for laws to limit strictly access to these drugs was becoming a matter of national legislative concern and that provincial pharmacy laws were expanding to control cocaine more tightly than other drugs.

Treatment of Addiction in the Nonspecialist Asylum

How did physicians treat addiction in nonspecialist institutions? In the discussions of treatment presented in Chapter 5, Stephen Lett, J.B. Mattison, and Edward Mann were all asylum-based practitioners who made addiction their professional speciality. Yet, as we have already seen, general-asylum physicians were not looking for addiction, so their approaches were not necessarily in keeping with the approach of the specialists. Addiction was not within their field of visibility unless it appeared in a different form. Indeed, as Clark's and Bucke's contradictory interpretations of Edward C.'s case indicate, alienists were not in agreement about diagnoses; how could they be in agreement about treatment?

Across the country, medical superintendents at provincial asylums were facing the problem of how best to treat addicted patients. In one respect, a misdiagnosis may not have hampered the resulting treatment. The general approach of asylum therapeutics from the middle of the century favoured moral treatment, supporting patients with a firm hand, salubrious distractions, and some medications as they recovered their reason. So it was possible that an addict, arriving at an asylum in a state described as melancholy or "morbid introspection," could pass relatively unnoticed through the process of detoxification without the attendants suspecting any afflictions different from those that often appeared at the asylum. Indeed, during detoxification from opiate addictions that had required low doses of opiates to maintain, a minimal degree of medical intervention may have been necessary, and asylum therapeutics could have been effective simply due to the controlled conditions under which the patient was placed.

Moral treatment, however, was of limited value in combatting detoxification from more profound addictions. Some conditions were so severe that nothing less than a substantial therapeutic regimen was necessary. At the Homewood Retreat in Guelph, Ontario, Stephen Lett envisioned extended stays of at least several months to slowly wean his addicted patients off their habit.[94] Although the length of Lett's treatments may have been extreme, a stopover of a few days would be relatively ineffective to treat a physical addiction. Several examples illustrate the potential ineffectiveness of therapeutics based on incomplete diagnoses. Dr. T.E. spent six days in the Saint John Asylum in September 1880. His first admission record noted that he had a "mind disturbed by drinking." His second and third visits, during which drug use was part of a broader condition of the insanity, also lasted less than a week.[95] On the fourth admission, Dr. T.E. received longer-term care. The admission records identified addiction as the main reason for his condition: he was taking morphine and stimulants and had reached the considerable dosage of 30 grains a day, administered hypodermically. His fourth stay lasted nearly three weeks. Whether this treatment worked is unclear, although Dr. T.E. did not return in the next eighteen months for which we have records.[96] Other addictions were also apparent after repeated visits. Sarah M. arrived at Toronto from Homewood, supposedly relieved of the chloral hydrate addiction for which she had entered that institution.[97] She returned to the Toronto Asylum to be treated specifically for her addiction at least three more times.

Whereas physicians in other provinces had recognized and learned to treat opium habits by the turn of the century, things were different in British Columbia. Familiarity with opium use among both Chinese and non-Chinese residents, along with the general attention to opium habituation in the media and in politics, may have caused asylum staff to pay careful attention to the conditions of opium use and its treatment. We have already seen how Chinese patients were linked to the habit of opium smoking, even though it appears that their mental distress was deeper; in non-Chinese patients, opium use was also found, and its treatment suggests a sophisticated understanding of how opium addiction should be addressed. Consider, for example, the August 1899 arrival of the twenty-eight-year-old physician Dr. I.M. The remote cause of his condition was "the excessive use of morphia for some years," and the recent cause was a double addiction to "cocaine & morphia in excessive amounts." The name of his diagnosed disease was "morphinism & cocaine poisoning." Dr. I.M. gave himself up to the police authorities in the interior mining and railway town of Revelstoke "because he felt the necessity for restraint as he had tried to control his habits of taking morphine and cocaine and was unable. This seems to have been his sole trouble." He had been taking up to 30 grains of both morphine and cocaine a day, and when he arrived at the asylum, he had reduced his consumption to 10 grains. He was fully equipped, having brought with him several packets of morphine and a bottle that had contained a 4 percent solution of cocaine. The records describe the gradual withdrawal from both substances, although it may not have been gradual enough, for in under a week they had reduced his intake to about 2 grains of morphine and 2 grains of cocaine, and he suffered cramps and poor sleep. Unfortunately, the records for this case are incomplete, being continued in a casebook that is no longer available.[98]

By the turn of the century, drug use had begun to emerge as a viable diagnostic category for admission to the state-run lunatic asylum but generally only when it manifested itself in socially disruptive behaviour. Although doctors differed in assessing how to treat addiction and what sort of damage it could wreak on the individual's mental apparatus, they increasingly recognized that addiction alone was a form of mental disorder and could potentially benefit from the treatment provided by the state-run asylum. As asylum physicians carved out their domain of authority from the broader field of medicine, they enforced their role in determining the proper care and treatment of mental deviance and reinforced the need for expanded authority for the medical profession. The experience of doctors at the asylums, however, should not suggest that addiction had become a widespread social concern, since the patients who arrived at the gates of the hospitals were individuals whose condition had become extreme enough to disrupt the family and the community. Addiction slowly became a problem that many expected the state to control because apparently addicts could not control themselves.

In the asylum, addiction presented a further means for physicians to demonstrate their essential role in guiding and protecting social development and the integrity of the nation. Not only was mental alienation a growing problem, they argued, but inherited and developed mental damage (characterized by the diathesis) would also result in socially deviant behaviour like drug and alcohol consumption. Habitual substance use would subsequently cause further damage to the physical, mental, and moral fabric of the individual. Since the addicts who appeared at the asylums often came from the middle or upper classes, their cases reinforced the interpretation of a potential threat to the integrity of the nation. Although the numbers were low, the severity of family upheaval and the apparent solution to the problem – getting rid of the drug – made the issue immediate and socially significant. Nationalistic justifications for state control of the addict became enmeshed with broader justifications for the control of pathological social deviance. These arguments were likely bolstered by an upper-class belief that elites were particularly susceptible to drug addiction due to the fragile organization of their more sophisticated mental faculties.

Since investigations into the causes of addiction began increasingly to centre on the physical causes wrought by drugs themselves, the experience of asylum physicians provided further validation of state-centred control of drug addiction and eventually drug prohibition. As the nineteenth century ended and the twentieth century began, concerns over drug addiction were integrated into a broader discourse of national and social integrity, which permeated policy arguments and decisions at both the provincial and national levels. The place of drug use in the etiology of insanity, treatable under the auspices of the state institutional system, fed into a discourse that equated mental dysfunction with social danger and conversely viewed confining or curing the insane with social elevation. Prophylactic means of dealing with detrimental misuse of drugs could therefore contribute to a more expansive program of social elevation. Improving society and defending its integrity required vigilance over the causes of debasement. Since drug use, unlike masturbation, was a behaviour directly related to a commodity, one way to reduce or even eliminate insanity resulting from drug use was to strictly control the sale of drugs. In the next chapter, I examine how the potential danger of drug addiction informed and reinforced arguments over the regulation of the patent medicine trade and how this debate affected the initial legislation to prohibit the sale and use of opium for nonmedical purposes.

7
Proprietary Medicines and the Nation's Health

By the last decades of the century, the streams of unease feeding ideas about habitual drug use had begun to merge into a river of worry that would cascade into panic as the next century opened. The perceived infiltration of the Chinese opium smoker into Canadian life, the reframing of habituation as something that should be treated medically, professional lobbying to pass laws ostensibly to protect the public from dangerous substances, and the asylum-based recognition of addiction as a deviance worthy of social concern all informed turn-of-the-century discussions of drug use and addiction. As a result, physicians, pharmacists, legislators, and the general public began to explore the best way to control access to and use of these substances.

It was not a simple issue, however. Opium and its derivatives, especially morphine, remained common, even essential, medications. Notwithstanding the potential for habit, physicians had few other palliatives for many of the pains and conditions of modern life. Although the emerging pharmaceutical industry, led by the innovations in German dye manufactories, began to offer up new chemical treatments for a variety of illnesses (such as Phenacetin, mentioned in the records of physician William Reinhardt of Vernon, British Columbia, soon after it was introduced to the market), opiates remained fundamental to medical practice. Moreover, cocaine, one of the newest medical innovations, was also becoming rapidly problematized. Cocaine offered tremendous value in treating a variety of illnesses, especially catarrh (nasal inflammation and discharge), as well as functioning as a remarkably effective topical anaesthetic for surgeries. Doctors also tried to use it in treating opiate addiction, which was ultimately an ironically bad choice. Soon cocaine found a place among what we would now call recreational drugs. It, along with the opium derivative heroin, which Bayer began to market at the end of the century, joined opium and morphine as problematic habitual drugs.

Complicating the issue further was the limited effectiveness of pharmaceutical legislation in controlling the distribution of and access to proprietary substances. Although provincial pharmaceutical legislation, which was in effect in all provinces and territories except Prince Edward Island by the middle of the 1890s, made it relatively easy to add substances to the poison schedules and thereby restrict their distribution, this legislation was limited to specified compounds. Consequently, there were several avenues people could take to access restricted drugs without breaking the law. The expansion of the patent and proprietary medicines industry was central to this approach. (The labels "patent" and "proprietary" were used interchangeably, although many of these products were proprietary in their nature but were not patented.) These terms refer to a wide variety of products, from standardized preparations of well-known medications, such as tinctures of opium; to remedies with unknown ingredients that targeted a specific condition, such as cough syrups and pain killers (likely containing opium); to the dubious nostrums advertised in newspapers that claimed to heal every illness.[1] Regulating these substances was terribly tricky since the former products were legitimate medicines of reliable strength prepared by respectable businesses, the latter products offered hope to the desperate, and the substances in the middle often did precisely what they claimed, although the secrecy of their recipes made them questionable.[2]

Then there were the various vested interests involved in the patent medicine trade. *Proprietary* medicines were literally the stock in trade of major medical manufacturers, like Montreal's Lyman Brothers Company, Detroit's Parke-Davis and Company, and numerous smaller wholesale manufacturers, which often had their roots in a relatively modest neighbourhood pharmacy. Physicians often appreciated the reliability of many of these substances, both the standardized tinctures and also, at times, more "secret" remedies like Lydia Pinkham's Pills or Browne's Chlorodyne. Newspapers were loath to print articles that criticized proprietary medicines. Peruse *any* issue of the *Toronto Globe* newspaper before the beginning of the 1900s on which advertising appears, and you will find ads for a variety of proprietary medicines. Finally, and significantly, proprietary medicines were offered by the increasingly powerful and ubiquitous "departmental stores" like the businesses run by Timothy Eaton and Robert Simpson. These businesses advertised and sold many proprietary medicines and attempted to include a pharmacy as one of their departments. Often opposing these interests were the smaller retail druggists, whose professional status was based on their skills as compounders of medicine. The retail druggists found themselves in complicated arguments with wholesale manufacturers, who were normally fellow professional pharmacists; with physicians, who were their erstwhile allies in the professionalization process; and with the retail grocers and departmental stores, which were rapidly becoming their nemeses.

The patent medicine issue was related, then, to professional status and the ability for the two key health professions in this story, physicians and pharmacists, to protect the health of the people. And with the drug habit being considered a growing threat both to individual health and to the integrity of the nation, it informed many discussions about the availability of and attempts to restrict access to medicine. Doctors and pharmacists looked at their own practices, at the public's means of acquiring dangerous substances, and at the types of new drugs available to define the types of substances that needed to be under their professional control. Being intended both to manage the image of their profession and to protect the health of the people (the two ideas were intertwined), their actions reflected a different kind of governmentality. Professional bodies attempted to conduct the conduct of professional brethren, of course, but also to affect the actions of those outside the professional purview who infringed on the legislated territory of doctors and druggists. The pharmacists' and physicians' efforts were hampered by the complexity of the issue and by the fact that neither group could agree about the scope of the problem or the best course of action to address it.

By the beginning of the twentieth century, commentators increasingly drew the public's attention to the dangers of the patent medicine trade. Despite these warnings from some doctors and pharmacists about secret nostrums, the public continued to use proprietary medicines, and the industry remained relatively unchecked until the first decades of the twentieth century. Although the *Ladies' Home Journal* had been vocally opposed to the secret-remedy business since ceasing to accept patent medicine ads in 1892, the most notorious publicity against proprietary medicines came in a series of articles by reformer Samuel Hopkins Adams called "The Great American Fraud."[3] These articles first appeared in *Collier's Weekly* in 1905 and continued until 1907. Canadian commentators discussed Adams's and others' "muckraking" revelations.[4] Nevertheless, although this series likely inspired the growing urgency in the drive for Canadian legislation, Canadian doctors and druggists had been urging government intervention long before 1905.[5] Indeed, as we saw in Chapter 3, an early draft of the Ontario Pharmacy Act of 1871 included restrictions on patent medicines.

The emergence of legislative concerns over the relatively unrestricted access to and use of addictive and dangerous drugs in proprietary medicines began at the provincial level and then shifted to the Dominion Parliament. The Proprietary or Patent Medicine Act of 1908 was passed in the same session of Parliament as the Opium Act of 1908, and as we will see in the next two chapters, these two pieces of legislation were more intricately linked than most historians have acknowledged. The Opium Act also fitted into a broader concern over addictive drugs and dangerous substances, which in turn was related to the health of the nation. Pharmacists and physicians, attempting both to control perceptions of their profession and to protect the health of the people, persistently debated various aspects of the issue.

Neither profession was of one mind on the issue, and the debates allow us to see how the medical prescription and the product that challenged its authority – the proprietary preparation – sat on the uneasy boundary between these two professions. As they sought to conduct the conduct of their own profession and to constrain the problematic behaviour of those outside their professional purview, the physicians and pharmacists careened through hazardous rapids toward the dark water of national drug regulation. This chapter explores the issues surrounding the expansion of the patent medicine industry and its relationship to the medical and pharmaceutical professions. The next chapter charts the push, first at the provincial level and later at the federal, to restrict the sale of proprietary medicines.

Defining a Problem

Medical professionals' growing concern over public use of patent or proprietary medicines coincided with changes in doctors' therapeutic practices and in the business of pharmacy. Concerned about the apparently ineffective drugs that their predecessors had used so extensively and faced with a therapeutic skepticism from their confreres and their patients, physicians looked for new means of treatment.[6] Many doctors began to rely on milder, less "heroic" therapies, while also finding in the expansion of their pharmaceutical colleagues' chemical and scientific knowledge a more refined understanding, if you pardon the pun, of the benefits of some drugs, including opiates. The elusiveness of the nature of opiates expressed by Dr. F.A. Fluckiger in 1870 began to fade as analysis and refinement procedures became more advanced.

These chemical advancements were both fuelled by and caused changes in the business of the druggist. By the turn of the century, the pharmacy was no longer characterized by the traditional small shop with a drug compounder and apprentice. Some pharmacists, most of whom became successful in larger communities, gradually expanded their business. Some pharmacists, like Victoria's Thomas Shotbolt, opened new stores around the city. Other drug retailers, like the businesses of Montreal's Lyman family and of W.W. Bole in Moosejaw, expanded from smaller companies into large national firms. The Lyman Brothers Company eventually merged with several others to form the the National Drug and Chemical Company (a move lauded by many pharmacists as a step toward rationalizing an out-of-control competitive pharmaceutical system).[7] Similarly, B.A. Mitchell of London was bought by the London Chemical Company. Still others remained smaller but also expanded their reach. All such companies tapped into broadening transportation and communication networks, which were made more substantial as rail and telegraph service expanded across the country. The invoices of Stratford's J.H. Nasmyth and Company Pharmacy from the 1870s and 1880s illustrate well this network. Nasmyth and Co. received products from firms in Windsor, London, Waterloo, Toronto, Montreal, and cities across the United States. It also purchased from British firms, usually through Canadian representatives. Indeed, some of the Canadian sellers were well-known names to the Canadian pharmacy business, being founded or co-owned by prominent pharmacists intricately involved in the pharmaceutical profession: along with the aforementioned Lyman Brothers and B.A. Mitchell, wholesalers selling to Nasmyth included William Saunders (London, Ontario); Evans, Sons and Mason (Montreal and Toronto); Davis and Lawrence (Montreal); and Elliot and Company (Toronto). The products that these companies sold ranged from standard prescription ingredients such as opium, quinine, morphine, gum camphor, and potassium bromide to substances of dubious provenance such as "Shiloh's Consumption Cure" and "Fountain of Health."[8]

Nasmyth's business was typical of what was going on in small towns across the country. By the end of the century, the small, individually owned pharmacies in which druggists compounded medicines for the patient were selling more ready-made products while also competing with large drug firms that served a variety of everyday needs of the customer, from cosmetics to fountain soda. Drug compounding was a small part of a large business. Nasmyth's invoices, for example, included many dry good and grocery products beyond the normal scope of pharmacy: combs, jars, baskets, and various manufactured "Indian" goods. Discussing the growth of the patent medicine trade in 1906, Toronto physician John Hunter reminded his audience that "twenty or thirty years ago the drug store was practically a medical laboratory, and the druggist ... belonged to the learned professions ... [Now he] must be a man of business aptitude and training ... The dispensing of prescriptions is only an incidental part of the commercial enterprise." Hunter was not amused; his was a criticism of the dangers of corporate pharmacy, where individual attention to customers/patients was in decline, and the individual's health could be threatened. With the compounding of prescriptions now the responsibility of a clerk, safety was compromised:

> During the one, two or three, hours the clerk is at work on a doctor's prescription he serves many swains and their sweet-hearts with ice cream sodas, washes the tumblers and spoons, selects the best brands of cigars for young and old sports, sells brushes, nursing bottles; in short, everything pertaining to the needs, fads, or fancies of the nursery, bath or lady's boudoir ... Is not the commercial spirit the most dominant and rampant factor in pharmacy and therapeutics?[9]

Even the part of the business that still involved the sale of medicines, the actual compounding of remedies, which was once the cornerstone of the pharmacist's claim to professional credibility, often became secondary to selling proprietary substances. Indeed, the delineation between respectable and disrespectable company was not based on the products they sold. Wholesale manufacturers of patent medicines could also become agents for international brands. For example, the header of the invoice for Northrop and Lyman boasted that the company, based in Toronto, was "Wholesale Agents for Most of the Popular Patent Medicines of the Day." Among their products were the who's who (or what's what) of secret remedies, including Ayers Cherry Pectoral, Holloway's Pills, Radways Ready Relief, and Kennedy's Discovery, as well as various hair balms, salves, and beef extracts.[10]

Although the network of distribution was expanding along with the product lines, patent and proprietary medicines were not new to late-nineteenth-century medical practice. Physicians had relied on numerous proprietary preparations for decades; not the least among them was Dover's Powder, a therapeutically versatile mixture of opium and ipecac first compounded by Thomas Dover in 1732.[11] We saw Dover's being used in a significant proportion of the prescriptions written by Dr. Thomas Geddes of Pictou, Nova Scotia. Even laudanum, or tincture of opium, bore the marks of a proprietary preparation. The form of laudanum made popular by Thomas Sydenham in the seventeenth century, a mixture of opium, brandy, cinnamon, cloves, saffron, and other spices, was both a valuable medicine and potentially a substance for leisurely nonmedical consumption.[12] Thomas De Quincey, Samuel Taylor Coleridge, and Wilkie Collins were addicted primarily to laudanum, and notable Romantic writers like Percy Shelley, John Keats, Sir Walter Scott, and Lord Byron purportedly used laudanum, although whether they were addicted is unclear.[13]

By the turn of the nineteenth century, patent and proprietary medicines had changed significantly and were taking a larger role in medical practice.[14] In 1903 Andrew Macphail, the editor of the *Montreal Medical Journal,* distinguished between potentially useful proprietary medicines and dubious "secret" proprietaries. The former, he observed tautologically, is a "preparation which is proprietary," manufactured by a specific company, but the ingredients of which the manufacturer made clear. Identifying a specific brand name of a "tincture of opium" or "nitrous spirits of ether" enabled physicians to avoid the uncertainty engendered by the growing number of pharmaceutical manufacturers plying their wares since they could ask for a brand name that they trusted.[15] They could then be assured that patients were being treated with a reliable substance.

Macphail used official reports to support his claim that the quality and consistency of the products manufactured by large pharmaceutical firms would be a boon to medicine. In 1899, a public inspector for the Department of Inland Revenue issued a routine analytical bulletin (which became the notorious "Bulletin 60") outlining the results of an analysis of samples of tincture of opium obtained at pharmacies throughout southwestern

Ontario. He found that 50 percent of the samples were below the standard set by the British pharmacopoeia, and all but one had come from a neighbourhood pharmacy. The one that was obtained from a wholesaler was found to be properly compounded.[16] Macphail's article, written four years later, drew on several analytical bulletins released over the past few decades. Along with Bulletin 60, the Department of Inland Revenue had issued Bulletin 34 that studied "Compound Tincture of Gentian, of Cardamoms, Camphor, Myrrh, Rhubarb, Calumba, Ginger, Squills, Jalap, Arnica and Buchu."[17] All examinations found notable adulteration, in some cases up to 60% of products analyzed. Bulletin 77, released in 1901, was a nationwide study looking at a relatively new preparation, effervescent Sodium Phosphate, finding that only 20%, 13 of 64 preparations, were made correctly.[18] "Nearly all were below the standard in Sodium Phosphate, some were carelessly compounded, some adulterated with Magnesium Sulphate, and many deteriorated with age."[19] Macphail used these results to argue that, since preparations made by druggists were not reliable, the existence of brand-name preparations enabled physicians to base their reputation on that of the firm. "If a physician thinks that a preparation of opium, manufactured by a certain firm, is better than any other, he may prescribe that it be drawn from the stock manufactured by that firm."[20] Possibly most troubling for pharmacists: the Bulletins listed the names of the pharmacies from which all samples were obtained, and the results of each study. These were not fly-by-night operations: some of the pharmacists were big names in the pharmaceutical fraternity.

Such statements touched raw nerves among retail pharmacists, who saw many of these same proprietary preparations as undermining the authority and acumen of their profession. Pharmacists based much of their main professional identity on their skill as compounders of prescriptions and as the gatekeepers of dangerous drugs. To be circumvented by prepackaged versions of drugs that they could make up themselves undermined this professional identity. Indeed, many by the 1890s would anticipate Hunter's lament about the changing character of the pharmacy business. However, they would not be issuing it as a criticism of their pharmacy confreres but as a challenge to physicians, many of whom pharmacists saw as undermining pharmacists and disrespecting pharmacy as an honourable profession. When in 1895 the *Ontario Medical Journal* accused druggists of being responsible for the sale of proprietary medicines, William Dyas, editor of the *Canadian Druggist,* was livid, saying that the arguments and evidence "are so weak that it might be allowed to pass without criticism, but the frequency with which articles of a similar kind ... appear in medical journals ... makes it advisable that some notice should be taken." The *Druggist* turned the issue around, arguing that the glut of physicians in the countryside was responsible for the increase in patent medicines. In 1897, the *Canadian*

Pharmaceutical Journal published an article by physician J.T. Fotheringham that expressed a contrasting, pharmacists-friendly view of the relationship between doctors and druggists. Fotheringham noted that the retail druggist "is the one on whose probity and accuracy we [physicians] must rely for our success ... the centralization of trade in the hands of large manufacturing houses is slowly driving him to the wall, and we help in that process every time we prescribe a proprietary article."[21] The *Canadian Druggist*'s Montreal correspondent complained in 1899 about physicians who are "always growling at the pharmacists." Yet, the correspondent asked, why is it that "these high-toned gentlemen do not appeal to the College of Physicians to put a stop to [duly licensed] physicians ... being proprietors or shareholders in some of the worst quack medicine, advertised in a most unblushing manner, and sold broadcast all over the Dominion?"[22]

Some doctors suggested that the growth in the sale of patent medicines was the fault of "our weak-kneed friend, the druggist," who, by repeating prescriptions and selling patent medicines that could be dangerous, helped the patient to avoid a doctor's fee.[23] They were alluding to a reported practice by which a pharmacist, finding that a physician's prescription had been especially helpful to a specific condition, would take the recipe, make it up in large quantities, and sell it to his or her customers, sometimes as an alternative to a doctor's written prescription or even sometimes without the patient first consulting a physician at all. In contrast to blame being placed on pharmacists, the *Canadian Pharmaceutical Journal* reprinted an article from the *California State Journal of Medicine* that defended pharmacists against the attacks by doctors:

> There is hardly a pharmacist in the country who would not gladly rid himself of half his stock of clap trap stuff, if he could; but the physician will not let him, because, forsooth, he does not know enough about his own profession to know what he is making the druggist do. If doctors would cease prescribing patent medicines, the pharmacists would no longer have to stock them.[24]

This statement suggests that we need to be cautious when looking at records like those of Stratford's Nasmyth. We do not know where the demand for so many products originated: was it the customer, the doctor, or the convincing sales person?

Although clearly the blame could be cast in both directions, druggists were aware that they needed to keep the physicians on their side. When Dyas of the *Canadian Druggist* responded to the *Ontario Medical Journal*'s accusations, he called for professional collegiality in the interest of the good of society: "Let us ... work harmoniously together, as we should do, each keeping as much as possible within his own limits, and be co-laborers in the main aim and end of both professions – the relief of the suffering and cure of the diseased."[25] Eight years later, Dyas noted that the pharmacist needed to work to ensure that the physician was aware of the quality and integrity of the local pharmacy, apparently by boring him with sycophancy:

> The thing to strive for is his good opinion of your store, your methods, and above all, your reliability. Speak about the care exercised in the preparation of galenicals, dwell upon the purity of your chemicals, call attention to your stock of gauze, cotton, bandages and antiseptic dressings; state your willingness to make up his private formulae and keep the preparations in stock for his prescriptions.[26]

For pharmacists, good relationships with physicians were fundamental to business success. As the evidence from many pharmacies' records suggest, however, so was the stocking of many proprietary preparations.

Clearly, debates over proprietary medicines were multifaceted and drove different fissures into professional ranks since physicians and pharmacists disagreed among themselves about the utility or danger of these substances and their availability to the general public. Macphail may have been enthusiastic about reliable forms of familiar remedies such as the tincture of opium tested by the Dominion analyst, but the problems with proprietary medicines eclipsed the simple convenience of obtaining a tincture of opium in the correct proportions. Most proprietary medicines were secret, they were easily obtainable outside of the pharmacy, and they therefore denied a physician and a pharmacist the fee for prescribing and dispensing. Yet many pharmacists also compounded their own versions of popular medicines, many often renamed as a cough remedy or painkiller, with the recipes kept secret. Other pharmacists, such as those from whom Nasmyth ordered many of his products, were building their business on eponymous proprietary medicines, such as West's Cough Syrup, from John C. West Company. In 1901, the owner of Merrill's Drug Store in Brantford, Ontario, found that the sales of his preparations "Merrill's Four Ts" and "Merrill's System Tonic" were growing beyond his capacity to make them. He advertised for a business manager who would help him to keep up with the demand.[27]

Yet some physicians were not entirely opposed to secret remedies as long as the companies were trustworthy and their business methods were reputable. In 1906, the editors of the *Dominion Medical Monthly*, commenting on agitation against secret remedies containing dangerous drugs, observed that "formerly, proprietary articles were looked upon with favor by the medical profession, and could, consequently, be styled as ethical." Ethical preparations "were made expressly for the dispensation of the [medical] profession, and were in no way advertised to or brought before the people at large." Lately, the editors noted, a movement had begun to style as "unethical" any preparation whose manufacturer kept the recipe secret. In response to calls for legislation requiring such manufacturers to place the entire recipe of the remedy on the label, thereby informing physicians and patients of what was inside, the editors balked: "We remain so far unconvinced that it has been wrong to use these [secret] preparations; for we have seen many times prescriptions [by physicians] which when compounded would floor their master to tell what form the combinations took when it had entered the stomach of his patient and what its therapeutic effect would be."[28] According to these doctors, many physicians were unable to write a useful prescription, so proprietary medicines might permit physicians to free themselves from their own ignorance. The status of the profession would benefit from the uniformity of prescription medicine, and the public would benefit from improved health.

In this view, ethical proprietary medicines helped physicians to do their job better, but in most discussions physicians saw proprietary medicines as hindering their ability to protect the health of the people, if not actually doing real physical damage. Doctors felt that their influence was limited because people could, and did, self-medicate. It did not matter whether these substances were manufactured by (questionable) companies, published in volumes like *Dr. Chase's Recipes*, or transmitted through oral tradition: it was all self-medication and therefore, to the physicians, replete with problems. The *Maritime Medical News* often printed articles in which doctors scratched their heads over why the public did not trust the medical profession.[29] Most astonishing to them was the fact that many people seemed to prefer the patent medicine "quack" or "charlatan" over the educated doctor. Although doctors lost business, the biggest loser, they argued, was the public. "Pharmacy and the medical profession are injured by this open system of quackery, but not one fraction of the extent of injury that is inflicted upon the public by the sale of these secret nostrums," wrote R. MacNeill, president of the Maritime Medical Association in 1899.[30] This rejection by the public was more startling because, doctors argued, the medical profession was most capably armed to protect the public's health.

Physicians had to strike a balance between their role as guardians of the public health and their economic and professional interests. They worried that people would believe that doctors who opposed unrestricted patent medicine sales were merely hoping to strengthen their economic power rather than acting in the interest of the public. John Fulton, the editor of the *Canada Lancet*, sought to overturn this charge when he declared that physicians were the only people "in a position to fully comprehend the magnitude of this ever-growing evil." He argued that an inquiry into the selfless actions of physicians need look no further than the numerous positions that physicians held: "We are continually making strenuous exertions in the public interest against disease in many ways, and devoting our time and talents often gratuitously to hospitals, homes, asylums, infirmaries, boards of health, etc. ... Therefore we claim credence and confidence when our advice is given."[31] Physician J.T. Fotheringham, who had defended pharmacists' integrity in the *Canadian Pharmaceutical Journal,* wrote that prescribing patent medicines undermined the physician's profession because he was subsuming his professional skill beneath the commercial interests of a "layman": "The man, I had almost said physician, prescribing them is making himself the agent of a layman, allowing the layman to use him for selfish ends and not for the good of the patient."[32] Likewise, Dr. John Hunter of Toronto wrote that "the preservation of life is a sacred trust, committed to the individual, to society, to the nation, and to the race. Any act that imperils it unlawfully is a crime."[33] To Hunter, proprietary medicines were "a stain on the medical profession" precisely because the medical profession should have been able to stop their proliferation and thereby protect the health of the people.[34] Although they stood to gain more control over the medical treatment of the nation, doctors argued that eliminating the threats posed by unscrupulous and uncontrolled medicine vendors would be a significant benefit to the public.

Critics of the patent medicine trade contrasted the idea of the doctor's honourable calling with denigrating images of the patent medicine vendor. These images painted the vendor as inferior by class, profession, and occasionally race.[35] In 1902, the *Canada Lancet* argued against proprietary medicines containing "stimulants and interdicted drugs," noting that "any one, a carpenter, a stableman, a farmer, a blacksmith, or a scrubwoman, for example, may put up compounds."[36] In 1893, the *Toronto News* argued that the government needed to enact some form of legislation. The editor noted that, whereas a doctor had to undertake years of education, "here we find a blacksmith on the one hand patenting a narcotic that is to insure baby's sleeping well, while on the other hand a shoe maker or a railway navvy [patents] the sure cure' for consumption."[37] In 1899, during special committee hearings on patent medicines in Quebec, Professor J. Morrison warned that unless pharmacy was protected, prescriptions could be made up by a "cook or coachman" instead of a druggist.[38] Morrison's class-based argument extended to racial concern. As the editor of the *Canadian Pharmaceutical Journal,* he told his readers about "an Indian of the Caughnawagas" who was marketing "Dr. White-Cloud's No-Dac Pain Reliever."[39] The man's modus operandi was cleverly deceptive: he would send a bogus order to a druggist for the substance (of which the druggist had never heard) and then arrive at the place of business a few days after the order, posing as a legitimate trader to sell this new cure, which was obviously in demand. Morrison suggested that the reader "keep a good hefty club on hand for the entertainment of all such redskin swindlers, and when they call invite them out into the back yard to attend a seance."[40] In 1900, Dr. D. MacKintosh, president of the Medical Society of Nova Scotia, suggested a racial aspect to the danger of patent medicines when he criticized the mysticism and nonscientific nature of medicines advertised "by the picture of a Red Indian with feathers in his head."[41] Owing to the danger posed by lower-class, uneducated, and occasionally nonwhite swindlers, ran the arguments, the sale of patent medicines needed to be restricted.

The professional, racial, and class-based imagery paralleled arguments about the actual physical effects of patent medicines on the health of the people. Not only did these products contain unknown and potentially dangerous drugs, but the science of medicine required a more nuanced understanding of the specific condition under which the individual suffered before jumping to a therapeutic conclusion. Mackintosh contrasted the mystical and mysterious allure of "quack" remedies with the pragmatic work of the medical profession. In contrast to the extravagant claims of patent medicine vendors, doctors could identify diseases only "after patient waiting and watching." The physician's role was scientific, empirical, and interactive: "learn [the patient's] peculiarities, adapt our treatment to the conditions as they arise." Sometimes, Mackintosh reminded his readers, all the doctor could do was make the patient's final hours bearable.[42] Even this recognition of medicine as part of a scientific process did not always lead to success. The editors of the *Maritime Medical News* stated that people would avoid dubious patent medicines if they "only realized how difficult it is at times for even the best trained physicians to decide upon the best course of medication."[43] Likewise, Victoria physician C.J. Fagan noted, even educated physicians could make mistakes in their prescriptions: "The question as to when, how, and how much is to be given in each individual case, is often a perplexing one even to the medical attendant."[44] How, these doctors argued, could self-medication avoid some of the pitfalls into which properly trained physicians sometimes stumbled?

Pharmacists also had mixed feelings about patent medicines. Some, like Joseph Constant, the president of the Pharmaceutical Association of Quebec, was uncategorically critical. "Patent medicines are a curse to the physician, the pharmacist and the public," he argued in an address to the association in 1895.

> They are an unjust and direct opposition to the physician by preventing the sick from obtaining proper advice; they deprive the pharmacist of the sale of his own preparations, and force him to keep in stock a large number of preparations which have only a limited sale; and they are injurious to the public, which, allowing itself to be cajoled by the certificates of cure, which are the complement of the advertisements, purchase the famous remedy, which often does more injury than good.[45]

In the *Canadian Pharmaceutical Journal,* a correspondent calling himself "Medicus" couched the pharmacists' opposition to patent medicines as being in sympathy with the view of physicians, who were losing business, just as were the retail druggists. He predicted that both professions would suffer. "Unless something is done to cause an awakening," he argued, "in ten years from now the doctor will not know how to write a prescription for his patient, from his own knowledge of medicines, but will be using patent nostrums, of certain manufacturers who now play him, as well as the druggist, for a sucker, while the druggist ... will not require any knowledge of dispensing, as there will be no use for it." Medicus placed the onus on the pharmacists to enlighten physicians to the evil: "We druggists are in a position to take each and every doctor into our private sanctum, and show them the large amount of patent medicine business being done, and the number of cases we might have sent to him had he treated us, as he should, by writing prescriptions ... show him, also, reasons why he should support the druggist at home, instead of Physicians' Supply Houses," which were large wholesale drug businesses.[46]

Yet proprietaries were not entirely problematic to pharmacists either. As noted earlier, many pharmacists sold their own proprietary medicines, and many of the executives of various pharmaceutical councils and colleges were the heads of growing drug-manufacturing firms. The *Canadian Pharmaceutical Journal* published glowing reports of the banquet held by the Proprietary Association and often editorialized positively on the growth of the proprietary business.[47] Even Merrill's Pharmacy of Brantford found that its trade in eponymous proprietaries was boosting sales, leading to the aforementioned ad for a business manager. So the pharmaceutical press walked a fine line between supporting restrictions on proprietary medicines in order to protect the people and opposing such restrictions in order to protect the free market. Indeed, as we will see, when it came to legislating restrictions on proprietary drugs, the divisions within pharmacists' ranks caused setbacks and even outright reversals in the fortunes of pharmacists.

By the 1890s, however, the discussions about proprietary remedies involved a new player, one who was of deep concern to pharmacists. Previously, the relationship was positioned as one between pharmacist, physician, and patient, but in the 1890s new, large "departmental stores" like the Timothy Eaton Company and the Robert Simpson Company complicated the situation.[48] These large, multifaceted stores, which were located on prime retail real estate in the centre of cities like Toronto and Montreal, had the purchasing power to negotiate discounts with the wholesale drug companies and proprietary medicine manufacturers. Consequently, in several provinces pharmacists began to push back against what they saw as encroachment on their legislated territory. Several high-profile prosecutions resulted in mixed outcomes and often in appeals to higher courts in order to determine whether the type of sales undertaken by these departmental stores contravened the pharmacy acts.

Departmental stores were triple threats to the pharmacists. First, they attempted to sell drugs that the pharmacists believed should be the purview only of licensed pharmacists. Second, they were thereby drawing people into their stores and away from associated product lines such as toiletries and perfumes that were often featured in pharmacies and often essential to the survival of a drug store. Finally, and most crucially to the business of pharmacy, the departmental stores engaged in the practice of price cutting, which the pharmaceutical press spit out like an obscenity as "cutting." It had become a scourge of the competitive retail sector by the last quarter of the century.

The rise of the departmental store cast in sharp relief the distinction between the nobility of the medical professional and the dangers of competitive capitalism. As the druggists' advocates were quick to remind anyone willing to pay attention to them, departmental stores were not interested in selling patent medicines for the sake of healing the public; they wanted to offer them at deeply discounted rates simply to draw customers into the stores. A letter in 1887 to the *Canadian Pharmaceutical Journal* signed "HGE" outlined the issues that would continue to reappear in subsequent discussions: the future of the pharmaceutical profession, the honourability of the trade, and the degradation that cheap drugs could cause the profession and the public at large:

> It is far from being encouraging to a young man engaged in the drug business, to walk into a grocery and see poisons and drugs handed out at prices lower than he can afford to sell, and regardless of any registration. They have their own business, and if motives of principle will not incite them to act fairly, I think some action should be taken to compel a recognition of our rights. If we retaliate it is by making a farce of our profession by handling goods far from our line.[49]

When legislation was proposed in Quebec to allow department stores to sell patents, the *Canadian Druggist* argued that this was a simple but debasing business strategy that had nothing to do with the health or safety of the people: "Of course the departmental stores only want patent medicines for advertising purposes, and their great point will be to advertise the most popular ones at about cost."[50] Such tactics were fundamentally at odds with the noble calling of pharmacy.

Pharmacists had the recourse of their legislation, but its effectiveness was limited. By 1892, the *Canadian Druggist* was calling on the Ontario College of Pharmacy to deal with the issue, noting that department stores selling patent medicines appeared to violate the legislation, which "has been framed

for the protection of the druggist as well as the general public." It argued
that the college should charge one of the offenders in a test case "to see
whether the Pharmacy Act does not apply."[51] The issue usually related to
how the provincial legislation defined a pharmacy and to whether a pharmacy had to be owned by a licensed pharmacist or whether only the compounders and dispensers of drugs needed to be licensed. A month later, the
Druggist told of pharmacists in London, Ontario, taking a merchant to court
for selling a poison (they reached a settlement).[52] In October, the lead story
for the *Druggist* was about the finding against the T. Eaton Company for
breaching the Pharmacy Act by selling Browne's Chlorodyne and Boschee's
German Syrup. The sale of the latter product had resulted in a child dying
from poisoning.[53] J.N. Woodward of Vancouver was not so sure that legislation could stop the departmental stores. He argued that in the modern era,
pharmacists' "old-time method of charging seventy-five cents for a prescription, fifty cents for time, and twenty-five cents for a good average profit on
drug and bottle, will have to be substituted for the honester [*sic*] and better
method of charging twenty-five cents for the same." To Woodward, protection would not do; he believed that pharmacists had to compete freely,
using whatever trade tactics they could. He blamed druggists for this situation since "no legislature would prohibit [the departmental stores] trading
in drugs, and as long as there are druggists whose avarice and cupidity are
greater than their professional honour, so long will we have to compete ...
which virtually means annihilation to the drug trade."[54] As we will see below,
the ability for pharmacy acts to effectively curtail the sale of proprietary
medicines was limited and contested.

One of the strategies that pharmacists used to address the problems they
perceived from the patent medicine trade was to unite in municipal, provincial, and national retail druggists associations, such as the National Association of Retail Druggists in the United States and the Ontario Society of
Retail Druggists. The rhetoric of these associations demonstrates the conflicted nature of the self-perception of the pharmacist as a professional. For
the most part, the retail druggist associations sought to push back against
what they considered unfair practices by large manufacturers and larger retail
vendors, including departmental stores. Fighting the big departmental stores,
retail pharmacists reiterated the role of pharmacists in protecting their customers. They argued that departmental stores were making dangerous drugs
available without the proper screening and recordkeeping embedded in the
spirit, if not the letter, of the pharmacy acts. Yet in other cases, the retail
druggists sought to address specific financial arrangements that had little
to do with the health of the public and that may even be considered to have
run contrary to a sense of public well-being. For example, these organizations targeted both the proliferation of cheap proprietaries sold by large
manufacturers and price cutting on prescriptions and other goods in highly

competitive environments. The latter practice was sometimes blamed on competitive individual pharmacists but more often on overly hungry sales-people for the wholesale drug firms and proprietary manufacturers, who were trying to get as much product into the stores as possible and to move as much through as possible. Although the retail druggists occasionally suggested that the result was substandard prescriptions, more often they argued that these practices simply undermined the fiscal health of individual drug stores, not the health of the people.

Self-interest and selflessness might be rhetorically intertwined (keep small pharmacies financially viable to avoid dangerous prescribing practices), but they were discursively distinct. A pharmacy that placed its self-interest first may have a hard time arguing that this self-interest in all things was actually for the benefit of the health of the individual. This was especially a challenging disjunction since large pharmaceutical companies were producing standardized products, like various popular tinctures, using increasingly advanced quality-control methods. Thus, when the 1899 and 1903 reports of the Dominion Analytical Chemist found that common remedies compounded by individual retail pharmacists were often less reliable than mass-manufactured versions of the same remedies, the retail druggists' arguments about purity and safety rang hollow.

The legal status of proprietary medicines further complicated the issue. Although the recipes were not known, most pharmacists had a good idea of some of the drugs that these products contained, especially when the drugs were things like opiates, which had discernible physical effects. Cough remedies, sleep medicines, and anti-diarrheal medicines, for example, were likely to contain opiates. Moreover, by the last decades of the century, pharmaceutical journals were in the habit of publishing their estimations of the recipes of proprietary remedies.[55] Such recipes and pharmacists' pharmacological knowledge convinced them and many physicians that these substances needed to be more consistently controlled and that their distribution should somehow be tracked. Yet, given that these were retail products, and that many came from reputable manufacturers, it was more difficult to argue convincingly that these were going to be used for intentional or unintentional poisoning, which was the main public-safety issue that advanced the first round of pharmacy laws. The definition of "dangerous substances" was broadening.

Status, National Health, and Patent Medicine Advertisements

Commentators who argued against the patent medicine trade did not just present concerns about the damage that these substances could wreak on the patient; they were also concerned about the repercussions of the unscrupulous methods of advertising.[56] Much of this concern related to how ads for the products represented physicians. Doctors, who idealized the concept that professionalism transcended the corruption of competitive capitalism, saw patent medicines ads, which used doctors' testimonials to support extravagant claims, as a challenge to medical authority. To combat this practice, the *Montreal Medical Journal* provided an illustration of how patent medicine vendors elicited testimonials from physicians regarding the effectiveness of their product. A "patent medicine man" offers a physician sample bottles of his medicine:

> He tells [the physician] what is in these bottles, being careful to suppress the quantities and the exact composition, at the same time impressing [the doctor] with the important fact that no one else can prepare this medicine ... Finally, he insinuatingly requests, as a return for the amount of the doctor's time that he has wasted[,] the small favor of a testimonial setting forth the merits of the preparation ... The wearied doctor hesitates and is lost. To get rid of his persecutor he signs.[57]

Medical associations saw this tendency to provide testimonials to patent medicine vendors as anathema and tried to put an end to the practice. The Montreal Clinical Society, for example, passed a resolution to condemn this "reprehensible" behaviour. The society would permit its members to recommend and prescribe secret remedies when they felt the remedies were effective, but they were not to be quoted or named in ads. The *Montreal Medical Journal*'s editors questioned this permission, noting that, since the recipe of a patent medicine was secret, there was no guarantee that it would remain the same.[58] Some evidence bears out this suspicion. In July 1904, for example, the *Canadian Pharmaceutical Journal* recounted the details of a libel case launched against the *Ladies' Home Journal* by the R.V. Pierce Medical Company. In an examination of the patent medicine trade, the editor of the *Ladies' Home Journal* had alluded to the existence of opiates in one of Pierce's products. After the Pierce Company threatened court action, the *Ladies' Home Journal* printed a retraction, noting that its original article had drawn on studies of the products from twenty-five years earlier. A new chemical investigation of the medicine demonstrated that its formula had changed and that it contained no opiates.[59]

Along with the trade in reliable substances came both aggressive marketing tactics and an overabundance of fraudulent substances. "We have been 'circularized,' we have been overwhelmed with 'literature,' we have been patiently waited on by 'representatives,' of this firm and of that," complained the editors of the *Montreal Medical Journal* in 1903. The problem was that doctors were being overwhelmed by such attention and could neither distinguish the good preparations from the bad nor handle the persistent harassment caused by manufacturers' advertising methods: "Frankly, we cannot do without the products of the manufacturers; we can and shall do without the products – good or bad – of those firms which push their wares with undue zeal. If they wish to adopt a suggestion, it would be, to take to heart the wisdom of hastening slowly."[60]

Despite cautions and resolutions of this sort, physicians and pharmacists continued to agitate for restriction of the growing trade. Professional integrity and the health of the people coincided with arguments against patent medicines. C.J. Fagan of Victoria, British Columbia, noted the intersection of professional and public interest when he illustrated a hypothetical case with which he figured that all physicians likely had experience. A patient, the treatment of whom occupies a great deal of the physician's time and energy, "is lured away by some glowing advertisement of alleged miraculous cures." The patient purchases "bottle after bottle, it may be case after case," of the medicine but with little improvement. "After utterly ruining his system ... [the patient] struggles back to our office, more dead than alive," and complains that he does not seem to be getting better. If subsequent attempts to cure the now even weaker condition should fail, the physician, not the patent medicine, would take the blame.[61] Fagan proceeded to introduce examples of his experiences with patients who had been duped by the claims of patent medicine vendors and, in the process, had lost money and health. He likened the morality of the business of patent medicine to highway robbery and reminded his reader that the methods of the successful patent medicine vendor centred around preying on the fears and anxieties of the sick.

Pharmacists also looked to legislation to control the dubious patent medicine trade, but they were decidedly disunited. Retail druggists hoped to place or keep proprietary medicines within the scope of provincial pharmacy legislation. In 1890, the *Canadian Druggist* argued that there were enough laws constraining the operations of the pharmacist but agreed with the idea of amending the pharmacy laws so that sales of any proprietary medicines and "other articles containing poisons" were recorded, just as other poisons were already controlled.[62] The *Montreal Pharmaceutical Journal*, which was operated by the Lyman Brothers Company, argued in 1891 that at least "some of the abominable preparations now sold under patents and elegantly enough arranged to catch the eye of the suffering" should be controlled, but it drew the line, not surprisingly, at overly sweeping legislation since it would "throw inestimable wealth into the hands of the Doctors" and financially undermine the pharmacy business, which it argued relied on patent medicines.[63] The journal was using the tension between doctors and druggists to push its self-interested agenda. In contrast, the *Canadian Druggist* noted that the responsibility had to lie with the government because, although a druggist could register a proprietary medicine that he knew included restricted poisons, the composition of most proprietaries was unknown. Thus legislation requiring some kind of disclosure or chemical analysis would have to come before any comprehensive control on patent medicines could be feasible.[64]

Wholesale pharmacy houses expected that trade associations and formal or informal agreements among the manufacturers would eliminate the most problematic excesses and violations of the spirit of pharmaceutical control. At various times, they sought to curtail price cutting, a standard tactic of larger retailers, which involved dropping prices on selected proprietaries in an attempt to outsell the competition. Some agreed to cease selling to retailers who indulged in cutting. W.G. Evans, the director of Evans and Sons, claimed in 1898 that he had withdrawn his company from the Canadian Wholesale Druggists Association because its members were breaking their "solemn promises" to the retail druggists not to engage in price cutting.[65] Evans's withdrawal effectively killed the association.[66] Other wholesalers advertised to pharmacists the fact that they would sell their products only to duly licensed pharmacists. In a victory of sorts for retail druggists, and a demonstration of unity among the various branches of the trade, in 1903 the Wholesale Druggists Association agreed to follow a "Price Restrictive Plan," which was intended to eliminate the practice of cutting.[67] In subsequent advertisements to pharmacists, many wholesale manufacturers noted that they were following this plan.

Some wholesale pharmaceutical companies used fears about dangerous drugs in secret patent medicines to their advantage. By the turn of the century, several advertisements in the pharmacy trade papers included declarations that the medicine in question was free of all dangerous substances. In 1900, the *Canadian Pharmaceutical Journal* endorsed the "Indian Catarrh Cure" as a valuable alternative to the many catarrh cures on the market that "contain cocaine, and are as a consequence dangerous to the user, and such as no pharmacist can recommend." In contrast, this cure was "absolutely free from opiates of all kinds," by which misnomer the advertiser also included cocaine.[68] Restrictive legislation could also serve to bolster the credibility of those proprietary medicines that, when analyzed, were proven free of opiates. An advertisement entitled "NO POISON in Chamberlain's Cough Remedy" explained, "Owing to special legislation regarding the Poison Act, the Pharmacy Board of New South Wales had an analysis made of all the cough medicines that were sold in that market." The results showed that only Chamberlain's remedy was "entirely free from all poisons." The company played on fears of infant doping, which were often expressed in condemnations of patent medicines. "The absence of all narcotics makes this remedy the safest and best that can be had, and it is with a feeling of security that any mother can give it to her little ones."[69] The advertiser did not mention the effectiveness of the remedy but rather asserted that it was a safe alternative to dangerous medicines.

Professional commentators disparaged this tendency to manipulate public sentiment as favouring the business of advertising over the science of creating better remedies. In 1906, G.E. Gibbard of the *Canadian Pharmaceutical Journal* provided an example of a medicine manufacturer who, finding that his remedy was not selling as well as he had hoped, sought a new advertising manager rather than a new business manager. The result was an increase in sales, with no change in the product. Although this process may have appeared to business people as not unusual, Gibbard was disgusted, and he alluded to the problems presented when competitive capitalism overwhelmed the medical industry: "The truth and nothing but the truth is too much to expect in a condition where the advertiser's art is so potent a factor in producing successful results, but so grossly have the bounds of truthfulness been overstepped that the over-advertised patent medicine has almost become a public nuisance."[70] A similar opinion came from the *Canada Lancet* when its editor, John Ferguson, responded to the *Toronto Globe*'s defence of the right of patent medicine vendors to keep their preparations secret. The *Globe* likened a medical innovation to any other invention, for which a patent protects the creator. Ferguson simply stated,

> Medicines are not on the same level at all as a patent. If a man gets hold of a formulae [*sic*] for a mixture for whooping cough, and then places it upon the market, it is absolutely necessary that its composition should be made known. The medical profession is then in a position to inform its clientele of the safety, or otherwise, of such a mixture.

Ferguson rejected the credibility of arguments favouring the protective devices of capitalism, such as the patent, because they were made by a newspaper editor who relied on patent medicine ads for revenue. The doctor's duty was to protect the "public weal in all sanitary and healthful measures."[71]

Patent Medicines and the Drug Habit

The lethal or generally debilitating result of improper administration was one of several grave dangers that patent medicines posed to the general public; addiction was increasingly becoming another. By the first decade of the twentieth century, entreaties for the need to restrict the sale of patent medicines argued that many secret cures were addictive.[72] "Alcohol in some, cocaine in others, opium in a third, impotent stuff in a fourth, no alcohol advertised in a fifth, and yet full of it, etc., etc., is the every-day experience of every doctor," observed the *Canada Lancet* in 1906.[73] John Herald, editor of the *Queen's Medical Quarterly*, stated that "almost every day the practitioner meets some victim of the medicine habit who is as great a slave to some patent nostrum, manufactured for the purpose of enriching its proprietor, as the ordinary alcoholic or 'dope' habitué."[74] In the *Montreal Medical Journal*, Andrew Macphail tied his charge to the dubious advertising tactics of the patent medicine vendors:

> A person suffering from a "tired feeling" is stimulated with a tonic wine containing alcohol and cocaine; another has his catarrh dried up by morphine; constipation is cured with senna under the guise of some fanciful syrup, and children are soothed into a lethal slumber by some preparation of opium. It is no wonder then that the victims are ready to adduce sworn testimony that they cannot get along without their favorite medicine; any drunkard or morphinomaniac will attest to as much.[75]

The *Dominion Medical Monthly* agreed, arguing that the doctor had the duty to warn the public of the danger of "the evil habit of drug taking, for nefarious habits in this respect are soon and easily formed." These writers called for legislation to regulate the trade.[76]

The inclusion of addiction in the list of dangers presented by patent medicines drew on a growing view of addiction as a problem, along with a shifting perception of the best means of presenting potential public "dangers." In the 1870s, commentators attacked proprietary medicines because they purportedly "cured" diseases that the regular medical profession knew were incurable and because they could kill if taken in excess. Just as the unrestricted trade in patent medicines presented a challenge to the authority of the medical profession, so too did the growth of concerns about addiction threaten the authority of doctors and druggists. When discussing addiction, pharmacists and physicians once again clashed in defining the borders of their professional domains.

As with the proprietary medicine trade in general, when discussing the apparent spread of addiction, druggists and doctors could not agree on who was to blame. In 1900, the *Canadian Pharmaceutical Journal* cited an article by E. Toussaint in *La Dosimetre au Canada* that attacked the "hundreds of unscrupulous pharmacists who sell morphine to anyone who asks for it." The editor, J.E. Morrison, responded that "if there are so many morphinomaniacs it is due to the carelessness, and, we might say, laziness of a certain class of physicians who prescribe morphine for every little pain and ache of which their patients may complain."[77] Morrison's successor as editor, G.E. Gibbard, cast the net of blame wider, although he was less willing to admit the growth of addiction. In 1903, he noted that drug addiction was on the rise in other "civilized" countries, especially the United States and Europe, but that Canada was less affected by addiction. He attributed this condition to "the strenuous life we lead, the rigor of climate in which we live, and, with all, the quality of material out of which Canadians are built ... Alcohol, rather than 'dope,' is our tendency, and even this habit is created and fostered more by social tendency than by desire or appetite."[78] Despite these conditions, he noted, "there are amongst us unfortunates who have acquired drug habits." Two years later, this confidence had diminished to a certain resignation. "Almost every member of the craft [pharmacy] has to deal with the habitués," wrote Gibbard in 1905. He speculated on three principal causes of the growth of addiction: "the carelessness on the part of physicians ... a certain class of patent medicines ... [and] the aid rendered by unscrupulous druggists."[79]

Although they fought against the idea that this unscrupulous druggist created or exacerbated drug habits, pharmacists were aware that there were some among them who were not so honourable and who thus challenged their profession's integrity. In 1899, William Dyas of the *Canadian Druggist* declared that any druggist who was selling addictive drugs to an individual in order "to sustain the cumulative influence of a drug habit is guilty of a moral crime of a very serious nature."[80] Another writer concluded that, compared to the immoral vendor of habit-forming drugs, the liquor dealer "is angelic."[81] Yet despite the potential damage that an unprincipled druggist could do, Gibbard asserted that the pharmacist's "influence in combatting and remedying the evil is all powerful if he chose to exert it."[82] This power came from the pharmacists' ability to control the trade in dangerous drugs, established in the campaigns to expand pharmaceutical legislation and in the self-regulating powers of the various provincial and local pharmaceutical societies. When, in 1903, the Council of the Ontario College of Pharmacy and the Toronto Drug Section of the Retail Manufacturer's Association passed resolutions condemning the sale of narcotics to habitués, Gibbard called on medical associations to join the pharmacists in condemning the practice and to secure legislation that would "properly restrict the traffic."[83]

This call to the physicians is indicative of the unsteady relationship between druggists and doctors in the area of controlling drug addiction. The medical associations generally recognized their members' own culpability in causing iatrogenic addiction, and they pointed out the pharmacists' role in the increase of drug habituation. In 1879, a Montreal druggist wrote to the *Canada Medical and Surgical Journal*, arguing that the city's doctors needed to arrive at some "understanding ... with pharmacists regulating the repetition of prescriptions containing Morphia, Chloral, &c."[84] He explained that his confreres faced a dilemma when asked by patients to repeat prescriptions containing these dangerous substances. The editors of the journal in 1880 agreed, citing a case from the *Medical Times and Gazette* of a woman who took advantage of the practice of repeating prescriptions to procure enough bottles of a remedy to compile a fatal dose. The editors' concern included the danger both to the public and to the physician's reputation. Often an individual who found that a certain prescription was effective would circulate it "among the members of the family or kindly friends in the neighborhood. Surely under such circumstances it is grossly unfair to hold a physician answerable for what may happen."[85] So, although commentators like Alfred H. Mason argued that "medicine and pharmacy ought ever to be united in friendly co-operation," when confronting the issue of drug addiction through the patent medicine trade, doctors and druggists continued to eye each other with suspicion.[86]

The Cocaine Addiction Panic

Intersecting the growing concern over the trade in patent medicines and the problem of addiction was the issue of the use and abuse of cocaine.[87] Isolated from the coca leaf in 1855, cocaine entered the *materia medica* quickly in a number of forms. The Parke-Davis Company became an enthusiastic marketer of cocaine in numerous stimulant preparations, including cigarettes, cordials, and tablets.[88] Cocaine's anaesthetic properties made it valuable in eye and dental surgery. Like opium, cocaine's flexibility resulted in a degree of enthusiastic confusion regarding its value. In 1882, Dr. E. Palmer touted cocaine as a remedy for the opium habit, stating that his patients took the fluid extract of coca a few times and never felt the need for opium again.[89] By the turn of the century, cocaine was part of a broad array of proprietary products, the most notorious of which was Coca-Cola.[90]

The dangers of cocaine addiction emerged quickly as its use spread. In 1886, Dr. James Stewart of McGill College reported in the *Canada Medical and Surgical Journal* that, although cocaine was a valuable therapeutic medicine, doctors must use it cautiously; "otherwise we may bring about a cocaine habit which, if all reports be true, is even worse than that of opium."[91] Stewart's tempered interpretation of cocaine use contrasted with a report that the same journal printed eighteen months later. The editor quoted an article from the *Journal of Mental Science* condemning the moral effects of cocaine habituation:

> The patients lie when they open their mouths, they steal on the first opportunity, and they desire to do that which they are unable to perform. They are irresolute in their action, and should they have begun anything, their activity is of the shortest duration. In their being they become apathetic, indifferent to everything, untidy in their belongings, unclean in their person – in short, they are demoralized.[92]

Not all commentators, however, were so cautious about cocaine. In 1887, the *Canada Lancet* quoted a Dr. J.R. Rankin of Muncy, Pennsylvania, who said that "he has never seen any alarming effects follow the use of cocaine in his practice, although he has employed it quite extensively."[93] Enthusiasm like Rankin's declined as the century drew to a close and as newspapers printed increasingly concerned stories about cocaine habituation and criminal behaviour.

Often the effects of cocaine habituation were compared with opium's effects on the body and soul, and many commentators determined that cocaine was a more significant problem than opiates. Charles M. Pratt told the Saint John Medical Society that the cocaine habit was "even worse than the morphine habit," and W.S. Muir of the Dominion Medical Association said the habit was harder to break "than that of opium or alcohol."[94] For another, the physical effects of the drug were worse than those of opium, precisely because cocaine created such an overwhelming change in the body: "The opium habitué may have a fairly steady hand and a reasonably steady head for years ... the cocaine user finds a complete and ever increasing lack of power to co-ordinate the muscles of the body."[95] One writer's descriptions of a "coca smoker" paralleled earlier characterizations of the opiate habitué: "a tall, thin individual, with sallow complexion, and queer, expressionless eyes."[96] Physical effects were not as significant to many writers as the moral impact of cocaine addiction. In 1898, the *Canadian Pharmaceutical Journal* quoted Dr. W.F. Waugh, who wrote in the *Quarterly Journal of Inebriety* – the journal of the American Association for the Study and Cure of Inebriety – that cocaine was "the most disastrous in its effects of any habit-drug ... It destroys the soul, the moral consciousness is dead."[97] In 1906, Charles Heebner, dean of the Ontario College of Pharmacy, called the unrestricted trade in cocaine "the traffic in human souls."[98] The *Canadian Pharmaceutical Journal*, discussing the "diabolical traffic in cocaine" in Montreal during 1910, called it "this soul-destroying evil."[99]

Some writers saw in cocaine the central reason for the growing numbers of "drug fiends" in Canada. Heebner argued in 1906 that public and legislative sentiment against habit-forming drugs was virtually nonexistent until "the Cocaine Monster came upon the arena ... Cocaine proved to be a far more enslaving drug than opium or morphine."[100] Two years later, Gibbard of the *Canadian Pharmaceutical Journal* reported that a pharmacist was suspected of selling exorbitant amounts of morphine and cocaine. He argued that all pharmacists would recognize that the amounts this druggist ordered far exceeded the requirements of normal business, and he called the practice "diabolical," particularly because of cocaine's addictive nature. "In the case of whiskey and morphine, victims may and frequently do reform, but with cocaine never."[101] Other writers were not convinced that cocaine was the driving force in the rise of addiction but argued that restrictions on cocaine would be "a much needed safeguard" against potential addiction. In 1908, two Montreal druggists were threatened with legal action "for causing grievous injury in selling cocaine to parties addicted to the habit."[102] Some argued, then, that restrictions on the sale of cocaine and other drugs could prevent the spread of addiction, while protecting pharmacists from prosecution.

Pharmacists became concerned particularly about cocaine's prevalence in various cures for catarrh, an inflammation of the mucous membrane in the nose and throat. Many catarrh cures were inhaled into the nose. The Canadian pharmaceutical press repeated stories of "cocaine fiends" fraudulently obtaining catarrh cures from local druggists. In 1898, one of the Toronto wholesale houses discovered "a pile of empty bottles and lengths of rubber tubing" near the basement water closet.

> An inspection revealed the fact that the bottles were the empty containers of a much advertised catarrh cure, and the rubber tubing the instrument used for puffing up the nostril. The pile of bottles on counting was found to contain 20 dozen. The suggestiveness of the find comes in from the fact that this particular catarrh powder is said to contain a large percentage of cocain [*sic*].[103]

In 1908, a Toronto druggist reported that he had received dubious calls for the delivery of a catarrh cure that contained cocaine. When the messenger arrived on the street where the customer lived, he encountered a man who said that he had ordered the cure and then took the medicine without paying. The messenger demanded the product back, and the man, through a sleight of hand, returned an empty bottle. After this initial story was printed in the *Canadian Pharmaceutical Journal*, over forty Toronto druggists reported similar incidents. Later that month, "that cocaine fiend" was apprehended.[104]

Behind the growing cocaine panic was its mutable relationship to class and social order. As a stimulant and an anaesthetic, cocaine had a variety of applications and hence a variety of forms of abuse. Several writers linked cocaine use to concerns based on class, gender, and race. In 1897, the *Dominion Medical Monthly* abstracted an article first published in the *Eclectic Medical Journal* by Dr. E.R. Waterhouse, who described a "cocaine joint" in St. Louis: "The patronage was largely from the lower class or fallen women, men seldom using [cocaine]."[105] The *Canadian Pharmaceutical Journal* reported in 1900 that the sale of cocaine was attaining "alarming proportions in certain parts of the Southern states." The alarm came mainly from the impression that "the consumption is mostly amongst the negroes. In Louisville it is said that 90% of the colored population are cocaine fiends."[106] In 1903, the *Canadian Pharmaceutical Journal* published an article by E.G. Eberle of Dallas who linked cocaine to social deterioration. Eberle stated that it was "most used amongst the lower classes of society. The habitués fill our insane asylums, almshouses, city hospitals, and the acts they commit as a result of the dissipation, bring them into the courts for crimes and offences of every description."[107] Eberle's assertion contrasts with the presence of cocaine addicts like Edward C. in the lunatic asylums of Canada. Many of these patients came from the wealthier families.[108] Accordingly, the *Canada Lancet* noted in 1896 that "it is almost entirely in our own profession that the [cocaine] habit has taken root."[109] Heebner noted in 1906 that "the cocaine habit claims those following the higher callings of life, such as pharmacy, medicine and law."[110] Cocaine use, then, occupied a bifurcated realm of social concern related to status-based fears over a dangerous lower class, violent racial others, and the potential deterioration of the upper class. Although many of the examples came from the southern United States, the images that they presented resonated in the debates in Canada. Indeed, they may have suggested a creeping threat from south of the border.

The danger of cocaine "mania," and the social panic that it often engendered, underpinned legislative change in the first decade of the twentieth century. In its restrictive nature, this legislation often exceeded the controls placed on opiates. Compared to patent medicine legislation, which pharmacists had been advocating and debating for decades, defining a drug like cocaine to be a controlled substance within the meaning of a pharmacy act was normally a straightforward matter of a pharmaceutical association or college declaring it as such and a governor-in-council agreeing to the change. Thus, by 1908, before either the Opium Act or the Proprietary or Patent Medicine Act became law, most provincial legislatures had modified their pharmacy legislation to limit access to cocaine. In some, the limits were stronger than those imposed on other poisons. The Quebec Pharmaceutical Association had cocaine (spelled "cocoaine") added to its poison schedule in 1890. By 1900, the Nova Scotia Pharmaceutical Association had added a remarkable thirty-seven new substances to its poison schedule, including cocaine; the Prince Edward Island Pharmacy Act of 1905 also included cocaine in its original poison schedule.

Yet, whereas pharmacy acts could generally be modified by such additions to the poison schedules, most amendments placed cocaine in a separate category of restriction. Legislatures and pharmacists clearly viewed the older poison provisions as not strong enough to deal with the growing problem of cocaine use. In 1908, the laws in both Ontario and Manitoba were changed to deal with cocaine separately from other poisons. The Manitoba legislation, for example, maintained the packaging requirements for all listed poisons and allowed pharmacists to sell these poisons to people with whom they were familiar. But the law included a separate paragraph making it "unlawful to sell cocaine by retail, except to a duly registered medical practitioner or dentist, or upon the prescription of a duly registered medical practitioner."[111] There was no room here for the subjectivity of the pharmacist's attention to packaging requirements or familiarity with the customer.

Cocaine was the most strictly controlled drug in the province. By 1911, when the federal Opium and Drug Act was passed, British Columbia, Alberta, Saskatchewan, and Quebec had also amended their pharmacy acts to restrict specifically the sale of cocaine without a prescription, with British Columbia's law referencing its subsumption under the new Dominion laws.[112] The fact that separate paragraphs were also added to specify prohibitions about cocaine indicates the increased concern over this drug. As we will see in the next chapter, the provincial efforts to restrict cocaine came at least a decade after attempts to address concerns about patent and proprietary medicines, and all of these efforts faced the sort of opposition that cocaine legislation never saw.

The proprietary medicine trade presented a complex dilemma to Canada's medical professionals at the turn of the century. Not only were there a variety of substances, some reputable and some disreputable, but the different ways that medical practitioners used them, the different types of pharmacy business, and the demographic diversity of the country also meant that consensus would be difficult to achieve. Some physicians appreciated the reliability of some substances, which they could prescribe knowing that their patient was getting the same product each time. Many physicians in rural areas relied on such standardized remedies given that it was impractical to send a patient to a far-away pharmacy and that the physician may not want or be able to compound the remedy himself. Many pharmacists generally found this situation to be unacceptable since it undermined their claims to be skilful compounders of complex remedies. At the same time, some pharmacists liked the ease and profitability of creating their own proprietary remedies for common complaints. Physicians were not so thrilled about this practice since it got in the way of the physician-patient interaction, denying doctors a fee and denying patients the authoritative interpretation of the trained medical gaze.

The one issue on which most pharmacists and physicians could agree was the problem of the availability of dangerous drugs in the proprietary medicines whose ingredients remained secret. These dangerous drugs were normally addictive substances, and the prevalence of intense stimulants like cocaine in things like catarrh cures joined the more familiar problems of infants doped up with cough syrup and dreamy individuals chasing sunflowers and butterflies to a laudanum-scented Xanadu. When the effort to address the generally unfettered trade in patent and proprietary medicines arrived at the steps of various legislatures, it was these addictive substances, not just the secrecy of remedies, which dominated the spotlight.

8
Regulating Proprietary Medicine

Concerned with the growing market in patent medicines, pharmacists and physicians debated and advocated a range of options for controlling the trade. Their approaches ranged from simply educating the public about the dangers of these dubious remedies to pursuing legislation at the provincial and federal levels. Having failed in the early 1870s to include proprietary medicines in their provincial pharmacy acts, pharmacists in both Ontario and Quebec continued to insist that modification of the existing pharmacy legislation was the most efficient means of controlling the distribution of the proprietaries. By the turn of the century, they were joined by pharmaceutical societies in other provinces. Pharmacists faced opposition from retail businesses, especially the departmental stores and some patent medicine manufacturers, which framed the issue as about unnecessary restrictions in a free market. So to achieve a measure of control over the expanding trade, pharmacists had to couch their discussions, yet again, in the language of social protection since the unrestricted trade of drugs containing unstated dangerous ingredients could threaten the health of the people. Both pharmacists and physicians saw themselves as responsible for the public's well-being; to them, their professional status validated their role as guardians of health.

In the push to regulate proprietary medicines, Canada's efforts sat somewhere, literally and figuratively, between its neighbour to south of the border and its motherland across the Atlantic. In Britain and the United States the dubious ingredients of secret remedies had become a major concern by the turn of the century. British physicians had begun campaigning for a patent medicine act in the 1880s, an effort aimed especially at combatting the problems presented by the popular and reportedly addictive remedy Chlorodyne.[1] In the United States the issue did not become a matter of national concern until the turn of the century, although pharmaceutical associations had been lobbying to place some control on the proprietary medicine trade long before Samuel Hopkins Adams's exposé appeared in

Collier's Weekly.[2] Canada was influenced by the market and policy changes in both countries. However, although national restrictions on patent medicines were enacted in 1908, two years after the US Pure Food and Drug Act of 1906, the Dominion government and provincial governments had been paying attention to the problem long before then. Indeed, the Canadian government had passed the Inland Revenue Act of 1875, which included provisions for testing adulteration of food and drug products that were virtually identical to those of a similar British law passed in 1872.[3] And as we will see, some provincial governments began to legislate controls on proprietary medicines in the last decades of the nineteenth century.

Achieving legislative restrictions on proprietary medicines was not the only means that commentators envisioned to protect the public from dubious nostrums. In 1873, James Neish, editor of the short-lived *Canadian Medical Times,* argued that "moral means are probably the only effective ones" when dealing with the patent medicine trade. Moral means reinforced the doctor's social status but also relied on that status for legitimacy. Physicians should make every effort, he explained, to inform their patients of the potential dangers of patent medicines and to suggest legitimate remedies, "which may be more cheaply obtained from a respectable druggist."[4] Neish rejected legislative restrictions on patent medicines. He likened such legislation to a heavily value-laden scheme for government restriction of alcohol: "high license." High license was the means of attempting to restrict the sale of alcohol by imposing high taxes on the manufacture and sale of liquor. Opponents argued that this elitist practice restricted access to alcohol only among the poor but did not effectively deal with the social problems of the liquor trade; it also legitimated the liquor trade by equating government taxation with government endorsement. Neish saw the parallels in the patent medicine trade. By making vendors or manufacturers pay expensive fees, the government could price patent medicines out of reach of most people. He opposed this approach on the principle that it would appear to provide government-sponsored legitimacy for any patent medicine, regardless of the substance's ingredients or effectiveness. The *Canada Lancet* also viewed moral suasion as a key aspect of a broader-based reform effort. In 1886, John Fulton, the *Lancet's* editor, recognized that gaining legislation against patent medicines would require concerted efforts on the part of physicians to educate the public on the issue. This job would be particularly difficult since doctors faced the opposition of the many newspapers that derived a large proportion of their advertising revenues from patent medicines. However, Fulton explained, only physicians could help society to resist the "tide which threatens to overwhelm us."[5]

Vain attempts at moral suasion were soon eclipsed by pushes for legislative solutions. Concerted attempts to bring patent medicines under the purview of the pharmaceutical and medical associations began in Ontario and Quebec in the 1880s and gained momentum as the century drew to a close and as other provinces' pharmaceutical associations gained enabling legislation and an authoritative voice in discussions about the drug trade.[6] In 1885, Quebec's Pharmaceutical Association successfully sponsored a new Pharmacy Act through the legislature. The poison schedule of this act was divided into two parts (Schedules A and B). Schedule B included substances that could be sold by nonpharmacists only if the package or bottle remained unopened. Most of these substances were moderately safe products such as linseed oil, bicarbonate of soda, and castor oil. The new schedule was designed not to control access to dangerous substances but to address the generally widespread problem of adulteration.[7] Nevertheless, patent medicines headed this list.[8] Their inclusion had two notable implications. First, by identifying patent medicines as potentially problematic substances, pharmacists suggested that their profession should have authority to control these products. At the same time, the fact that they were on a secondary schedule, with the key issue on this schedule being the integrity of the packaging, suggests that the legislature continued to accept that, in general, patent medicines did not need further controls. In this reasoning, it was not the manufacturers who were a problem but nefarious individuals who sought to dilute or otherwise alter the medicines.

In 1890, the Quebec Legislature passed an amendment to the Pharmacy Act that shifted the situation once again. This amendment included a clause that gave pharmacists nearly unrestricted power to define poisons; the Quebec College of Physicians and Surgeons no longer had input in the process. Further firming up pharmacists' authority in the province, the act required any physicians who wished to open pharmacies in Quebec City or Montreal to cease practising as physicians. This provision was a significant coup for pharmacists, who, across the country, had been complaining that, since pharmacy acts normally exempted physicians from needing a pharmacy licence to sell drugs, some physicians were opening pharmacies. Yet the 1890 amendment also eliminated Schedule B, removing patent medicines altogether and any provisions for the protection against adulteration. The clause discussing Schedule B was replaced with a clause specifically dedicated to labelling and sales of arsenic-based pesticides Paris Green and London Purple. Although the act no longer included patent medicines explicitly, by subjecting all poisons to the same form of restrictions, and by giving pharmacists the power to identify specific poisonous substances, the act enabled druggists to control a broader range of medicines.[9] The power of the pharmaceutical profession over the trade in patent medicines, therefore, became nearly absolute, as the definition of what constituted a "dangerous medicine" was placed entirely in the hands of the pharmacists.

In 1892, the physicians in Quebec petitioned for amendments to the Quebec Medical Act that would give them some control over the distribution of patent medicines. Their amendment would have defined all who advertised a patent or proprietary medicine, dispensed these medicines, or "gave consultation" before selling a remedy or patent medicine" as practising medicine. If they were not registered under the Medical Act, such people would have violated the law. Edward Shuttleworth, in the *Canadian Pharmaceutical Journal*, called on the druggists of Quebec to oppose this bill since it would make it illegal for a druggist to recommend even a simple remedy to a common ailment, like a cough medicine or liniment, without breaking the law.[10] Indeed, the idea of "over-the-counter prescribing" had been a sore point between physicians and pharmacists for many years. Physicians insisted that only they could recommend specific remedies for specific illnesses, whereas pharmacists countered that there was nothing wrong with a pharmacist recommending a remedy when a customer provided general symptom information. Some of these instances were discussed at the end of Chapter 4. The nuances of these distinctions are too intricate to address here; suffice it to say that that the Quebec physicians' amendments did not pass.

The legislative initiatives against the unrestricted sale of patent medicines in Ontario reflected similar tensions between pharmacists and general merchants. In 1892, the Council of the College of Pharmacy proposed an amendment to the Pharmacy Act of 1871. Initially, the council looked to follow Quebec's lead and include in Part 2 of Ontario's poison schedule the phrase "any and all patent or proprietary medicines, of whatever nature, that contain any one or more of the poisons contained in the schedule." This amendment would have placed many dubious or dangerous patent medicines under the pharmacists' purview. A committee of the College of Pharmacy modified this clause so that only patent medicines that contained poisons listed in Part 1 of the schedule would fall under the amendment's provisions. Shuttleworth questioned this alteration and predicted that the entire proposal would fail. He argued that the amendment had to be more specific than "any and all patent and proprietary medicines," that poisons in Part 2 of the schedule were also dangerous when hidden in patent medicines, and that no official means of determining the content of patent medicines existed. Any law that restricted patent medicines on the basis of their contents, he said, would be meaningless without a provision to test these medicines.[11] Shuttleworth was arguing for the increased power of pharmacists over the definition and control of patent medicines, as had been achieved in Quebec, an achievement that, we will see, was fleeting.

It must have been bitterly ironic for the Ontario pharmacists when, instead of restricting the trade in patent medicines, the legislature opened the trade up to more vendors. Many legislators and newspapers had opposed the amendment to restrict patent medicines, charging that it was once again an attempt by the pharmacists to extend their monopoly over one aspect of trade. Pharmacists, fearing a total collapse of their initiative, attempted compromise. In March 1893, R.W. Elliot, one of the founders of the Ontario College of Pharmacy, who had helped to draft the original Ontario Pharmacy Act and was a co-owner of the large drug-wholesaling firm Elliot and Company, suggested an amendment to the clause that "would have been acceptable, possibly even to the patent medicine men." Elliot proposed that instead of including a blanket provision to restrict all patent medicines under certain conditions, all patent and proprietary medicines should be exempted from the Pharmacy Act. Patent medicines could face the scrutiny of the Board of Health if,

> on the petition of the College of Pharmacy or any licensed medical practitioner, the Provincial Board of Health shall cause to be made a full and sufficient analysis of such patent or proprietary medicine by the official analyst or some other competent person, and if on such analysis it appears that such patent or proprietary medicine contains any of the poisons mentioned in any of the schedules to this Act to an extent that renders their use dangerous to health or life.[12]

The Board of Health would then request the lieutenant governor to add the specific patent medicine to the schedule. The proposal clearly targeted what would be considered illegitimate proprietary medicines, those nostrums vended by grocers and general merchants, as well as pharmacists. The suggestion was, of course, that legitimate proprietary medicines, manufactured by reputable pharmaceutical companies like Elliot and Company, would not be a danger at all.

This compromise, which appeared to satisfy all of the requirements of opponents to the earlier amendment, passed through the legislative committee but was defeated in the legislature. Not only did the pharmacists' compromise fail to sway the legislature, but the legislators reacted to the pharmacists' initiative by *opening up* the trade in patent medicines. While debating another amendment to the Pharmacy Act, which was intended to lift restrictions on the sale of Paris Green, the legislature added a temporary clause that eliminated entirely restrictions on patent medicines for one year.[13] This temporary clause was extended for a second year in 1894.[14]

The attempts to restore some legislative – and pharmaceutical – control over the sale of patent medicines resumed two years later, and initially the pharmacists were not satisfied with these efforts. While preparing to lift the annulment, the Ontario Legislature added a significantly modified version of Elliot's clause. Shuttleworth thought that this change was laughable and that "attempts at pharmaceutical law making have of late years been characterized by absurdity and sometimes utter puerility."[15] Instead of a concise program by which suspected patent medicines could be analyzed and restricted, Shuttleworth found the new clause to be vague and unsatisfying:

> This rigamarole simply amounts to this: That "in case of there being reason to apprehend" – by whom the provisio does not specify – that a medicine contains any of the poisons in the schedule, in such quantity as would render the use of the medicine, *in the prescribed doses,* dangerous to health or life, the health authorities may ascertain that this is the case, and may submit to the Lieut.-Governor in Council, or report to this effect, and after considerable circumlocution the medicine may, subject to appeal, be considered as being under the poison provisions of the Pharmacy Act.[16]

Shuttleworth concluded that not only did the new law fail to provide an effective check on secret medicines, but it also reduced the power of pharmacists to influence legislation. Unlike Elliot's compromise, which had empowered both the College of Pharmacy and medical practitioners to request analyses of specific medicines, this clause provided no such authority. Also, Shuttleworth suspected that the amendment allowed "poisonous medicine" to be sold by "others" besides registered pharmacists. According to Shuttleworth, the initial concerted attempt to restrict the sale of patent medicines in Ontario through extant legislative means had failed, given that the pharmacists had not achieved the power to define and act on concerns about potentially dangerous patent medicines and that their authority over this area of the distribution of problematic substances had not been extended.

The pharmacists in Quebec were more successful. In 1898, the control that Quebec pharmacists had gained over the distribution of patent medicines earlier in the decade came under the scrutiny of the legislature and the public press. In that year, the Grocers' Association lobbied the legislature for broad-based amendments to the Pharmacy Act that would have effectively permitted any retail vendor to sell patent medicines. The grocers accompanied this legislative initiative with a concerted attack on pharmacists in the public press. In December 1898, several newspapers in the province began to print letters denouncing "the druggists' monopoly."[17] The pharmacists were concerned that they seemed unable to present their side of the story to the press, which they charged had too much to gain from the unrestricted sale of patent medicines since a large proportion of many newspapers' ads were for these nostrums. When the grocers had the bill reintroduced in 1899, the results were less than ideal for the opponents of pharmacists' control. This time, the legislature formed a select committee to investigate the viability of the amendments. After several days of hearing testimony from notable doctors, druggists, and grocers, the committee recommended as a compromise limiting the sale of only those patent medicines that a chemical analysis determined to be dangerous to the public.[18]

Unlike the Ontario legislation, the result of the debates in Quebec was an expanded role for scientific investigation in the policy decisions of the province. No longer would commercial interests have such an extended control over an aspect of provincial health. In the amended act, the Pharmaceutical Association "could declare that any substance ... shall be a poison within the meaning of this act," but it had to submit this recommendation to the lieutenant governor for approval. The lieutenant governor had two options: he could simply approve the recommendation, or he could "cause to be ascertained, by an expert, at the expense of the Pharmaceutical Association of the Province of Quebec, whether the substances mentioned in the regulation are or are not poisons within the meaning of this act." Patent medicines were not subject to a blanket restriction, but they were now liable to government scrutiny. As in Ontario, suspicions about the contents or safety of any medicine could result in the Board of Health requesting an analysis, a process that could lead to the restriction of a specific product. The 1899 amendments to Quebec's Pharmacy Act, then, maintained the control of the pharmacists, while extending the power of scientific investigation to define policy decisions. Trained, professional chemists would use their skills in unbiased scientific analysis to protect the public, and the Board of Health, generally dedicated to concerns about contagious diseases and the health-related infrastructure of the province (such as drinking water, ventilation, and pollution), expanded its role in overseeing the health of the people. Ironically, a movement begun by the grocers to curtail the pharmacists' power and to extend their own commercial interests had further legitimated the status of pharmacy and had reinforced the place of medical science in policy formation.

The approach to the issue was different in British Columbia. Whereas both Ontario and Quebec attempted to control patent medicines by expanding the pharmacy legislation, in British Columbia the government of Richard McBride drafted a distinct patent medicine law, which it presented in February 1906. This legislation came after several months of agitation in the province, led by Victoria physician C.J. Fagan, who had presented his article condemning patent medicines to the Canadian Medical Association when it met in Vancouver in 1904. Samuel Hopkins Adams's articles on patent medicines were published in 1905, and in January and February 1906 two subsequent cases of infants dying after being treated at home with patent medicines shocked the city of Victoria. When several British Columbia newspapers picked up on the issue, it seemed the sort of topic that the premier, at the end of his first mandate, could champion. Consequently, the bill was brief and to the point, targeting specific drugs of special concern and the overabundance of alcohol in these medicines. It forbade anyone from selling any patent medicine "that contains chloral hydrate, ergot, morphine, opium, belladonna ... cocaine ... acetanilide, sulphuric, sulphurous, nitric, and nitrous acids" unless the packaging was clearly marked "poison" and indicated the percentage of poisonous ingredients. The legislation also placed controls over any patent medicine that contained more than 10 percent alcohol by weight, requiring permission from the provincial Board of Health to use that amount of alcohol.[19]

The professions were not impressed. Just as in 1891, when the province's pharmacists found that the government had disrespected their profession by significantly modifying the initial pharmacy legislation to their dissatisfaction, so too was the patent medicine bill considered by the pharmacists to be unsatisfactory. When they met with the premier, Minister of Finance and Agriculture R.J. Tatlow, and Dr. Fagan, the pharmacists learned that physicians were also dissatisfied with the legislation and had met with McBride the day before. The pharmacists and physicians both asserted that the law was too overarching to be effective, with pharmacists arguing that it would unnecessarily affect pharmacists who compounded valid preparations and sold them under their own names. The BC Pharmaceutical Association's delegation was proactive, proposing to McBride that the legislation be set aside until the next session so that further consultation could take place or significantly amended so that it would be, as the pharmacists reckoned, more suitable to the current state of business and medicine in the province.

The BC Pharmaceutical Association's amendments cut to the heart of the matter. They ensured that the normal operations of the Pharmacy Act were not circumvented by this new legislation and targeted narcotics specifically. First, the association recommended that the list of prohibited drugs be deleted and that a more specific list be substituted. The recommended list demonstrated a more nuanced approach to patent medicine legislation but also one that allowed milder products to continue to be sold. It would restrict "cocaine or its salts in any quantity or more than one-fourth of a grain of morphine, or more than two grains of opium, or more than one-fourth of a grain of Extract of Belladonna or its equivalent in one fluid ounce." The amount of alcohol that would require acquiescence of the Department of Public Health would increase from 10 to 15 percent. To protect pharmacists, it offered a reworded section that no longer placed anyone who sold such substances in the law's sights, making it clear that the culpable parties should be manufacturers:

> No person except the manufacturer of such patent medicine, proprietary medicine, nostrum or specific, shall be deemed to have contravened the provisions of this Act, in selling, furnishing of [*sic:* or] giving away any patent medicine, proprietary medicine, nostrum or specific, not in conformity

of the provisions of this Act, unless [the substance] has been analyzed by
the authority of the Provincial Board of Health, and the result of the analysis,
together with the declaration that such [product] contravenes the provisions
of this Act.[20]

As with attempts to address the problems of proprietary medicines in Ontario
and Quebec, this solution drew on the existing analytical facilities of provincial public-health authorities to determine the healthfulness or dangers
inherent in such potentially problematic products.

The pharmacists and physicians were concerned about how the legislation
upended their own authority in dealing with a problem they agreed was
serious; the manufacturers saw this legislation as an affront to all that was
good about liberal democracy. Soon after the first Proprietary Medicine Act
was introduced in 1906, Premier McBride received a letter from the lawyer
representing the Proprietary Articles Trade Association of Canada (PATA),
based in Toronto. The letter reproduced a detailed (and therefore expensive)
telegram listing seventeen points on which the PATA objected to the legislation. The PATA appealed to McBride, a Conservative, on mainly the grounds
of fairness in business dealings, drawing on a range of issues that were often
used to criticize new regulatory legislation. They argued that the bill's object
is "not to regulate but to destroy the proprietary business," calling it "class
legislation," allowing "one class of people to place any drug before the public
without label, while the other people have to label their drugs in such a way
that their sale is practically prohibited." Therefore, they argued, it unfairly
discriminated against the manufacturers when it allowed physicians and
pharmacists to prepare medicines that contained any number of the substances of concern in any volume. Moreover, the requirement to put ingredients on the label violated the intellectual property of the manufacturers
since the "formula ... is a private and valuable property that has its original
value in its merit and further value in the years of labor spent in bringing
it before the public." Turning to the issue of respectable business practices,
and alluding to the concerns that these substances were inherently dangerous, the PATA noted that proprietary medicines "are carefully prepared, as
a mistake would ruin the medicine. You cannot get such careful preparations
if the formula were filled indiscriminately." Finally, the PATA argued that
the public did not want the legislation, that the public wanted unfettered
access to proprietary medicines, and that the legislation would put an undue
hardship on people in remote districts.[21]

The PATA's letter, then, drew on a range of key themes in the regulation
of substances and on objections to government oversight of the health
industry in general. Concerns about monopoly were at the root of the professionalization of medicine and of pharmacy. Access to medicines in remote
locations was a key concern for physicians when limits on their ability to

dispense their own medicine were sought by pharmacists and might have had added significance in British Columbia, where the Pharmacy Act's restrictions had originally operated only in larger towns and cities in the province. Moreover, the appeal to the needs and demands of the public was strong because it drew both on issues of laissez-faire economics and on the importance of the free market, not to mention subtly suggesting that McBride's government would lose the next election if it passed such a heinous affront to the free market.

With opposition like this, it is not surprising that the legislation did not go beyond first reading. It was "set aside" in the legislature and was never discussed in committee, and without it being discussed in the house, we cannot assess legislators' reaction to the pharmacists' proposed amendments or whether the proprietary medicine industry would have presented its own modifications. Certainly, the PATA was quick to rally the local newspapers to oppose the legislation, sending a circular that called the bill "a specimen of unadulterated gall." A short editorial comment in the *British Columbia Pharmaceutical Record,* the organ of the BC Pharmaceutical Association, noted wryly that the Victoria newspaper the *Week,* which was well known for taking a stand against proprietaries, was not astute enough even to know the difference between "Preparatory" and "Proprietary" when discussing the circular. (The *Record* also noted that the *Week* had jumped on the anti-proprietary bandwagon by plagiarizing an article in the *Ladies' Home Journal.*) Meanwhile, the physicians who had also opposed the legislation turned quickly to the Dominion government. In a meeting on 12 March 1906, after a rousing talk by Dr. Fagan, the Vancouver Medical Society passed a resolution expressing its concern about patent medicines and hoping that the issue could be taken out of the highly charged atmosphere of provincial interprofessional wrangling. "Whereas the evils are so complex that a proper solution can be arrived at only by competent disinterested persons," it resolved "that the Dominion House of Commons ... be petitioned to appoint a commission to investigate this whole matter with a view to enacting laws which will eradicate these evils."[22]

A month after the Vancouver Medical Society passed this resolution, Nova Scotia's government also attempted to enact a patent medicine law. Unlike British Columbia, here the legislation was at the prompting of the Halifax and Nova Scotia branch of the British Medical Association.[23] The bill's provisions were similar to those of other provincial legislation, establishing a limit of 6 percent alcohol and targeting medicines that contained more than one-twentieth of 1 percent of morphine, heroin, or cocaine, the unholy trinity of the drug panic. Also similar to the BC bill, the Nova Scotia proposal placed authority for analysis in the hands of the provincial health officer. The *Acadian Recorder* joined a chorus of newspapers opposing the legislation. Calling the legislation "A Bill to Kill Patent Medicines," the *Recorder's* editor manifested the ideal of the free market in arguing that the medical profession, which he called a "close combine," was "at the bottom of it." The rest of the editorial made the same kind of arguments that the PATA had done in British Columbia, with the added observation that, in any case, it was up to the Dominion Parliament to regulate trade.[24] The *Halifax Morning Chronicle*, also opposed, published an editorial reiterating the simple message of its title: "Kill This Bill."[25] And it was done.

The attempts to regulate the patent medicine trade at the provincial level resulted in repetition of the same battle cries and arguments from various directions. Newspapers, proprietary medicine manufacturers, wholesale and retail druggists, and physicians all saw the issue as involving the proper direction of the nation and the role of government in forging that direction. Placing themselves in the role of guardians of the public's health, pharmacists and physicians saw their duty as one of presenting rational and scientifically grounded perspectives that would help to forge effective legislation that did not interfere with their legitimate attempts to heal, or at least soothe, the sick. The patent medicine manufacturers also saw themselves as working to maintain the health of the people, but they paired this noble discourse with ideas about the importance of the free market and about the need to keep the government at an arm's length from the operations of respectable businesses. The newspapers, financially reliant on advertising from patent medicine manufacturers of varying reputations, kept the pressure on governments to view such efforts as bald-faced attempts to dominate the industry by the pharmacists and the physicians, whose monopoly was considered antithetical to the smooth operation of the economy. In the end, the only thing that the newspapers, pharmacists and physicians could agree on was the direction the process had to take. The legislative solution to this proprietary medicine problem, intertwined as it was with issues of the jurisdiction of pharmacy, medicine, and private industry, the health of the people, and the integrity of the nation, lay in Dominion-government hands.

Arguments about the need for Dominion action on proprietary medicines were not new in 1906. In 1893, the *Toronto News* had suggested that the federal government should use extant mechanisms to bring the patent medicine trade under check. The correspondent called on "controller Wood, of the Inland Revenue Department, to exercise his genius and devise some means by which he may secure a considerable amount of excise revenue" and to "cause these medicines to be compounded under Government inspection."[26] In 1888, under the authority of the Adulteration Act of 1884, the chief analyst of the Department of Inland Revenue began to issue bulletins of analyses of food, drugs, and agricultural products (e.g., Paris Green) in annual reports to the federal government.[27] As we have seen, the department included proprietary medicines, purchased from pharmacies and wholesale drug manufacturers across the country, in its analyses, the results of which did not always place the neighbourhood pharmacists' compounding skills in a favourable light.

To some, the suggestion that the Department of Inland Revenue create higher taxes on patent medicines was not a viable solution. Like the *Canadian Medical Times* in the 1870s, other journals declared that any form of licence or tax would not serve the purpose of restricting the trade adequately. Responding to a doomed bill presented to the Ontario Legislature that would have required all patent medicine manufacturers to take out a licence for $1,000,[28] the *Dominion Medical Monthly* argued that this provision would serve only to "freeze out ... all the small concerns, so that the large firms may have the dear public ... more entirely under their care." The *Monthly's* solution was twofold: first, no remedy should be permitted to be sold "unless it were first proved to the satisfaction of a competent authority that it could reasonably be expected to be of value to the conditions for which it was supposed to give relief"; and second, "the ingredients should be plainly stated on the bottle or package."[29]

These legislative initiatives and the responses by the professions underscore the main difference between pharmacists and physicians on how to address the problems that each saw in the unregulated proprietary medicine trade. Although both professions considered the trade to be problematic, with the undisclosed ingredients of these medicines posing a real danger to the health of the people who could buy and consume them at will, pharmacists saw this as a problem with distribution outside of the purview of professional pharmacy, and physicians saw the drugs as interfering with physicians' ability to treat their patients. In 1898, while the Quebec Legislature debated its amendments to the Pharmacy Act, R.W. Williams, president of the Quebec Pharmaceutical Association, in an instance of interprofessional collegiality, wrote to the College of Physicians of the province asking that it form a committee to investigate the possibility of federal legislation of the patent medicine trade. The pharmacists resolved to "give our aid to this committee," arguing that it "is of the greatest importance" that the trade be regulated since "these remedies are injurious to the public health." In response, the Board of the College of Physicians and Surgeons drafted three motions to deal with the issue. It agreed to approach the federal government about legislating against patent medicines and specifically intended to ask the provincial legislature not to "legislate on the sale of secret remedies before the Federal Parliament has taken the matter into consideration."[30] J.E. Morrison, editor of the *Canadian Pharmaceutical Journal*, applauded this initiative but cautioned that, although representative bodies of pharmacists and physicians working together might be able to secure this type of legislation, "perhaps the medical societies will not take such an active interest in the question."[31]

Morrison's reservations reflected a general disagreement between pharmacists and doctors on the best way to ensure that the public would be protected from these medicines. From the 1880s until the passing of the 1908 federal law, the editors of the *Canada Lancet* repeatedly argued that Canada should adopt the practice of printing the entire recipe of the patent medicine on the label.[32] In 1903, Dr. W.H. Moorehouse, the president of the Canada Medical Association, endorsed the system used in France, "by which all makers of patent medicines are obliged to put the formula, both qualitative and quantitative[,] upon the package."[33] The Vancouver Medical Association resolved in 1906 that "if persons know, as they should know, what is offered them, they would be able to discriminate between the beneficial and harmful."[34] This association's discussion took place soon after a provincial bill to regulate patent medicines, which included the "formula on the label" requirement, failed to become law in British Columbia. For physicians, placing the formula on the label would enable them to determine whether the substance was indeed useful based on accepted contemporary pharmacology.

In general, pharmacists condemned the "recipe on the label" approach. To them, it was a violation of the rights of pharmaceutical manufacturers and, in any case, would not adequately inform the purchaser of the efficacy of the medicine. When the BC Legislature considered the 1906 bill to regulate patent medicines, G.E. Gibbard argued in the *Canadian Pharmaceutical Journal* that placing the formula on the label was problematic for three main reasons. First, it would interfere with the legitimate practice of pharmacists, whose proprietary knowledge should be protected. Second, it would be essentially meaningless to anyone who had no pharmacological background; unless the purchaser had specific understanding of *materia medica,* Gibbard explained, people would not be able to assess the efficacy of the cure or its danger. Third, it would not guard against fraudulent claims since unscrupulous manufacturers would misrepresent what was in their products. Such reasoning underlay the pharmacists' arguments that provincial boards of health should be authorized to analyze suspected products and was reiterated in discussions over Dominion legislations. An "impartial board of commissioners appointed by [the] government and possessed of the professional and technical knowledge requisite to arrive at a correct conclusion as to [the medicine's] merits or fitness to cure a specified disease" would be far superior to relying on the ability of individual consumers or physicians to understand complex pharmaceutical recipes.[35]

As with the creation of the poison acts in the last third of the nineteenth century, discussions about how to deal with proprietary medicines highlighted different professional priorities. Doctors, insisting that they could benefit from premixed medicines, which would provide physicians with a consistently reliable preparation, preferred to know as much about the medicine as possible. Their patients would trust the doctors' assessments and follow their advice. Legislation, therefore, needed to ensure only that the patent medicine vendors were operating within parameters of professional conduct and honesty. Pharmacists were concerned with protecting both their authoritative role in distributing dangerous drugs and their proprietary rights to the knowledge embedded in medical preparations. They did not think that the entire formula needed to be on the label since that could potentially interfere with the individual medicine manufacturer's ability to compete in the market. The solution of using chemical analysis permitted an objective method of scrutiny to cut through the dubious claims and obfuscatory tactics of disreputable manufacturers. Scientific analysis would protect the integrity of legitimate pharmacy while simultaneously protecting the health of the people.

The Dominion Legislation

Starting in 1904, the federal government began its own efforts to control patent medicines. That year, Senator Michael Sullivan, a physician and former president of the Canadian Medical Association who was acting on behalf of his confreres in the Ontario Medical Council, moved that the governor general take actions to investigate the patent medicine business. The Senate agreed to the motion, and on the same date, the secretary of state, Mr. R.W. Scott, asked the minister of inland revenue to investigate the issue. This investigation wound gradually through the bureaucracy. In April 1905, eight months after the initial request, the minister of inland revenue asked A.E. DuBerger, an analytical chemist, to prepare such a report. DuBerger submitted the report in April of the following year.[36]

DuBerger's report examined specifically how the Adulteration Act could be modified to ensure against both adulteration of medicines and unethical medicines. DuBerger's conclusions paralleled those of his pharmacist cousins, reiterating the importance of the pharmaceutical sciences in defining the dangers of certain patent medicines. He explained that sometimes patent medicines "possess real merits and their formulae are the fruit of long work and often the result of several years of experience and observation." In these cases, publishing the formulae would "favour indelicacy and abuses on the part of unscrupulous persons" and would be "unfair." DuBerger concluded that the government ought to form a committee composed of "two physicians and two pharmacists and of the chief of the pharmaceutical or drug section of the Department of Inland Revenue ... to take into consideration all formulae of preparations submitted to them." This solution reflected the proffered solution of pharmacists while also accepting physicians' claims of authority over issues of public health.[37]

The subsequent events surrounding the creation of the Proprietary or Patent Medicine Act of 1908 illustrate the legislature's (and the public's) willingness to accept the authority of pharmaceutical chemistry and medicine as determinants of social policy, as well as indicating the importance of the cocaine panic in legislative debates. DuBerger's report was not formally discussed in the House of Commons, but a few weeks after its submission, Alfred Stockton, the member for St. John, moved that a committee be formed to consider the best way to deal legislatively with the trade in patent and proprietary medicines. Stockton's request, and the subsequent committee's investigation, may have come from the growing public concern over the patent medicine trade rather than from Sullivan's earlier initiative.[38] Adams's muckraking investigations into the proprietary medicine trade had been published months earlier, as had the cases of the BC infants who died after taking proprietary remedies. The subsequent committee resolved that a law "regulating the sale and manufacture in Canada of patent medicine and the advertising thereof" was necessary.[39] In 1907, William Templeman, the minister of Inland Revenue and (possibly coincidentally) the member of Parliament for Victoria, presented a bill to the House and sent copies of it to "those interested in the trade."[40] The main issue voiced in the House in 1907 was not a concern over the details of the bill but a concern that the bill would not make its way into law that year. When Templeman added the post of acting minister of marine and fisheries to his portfolio, Mr. J.G.H. Bergeron asked whether Templeman's new duties would kill the bill's chances. Templeman admitted that, since some of the responses he had received to the initial drafts of the bill had been critical, it would be difficult to present an acceptable form of legislation in that session. When the legislature debated the final decision to set back the bill, members of both the Opposition and the government noted their disappointment. As Mr. Bergeron observed, "the public are waiting for the passing of that Act with a great deal of interest." Despite support from both sides of the House, the concern to ensure that the legislation did not violate pharmacists' interests, combined with administrative complexity, resulted in the legislation being set aside until 1908.

Although legislators expressed few concerns about the proposed proprietary medicine act, the pharmacists viewed it differently. Druggists had serious reservations about the bill and saw the issue as so fundamental to the future of pharmacy that the issue unified the profession across the country. The impending legislation was the single most important factor leading to the creation of the Canadian Pharmaceutical Association. In an article tellingly entitled "Up, Pharmacists!" Joseph Emery, the editor of the *British Columbia Pharmaceutical Review* and president of the BC Pharmaceutical Association, observed that "druggists everywhere in the Dominion are anxious to blot out the narcotic evil, but hesitate for the lack of some governing spirit, some definite reliable instructions." Arguing against "this idea that 'it does not concern us,'" he claimed that "the health of the public is at stake, and an insidious foe more deadly than alcoholism even is sapping the character, energy and life, out of the nation. It is our duty to do our part – and it is a big part – to help suppress it now." Noting that "we are custodians of the public health and as such are held responsible," he asserted that "druggists must help themselves ... by uniting; by forming an association which shall extend from the Atlantic to the Pacific."[41] His lead editorial in the next issue was entitled "Will somebody please wake up the drug trade?"[42] Apparently, somebody did. A year later, with another version of a Dominion proprietary or patent medicine act about to be presented to Parliament, the Canadian Pharmaceutical Association was formed on 3 September 1907, with G.E. Gibbard as its president.[43] One of its first actions was to strike a committee that would propose alternative proprietary medicine legislation. After the committee deliberated for three days, its report was accepted by the conference with few amendments, and it laid its proposed legislation before the minister of inland revenue.

When Parliament sat the following year, legislators, who for two sessions had discussed the idea of restricting the proprietary medicine trade, were presented with a bill that had been changed to accommodate the interests of the druggists. Gibbard noted in the pages of the *Canadian Pharmaceutical Journal* that it was both "a complete justification of the formation of the Canadian Pharmaceutical Association and a testimony to the effectiveness of work done by it" since it included "every important suggestion" that the association had made.[44] It defined a proprietary or patent medicine as a remedy not found in any formulary adopted by pharmaceutical societies or in "the British Pharmacopoeia, the Codex Medicamentarious of France, the Pharmacopoeia of the United States, or any foreign pharmacopoeia approved by the Minister." It required all manufacturers to register their products after providing the minister of inland revenue with a list of the medicines that they proposed to manufacture. It forbade including cocaine in the remedies, it required the manufacturer to print the name of any substance included in an attached poison schedule on the label of the package, and it placed the burden of proof on the manufacturer for ensuring that the rules were being followed. As far as dangerous drugs were concerned, the legislation allowed manufacturers to choose between either printing the name of the restricted substance on the label or sending a statement to the Department of Inland Revenue that listed the items; in the latter case, if the mixture was approved, the manufacturer would be permitted to sell the substance without listing the problematic ingredients on the label.

Introducing the bill in April, Templeman summarized the main issues facing the legislation. Provincial enactments to restrict the trade almost always failed, he noted, "because it was felt that any Act of the kind should be of a Dominion character" to ensure uniformity in manufacturing parameters. He called the new legislation less "drastic" since it did not *require* a full formula to be printed on the label. Templeman explained the key aims of the bill in June, two months after consultation with interested parties: "We aim to prohibit absolutely the use of cocaine; we propose to prohibit the excessive use of alcohol; and we propose to require that any manufacturer who will put the formula on the label will not come under the act."[45] The bill was passed by the House after a debate that involved discussing specific aspects of the poison schedule and how much time pharmacists would have to get rid of their stock.

The debates in the Senate turned to broader issues of who should hold authority over the regulation and distribution of dangerous drugs. Many of the discussants were physicians. Senators scrutinized the clause outlining specific restrictions of the legislation. In three subsections, Clause 7 provided that no proprietary or patent medicine should contain "cocaine or any of its salts or preparations[,] ... alcohol in excess of the amount required as a solvent or preservative," or any drug in the attached schedule that was not listed on the label of the medicine. Senator Philippe Roy, a physician, proposed an amendment that created a proviso to the clause, stating that a manufacturer could have its substance exempted from the third restriction if it "transmit[ted] to the minister an affidavit specifying such drug and the proportion of it contained in the mixture and dose."[46] The provision gave the minister the authority to exempt the substance from the requirements of the bill. Several senators objected to this exemption. Dr. Sullivan argued that "by this clause you are ... authorizing the Minister of Inland Revenue to permit the sale of the most virulent poisons ... It is outrageous ... damnable unless the minister has supernatural knowledge."[47] At issue was the capability and authority of the minister to make distinctions better left to pharmacists and doctors. Senator James McMullen replied that the minister would act only on the recommendations of the analysts of the Department of Inland Revenue, whom he called "some of the best analysts in the country." He added that he "would rather trust the analysts of the department than the doctors ... We are safer in the hands of the analysts than we would be in the hands of the doctors."[48] The minister's position to decide would be reinforced by the authority of the chemists.

This assurance did not end the debate, and the Senate considered the broader definition of drugs. Several senators were concerned about how the bill would relate to the forthcoming Opium Act. Given that the latter legislation required opium to be sold only on the prescription of a physician and that the Proprietary or Patent Medicine Act allowed opium to be sold in proprietary medicines not controlled through the pharmacy, the senators were concerned that the latter could affect the proper operation of the former. Repealing the proviso to Clause 7 would not, Mr. Scott claimed, be detrimental to the operation of either legislation. In fact, it would allow the buyer to be aware of the existence of opium in the medicine. "In view of all the evidence we have of the harm that opium is doing, it will scarcely do for the Senate to say that a person buying a patent medicine or accepting a prescription at the druggist's shall have to take it without knowing whether or not opium forms an element in it."[49] He proceeded to challenge the priorities of the bill, which he saw as comparing "the lives of the public" to "the money invested in the drug business." When the Senate voted to retain the proviso, Mr. Scott grumbled that this was a case of "money over human life."[50]

In the debates over the Proprietary or Patent Medicine Act, the needs of the health of the public were weighed against the requirements of the pharmaceutical industry and the authority of the government. The legislators recognized the importance of the pharmaceutical societies, consulting with them at all stages of the legislation, both inside and outside of the standard committee channels of consultation. In drafting and refining the bill, the legislators recognized the dangers that the unrestricted sale of certain drugs, specifically cocaine and opiates, presented to the public. They also recognized and validated the potential role of the pharmaceutical industry and the retailers in controlling this trade under the auspices of the government. At the same time, the senators did not see a major role for physicians in protecting the public from patent medicines. As Scott's opposition suggests, the Senate also viewed as legitimate the authority of professionals to constrain the public's actions regarding health decisions. These events demonstrate how the government was erecting a more elaborate legislative framework, ostensibly to protect the public but also to guide public actions along lines determined by government policy. The legislation would conduct the conduct of the people, directing them to take proper action in order to defend their own health within parameters established by knowledgeable professionals.

The Proprietary or Patent Medicine Act saw a variety of reactions. Historian Glenn Murray has called the act "a very weak instrument," but the reaction by the doctors and druggists suggests that this weakness was a matter of interpretation.[51] According to the *Canadian Pharmaceutical Journal*, the legislation was almost exactly what the pharmacists had wanted. Gibbard explained that "this bill as it passed parliament is practically the recommendation of the [Canadian Pharmaceutical Association]."[52] Yet pharmacists, many of whom had their own lines of proprietaries, may have approved of the legislation specifically because of its limits. We see these limits in the doctors' reactions, which, although less precise, were certainly less positive. The *Canada Medical and Surgical Journal* printed a mixed review of the act. It noted that the schedule of poisons was comprehensive and important, but it condemned the mild restrictions that the legislation placed on the products themselves. It cited as an example the case that Mrs. Winslow's Soothing Syrup for Infants could still be sold, providing that it had "Morphine" printed on the label. The editor still wanted a formula on the label. In contrast, the *Canada Lancet* either ignored the legislation or saw it as so weak as to be meaningless. In September 1909, fully one year after the act received royal assent, the *Lancet* printed an editorial demanding that physicians lobby for some form of restriction on the patent medicine trade. In a move that reflected Gibbard's earlier concerns over the integrity of some proprietary medicine manufacturers, the writer observed that some manufacturers fraudulently indicated on their labels the presence of a variety of ingredients that were not in the remedy. Whereas Gibbard thought that manufacturers would mislabel their remedies to hide the presence of dangerous drugs, the *Lancet* was suggesting the opposite: manufacturers were stating the presence of drugs that were not in fact part of the formula. This, the *Lancet* speculated, may have been to bolster the claims of effectiveness in their advertisements. The article called on organized physicians to vigilantly voice their opposition to such behaviour.[53]

The law also garnered unwanted international attention, with varied opinions on its usefulness. In September 1909, the *Journal of the American Medical Association* printed an article that condemned the act. The editor's criticisms were extensive:

> A careful perusal of the new Canadian Act respecting proprietary and patent medicines will leave the impression that the law has been framed with a view rather to appeasing public clamor than to furnishing public protection ... It would seem that the new law will actually protect the Canadian public against cocain-containing [*sic*] nostrums; but from the innumerable other vicious forms of self-administered medicaments the Act seems to offer tempting opportunities for the unscrupulous manufacturer to profit at the expense of the people.[54]

Canadian medical journals gave this article a mixed reaction. The *Canadian Practitioner and Review* simply printed the article verbatim, with no comment.[55] W.A. Young, the managing editor of the *Canadian Journal of Medicine and Surgery*, however, took exception to the "quite uninvited" criticism. Carefully avoiding any specific support for the legislation, Young noted that Canadian doctors "are a unit on the subject of pure drugs and proper public protection" and argued that the *JAMA*'s editor had no place criticizing the Canadian lawmakers. "We are at a serious loss," Young observed, "to learn the ingredients of the self-esteem nerve tonic this gentleman takes. It really should be writ large on the label and filed away in the archives of drugdom."[56] Nevertheless, Young did not frame his criticism of the *JAMA*'s charges by defending the legislation, preferring instead to defend Canadian institutions from an American critic. Doctors' reactions to the Proprietary or Patent Medicine Act, therefore, suggest that they recognized the weakness of the legislation but saw it as a better condition than the unregulated trade. In contrast, the *British Medical Journal* congratulated "the Colonies" of Canada, South Africa, and Australia for "vigorously attacking" the "quack medicine traffic." This article was designed as a criticism of the "apathetic" stance of the British government toward the trade.[57] With a more vigorous law on the books in the United States, the American journal could be critical of the Canadian law; the British journal simply sounded envious.

The efforts to enact restrictions on patent medicines were part of a broader movement to protect the health of the public by reducing the perceived social threat presented by easy access to unrestricted medical products. The rising panic over cocaine, a persistent vigilance over alcohol sales, and a concern over the availability of habit-forming opiates combined to present restrictions on patent medicines as a viable and necessary public-policy issue. What remained were questions about who would control the distribution of the substances and about what role the government would play in regulating the drugs. Limited provincial efforts to restrict patent medicines led to a recognition of the need for federal legislation. The result of this legislation was an increased reliance on the knowledge and skill of chemists, the strengthening of a government bureaucracy overseeing the nation's health, and an acceptance of the pharmaceutical profession's role as a guardian of society. The process of creating patent medicine laws recognized the doctors' credibility when identifying problematic substances; but this power of definition did not equate with social authority in policy. Given the conflicting perspectives on how best to ensure that dangerous substances would be properly regulated, the government elected to extend an existing administrative system and to reinforce it with the knowledge and skill of chemical and pharmacological investigation. The government's measures were driven by concerns about the dangers of drug misuse as articulated by physicians, pharmacists, and social reformers, but they resulted in more authority for pharmacists and more oversight by government agencies. Substances defined as dangerous, habit-forming, or poisonous were now the subject of the attention of federal regulatory agencies. Regimes of control were growing, authoritative voices were becoming stronger, and the field of visibility over the manufacture, sale, and distribution of problematic drugs was widening.

9
Drug Laws and the Creation of Illegality

By 1908, the various streams of meaning attached to drug use combined and flowed freely. Addictive drugs, especially opiates but also cocaine, the newcomer to the psychoactive party, had been transformed in the popular imagination from medications that might cause habituation into dangerous drugs associated with a range of problematic behaviours. Medical and pharmaceutical professionalization, changing ideas of mental and physical health, international diplomacy, and concern for the future of the nation all intersected in a series of legislative initiatives to restrict the access to and use of drugs in Canada. Pharmacy acts in all provinces and territories placed "poisons" under the control of professionals whose training and respectability would enable them to make, so the argument went, judicious decisions on who could access the drugs. Physicians' prescriptions were normally the means by which individuals could purchase controlled drugs, but many pharmacy acts also permitted pharmacists to provide drugs to individuals with whom they were familiar. Some laws placed even stricter controls on cocaine, making it available only by medical prescription, with no room for discretion of the vendor. Outside of professionally recommended medication, the Dominion Proprietary or Patent Medicine Act of 1908 placed many commonly sold substances under more systematic scrutiny by professional analytic chemists and by the Dominion government, while simultaneously informing consumers about any problematic substances they might be taking.

Yet, such regulations could not deal in any satisfactory way with the importation, manufacture, and distribution of drugs that would not be used for medical purposes – at least not insofar as "medical" meant "under the direction of a physician." In discussing the proprietary medicine controls initiated by the US Pure Food and Drug Act of 1906, Tim Hickman reminds us that this was a labelling and a product-safety measure more than a prohibition measure. The Canadian legislation was arguably more prohibitory for certain substances since it absolutely forbade remedies containing cocaine (which the US legislation did not do), but it also constrained, rather than prohibited, the distribution of problematic substances. Since it was dealing with manufactured medical products, the Proprietary or Patent Medicine Act, regardless of how effective it may have appeared to be, did not address substances that were rapidly becoming associated with a criminal subclass. Nevertheless, what is important to note about the proprietary medicine legislation is that, as was the case in provincial pharmacy acts, the Dominion law's provisions added another degree of danger to opiates and other listed substances. The association of opiates with problematic behaviours and criminality, then, helped to sharpen the focus on the potential social dangerousness of these increasingly restricted substances. Moreover, the Proprietary or Patent Medicine Act of 1908 was part of a broader set of restrictive measures framed as socially progressive, which placed more constraints on what could be consumed and on who could consume it. These measures were all about nation building: constructing and strengthening an imagined community of Canadians.

Another piece of legislation, which affected fewer people but was also related to the nation-building project, was the Opium Act of 1908, which prohibited the importation, manufacture, and sale of opium for nonmedical purposes. This act has normally taken centre stage in discussions of the origins of Canada's drug laws. But it is better viewed as one of a set of measures, spread out over three years, that ushered in the criminalization of drugs in Canada. It was one part of a broadening regime of control over substances that were being decried as dangerous to the health of people and the nation. This notion of danger was complex, including not only the simple physiological functioning of the body but also the integrity of the will and the moral capacity of the individual. As this book has argued, this process began long before 1908. But the circumstances around the creation of the act, and the causes of subsequent modifications, shaped the specific form of this legislation.

The Opium Act of 1908

When Deputy Minister of Labour William Lyon Mackenzie King's investigations into the race riots of 1907 found opium manufacturers seeking compensation, his reaction to this situation was part of a much broader process of growing concern than may be obvious at first glance. His story is often presented as a one-man morality play about a zealous moral entrepreneur pushing a racist agenda to target a behaviour of an undesirable racial out-group. The narrative concludes with King as a moral entrepreneur, whose efforts are held up in most historical accounts as singularly influential in driving drug prohibition, both in 1908 and in 1911, when the law was expanded to include morphine and cocaine. Yet the "moral entrepreneurship" argument, although appealing, is focused on individual moments as driving policy change. It misses both the gradual change in public and medical opinions about opium and the sudden jolts to public opinion that can occur during specific moments of crisis or media attention, such as the one created with the magazine articles on patent medicine fraud earlier in the decade. To be sure, the 1908 act, a one-page document of two paragraphs, was not earth shatteringly new, but it did establish a precedent of restriction that informed subsequent laws. Thus we begin with the context and creation of the 1908 law as a way of understanding the creation of federal drug legislation.

Concern over nonmedical opium use was growing in newspapers across the country far before 1908. Editors and reporters presented to their readers the multiple meanings and understandings of opium and, by the beginning of the twentieth century, cocaine. By the 1880s, although opium's medical nature remained a topic of debate among physicians, its habitual use had begun to take on the trappings of a moral panic, with the elements of the drunkard's progress embedded in the story. In 1881, the *Manitoba Daily Free Press* reproduced a story of the deaths by morphine injection of "persons more or less prominent" in New York City. It was a tale of the dangers of pleasure seeking but one overlaid with the dangers of medical treatment. "Most of them had ... begun the injections in order to relieve themselves of pain ... The effect was so pleasant, so delicious, indeed, that they were seduced into the use of morphine when they had no need of it, and, soon yielding completely to the habit, were destroyed by it."[1] The *Free Press* told its readers about "Noble Victims of the Fatal Vice," citing the case of a young society woman who had died of an overdose at a party, although an investigation found that she had been using opium for years.[2] The *Toronto Globe* published an editorial in 1887 explaining that the new drug of choice for the elites was morphine, whose "effects are said to be still more frightful than those which De Quincey has made immortal." Moreover, its demographics and reasons for consumption were becoming worrisome: "Whole circles of ladies it seemed [sic] take it for pleasure, not because they have been initiated into its use by its being prescribed as an antidote to pain, but simply because they have learned that for the time being it makes them comfortable and bright, and helps amazingly to pass the time and even to stir the fancy." The editorial was steeped in references to indulgence by the refined, but profligate, class. These were "fine ladies" or "fashionable people" who took morphine to deal with "ennui." They belonged to "the most elegant classes of society" and concealed their "syringes and artistically made bottles" in jewellery. Such stories, twisted variations on the themes of society-page gossip columns, revealed dangers. The morphinomaniac's life, then, followed an opium drunkard's progress:

The end of course comes, and speedily, and comes in the shape of the direst troubles and the deepest darkness. Rapid degeneracy, both physical, mental and moral, sets in. The body takes on a lean, emaciated appearance. The brain loses its power. The conscience becomes debauched. The victim very speedily can neither speak the truth nor do the right. The morphia habit, we are told, frequently transforms the tenderest affection into hate.[3]

The opium habit's victims, whether the once ill but respectable citizens who had taken pain relief to the extreme or the capricious society ladies who sought stimulation, represented a perilous outcome of the uncontrolled quest for palliation.

Such tragedies needed their villains. These were the smugglers and dealers who preyed on these victims. Winnipeggers may have been shocked to learn, as a *Free Press* headline cried in 1901, that there was "Trafficing [*sic*] in Opium Here" and that "The Vice [Is] Prevalent." Winnipeg had attained cosmopolitan status since it had "become infected with vices which are generally supposed to be peculiar to the Chinatown dens of San Francisco or the slums of Chicago."[4] This observation was made in a story about Chinese opium smugglers, who provided the drug to "women of the town and inmates of houses of ill-fame" and whose dangerous nature was inscribed in both racial and moral discourses, as we saw in Chapter 4. But other stories spread the net of guilt more broadly, identifying other types of opium users (who were probably white people because their race was not mentioned). When Jack Lynch was arrested in Detroit for smuggling Chinese men into the United States, he told about "an organization which had for its purpose the smuggling of Chinamen and opium."[5] Presumably, given that they were smuggling Chinese men, these smugglers were not Chinese themselves since such racial outsiders would not likely have such easy passage across the border. In 1895, the *Free Press* informed its readers of "A Novel Method" of opium smuggling. "Large quantities of opium are smuggled from this side in the stomachs of live cattle, and that a great many of cattle are also smuggled."[6] Here, as in Jack Lynch's Detroit adventures, opium was a component in broad networks of contraband smuggling, with some clearly innovative techniques.

The attention of the Manitoba newspaper was not coincidental. Since Winnipeg was a major transportation hub for the railway, its province was also a major conduit for the opium traffic. In 1887, a man named George Cannon, arrested in San Francisco with 386 boxes of smuggled opium, explained that he could make a lot of money by bringing opium from Minneapolis. This opium, the paper reported, "was received at Victoria from China, and taken thence over the Canadian Pacific to Winnipeg. It crossed the border in Manitoba and made its way to California by way of Minneapolis and Omaha."[7] In 1888, the *Brandon Sun Weekly* reported that Dominion officials had confirmed the Manitoba connection. When residents of Dakota Territory complained about opium and lumber smuggling from Manitoba to their side of the line, a Canadian customs officer charged with investigating the complaints found four roads into the territory over which opium and lumber were transported illegally. He recommended that the North West Mounted Police step up their border patrols.[8]

Smuggling had become big business, and the Canadian Pacific Railway allowed opium to reach distribution points across the country. The rapid increase in opium imports between 1886 and 1894, shown in Figure 1, was likely due to a different excise regime in Canada than in the United States. Although the duty on opium imported into both countries was $1.00 per pound, the US authorities exacted a tariff of $10.00 per pound on refined opium, whereas the Canadian authorities did not. Consequently, a significant opium-refining industry had developed, for which the *Toronto Globe* noted that "the Government does not want any credit." One report numbered the refining factories in British Columbia at sixteen in Victoria and Vancouver, "any one of which could produce more of the refined article than could possibly enter into the consumption of Canada for medical purposes."[9] So the smuggling industry became big business.[10] In 1887, US customs officers came to Kingston, Ontario, to investigate reports that the city was a major hub for opium smuggling. Having "ascertained that Kingston had been the distributing point in the opium business," they kept an eye on two trunks, each containing 450 pounds of opium. But the smugglers were wily and did nothing while the customs officials were in the city. Once the officers left, the opium did too.[11]

This network of smuggling and criminality, infused with an element of foreignness and debauchery, gave rise to a bifurcated understanding of the dangers of opium. In an extensive article on "The Drug Habit," published in 1903, the *Toronto Globe* provided some sensationalized descriptions of who was using the drug. This article was focused mostly on social and even eugenic subclasses and less desirable elements among society. Drugs, the *Globe* argued, appeal to "the mentally weak ... to produce hilarity, stupor, or morbid dreams of happiness." Such mentally weak individuals could be everywhere, but the demographics of opium users were, to the *Globe*, more specific:

> It has been shown that a majority of the class known as habitual criminals are addicted to the drug. Both in the army and navy the use of opium has developed very rapidly. Some of the soldiers acquired the habit of opium-smoking in the east, and the practice has found fruitful soil in the idle routine of soldier life. In the navy this method of taking the drug is less common, but the habit of opium-eating has been acquired, to some extent, in the intercourse with natives of foreign countries.[12]

The profligate, debauched, and criminal residuum was the flipside of the elite, noble, and fashionable individuals whose tragic tales had served as harbingers of the widespread, habitual use of opium a generation earlier. Thomas De Quincey, as the *Globe* illustrated in the 1887 article, remained a dominant image in the stories of opium habituation. Yet decades of cultural change, the rhetoric of social reform, evangelical temperance movements, and the emergence of eugenics sentiments as an extreme form of national and racial protectionism transformed such debauchery from an amusing spectator sport for social observers into a pressing problem that threatened the nation. So in the *Manitoba Daily Free Press* in 1908, just after the Opium Act became law, a women's columnist with the evocative name of Mary Markwell reproduced the tale of the opium drunkard's progress before warning mothers to protect their sons, the future of the nation. Markwell told of a "wreck of a man" who had owned "a large and prosperous business" but who followed a trail of increasing danger until he was ruined. He began with smoking tobacco and then moved to drugs, becoming "a victim to the morphine habit," from which "his downfall was rapid." The article concluded with a warning to mothers to speak to their sons about the dangers of tobacco, which would "injure his mental as well as his bodily growth" and lead him into the opium habit and its decline.[13]

These articles are samples of a change in the perception, if not the reality, of the demographics of opium use. Understanding the shift to the criminalization of habitual opium consumption requires us to be aware of the power of perception over fact. As I discussed in relation to the Chinese opium smoker in Chapter 4, in law creation (as with reform agitation), sometimes it is not the actuality that matters as much as the perception. In *Dark Paradise,* his ground-breaking work on the creation of American drug laws, David Courtwright argues that by the time national drug laws were passed in the United States, the demographics of users had shifted away from the iatrogenic addicts and toward the criminal subclass and its recreational use of drugs.[14] Courtwright uses insightful analyses of statistical data and other material to challenge the labelling interpretation of drug laws, which posits that everyday, law-abiding people are labelled outlaws by legislation that criminalizes their activities. Instead, Courtwright argues that, by the time the Harrison Act of 1914 was passed, iatrogenic addiction had been on the decline and that recreational use by a more undesirable social subclass was on the increase. They were already criminals and didn't need to be labelled as such by a legal change.

This view of the demographic shift, based on a brilliant examination of complex data, although insightful, may be beside the point. Since most citizens would have little personal interaction with opium addicts of Courtwright's subclass variety, more important is the *impression* of criminality associated with opium, whether or not the addict demography had begun to shift toward a preponderance of recreational, criminal-subclass users. Moreover, as Louise Foxcroft has argued, by the end of the nineteenth century in the United Kingdom, there were two streams of understanding of the opium user: the innocent victim of iatrogenic addiction, who was often drawn from the more respectable classes; and the profligate abuser of psychotropics, who came from a pleasure-seeking criminal subclass.[15] It was this perceptual shift that affected understandings of opium use and that created deeper notions of its baneful influences. So, although the numbers are strong indicators of a shift in the demographics of use, Courtwright does not discuss in detail the discursive reconstruction of opium prior to the advent of legislation to criminalize it. State-level pharmacy legislation, high customs duties on importation, and additional excise fees on opium refining made it lucrative to smuggle opium. These factors, in turn, gave a criminal aspect to opiates before national legislation outlawed their use, a sort of cultural labelling of opium as criminal, if not yet criminalized. So the critique of the labelling interpretation may be technically accurate because the shift toward criminal use happened before the national criminalization of opiates, but it may not appreciate the scope of the perceptual shift that was taking place. In other words, before opium was made illegal, it was discursively linked to crime and criminal behaviour since what people normally read in the newspapers was that opium was smuggled, consumed by criminals, used in poisoning cases, anathematized in patent medicine advertisements promising "no opium" (or "no cocaine"), and (like cocaine) stolen from pharmacies or obtained through other nefarious means. Both opium and cocaine were thereby associated with deviance, notwithstanding the number of legitimate iatrogenic addicts and respectable mothers, grandmothers, businessmen, and physicians who may have also been jonesing for a regular fix. It was within this smithy of belief that drug laws were forged.

By 1908, the popular understanding of opium was complex, and it occupied several different cultural spaces, all related to ideas of national integrity. Smoked opium was a substance indulged in by Chinese sojourners, foreigners who would never be able to assimilate but who might entice young men and, most alarmingly, women to surrender their virtue and be ruined. Opium, in the form of hypodermic morphine, was a secret indulgence of a wide range of people, not only the rich, although they were the ones with the custom-made hypodermic needles and gem-encrusted carrying cases. These were images of decadence that paralleled the concerns of eugenicists and temperance reformers that the social elites, the supposed leaders of society, were debasing and degrading their stock. Other forms of opium use had a rougher demographic, being an indulgence of sailors, soldiers, and other members of a distasteful (yet often economically necessary) subclass. At the same time, opium remained a valuable medicine. Despite the advent of new and less troublesome pharmaceuticals, opiates remained heavily prescribed, and its derivatives, especially morphine and heroin, remained essential palliatives for many common symptoms.

These threads of cultural understanding, the ways that Canadians thought of opium, began to converge in the early twentieth century. The anxiety was intensified, and opiates could even be eclipsed by the newer and (to some) more dangerous drug of cocaine, although as we saw with the story of Edward C., often these substances worked as a tag team of psychotropic indulgence. Doctors and druggists had expressed elements of the panic in the rhetoric around their concern over the trade in patent and proprietary medicines, but they were not the only ones to discuss the pernicious influence of cocaine. The widespread understanding of the perceived dangers of drug use became embedded in casual rhetorical forms. Advertisements for patent medicines often appeared as large exposé articles engendering or drawing on panic toward drugs. An article in the *Manitoba Daily Free Press* cited "prominent city druggists," empowered as guardians and harbingers of danger, who were "lamenting the terrible increase in the use of opium." It reminded readers that authors Thomas De Quincey, Wilkie Collins, and Samuel Taylor Coleridge had all been addicts, asserted that "the sombre, joyless melancholy state of servitude to this ruinous drug is the sure end," and then concluded with the fortunate information that "there is but one thing known that will 'stimulate the brain and steady the nerves,' in a natural and harmless way. That is Paine's Celery Compound."[16] In 1897, the top half of a page in the *Toronto Globe* included a tabloid-style exposé of "a whole Town enslaved by the Cocaine habit," linking the habit to cocaine-laced catarrh cures and then reminding the reader that Chase's Catarrh Cure was cocaine free.[17] Even reputable drug companies were not exempt from such sensationalization, drawing on fears of unscrupulous, although legally certified, drug vendors. A 1907 ad for the Gordon Mitchell Drug Company in Winnipeg informed the readers, "We do not abuse our privileges as druggists. We will not on any account sell cocaine, morphine or other injurious drugs ... without a doctor's prescription."[18] Less seriously, but equally significantly, when mocking attempts to deal with dyspepsia through trade negotiations, the *Globe* editorialized in 1908 "that the greatest menace portentously assailing the human race today is not alcoholic liquor, cocaine, morphine, race suicide, gambling, trades unionism, or bargain-hunting, but the little-suspected though invidious mince pie."[19] In all of these examples, the awareness of opium and cocaine as dangerous and troublesome products and the idea of their habitual use as socially ruinous were necessary for the advertisements or parodies to have any positive commercial effect or satirical punch.

William Lyon Mackenzie King himself was not a stranger to nonmedical opium use and to the potential problems it engendered. As a young man,

King's experience of opium and its derivatives was – like most, if not all, Canadians of his time – as valuable for treating a variety of illnesses. When helping to take care of his brother Max during an extended bout of quinsey (a complication of tonsillitis), he purchased morphine after Max "had both cheeks lanced."[20] As a law student, he worked in the police courts, and his diaries include accounts of people who were morphine or opium users and found themselves in trouble with the law. Moreover, an acquaintance, Irene Shields, appears to have been addicted to morphine. In 1894, he mentions that she promised to leave off morphine if her father quit drinking. Shields entered the Toronto Asylum in March 1895, and when King visited her in June, just before her discharge, "she told me all about the Morphine habit which she had acquired, how she had secretly stolen it and had at times asked God to help her & then got up from her knees and given way to temptation – who has not experienced this? A tear came falling down her cheek as she told me all."[21] Shields remained in the asylum for just under five months with a condition diagnosed as mania, and when she was discharged, her record noted that her insanity had lasted only two months.[22] Although King's rhetorical question – "who has not experienced this?" – may have been a reference simply to the inability for a human to resist temptation in general, it may also suggest, in his nonchalance, a general familiarity with the problems of opium addiction. Later in 1895, King read De Quincey. But instead of condemning the opium habit, which one would expect of someone with King's experiences and deep Presbyterian devotion to moral uplift, King admitted that he was searching for "thrilling experiences in the effects of opium." He complained that, at least in the first half of the book, "[one] gets only the history of a life which would be extremely interesting if one were looking for that."[23] King was looking for something more sensational.

Such statements are indicative of the complexity of King's understanding of opium, belying a simple assertion that King's report was exclusively about Chinese exclusion. First, King was intimately familiar with the problems caused by opiate habituation. He saw it as leading to personal distress in close friends and witnessed the association with criminality and dissolution. Second, King was not initially repulsed by opium. He, a young legal student from a good family, was interested in opium as a provider of thrills, although as far as we know he sought that thrill not from opium, only from its literary representation. Even though there is no evidence that he reflected on these experiences in 1908 when he penned his report to Parliament condemning the opium trade, King's personal familiarity with the effects of opiates, not just his knowledge of Chinese opium smoking, suggests a broader understanding of the drug's manifestations. King was aware of opium in its form as a medicine, intoxicant, and bringer of fantastic visions; opium's baneful influences, and its many forms, were well known, indeed.

Yet, a focus on King's role reduces the history of the opium laws in Canada to a "great man" approach and tends to minimize the social and political context in which King operated. There can be little doubt that King's report set in motion the process of creating the Opium Act of 1908, but the fact that the legislation passed a mere month after King returned from British Columbia should suggest that there was more going on behind the scenes than embodied in a report from a deputy minister and the subsequent push toward legislation. Indeed, the years prior to the passing of this "Act to Suppress the Importation, Manufacture, and Sale of Opium for Other than Medical Purposes" had seen increased pressure on the government to do something about the opium trade, with several other individuals taking an active role in both investigating the issue and lobbying for change. King's investigation was the final step in a process of lobbying and alliance building. It was this process that resulted in the legislation being agreed to immediately and unanimously by all parties in the House of Commons.

The government had been facing demands to do something about the opium traffic for years prior to 1908. In 1905, various evangelical organizations, concerned about the continued British trade in opium, organized to send a series of petitions to King Edward VII via the secretary of state and the governor general. Many of these petitions cited the immorality of forcing opium on China, contrary to the wishes of the Chinese government itself. For example, the petition from the Annual Conference of the Methodist Church in the Province of Nova Scotia asserted that "the conference and the great bulk of the members of the Church we represent have long regarded the Opium Traffic with China as a reproach to the British Nation, of which we are loyal citizens."[24] This language was similar to that of petitions sent by conferences in Alberta and Manitoba and by Anglican Synods in Toronto and Niagara. All petitions referred to the immorality of the traffic and to how its continuation was a blot on a Christian nation. The Anglican Synod of Toronto pleaded "for the relief of the Empire from the great responsibility for the Opium Traffic" and denounced the traffic as a "terrible hindrance to Christian Missions."[25] Similar messages were sent periodically in the years prior to 1908, most of which were focused on the trade in Asia.[26] In March 1907, the Board of the Department of Temperance and Moral Reform of the Methodist Church endorsed a petition that was being sent to "all civilized governments to take separate and united action to prohibit the selling of intoxicants and opium to uncivilized races."[27] Several petitions with such language arrived at the secretary of state's office over the next few months.

Making the transition from a concern that the trade in opium in foreign countries would corrupt "uncivilized races" to arguments against the domestic trade was relatively simple. In June 1907, three months before the race riots in Vancouver's Chinatown, the Health and Morals Committee of the City of Victoria, British Columbia, sent a petition to the Dominion government asking it "to prohibit the manufacture and sale of opium."[28] This petition arrived in Ottawa even though a resolution to send the message had not been passed by the Victoria City Council. It had been defeated on a vote of five to four, although one councillor later admitted that he had voted against it only because, as he understood the constitutional division of authority, the Dominion government could not restrict drug sales; it was a provincial matter.[29] Such efforts were supported further east, where, in June, while Mackenzie King was calculating reparations payments for race-riot damages, Ontario Methodist conferences in London and the Bay of Quinte called on the Dominion government to restrict the sale of opium "in any of its forms except for medicinal purposes."[30] The *Victoria Daily Colonist* lauded these efforts from "various bodies in Eastern Canada" and observed that

> it is difficult to understand on what grounds this request could be refused. It requires no argument to secure an admission that such a deadly drug ought not to be dispensed indiscriminately to all who care to buy it; and when one comes to think about it the wonder is that such prohibitory legislation was not long ago placed on the statute books of the country.[31]

A month later, the *Colonist* reiterated this bewilderment when, explaining that "a movement will be initiated to suppress the opium traffic in Canada," it wondered "why a similar proceeding was not taken long ago."[32] Five days later, the Opium Act was presented to Parliament.

The *Colonist* may have wondered why such a movement did not emerge earlier, but it did not question why it was emerging at that time; a historian should do so. Part of the reason for the amplified volume of concern being transmitted to the government was the rising chorus against the opium trade in China. As we saw in Chapter 4, this outcry was orchestrated by the networks of evangelical missionary societies and their local auxiliaries, who hosted talks and raised funds for their evangelical campaigns. Another influence was the efforts of certain key individuals within Canada. In early 1908, S.D. Chown, the general secretary of the Temperance and Moral Reform Department of the Methodist Church of the Dominion of Canada, Newfoundland, and Bermuda, met with Sir Wilfrid Laurier and asked him whether the prime minister would like Chown to "look into the Opium question and report my results to you."[33] Apparently, the prime minister agreed, for on 26 May, while King was en route to British Columbia, the Methodist gentleman sent a detailed four-page report about his observations while visiting Canada's western provinces, including descriptions of how opium was made, the degree of opposition to opium from Chinese officials in China and Canada, and what western municipalities were doing to deal with the Opium question. In his conclusions, Chown asserted that "the Chinese government greatly desires to put an end to the opium habit among its people ... The better class of Chinese in Canada are strongly in favor of putting an end to it, and ... the Municipal councils want to prevent its sale." Chown then reminded Laurier that the British government had recently resolved to take steps "for the speedy abolition of the system of licensing opium dens in crown colonies" and that an international conference on the opium trade was to be held in January 1909. With all this evidence, he argued, "the Canadian Government will surely not hesitate to pass a law preventing the importation, manufacture and sale of opium except for medicinal purposes. Only the Dominion government has the necessary power to meet the situation, and we trust you will soon make use of it."[34]

King's and Chown's visits to British Columbia overlapped, and although it is tempting to speculate about whether they met each other while there, they did meet with some of the same key advocates for the suppression of opium. One of these was P.T. York, the editor of the *Wa Ying Yat-Po* daily Chinese newspaper published in Vancouver. He informed Chown of the cost of opium smoking to individual users and said that about one-third of the Chinese men in Vancouver smoked, along with "immoral white women." York's discussion was translated by Peter Hing (Chown misnamed him Hong), a moral entrepreneur in his own right. The son of Ng Mon Hing, a Chinese lay missionary, teacher, and Presbyterian minister who had arrived in Victoria in March 1895, Peter Hing had studied law at McGill University, from which he graduated at the top of his class.[35] Both King and Chown were impressed with Hing's efforts to reform his countrymen, and he had an ongoing correspondence with the deputy minister of labour prior to returning to Canton to take a government position.[36] He saw himself as an advocate for his compatriots while in Canada, noting to King in November 1908 that many of his countrymen "in various parts of Canada" were concerned about the effect of opium on "morality, society and standard of life." He argued that "they all condemn the further existence of this evil."[37]

Hing was a motivated individual. Almost immediately after receiving his law degree, he took a leadership role in the Chinese Anti-Opium League of Vancouver. He may also have been instrumental in founding a similar organization in Victoria, although the *Colonist* mentions only a "well educated Chinaman" as an organizer of the provincial capital's league.[38] Writing to King in November 1908, Hing reminded the newly elected member of the federal Parliament and newly appointed minister of labour that Hing's reform efforts focused on several policies that he saw as oppressive to the Chinese in North America. In 1909, writing to King after the minister's trip to China for the first Opium Conference, Hing used his influential connection first to congratulate King on all the work he had done for Chinese people in championing the elimination of the opium trade and then to make an argument for the elimination of the head tax on bona fide Chinese students, an issue for which Hing himself had begun to advocate among his alma mater at McGill, law students at the University of Toronto, and "the leading citizens of Montreal."[39] Although King, newly enamoured of the Chinese people after his sojourn in "The Flowery Kingdom," was sympathetic to the issue of Chinese students and the head tax, Hing did not rely entirely on King for his support. He also wrote to Charles Doherty, a former professor at the McGill Law School and now a Conservative member of Parliament for Montreal's St. Anne riding.[40] Interestingly, as we will see, King and Doherty would clash in 1911 over the Opium and Drug Act.

In his report to Parliament on the opium trade, King acknowledged many of these precedents. He mentioned Chown's own investigation and cited letters from Hing regarding the hopes of the "better Chinese" in British Columbia to see opium eradicated. As Chown had done in his letter to Laurier, King outlined the domestic situation, including listing the volume of opium being refined and the dire situation of white women being found to be opium habitués. Next, he referenced laws that were already on the books, including pharmacy laws, which the easy access to opium seemed to flaunt. King then turned to contextualizing the legal status by referencing the international situation. He listed several countries whose laws placed excessive controls on opium, including legislation in the United States from several decades earlier and in the United Kingdom. In his conclusions, King, like Chown before him, made an argument for the integrity of the nation:

> Other instances of legislative enactments to suppress the opium evil, and to protect individuals from the baneful effects of this drug, might be given, if further examples were necessary. What is more important, however, than the example of other countries, is the good name of our own. To be indifferent to the growth of such an evil in Canada would be inconsistent with those principles of morality which ought to govern the conduct of a Christian nation.[41]

King mustered a broad array of evidence to reiterate the messages that had been sent to the government repeatedly over at least the past few years. Continuing to ignore the blight of the opium trade, domestically and internationally, was no way to conduct a Christian country. It harmed the integrity of the nation both by damaging its people's health and by damaging its reputation as a moral and upstanding international citizen.

The lobbying efforts of Hing, York, and various evangelical societies, Chown's visit to British Columbia and report to Laurier, and the growing international pressure to do something about the opium trade predated and reinforced King's observations about the problems of the manufacture and sale of opium for nonmedical purposes. So when, in his Royal Commission report, King noted that opium's baneful influences were too well known to

require comment, he could draw on a body of evidence to support that assertion. Growing awareness of a problem with nonmedical, or extramedical,
opium use (self-medicating without a physician's supervision), which had
nothing to do with Chinese opium smoking, reiterated in newspapers,
lamented in petitions from church missionary societies and temperance
organizations, and lobbied against by medical and pharmaceutical societies,
meant that the problems of opium use were indeed too well known to require
comment. But not so well known that they did not require action.

Consequently, when Rodolphe Lemieux, who was the postmaster general
and King's boss and whose department oversaw the Ministry of Labour,
stood in the legislature to move that it was expedient "to prohibit the
importation, manufacture and sale of opium for other than medical purposes," he was unable to finish his speech because a member of the Opposition immediately shouted "approved," and several others concurred.[42] In
response, Robert Borden, leader of the Opposition, made a joke of the
Parliament's unanimous agreement. He noted that Lemieux "is very much
in the position of a certain [law] practitioner, a friend of mine, who many
years ago made a motion in court in a certain case. The court was so much
in favour of the motion that they refused to hear him, and he complained
most bitterly because he was not allowed to make his argument."[43] When
the legislation came up for second reading, normally the point at which a
bill is sent to a committee to be scrutinized and, if necessary, amended
before being returned for a third reading, it was passed with no discussion
and received third reading immediately afterward, thereby being sent to
the Senate.[44] The only concern from the upper house was that businesses
currently holding stocks of opium should be allowed to have time get rid
of it, something that some argued would take years. The Senate's compromise
amendment allowed a six month window, during which time remaining
opium stocks would be held in bond; if not sold for medical purposes, they
would have to be exported.[45]

As it did in the House of Commons, the Opium Act was met across the
country with general approval, when it was noticed at all. The *Toronto
Globe* referred to the government's "commendable promptness in dealing
with the opium evil ... with a drastic measure of absolute prohibition."[46] In
the *Victoria Daily Colonist*, the enthusiasm was more effusive. Its Saturday
"Women's Realm" section commented that "there can be but one feeling
among women ... about the law ... It is to them a cause of thankfulness that
Canada will not become a distributing centre for a drug that does so much
to bring about the ruin of those who use it." The writer did note, however,
that "it is too much to hope that men or women who have already become
slaves of opium will be cured by any laws ... but it will, if rigidly enforced,
prevent the growth of the habit."[47] At its annual meeting, the Anglican
Synod passed a motion expressing its sincere gratitude to the government

for the law.[48] The Toronto Methodist Conference did the same at its annual meeting in June 1909.[49] The ladies of the Woman's Christian Temperance Union (WCTU) were positive but suitably moderate in their response. The WCTU's journal, the *White Ribbon Tidings*, observed that the Opium Act has come "not one moment too soon," a statement that was consistent with its observation of a month earlier that people in British Columbia had become worried about the opium trade in their province.[50] The only opposition, at least as far as newspapers reported, was from the manufacturers and importers themselves. After arguing for significant extensions to the deadline for getting rid of their stocks, on which, they argued, duty had in fact been paid, they were dismayed to learn that the legislature had agreed only to a three-month grace period. As noted above, this grace period was extended by the sober second thought of the Senate to six months, which, in the eyes of some, was half the time needed.[51]

The Meaning of 1908

By the end of 1908, Canadians' relationships to several problematic substances had been changed by federal statute. Patent and proprietary medicines had come under intense scrutiny, bolstered by fears of their ingredients and an emerging technocracy of analysts who could examine and determine the existence of dangerous substances in patented remedies. The federal control over medicines, begun with the adulteration acts of the 1870s, was joined by even more intense regulation over the nonmedical use of opium. Opium, a simultaneously dangerous and medically valuable substance, was thereby divided into discursively distinct categories. Acquired outside of channels controlled by appropriately trained and legally licensed (and themselves closely scrutinized) professionals, it could wreak tremendous social danger; obtained through proper means, under the wise guidance of statutorily empowered professionals, it was valuable and helpful. But it was always dangerous.

Why 1908? Were the patent medicine and opium acts just the result of a coincidental convergence? It is difficult to be certain, but nevertheless we should consider the timing. The patent medicine laws had been pushed for several years prior to the last session of the Tenth Parliament, so there is some argument for 1908 simply being a case of "the third time's the charm" for this legislation. But this was also a progressive, reform-minded government, and the Proprietary or Patent Medicine Act was joined by hard-won legislation against the sale of cigarettes to minors. The WCTU was much more vocal about that legislation than it ever was about even the patent medicine laws. It is the Opium Act that seems the anomaly, but again, the scant few weeks between its introduction and its royal assent came after years of increased agitation and lobbying from various sections of the country.

Yet, we must also exercise our cynicism. This was after all the final session in the Tenth Parliament; the year 1908 ended in an election. Patent medicine laws were reactions against the existence of habit-forming drugs and also alcohol in secret remedies. Campaigns against alcohol were the mainstay of many progressive supporters of the Liberal Party. Similarly, cigarette smoking by children was considered by many progressives to be a terrible scourge and dangerous to the healthy future of the nation. The laws passed in this session were the result of years of lobbying. The opium trade in all its manifestations, international and domestic, had also become an issue of progressive concern. What was being forced on the "uncivilized races" was also destroying the health and morality of the nation. It was not by accident that the City of Victoria's committee that petitioned the federal government against the domestic opium trade was named the "Health and Morals Committee," (and that the petition was presented to Victoria's city council along with a resolution to restrict smoking among boys).[52] These issues, in the minds of progressives, were deeply intertwined. In an era of eugenic language about strong Canadian (or British) stock, good health was moral, and morality was necessary for health. It should be no surprise, then, that in the election of 3 December 1908, the Liberals were re-elected with a healthy majority.

The Opium and Drug Act of 1911

The Opium Act's focus on the manufacture of and trade in nonmedical opium was intended to address its consumption, but it was soon found to be limited. The initial reasoning, as explained in 1911 by King, now minister of labour, was that suppressing the trade and manufacture of nonmedical opiates, both of which fell within the purview of the federal government, would eliminate their consumption.[53] In 1909, amendments to the Criminal Code made it illegal to keep "opium joints," grouping them with disorderly houses and illegal gambling houses. The modifications also gave police the powers of search and seizure in these places, noting especially that any smoking paraphernalia could be seized.[54] But although more expansive than the sparse Opium Act of 1908, these changes also did not punish use. When, in 1910, King presented a series of bills to add morphine and cocaine to the prohibition and to make illegal the possession and use of opium, morphine, and cocaine, he admitted that the Opium Act's strictures against trade and manufacture had not stopped the use of the drug. King presented to the House of Commons wide-ranging evidence, including the testimony of police chiefs, social workers, medical professionals, and reformers, demonstrating that more needed to be done to deal with the drug trade. His evidence represented a convergence of the various interests and arguments against nonmedical drug use. Most historians discussing the resulting Opium and Drug Act of 1911 use King's evidence to provide their own explanation for the law's implementation. Yet King's evidence was selective and is not necessarily reflective of the context in which it was passed. What is left to do is look at what happened between 1908 and 1911 to build the context for expanded control.

With the 1908 controls on proprietary medicines and prohibition of non-medical opium traffic, the drug's illegal status heightened concerns about opium's threat to the nation. As we saw earlier, opium smuggling was associated with the smuggling of Chinese people, bizarre bovine husbandry, and sophisticated criminal networks across the country. The newspapers did not stop presenting such stories after 1908. Indeed, since the manufacturers had six months to get rid of all of their opium stocks, there was some evidence that smuggling into the United States increased prior to January 1909, when the law would come fully into effect and the opium would be confiscated.[55] After that date, the importation of opium into the country was heavily controlled, so smuggling increased in both directions. As the *Victoria Daily Colonist* noted when reporting about new smuggling arrests in Vancouver in 1909, "since the prohibition of the importation of opium went into effect last April there have been several smuggling episodes reminiscent of the old days, when many ingenious schemes were used to run the prohibited drug."[56] Nevertheless, the market in the United States did remain the more lucrative, and attention was focused more on incidents of smuggling into the United States from Canada than on smuggling into Canada from elsewhere.[57] A major story about three Chinese men attempting to smuggle opium into Canada aboard the *Empress of Japan* in September 1909 made good sensationalist copy for Victoria and Vancouver newspapers, as well as those farther east, for several weeks.[58] The investigation uncovered an "extensive opium smuggling plot" on Canadian Pacific Steamship Company's Empress liners.[59] At the same time, newspapers were aware that the smuggling was to address the limited availability of opium. When one of these shipments of opium, which had been smuggled in the *Empress of China*, was capsized in the Vancouver harbour, the *Colonist* noted that the shipment had been part of a scheme "to replenish the stock in Vancouver's Chinatown."[60] Stories of opium smuggling to the West Coast were frequent features of BC newspapers.

As noted earlier, British Columbia was not the only destination for smuggled opium. In early 1911, authorities uncovered a plot to move the drug between China, Canada, and the United States. They found Montreal to be "the chief distributing point, although the smuggling of the drug has been continent-wide."[61] In 1910, the *Lethbridge Herald* noted Canada's continued shameful role in the smuggling of tens of thousands of tons of prepared opium to "victims of the opium habit" in the United States and Mexico.[62] Opium smuggling threatened the reputation of the nation and could simultaneously undermine the integrity of government officials. In November

1909, smugglers attempted to bribe customs officers in Victoria because "the great increase in the price of the drug ... caused a revival of smuggling."[63] The law, therefore, created more opportunities for criminality and added to the dangers to the nation.

The taint of smuggling could stain the highest levels of authority. The government of Sir Wilfrid Laurier, which had passed the Opium Act, was ironically wracked by a scandal that involved government employees being implicated in smuggling opium and Chinese immigrants into Canada and politicians apparently attempting to interfere with the course of justice. In the autumn of 1910, as King was preparing new drug legislation, the Liberals faced tough questions about its actions in dealing with a smuggling ring in British Columbia. When a Chinese-born government interpreter was accused of helping to smuggle opium, William Templeman, the member for the City of Victoria and the minister who had introduced the patent medicine legislation in 1908, was accused of interfering with the investigation. The scandal became the subject of a royal commission and rocked the Liberals, who faced questions from the Opposition when the House of Commons sat in 1911. Indeed, the concern over Chinese opium smoking appears to have expanded to general concerns over Chinese people smuggling other products and also misrepresenting themselves as merchants, who would not have to pay a head tax, rather than as general labourers. In these cases, the association between criminal networks and illegal immigration was also linked to illegal opium. So the racial undercurrents of the opium laws were reiterated due to the association, in this case and others, of opium smuggling with the smuggling of Chinese immigrants. The two illegal imports were viewed as two elements that threatened the nation, notwithstanding government attempts to stop them.

Along with smuggling Chinese people to evade the head tax, opium was linked in more general ways to criminal behaviour. For example, in September 1908 the murder trial of a man named Crooked Neck Smith included his opium-smoking tendencies as part of the evidence of his deviance and guilt, even though it had little to do with the murder itself.[64] Smith was sentenced to hang.[65] In November 1908, newspapers broke the story of an official at the Kingston Penitentiary who was smuggling opium (among other things) to prisoners.[66] An article about the police breaking up a Chinese-run "disorderly house" in Toronto included, of course, the requisite information that the police seized opium and opium pipes. When twenty-two Chinese men were arrested in a gambling house in Chilliwack, British Columbia, the *Chilliwack Progress* also reported the seizure of opium-smoking paraphernalia.[67] And on it went.

Smuggling was one aspect of the criminal context in which drugs – not just opium – now functioned; the other was the recreational use of such drugs and the sordid environments in which they were now seen to circulate.

Of course, prior to 1908 newspapers often printed stories of drug addiction and criminal acts related to drug use, but after 1908 the very illegality of opium, and the increased scrutiny of cocaine, could create some especially juicy news and some nefarious associations. A New York City correspondent to the *Ottawa Journal* observed that recent prohibitions of opium in the United States had caused Chinese people to substitute cocaine for opium. The correspondent noted that, in this behaviour, "John Chinaman shows his ability to assimilate the most pernicious" of American habits.[68] In Montreal a prominent local Chinese man was charged with selling cocaine illegally, a charge brought not by the police but by the pharmaceutical association. He absconded before his day in court.[69] Many articles continued the alarmist and prurient imagery, building on the images of Chinese opium smoking in darkened dens to include the sales of other drugs, especially cocaine. A white woman found in an opium den in Toronto was described as "a pronounced cocaine fiend."[70] A raid on the Winnipeg house of a Chinese man who was accused of selling opium found "several boxes of opium and one of cocaine."[71] The intersection of anti-Chinese sentiments and the anti-drug panic was potent, drawing on parallel discourses of a nation in danger and doubtlessly selling more papers.

Fear of the growth of the cocaine habit, indicated in the associations between cocaine and opium, was exceptionally volatile. As we saw in Chapter 7, many commentators considered cocaine to be a much more immediate danger to health and social order than opium, and by 1908 many provinces had passed specific amendments to their pharmacy acts that absolutely prohibited the sale of cocaine unless by prescription. The Proprietary or Patent Medicine Act also absolutely forbade manufacturers from including cocaine in their products. Thus, in most provinces, cocaine was the most strictly controlled drug in the pharmacopoeia. It is difficult to determine whether these restrictions increased the demand for the drug on the black market, but newspapers continued to print stories of illicit cocaine sales and to link them to broader social problems.

The heightened concern over cocaine use draws our attention away from the Opium Act and reminds us that the Proprietary or Patent Medicine Act would have had a greater impact on the drug-taking lives of a much larger proportion of Canadians. Although it was focused on only prepared manufactured medicines, these substances were ubiquitous and a major cause for concern. Indeed, there is some argument to be made that this act, not the Opium Act, is the more significant of the two pieces of legislation. After all, embedded within the Proprietary or Patent Medicine Act were all of the anxieties about the often unwitting consumption of alcohol, habit-forming drugs, and poisons more generally; unscrupulous vendors; and what effect such unrestricted commerce could have on the health of the nation. Moreover, the development of this act was a much more intricate process, involving lobbying from industry, pharmacy, and medicine, as well as expansive debates about the best way to judiciously regulate the market. The formation of the legislation received much more attention in both the popular press and more specialized publications, like professional journals and those of reform organizations. These latter specialist journals also commented on the Proprietary or Patent Medicine Act much more than the Opium Act after they became law.

Given this attention, it is worth reconsidering the place of the Opium Act in the history of Canada's drug laws. Simply put, since opium smoking was not a big deal for most Canadians, it seems incongruous to view legislation considered to be mostly an opium-smoking law as the acorn that grew into the mighty mutant oak of modern drug legislation. Keeping with the horticultural analogy, it might be more appropriate to see the legislation against opium smoking as a seedling, which was grafted onto a much more vigorous narrative of drug danger. Most studies of Canada's drug laws have seen the Opium Act as the starting place, but the formation of the law suggests that it was actually minor in the development of the anti-drug regime that exists today. Nevertheless, the Opium Act, along with the adjustments to the Criminal Code that were passed to make it effective, did create the legislative framework for subsequent laws, and the Proprietary or Patent Medicine Act was the first attempt to control widespread consumption of morphine, cocaine, and opiates. Much more important was the 1911 Opium and Drug Act, which combined the criminalization framework erected in the 1908 Opium Act with the broader social concerns over widespread consumption of cocaine and morphine that were first embodied in the Proprietary or Patent Medicine Act.

The Opium Act and the Proprietary or Patent Medicine Act legislated drug sales and health concerns, issues that were normally the purview of the provinces, but instead of creating constitutional disagreements, they built anti-drug momentum. The Dominion legislation spurred additional attention to the problems of cocaine and morphine use and drove new legislation that could go beyond the Dominion laws. Not six months after the acts of 1908 received royal assent, the Pharmaceutical Association of Quebec met with the provincial government to request "that the sale of poisonous substances, such as cocaine and opium, be placed under greater restrictions than at present."[72] This lobbying did not come to legislative fruition until over two years later when the pharmacists, bolstered by lobbying from groups such as the Children's Aid Society, saw a bill to create such restrictions presented in the legislature of 1910-11.[73] In British Columbia, the BC Pharmaceutical Association's president, Frank Mackenzie, who was also a Conservative member of the provincial legislature, introduced An Act Respecting Habit Forming Drugs in 1911. This legislation was considered to be supplemental to the Dominion legislation, forbidding sales of a list of drugs, mostly cocaine, opium, and their derivatives.[74] An amendment added a clause making it illegal for physicians to prescribe habit-forming drugs for nonmedical conditions.[75] These laws were designed to enhance the process of protecting the public from access to dangerous drugs by expanding the field of visibility of legal authorities to illuminate in more detail the numerous ways that Canadians could access and consume mind-altering drugs. It was a new regime of control, restructuring individuals' sense of their proper behaviour and of responsible citizenship as it affected and was affected by their consumption of medicines that could alter or enhance mood or mental state. This was a biopolitical project, influencing Canadians from legal, social, cultural, and medical directions, to reshape their behaviour in keeping with a specific vision of the integrity of the nation.

International Context

The national context was only one part of a larger equation. News stories alerted and alarmed the public about the danger of opium, morphine, cocaine, and other drugs among the young men and women of the nation; restrictive laws ensured that Canadians were protected from nefarious drugs and unscrupulous sellers; and increased oversight of the domestic distribution of drugs made sure that these newly alerted citizens had no chance to deviate from this national vision. The other part of the equation lay beyond the border. The international discussion over the opium trade involved Canada in a much broader debate and established William Lyon Mackenzie King as a national authority on the drug trade. His role in shaping Canadians' perceptions was not absolute, but his efforts to expand the restrictive drug regime that his report of 1908 helped to initiate were central to the change in Canada's drug laws. His participation in the 1909 Shanghai Opium Commission, this commission's resolutions, and the connections that King developed there with legislators in the United States and Great Britain informed and emboldened his perspective that Canada needed to do more to restrict the trade in drugs.

Soon after he was elected to Parliament, King was appointed to be a commissioner for the British delegation to the Shanghai Opium Commission of 1909. The commission was convened at the initiative of the United States. President Theodore Roosevelt was urged by Bishop Charles Henry Brent, a Canadian-born Episcopal bishop and former missionary to the Philippines, to hold an international meeting in order to "help China with its opium struggle." There was a more immediate interest for the United States since opium addiction was considered a pressing issue in the Philippines, which had recently come under US control. The resulting meeting, convened on 1 February 1909, was chaired by Brent. David Musto observes that Brent had hoped that the assembly would be a conference, "a diplomatic meeting that could lead to official action by represented governments." At the urging of Britain and the Netherlands, it was considered to be a "commission," tasked with gathering information and making recommendations but not commitments.[76] Nevertheless, the nearly four-week long meeting was an assembly of thirteen nations, which compared notes on their own domestic efforts at opium control and discussed how to deal with the international opium trade before issuing nine nonbinding resolutions aimed at constraining and then eliminating the trade, which was as much as such a commission could do.[77]

King's inclusion on the British delegation, urged by Governor General Lord Grey, confirmed the new member of Parliament's status as an international expert on opium. His investigation of opium in British Columbia and the resulting Opium Act were still attributed to his single-handed effort.[78] Yet King was hesitant since he had only recently become a member of Parliament and was concerned that he would be away from the legislature too long and should be in the House of Commons when the new parliamentary session opened. The reasons for King's change of heart are not clear. Lord Grey argued to him that this would be a good opportunity and then persuaded Laurier that King's mission should extend to India and that King should have a secretary and a budget for entertaining, thereby operating as a sort of travelling consul for Canada.[79] At the same time, he had been receiving letters of support and commendation from various moral reformers who thanked him for his work on the Opium Act and noted to him that he would be an excellent representative to the commission. The Board of Moral and Social Reform of the Presbyterian Church in Canada passed a resolution thanking King for his efforts to convince Parliament to act against the opium trade, and the Moral and Social Reform Association of Canada wrote to offer support. King saw these motions and resolutions as giving important moral leverage to his position in Shanghai.[80] When former missionary to Japan Rev. Dr. C.S. Eby, for example, wrote to King to applaud his appointment, the correspondence was typical. Eby told King that he was proud of the new minister of labour's appointment and hoped King would "stand for the position that no amount of money income can atone for the moral blight of a traffic forced by British guns on an unwilling people. Britain should know that Canada holds to a higher commercial ethical standard than that."[81] In his response, King reiterated a mildly self-congratulatory observation that he had been making to a number of supportive correspondents: "The action of our government in so promptly enacting legislation for the suppression of the opium traffic within the borders of the Dominion gave to my position a strength which nothing else could. Canada has already spoken with one voice."[82]

The tone of King's letters may have been more than a self-satisfied response to domestic changes; Canada was enjoying the position of trailblazer in domestic opium policy among many Western countries. In contrast, the

United States was embarrassed to be the commission's convening country but without a domestic anti-opium policy to show for itself.[83] (It did save face to a certain degree given that a law was passed by Congress on 9 February 1909, after the commission opened, which was to come into effect on 1 April 1909.)[84] Great Britain was also debating changes, but it was a fraught process that did not see fruition until the introduction of the Defence of the Realm Act of 1916, which included temporary wartime restrictions on the drug trade.[85] It is worth noting that the smugness was not entirely justified: Australia had instated a ban on smoking opium in 1905.[86] That the Shanghai commission was being planned prior to July 1908 may, therefore, indicate a further motivation for the quick adoption of the Canadian Opium Act. National pride and Canada's national pastime of showing up its southern neighbour could have added to the sense of urgency. In any case, King did see this commission as a chance for Canada to stand as a shining example to the world. As he wrote to Laurier on his arrival in Shanghai, "Naturally the part taken by Canada in the world movement for the suppression of the opium evil has helped to bring our country favourably to the fore."[87] However, whether this was actually the case is difficult to assess since, apart from being welcomed on his late arrival and the brief description of the situation in Canada, King and the country he represented were hardly mentioned in the commission's report. It is an absence suggesting Canada's international position in opium policy formation may have been more imagined than real.

Although the Shanghai Opium Commission was focused on the international opium trade, King clearly linked the opium trade and opium smoking generally to domestic efforts to restrict and control the distribution of opiates. Following the approach of the British delegation's leader, Sir Cecil Clementi Smith, whose report on the situation in "Great Britain, Australia, Hongkong [sic], Ceylon, the Straits Settlements and Weihaiwei" focused on opium and morphia, King's report likewise described the situation beyond the trade in opium.[88] Arriving after the commission had convened, and after Smith had presented his report, King was able to present Canada's position as being distinct from others. The report, entitled "Report on Opium and Morphia in Canada," first gave an overview of the Opium Act of 1908. It then turned to considering restrictions on morphia. First, it provided information on the operation of provincial pharmacy laws controlling access to most forms of opium and morphine. Second, it described the main provisions of the Dominion Proprietary or Patent Medicine Act, which, the report noted, was passed "on the same date" as the Opium Act.[89] Here King made clear links between the various threads of drug regulation, demonstrating that the baneful influences of opium reached beyond the opium pipe.

The Shanghai Opium Commission reiterated the connections between domestic pharmacy laws, patent medicine control, and restrictions on non-medical opiate use. The outcome of the commission was a series of nine resolutions about the distribution of drugs generally and about the responsibility of the member nations to control them. The resolutions focused mostly on the trade in opium in Asia and specifically on the efforts of China to eliminate the trade. Yet the resolutions were also conceived to be comprehensive while not interfering with the domestic laws of participating nations. For example, when the Netherlands delegation presented a resolution that governments adopt state control over the opium industry, removing the trade entirely from private industry, the other delegates saw this as both unworkable and interfering too much in the legislative autonomy of sovereign nations. The resolutions urged all nations to make more effort to reduce or eliminate the trade in nonmedical opium, urged governments to undertake scientific investigation into the properties of opium and into the potential for "anti-Opium remedies" to address addiction, and paid attention to the unrestricted trade in morphine, which was becoming a scourge of its own in China. The final resolution, written after considerable discussion about the ability of the commission to make demands on the participating nations to alter policy, urged all countries with "Consular districts, Concessions and Settlements in China" to apply their domestic pharmacy laws to these areas. The commission agreed that such an effort would not interfere with domestic law creation but would simply recognize the existence of laws that could already address some of the more egregious problems caused by the uncontrolled distribution of opium.[90]

King's involvement in the Shanghai Opium Commission provided him with important connections among a small group of influential legislators and lobbyists, and his participation as the sole representative for Canada certainly established his position as the leading authority on the opium trade in Canada. He corresponded and continued to meet with some of the major players in the opium-control efforts, notably Hamilton Wright, who included in legislation that he wrote for Congress in 1911, wording from an opium bill that King introduced to the Canadian parliament in 1910 (and that was modified to include morphine and cocaine in 1911). Wright also encouraged King to adjust the Canadian legislation to adhere more closely to some of the resolutions of the Shanghai commission.[91] Wright expressed considerable envy for the ease with which King was able to have the Opium Act passed in Parliament, alluding to the difficulties in passing effective legislation in the bicameral Congress in Washington.[92] King and Wright often spoke as brothers in arms, sharing legislative initiatives and consulting on strategies. At the same time, King also acted as an intermediary between Wright and Sir Cecil Clementi Smith, who had expressed considerable disagreement while in Shanghai over their visions of what should be the main resolutions of the commission. These careful discussions, an examination of which is beyond the scope of this book, may be read as components of King's education as an international diplomat.

A close examination of the development of the Opium and Drug Act of 1911 illustrates how the law came from several perspectives, while showing an intersection of several visions of the way to protect and strengthen national integrity. King's revised opium bill was not the first proposed legislation to deal with drugs in that session. Five days before King presented his bill, E.N. Lewis, the member for West Huron, Ontario, introduced a bill governing the sale of poisons, incorporating elements of provincial pharmacy laws and some unworkable aspects of patent medicine provisions that had been rejected by many pharmacists. It was to make illegal the sale of poisons without "the authority of a medical certificate or prescription" and dictated the type of oddly shaped container ("a blue glass, three cornered or square bottle with rough or corrugated corners") in which poisons had to be sold. Lewis argued that cocaine had become a popular alternative to liquor, especially in jurisdictions that had voted to ban the sale of liquor. He supported his bill with evidence that people were still being poisoned by mistakenly consuming dangerous substances and combined this evidence with stories of the illegal distribution of cocaine. Despite Conservative member, physician, and drug store owner Thomas Sproule's observation that a few years earlier similar legislation had been proposed and rejected because it might infringe on provincial rights, the legislation continued to first reading.[93] It did not return for a second.

Not a week later, King presented his opium bill. As the discussions with Hamilton Wright indicated, it was intended only to strengthen the 1908 Opium Act and to create provisions for making the actual smoking of opium illegal. During first reading, Richard Blain, the Conservative member for Peel, Ontario, attempted to use it to ban the manufacture and sale of cigarettes. When King said that cigarettes were "not an abuse so great an evil as the opium habit," Blain replied, "It is very much more widespread." This hairsplitting of vices aside, the bill passed first reading. When the House of Commons returned after Christmas, King presented two resolutions, to be considered in an upcoming sitting of the Committee of the Whole. His first resolution would expand the November opium bill in order to provide police with the authority to search for opium and destroy it when found and in order to permit the governor-in-council to "make such regulations as are necessary" – necessary for what, the resolution did not say. The second resolution was to add to the law "the sale and use of cocaine and morphine for other than medicinal or scientific purposes."[94] These resolutions, which would expand considerably the legislation's scope, were agreed to by the House. The following week, King presented a revised bill, incorporating the new resolutions.

King's discussions with Wright and the resolutions of the Shanghai Opium Commission, then, led to the expanding field of visibility of anti-drug legislation. After Wright advised King to incorporate "Resolution Four," which implored governments to stop permitting opiates to be exported from their territories into countries that prohibited their importation, King revised the draft legislation, telling Wright that he had incorporated "practically all the resolutions of the Opium Commission." He and Wright both agreed that the commission's resolutions should be applied to other drugs. Their discussions often linked cocaine and morphine, or what King called "this cocaine and opium evil."[95] King made specific, detailed, and slightly misleading references to the conclusions of the commission when supporting his bill. During the bill's second reading, he informed the House that expanding it to include cocaine and morphine was in keeping with the commission's findings:

> It was recognized ... that as the opium traffic was suppressed other drugs equally dangerous might take its place, such as morphine and cocaine, and the commission took the ground that it was desirable that every country which sought to suppress the opium habit should also pass effective legislation with respect to other habit-forming drugs. It is found that the morphine and cocaine habits prevail in some of our cities to an extent which, to say the least, is distressing. I mention these two drugs because of the bearing of the fifth resolution of the commission.[96]

The Shanghai commission's fifth resolution had focused on morphine; King's inclusion of cocaine involved some rhetorical licence and indicated that he, like many legislators, newspaper editors, and reformers, saw morphine and cocaine as similarly problematic substances, notwithstanding their unique biological properties, uncertain physical and psychological effects, and of course differing priority within the corridors of international diplomacy.

The Shanghai Opium Commission's report was not the only influential voice in drafting the legislation. After he placed the bill in the context of Canada's international responsibilities, King channelled authoritative domestic voices. The evidence allowed King to place the problem of opium, morphine, and cocaine, as well as other drugs that could be added by governor-in-council later, into a criminal and moral framework. His address drew on apparently unsolicited communications about the drug "evil" from the mayor and police chief of Montreal, the police chief of Vancouver, evangelical reformers, physicians, and pharmacists. Each of these commentators drew on discursive constructions of drug use that were rooted in modern anxieties and their ideas of nation. The problem of young men who were cocaine or morphine users appearing in court drew on the social panic of urban blight and decay. Drug legislation, King's correspondents argued, was necessary for the health and morality, and therefore the future, of the country. King also supported the law with evidence from the Canadian Pharmaceutical Association. During its annual conference of 1910, Robert Martin, the association's president, had encouraged his colleagues to request that the federal government "consider the advisability of enacting measures to more completely safeguard the public from the harmful consequences of the unregulated use" of cocaine and morphine. He linked the measure to a broader sense of national health: "The welfare of our public demands that inviolable laws be enacted by the parliament of our country to make it impossible to procure these peculiarly degrading drugs for any but legitimate professional treatment."[97] He also noted that the pharmacist is the person in whose hands legitimate control should be placed, and King quoted these sentiments in his argument supporting the legislation.

Wrapping up his presentation, King reiterated that he was bringing this evidence forward to show the House "how many different classes of people feel the necessity for legislation of this kind." He then placed it again in an international context and directed it toward a higher purpose. First, he reminded the House that the legislation was part of an international movement: "In this legislation Canada is not merely helping herself, but is helping also in a world-wide movement." Then came the money shot:

> A great deal has been said about the conservation of our natural resources; but natural resources are given to man for the use of man, and not for the destruction of human life. The first of all resources to be conserved are the health and life, moral as well as physical of our people, and it is to keep these intact, and to help to build up in Canada a strong, and happy, and a moral people, that the government brings forward this legislation and does so in the belief that it will pass this House without any opposition.[98]

With that broadly construed and hopeful conclusion, the bill was opened for debate.

In a Committee of the Whole, legislation is normally considered section by section, so once King's explanation was completed, the legislature proceeded to discuss specific elements of the proposed law. In the subsequent discussion, nobody disagreed that the law was necessary, but there was considerable argument about which drugs should be included in the legislation and about the advisability of adding new drugs by order-in-council. When asked about why only three drugs (opium, morphine, and cocaine) were included, King noted that the provisions of Section 14, which allowed drugs to be added to the law by a mere order-in-council, would allow the addition of "any [drug] that medical experts thought it desirable to include." Two physicians in the House did not feel such assurances were enough. Dr. Sproule was concerned that the law's summary of forms of opium ("crude opium, powdered opium, and opium prepared for smoking or in any stage of such preparation") was not comprehensive enough. Dr. Judson Burpee Black, the Liberal member for Hants, Nova Scotia, was likewise unconvinced. He wanted the legislation to be much broader:

In 47 years' experience in the practice of medicine I have found more people in eastern Canada suffering from the use of morphine than any other preparation of opium. I have found it taken by many people hypodermically, as well as by the mouth, and I think if legislation is required, as I am sure it is, to protect the people against the use of opium, it is equally required in the case of the alkaloids. Some persons drink laudanum, which is nothing less than opium and alcohol, but the great majority of people addicted to the opium habit take morphine, which is an alkaloid of opium, [or] codeine, another alkaloid, and I have found individuals who prefer to drink paregoric or any other form of opium. If we are going to legislate we really ought to include some alkaloids of opium.[99]

For Black, the medical view could not be gainsaid.

For some members, King's repeated assurances about the power of the governor-in-council to add items had the opposite effect. Instead of a palliative, it became a stimulant. Conservative Charles Doherty, the member for St. Anne, Quebec, who was a lawyer and a former Quebec superior court judge (and once a professor of BC anti-opium advocate Peter Hing), was focused on the way that provisions of the legislation took law-making power out of the hands of Parliament: "We are handing over the power of this parliament to make the criminal law to the Governor in Council ... It is going very far indeed for us to enact that the Governor in Council shall be free to make a crime, the possession of any substance whatsoever which in his judgement he may consider he ought to add."[100] His party's leader, Robert Borden, agreed, observing that, although he was "in sympathy with the purpose of and object of this Bill," it was the first he could think of that made criminal legislation by order-in-council. The claim that the governor-in-council needed the ability to make quick additions, he argued, required the legislature to agree with the suggestion that a new drug would "spring up to any considerable or even appreciable extent before another session of parliament." This seemed improbable to him. King reminded Borden that he had supported similar provisions in other bills. Notably, in the Proprietary or Patent Medicine Act, "exactly the same power was given."[101] King reiterated his insistence that this provision remain, but interestingly he shifted the voice of authority from the medical to the judicial profession:

Whatever is done by the Governor in Council, so far as criminal legislation is concerned, would be done upon the advice of the Minister of Justice, who, it may be expected, will zealously safeguard the administration of the criminal law were there any probability of this power being abused. I would withdraw this section were there likely to be any doubt as to the intention of parliament in the matter, but in naming the three drugs ... parliament makes it plain that it is legislating against what are known as habit-forming drugs, and it recognizes that as from time to time, one form of the drug is suppressed, a derivative of it may rapidly spring up which is desirable to check as speedily as possible.[102]

Unconvinced, Doherty restated his concern: "I think it is objectionable to delegate this power of making men criminals to any authority other than parliament itself."[103] King tried to argue that, since the legislation was about opium, morphine, and cocaine, it would be reasonable to presume that any order-in-council would relate only to preparations or alkaloids of those substances, but Doherty found this perspective risible.[104] As a result of these debates, the power of the governor-in-council was limited to adding any new derivatives or versions of the items on the schedule by order-in-council.[105]

The discussions in the Committee of the Whole ended by veering once again to the authority of medicine. Dr. Sproule returned to the earlier argument that the schedule was not comprehensive enough. Waving around his big pharmacological knowledge, Sproule asserted that there were "many drugs ... which are just about as dangerous as cocaine or opium," specifically naming "acetanilide, phenacetin, phenalgin, amonial and a number of those coal tar derivatives that injuriously affect the user and produce much the same results as does cocaine." He then argued that there were many products in drug stores that "affect you just the same as cocaine, and very much the same as morphine. Those who use them contract the habit." Seemingly contradicting his assurance to Doherty that additions to the legislation would be conservatively limited to opiates and cocaine derivatives, King reassured Sproule that the provisions to allow the governor-in-council to add items would make it possible for such substances to be added if they were found to be dangerous. Then, positioning himself as an expert in addiction, he argued that many of the drugs Sproule had listed "would hardly come in the same class as cocaine and morphine." Challenged by Sproule to name one, King said that he thought "phenacetin ... is not as bad as some of the others ... It is used, but I do not think we have many phenacetin victims." Sproule countered by whipping out his medical bona fides, along with a touch of condescension:

> I would not expect that the minister in his line of life would come in contact with them, but if he would speak with practical medical men who have been engaged in practice since this drug came into use they would be very likely to tell him that in their experience they have met quite a number of them. As a practicing physician, I know many who use these drugs simply because of the pleasant sensation, the peculiar soporific effect they produce, until they have become quite strongly addicted to them. Some of these are stimulant narcotics, and others sedative narcotics, but many of them produce much the same effect as cocaine.[106]

Sproule had the last word in the discussion, but his perspective did not carry the day. The schedule remained limited to opium, morphine, cocaine, and eucaine, a substance that was added on the recommendation of the director general of public health and the medical advisor to the Commission of Conservation.[107]

More than just an example of the rhetorical jostling that the Opium and Drug Act of 1911 faced, Sproule's final flourish tells us quite a bit about the contrasting views of dangerous drugs in the expansion of Dominion legislation. Apart from the insistence that phenacetin was addictive (and there is little indication that this perception was widespread), Sproule's comments suggest that, for some observers, there was a problematic link between any drugs that were taken for medical use, that were taken for pleasure, and that caused a habit. As a doctor who knew of people who had used medicines outside of the medical field of visibility, Sproule understandably perceived such use as deviant and in need of correction. Forty years of pharmacy laws, which constrained access to many pain killing and soporific medicines by labelling them as dangerous poisons and subjecting them to professional oversight, effectively shifted notions of "danger" in drug taking. Yet although the pharmacy laws set the groundwork for defining deviant use, the need for national regulation was seated in the perception of the dangerousness of the substances themselves. The Dominion laws were not intended to constrain the use of *any* medicines that could be used for pleasure. If that were the case, they would not have needed a list of restricted substances; they would simply have forbidden the nonmedical use of any medicines. Instead, the Dominion legislation was intended to deal with the intersection of specific drugs and dangerous or antisocial behaviour, which threatened the nation from inside and outside of the border. It was the moral baggage of challenges to national integrity embedded in these substances that drove the need to restrict them. Phenacetin and the other drugs that Sproule insisted were as dangerous as opium lacked the moral baggage and discursive complexity of opium, morphine, and cocaine. King's insistence that these new drugs were not an issue drew from his understanding, shaped by the broad-based evidence of danger embedded in the key substances of concern, that it was the responsibility of the government to restrict the drugs whose misuse threatened the future of the nation. These intersecting notions of health-giving, criminality-inducing drugs, and how to nurture the former characteristic by attacking the latter, would persist in drug-control rhetoric for decades.

The Opium and Drug Act of 1911 consolidated many of the lingering concerns introduced in 1908 with discussions about both the Proprietary or Patent Medicine Act and the Opium Act. The former dealt with the improper distribution of drugs of concern through medical channels, and the latter dealt with specifically nonmedicinal use. The Opium and Drug Act combined these concerns. It identified problematic substances that were much more threatening to the nation than smoking opium and the mythical Chinese smoker. By creating restrictions on the importation and sale of listed drugs, it broadened the field of visibility well beyond the dingy opium den. By making it illegal to export drugs to countries that prohibited their importation, the law aligned Canada with international sentiment about the need to control the traffic more comprehensively. Moreover, it added into its purview the fact that some physicians were prescribing drugs for nonmedical treatment. Finally, although the governor-in-council was not allowed to add new drugs to the schedule, the law did give powers to the governor-in-council to make regulations that would aid in the operation of the law and to add new variations on the listed substances. It was a significant expansion of government control over the drug-taking activities of citizens, but it did not make the consumption of those substances a crime. Instead, by making drug sales for nonmedical and nonscientific use a crime, it forced citizens who wanted these substances for personal, leisurely use to consort with criminals. The discursive associations strengthened, and the biopolitical process, however subtle, was affirmed.

Conclusion:
Baneful Influences

With the Opium and Drug Act of 1911, the Government of Canada had achieved the legal prohibition of drugs that were considered to be physically, morally, economically, and socially debilitating to the body of the individual and to the body of the nation. Such prohibition was something that its two closest allies, Great Britain and the United States, were still debating. The law established a framework for criminalization of drugs that echoed throughout the next century. The idea that certain drugs, taken for pleasure rather than for medically supervised treatment, were problematic and needed federal control increasingly had the character of an uncategorical truth. The biopolitical project of extending the authority of the state and its agents of health and policing into the lives of the citizens was well underway. In the next few decades, an expansive law enforcement bureaucracy was constructed within the aegis of discourses about health and around the government's health apparatus. Aspects of the original laws were clarified and expanded to deal with new issues previously unexpected or not fully considered. For example, the 1911 legislation did not define which government agency would enforce the federal law. Nor did it have a system for import and export licences to allow the legitimate traffic in controlled drugs. This became more of a problem after the Hague International Opium Convention of 1912, which resolved that importation and exportation should be carried out only by "duly authorized persons."[1] Although Canada was not directly involved in the Hague convention, being represented instead by a delegation from the United Kingdom and the British Dominions, the fact that all other signatories agreed to the need for greater oversight meant Canada could no longer see itself as a leader.

Although the complexity of the post-1911 legislation is beyond the scope of this book, some details connected to the main theme of this study provide a useful way of understanding the legacy of 1911. For example, the issue of how to enforce the law was addressed in 1918 with the establishment of the Department of Health, created soon after the Liberals (who had been ousted in the general election of September, 1911) returned to power in 1917. Although initially the Opium and Drug Act was not included in the department's ambit (whereas both the Adulteration Act of 1884 and the Proprietary or Patent Medicine Act of 1908 were), through an order-in-council, the Opium and Narcotic Drugs Branch of the Department of Health was established on 1 January 1920.[2] This branch was renamed the Narcotic Division in 1923. Its job was to control the legal channels of drug importation and exportation, and in doing so, the hopeful argument went, it would ferret out illegal distribution. The power to grant import licences fell under the purview of the minister of health, making it more properly a health issue than one of trade. The department did not have its own enforcement branch, so investigation of pharmacy records was undertaken by the newly created Royal Canadian Mounted Police.[3] In the early 1930s, the department hired its own "chemical auditor" to examine the records of the 109 wholesale vendors in Canada. As a result of these audits, the Department of Health constructed records of retailers who were selling inordinate amounts of drugs and of patients who were obtaining drugs from more than one doctor or having prescriptions filled by more than one druggist, and it subsequently created a database of known addicts.

To aid this surveillance, an amendment to the Opium and Drug Act of 1920 broadened significantly the scope of drug control in Canada. It strengthened enforcement procedures, created a catch-all crime of having drugs in one's possession without proper authority, detailed the processes of licensing vendors and dealers, and made it illegal for authorized vendors to fail to keep records or fail to produce them when requested by auditors. It included offences for traffickers and for physicians and pharmacists seen to be violating the legislation. In the 1923 overhaul of the act, now called the Opium and Narcotic Drugs Act, the offences were separated so that the health professionals would not be considered equal to criminal traffickers. P.J. Giffen, Shirley Endicott, and Sylvia Lambert argue that the complexity meant that the law continued to cause confusion, both to legitimate physicians and to pharmacists – the legal vendors of these products – as well as to legal professionals, who continued to have difficulty understanding the parameters of the act.[4] In 1929, the Opium and Narcotic Drugs Act was again significantly amended, increasing penalties, adding new offences including the possession of opium pipes and associated paraphernalia, and making it illegal for physicians to prescribe narcotic drugs to addicts. These changes came at the initiation of the Royal Canadian Mounted Police and the chief of the Narcotic Division. Just as Harry J. Anslinger, the first commissioner of the US Federal Bureau of Narcotics in 1930, has been credited with broadening the bureau's scope and expanding the range of problematic substances, so too in Canada, prior to 1930, did the chief of the Narcotic Division have an authoritative position in expanding the range of the division's activities and in encouraging the intensification of the criminalization of the sale and possession of drugs.[5]

By the 1930s, then, the initial law to control the importation, manufacture, and sale of opium, along with its companion law to ensure that problematic and dangerous substances were not distributed to and consumed by an unassuming public, had transmogrified into harsh criminal legislation subjecting both medical professionals and criminal distributors to significant penalties for transgressing the law. A powerful policing arm oversaw the enforcement of the law and recommended modifications to expand and strengthen its authority. The consumption of drugs for nonmedical uses was significantly constrained, and new drugs that appeared on the black market quickly entered the field of visibility, and the regime of control, of the expanding government agency. Indeed, the power to define "medical use" was also constrained since physicians were not allowed to prescribe maintenance doses of opiates for people they diagnosed as addicted; this was no longer legally considered to be medical use. Yet it is important to note how this legislative authority expanded the definition of health. The Proprietary or Patent Medicine Act and the Opium and Narcotic Drugs Act were both put under the authority of the Department of Health, which had as its mandate the oversight of all aspects of the nation's health. National integrity, at least inasmuch as it was tied to the physical health of the people, specifically included the manufacture, importation, distribution, and sale of drugs that were thought to be habit-forming and dangerous. The impact of these broader changes, and the legacy of troubling social and legal effects, has been told by others, and the story continues to unfold.[6]

The Biopolitics of Drug Use

Despite the weaknesses in the original laws, the 1911 legislation consolidated and strengthened a broad-based drug-control regime that had begun at the provincial level over half a century before, and initiated the break from medical control and the advent of judicial control, which was ironically administered through the Department of Health. Federal oversight of the importation, distribution, possession, and sale of specific habit-forming drugs was based on changing ideas about which drugs were dangerous, what habituation meant to the nation, and what role the state should have in managing these understandings. Pharmacy laws, which were founded on the idea that certain drugs were dangerous because they were poisons and could kill people when misused, established the idea of a selective control over specific substances. These laws were a product of the professional aspirations of pharmacists and the professional interests of physicians, and they were presented as measures to protect the public. The resulting drug-distribution system was established by governments and managed by pseudo-governmental bodies, the professional societies, colleges, and associations empowered by provincial legislation to manage the affairs of their members for the welfare of the citizenry. This alliance between government and professions established regimes of control that allowed professionals to gradually expand the definition of dangerous drugs and to entrench the importance of controlling these substances. In the aspirations of the professional associations, they asserted their authority over their colleagues, while attempting to constrain the behaviour of those outside of their direct influence.

These ideas, of course, were not shaped in a vacuum and were not exclusively bound to any kind of objective scientific process of evaluation. As many researchers have shown, scientific knowledge creation is a cultural process.[7] It can be affected by numerous factors, inside and outside of the knowledge-creating institutions. In the development of Canada's drug laws, the professional priorities of the medical and pharmacy professions combined with powerful cultural discourses. The final few decades of the nineteenth century and the first few decades of the twentieth saw a tremendous growth in concern over the future of the nation, and governments reacted accordingly. As noted, in 1908 the two drug laws were not the only progressive reforms on the agenda. The federal government passed the Proprietary or Patent Medicine Act and the Opium Act in the same session as restrictions on sales of cigarettes to minors. At the provincial level, reforms to social life included expanded public-health laws, which radically lengthened the reach of the state into the lives of the people; gambling laws, which protected the people from themselves by constraining access to games of chance; and liquor-licensing statutes, which restricted access to the highly value-laden waters of life.[8] In the debates over these reforms, grand narratives of the nation were informed by potent images and arguments about the moral and physical health of the people, fears of foreign elements undermining this moral and physical integrity, and Canada's responsibility both as a moral, Christian nation and as a member of the international community – especially, and ironically, with respect to the care and protection abroad of those same foreigners whose arrival in Canada could cause so much distress. Such elements became reiterated in the rhetoric of major social movements and cultural players. The temperance movement was interested in the future of the nation due to its concern that liquor and "narcotics," notably tobacco, were going to destroy the morality and health of the people, especially of the children. Medical and pharmaceutical professionals saw their role as keepers of physiological and pharmacological knowledge to be essential to protecting physical health. In a time when government committees with unironic names such as the City of Victoria's Health and Morals Committee could make proclamations on the issue of drug use, discourses of morality and physicality were tightly entwined. This interconnection is an essential biopolitical indicator. Moral behaviour was one of Quebec alienist Henry Howard's phenomena of matter. Morality is a way of defining the proper way to be and act in the world with respect to yourself and others, and physicality is about the treatment of the physical self. In these constructions, being a good citizen was about being morally and physically healthy and thus about how an individual's conduct was entwined in notions of good citizenship. This is an example of biopolitics: governments using the force of law to reshape the individual's relationship with his or her own body in conformity with a specific view of proper citizen behaviour. The embodied citizen, in turn, acts in biologically appropriate ways.

The drug laws that emerged in the first two decades of the twentieth century were, therefore, deeply entrenched in a cultural moment, but it was a moment that was decades in the making. It did not have its origins in 1907 when apparently racist Vancouverites ran rampant through Chinatown. It emerged through numerous streams of thought and springs of innovation related to ideas about self-control, physical health, sexual danger, mental strength, and hereditary disposition. It was a product of changing medical knowledge, a complex pharmacological market, inter- and intraprofessional conflict, national policy and international diplomacy, notions of personal responsibility to family and self, and the various ways that these ideals could be harnessed and could modify the understanding of the individual and the state.

In the end, the emergence of policy cannot be accurately analyzed by focusing on individual moments, notwithstanding the fact that one piece of legislation, be it a one-page Opium Act or some ill-conceived omnibus federal "tough on crime" legislation, can redirect the gaze of a legal system. The Canadian drug laws were products of a series of assumptions, prejudices, and predispositions driven by the efforts of specific professional, evangelical, and bureaucratic interest groups, to exclude those who fell outside their narrow vision of the nation. This exclusionist idea also required those who wanted to be part of this national vision – and who looked like they belonged – to behave in certain constrained ways. These are the baneful influences that created Canada's drug laws. Such complex ideas and intersecting forces are always involved when good drugs go bad.

Notes

Introduction

1 Virginia Berridge, *Opium and the People: Opiate Use and Drug Control Policy in Nineteenth and Early Twentieth Century England* (London: Free Association Books, 1999); Terry Parssinen, *Secret Passions, Secret Remedies: Narcotic Drugs in British Society, 1820–1930* (Manchester, UK: Manchester University Press, 1983); Geoffrey Harding, *Opiate Addiction, Morality and Medicine: From Moral Illness to Pathological Disease* (Houndmills, Basingstoke, Hampshire, UK: Macmillan, 1988); Louise Foxcroft, *The Making of Addiction: The "Use and Abuse" of Opium in Nineteenth-Century Britain* (Aldershot, UK: Ashgate, 2007). See also Elizabeth Lomax, "The Uses and Abuses of Opiates in Nineteenth-Century England," *Bulletin of the History of Medicine* 47, 2 (1973): 167–76; and Dolores Peters, "British Medical Response to Opiate Addiction in the Nineteenth Century," *Journal of the History of Medicine* 36, 4(1981): 455–88.

2 These ideas, recently challenged as simply reiterating some of the myths of opium in China, nevertheless drove paternalistic international movements to address the opium "problem." See Frank Dikötter, Lars Laamann, and Zhou Xun, *Narcotic Culture: A History of Drugs in China* (Chicago: University of Chicago Press, 2004).

3 David Musto, *The American Disease: Origins of Narcotic Control*, 3rd ed. (Oxford and New York: Oxford University Press, 1999); David Courtwright, *Dark Paradise: A History of Opiate Addiction in America* (Cambridge, MA, and London: Harvard University Press, 1982); H. Wayne Morgan, *Drugs in America: A Social History, 1800–1980* (Syracuse, NY: Syracuse University Press, 1981); Timothy Hickman, *The Secret Leprosy of Modern Days: Narcotic Addiction and the Cultural Crisis in the United States, 1870–1920* (Boston and Amherst: University of Massachusetts Press, 2007); Caroline Jean Acker, *Creating the American Junkie: Addiction Research in the Classic Era of Narcotic Control* (Baltimore, MD: Johns Hopkins University Press, 2002).

4 P.J. Giffen, Shirley Endicott, and Sylvia Lambert spend some time teasing out inconsistencies and simplifications in their introduction to *Panic and Indifference: The Politics of Canada's Drug Laws* (Ottawa: Canadian Centre on Substance Abuse, 1991). The most often cited articles on this issue are G.E. Trasov, "History of the Opium and Narcotic Drug Legislation in Canada," *Criminal Law Quarterly* 4 (1962): 274–82; Melvyn Green, "A History of Canadian Narcotics Control: The Formative Years," *University of Toronto Faculty of Law Review* 42 (1979): 42–79; A. Elizabeth Comack, "The Origins of Canadian Drug Legislation: Labelling versus Class Analysis," in Thomas Fleming, ed., *The New Criminologies in Canada: State, Crime and Control* (Toronto: Oxford University Press, 1985), 65–86; R. Solomon and T. Madison, "The Evolution of Non-Medical Opiate Use in Canada, Part 1, 1870–1929," *Drug Forum* 5, 3 (1976): 239–49; Shirley Small, "Canadian Narcotics Legislation, 1908–1923: A Conflict Model Interpretation," *Canadian Review of Sociology and Anthropology* 6, 1 (1968): 36–46. Small also published as Shirley Endicott and Shirley Cook.

5   Catherine Carstairs, "The Racist Roots of Canada's Drug Laws," *The Beaver* 84, 1 (February–March 2004): 11–12.
6   Neil Boyd, "The Origins of Canadian Narcotics Legislation: The Process of Criminalization in Historical Context," *Dalhousie Law Journal* 8 (1983): 102–36.
7   Giffen, Endicott, and Lambert, *Panic and Indifference.*
8   These laments are all over the blogosphere. See, for example, a narrow reading of Carstairs's article, which reproduced the anti-Chinese elements of the opium laws, by Pete McCormack, "Reform via Strange Circumstances: From Anti-Immigration/Racism to Canada's First Drug Law," n.d., http://www.petemccormack.com/blog/?p=707. Also, the Canadian Harm Reduction Network's library includes a topic on "Racism," which includes several of the articles targeted by Giffen, Endicott, and Lambert in *Panic and Indifference,* as well as some of Carstairs's work, which was published later. See http://canadianharmreduction.com/taxonomy/term/155. Most egregious is the statement by the John Howard Society, which quotes the Canadian Senate's statement that the drug laws are racist and then cites the contention of Giffen and colleagues that these laws are not racist but dismisses the academic research as "prejudicial categorizations based on race and class" and argues that since the law was applied in a racist fashion decades later, it must have been based upon racism. Such a statement demonstrates a tendency to use history only when it suits the political purpose at hand and to discard history when it seems to contradict a sensational narrative. See John Howard Society, "The Theoretical Realm: Balance or Contradiction?" n.d., http://www.johnhoward.ca/document/drugs/perspect/volume2/19.htm.
9   Giffen, Endicott, and Lambert, *Panic and Indifference,* 33–38.
10 W.L.M. King, *Report on the Losses Sustained by the Chinese Population of Vancouver, B.C.* (Ottawa: S.E. Dawson, 1908), 15.
11 Paul Starr, *The Social Transformation of American Medicine: The Rise of a Sovereign Profession and the Making of a Vast Industry* (New York: Basic Books, 1984), 14.
12 Ibid.
13 Benedict Anderson, *Imagined Communities: Reflections on the Origin and Spread of Nationalism,* rev. ed. (London: Verso, 1991).
14 "Moral Residents," *Halifax Morning Chronicle,* 17 March 1885.
15 Ramsay Cook, *The Regenerators: Social Criticism in Late Victorian English Canada* (Toronto: University of Toronto Press, 1985).
16 Philip Corrigan and Derek Sayer, *The Great Arch: English State Formation as a Cultural Revolution* (Oxford: Basil Blackwell, 1985), 4.
17 Mitchell Dean, *Governmentality: Power and Rule in Modern Society* (London: Sage, 1999).
18 Ibid.
19 David Courtwright has explored the shifting meanings of "alcohol, tobacco and other drugs" in "Mr. ATOD's Wild Ride: What Do Alcohol, Tobacco, and Other Drugs Have in Common?" *Social History of Alcohol and Drugs* 20, 1 (2005): 105–24.
20 See Mariana Valverde, *The Age of Light, Soap and Water: Moral Reform in English Canada, 1885–1925* (Toronto: McClelland and Stewart, 1991).
21 This is a vast and growing literature. See Suzanne Morton, *At Odds: Gambling and Canadians, 1919–1969* (Toronto: University of Toronto Press, 2003); Peter Baskerville and Eric W. Sager, *Unwilling Idlers: The Urban Unemployed and Their Families in Late Victorian Canada* (Toronto: University of Toronto Press, 1998); Tina Loo and Carolyn Strange, *Making Good: Law and Moral Regulation in Canada, 1867–1939* (Toronto: University of Toronto Press, 1997); Carolyn Strange, *Toronto's Girl Problem: The Perils and Pleasures of the City* (Toronto: University of Toronto Press, 1995); Sharon Ann Cook, *"Through Sunshine and Shadow": The Woman's Christian Temperance Union, Evangelicalism and Reform in Ontario, 1874–1930* (Montreal and Kingston: McGill-Queen's University Press, 1995); Angus McLaren, *Our Own Master Race: Eugenics in Canada, 1885–1945* (Toronto: McClelland and Stewart, 1990); Peter M. Ward, *White Canada Forever: Popular Attitudes and Public Policy toward Orientals in British Columbia,* 2nd ed. (Montreal and Kingston: McGill–Queen's University Press, 1978); Barbara Roberts, *From Whence They Came: Deportation from Canada, 1900–1935* (Ottawa: University of Ottawa Press, 1988); Richard Allen, *The Social Passion: Religion and Social Reform in Canada, 1914–28* (Toronto: University of Toronto Press, 1971).

22 The speech is reproduced at http://www.canadahistory.com/sections/documents/
    Primeministers/laurier/docs-thecanadaclub.htm. Laurier and Robert Borden both spoke,
    and Laurier's speech followed a toast by one Mr. W.L.M King, first vice president of the
    club.

Chapter 1: Medicating Canada before Regulation

 1 See J. Worth Estes, *Dictionary of Protopharmacology: Therapeutic Practices, 1700–1950* (Canton,
    MA: Science History Publications, 1990), 70 (Dover's Powder), 148 (paregoric).
 2 See Catherine Carstairs, *Jailed for Possession: Illegal Drug Use, Regulation, and Power in Canada,
    1920–1961* (Toronto: University of Toronto Press, 2006), 5–6; A. Elizabeth Comack, "The
    Origins of Canadian Drug Legislation: Labelling versus Class Analysis," in *The New Crim-
    inologies in Canada: State, Crime and Control*, ed. Thomas Fleming (Toronto: Oxford University
    Press, 1985), 65 (this article begins with the inaccurate generalization that "prior to 1908
    in Canada no legal restrictions were imposed on either the sale or consumption of opiates");
    Reginald G. Smart, *Forbidden Highs: The Nature, Treatment, and Prevention of Illicit Drug Abuse*
    (Toronto: Addiction Research Foundation, 1983), 4–5. Such an assumption may work for
    England, where a more densely populated country meant there was an easier access to such
    remedies, but even Virginia Berridge does not consider the nonopiate use, which reasserts
    the presumption that opium was the go-to drug of choice. See Virginia Berridge, *Opium
    and the People: Opiate Use and Drug Control Policy in Nineteenth and Early Twentieth Century
    England* (London: Free Association Books, 1999), 28. Similarly, see Elizabeth Lomax, "Uses
    and Abuses of Opiates in Nineteenth-Century England," *Bulletin of the History of Medicine*
    47, 2 (1973): 167–76.
 3 I am using the term "Canadians" somewhat anachronistically, since I intend it to refer to
    people living not only in Canada East and Canada West but also in the territories and
    colonies throughout the land mass that would become the Dominion of Canada.
 4 The import statistics list items "imported" and "imported for home consumption." The
    distinction is unclear to me. Although the former term could apply to all items imported,
    whereas the latter may apply only to items consumed in Canada, the numbers "for home
    consumption" were often higher than those for "imported." At other times, the numbers
    were the same, and roughly as often the former numbers were higher than the latter.
 5 Sources for import statistics come from annual records of the Department of Trade and
    Navigation, later the Department of Trade and Commerce, printed in the annual *Sessional
    Papers of the Dominion of Canada*. Canadian import duties were listed in the Trade and
    Navigation records each year. Statistics on per capita import numbers (Figure 2) come from
    K.W. Taylor and H. Michell, *Statistical Contributions to Canadian Economic History*, vol. 2
    (Toronto: Macmillan, 1931), 3.
 6 On American import duties, see David Courtwright, *Dark Paradise: A History of Opiate
    Addiction in America* (Cambridge, MA, and London: Harvard University Press, 1982), 16–17.
 7 In this analysis of the Niagara Apothecary records, I have changed the names of all the
    customers discussed.
 8 Jacalyn Duffin, *Langstaff: A Nineteenth Century Medical Life* (Toronto: University of Toronto
    Press, 1993), 47. This was the same rate charged by Thomas Geddes in Nova Scotia. See
    note 41 below.
 9 I discuss the Ontario Pharmacy Act in Chapter 3. On Chlorodyne and its relationship with
    patent medicine legislation, see Chapter 7.
10 I am speculating on this woman's identity, but her real name is and was unique enough to
    encourage me to cross-reference the Niagara Apothecary records with those of the Toronto
    Asylum. Unfortunately, owing to a research agreement with the archives that forbids me
    to disclose the names of the clients and that requires me to maintain a sufficient vagueness
    about the client's identity in order to eliminate the likelihood that a reader could find the
    person in other records, I cannot give more specific details of the client's life.
11 For the latter, see especially John K. Crellin, *Home Medicine: The Newfoundland Experience*
    (Montreal and Kingston: McGill-Queen's University Press, 1994); Vicki Busby, "'Doctors
    Can't Cure It': Traditional Medical Practices in Nineteenth-Century Upper Canada – Survival

Strategies in a Developing Society, 1783–1920" (MA thesis, Queen's University, 1993); J.T.H. Connor, "Minority Medicine in Ontario, 1795–1903: A Study of Medical Pluralism and Its Decline" (PhD diss., University of Waterloo, 1989).

12 Marion Robertson, *Old Settlers' Remedies* (Barrington, NS: Cape Sable Historical Society, 1960); Sheila Kerr, *Early Prairie Remedies* (Calgary: Barker Gifts, 1981).

13 Marion Robertson, "History and Folklore of Shelburne County," clipping from Shelburne *Coast Guard*, in clippings file, MG 9, vol. 34, Nova Scotia Archives.

14 Marion Robertson, *Old Settlers' Remedies*, 12.

15 Respectively, ibid., 14; and Jim Cameron, *Good for What Ails You: Self-Help Remedies from 19th Century Canada* (Burnstown, ON: General Store, 1995), 75.

16 Respectively, Cameron, *Good for What Ails You*, 77; and Robertson, *Old Settlers' Remedies*, 12.

17 Kerr, *Early Prairie Remedies*, "Popular Patent Medicines: Davis' Pain Killer," 44.

18 Jim Cameron, correspondence with author, c. 1995.

19 Victoria Sweet, "Hildegard of Bingen and the Greening of Medieval Medicine," *Bulletin of the History of Medicine* 73, 3 (1999): 381–403.

20 Hannah Jarvis, cook book, MS A210088, John MacIntosh Duff Collection, Archives and Special Collections, University of Guelph (hereafter JMDC/UG)

21 Anonymous manuscript, c. 1805, XM1 MS 117023, Una Abrahamson Collection, Archives and Special Collections, University of Guelph (hereafter UAC/UG).

22 Anonymous, housekeeper's book, n.d., XM1 MS A11Z017, UAC/UG.

23 Hannah Jarvis, cook book, MS A210088, JMDC/UG, 53.

24 A.G Higginson, recipe book, 1833–76, AM1 MS A117 064, UAC/UG.

25 Anonymous, recipe book, c. 1868–80, AM1 MS A117 030, UAC/UG.

26 Ibid.

27 Prof B.G. Jefferis, and J.L. Nichols, *The Household Guide or Domestic Cyclopedia* (Toronto: J.L. Nichols, 1894), 74.

28 Ibid., 156

29 Ibid., 169–70.

30 Ibid., 131.

31 Ibid., 132.

32 Elizabeth Driver, *Culinary Landmarks: A Bibliography of Canadian Cookbooks, 1825–1949* (Toronto: University of Toronto Press, 2008).

33 For a good overview of therapeutic skepticism (which was also called therapeutic nihilism), see Charles E. Rosenberg, "The Therapeutic Revolution: Medicine, Meaning and Social Change in Nineteenth Century America," *Perspectives in Biology and Medicine* 20 (1977): 485–506.   Paul Starr also discusses how it affected American physicians as a profession in *The Social Transformation of American Medicine: The Rise of a Sovereign Profession and the Making of a Vast Industry* (New York: Basic Books, 1982), 55–56, 408–11.

34 Connor, "Minority Medicine in Ontario."

35 Alvin Chase, *Dr. Chase's Recipes, or Information for Everybody,* 9th ed. (Ann Arbor, MI: Self-published, 1862), xiv.

36 Ibid.

37 Copies of *Dr. Chase's Recipes* are available at the Osler Library of McGill University and on microfiche through the Canadian Institute for Historical Microreproductions. Digitally, most can be accessed at archive.org and Google Play.

38 Chase, *Dr. Chase's Recipes* (1862), 154.

39 Duffin, *Langstaff.*

40 Dr. Thomas Geddes, casebooks, MG3, Nova Scotia Archives.

41 On phenacetin, see A.W. Jones, "Early Drug Discovery and the Rise of Pharmaceutical Chemistry," *Drug Test Analysis* 3, 6 (2011): 337–44, doi: 10.1002/dta.301; on adrenaline, see Andrzej Grzybowski and Krzysztof Pietrzak, "Pioneers in Neurology: Napoleon Cybulski (1854–1919)," *Journal of Neurology* 260 (13 February 2013): 695–96, doi: 10.1007/s00415 -013-6863-9; and on Protargol, see E. Vaupel, "Arthur Eichengrün: Tribute to a Forgotten Chemist, Entrepreneur, and German Jew," *Angewandte Chemie International Edition* 44, 22 (2005): 3344–55, doi: 10.1002/anie.200462959.

Chapter 2: Opium in Nineteenth-Century Medical Knowledge

1   F.A. Fluckiger, "What Is Opium?" *Canadian Pharmaceutical Journal* 2 (January 1869): 1–4.
2   S.E.D. Shortt, "Physicians, Science and Status: Issues in the Professionalization of Anglo-American Medicine in the Nineteenth Century," *Medical History* 27, 1 (1983): 51–68.
3   A fascinating discussion of the tensions between esoteric and common language may be found in Robin Valenza, *Literature, Language, and the Rise of the Intellectual Disciplines in Britain, 1680–1820* (Cambridge, UK: Cambridge University Press, 2009), esp. ch. 2.
4   "Text Books," in *Annual Calendar of Trinity Medical College, Session 1900-1901* (Toronto: Daniel Rose and Sons Printers, 1900), 63, in P78-0065-02, University of Toronto Archives.
5   I thank Jackie Duffin for the suggestion of looking at texts that were common at Canadian medical colleges.
6   John P. Swann, "Horatio C. Wood," *American National Biography,* online ed., http://www.anb.org/articles/12/12-00998.htm. Wood's son H.C. Wood Jr. is listed on that book's title page as having "thoroughly revised and rewritten" *Therapeutics: Its Principles and Practices,* 14th ed. (Philadelphia: J.B. Lippincott, 1908).
7   David L. Cowen, "George Bacon Wood," *American National Biography,* online ed., http://www.anb.org/articles/12/12-00997.html.
8   Jonathan Pereira, *Elements of Materia Medica,* 2 vols. (London: Longman, Brown, Green, and Longmans, 1842), vol. 2, 1758.
9   Ibid.
10   Ibid., vol. 2, 1750–56.
11   George Bacon Wood, *A Treatise on the Practice of Medicine,* 2 vols., 4th ed. (Philadelphia: Lippincott, Grambo, 1855), vol. 2, 24.
12   Ibid., vol. 2, 23–24.
13   See Pereira, *Elements,* vol. 1, 674.
14   Wood, *Treatise on the Practice,* 2, 24. Wood recommended leeches and blistering as well as bleeding with the lancet. Ipecac and calomel were both purgatives, with calomel, a mercurial, causing salivation; opium, along with drying up most secretions, increases perspiration.
15   Ibid., vol. 2, 24–30.
16   Ibid., vol. 1, 252.
17   Ibid., vol. 1, 679.
18   Ibid., vol. 1, 699.
19   William G. Smith, "An Inaugural Dissertation on Opium" (1832), in *Origins of Medical Attitudes toward Drug Addiction in America: Eight Studies, 1791–1858,* ed. Gerald Grob (New York: Arno, 1981), 16.
20   John Bell, "Materia Medica and Pharmacy Lecture Notes," 1863, 152–53, John Bell Fonds, MG 29 B40 vol. 2, Library and Archives Canada.
21   On isolation of strychnia, see Pereira, *Elements,* vol. 2, 1306; and on salicin, see ibid., 1074.
22   Robert Christison, *A Dispensatory, or Commentary on the Pharmacopoeias of Great Britain, Comprising the Natural History, Description, Chemistry, Pharmacy, Actions, Uses, and Doses of the Articles of the Materia Medica* (Edinburgh, UK: A&C Black, 1842), 646.
23   J. Moore Nelligan, *Medicines, Their Uses and Modes of Administration,* American ed. (New York: W.E. Dean, 1849), 216. Nelligan's textbook was the "class book" for *materia medica* at Queen's University's medical school; Pereira's text was the reference book. See Canadian Institute for Historical Microreproductions, 49693.
24   Sir Henry Holland, *Medical Notes and Reflections* (London: Longman, Brown, Green and Longmans, 1855), 513.
25   Ibid., 516–17.
26   Pereira, *Elements,* vol. 2, 1778–79.
27   Horatio C. Wood, *A Treatise on Therapeutics Comprising Materia Medica and Toxicology with Especial Reference to the Application of the Physiological Action of Drugs to Clinical Medicine* (Philadelphia: J.B. Lippincott, 1874), 194. This distinction notwithstanding, some writers continued to interchange the terms "opium" and "morphine." Notable for its author's conflation of the terms, in spite of the book's specific title, is H.H. Kane, *The Hypodermic*

Injection of Morphia: Its History, Advantages, and Dangers (New York: Charles L. Bermingham, Medical Publishers, 1880). Although he was mostly discussing injection of morphine, his examples combined opium and morphine without distinction.

28 See Horatio C. Wood, "Class VI: Analgesics. Opium," in *Treatise on Therapeutics*, 181–94.

29 Wood, *Treatise on Therapeutics*, 192.

30 On Geddes, see description in Nova Scotia Archives network database. http://memoryns.ca/thomas-o-geddes-fonds.

31 Alfred S. Taylor, *On Poisons in Relation to Medical Jurisprudence and Medicine*, ed. R.E. Griffith (Philadelphia: Lea and Blanchard, 1848), v.

32 Ibid., 18.

33 Ibid., 16.

34 Ibid., 460.

35 Virginia Berridge, *Opium and the People: Opiate Use and Drug Control Policy in Nineteenth and Early Twentieth Century England* (London: Free Association Books, 1999), 97–105; H. Wayne Morgan, *Drugs in America: A Social History, 1800–1980* (Syracuse, NY: Syracuse University Press, 1981), 2–3, 37–38.

36 The journal did not state where the deaths took place.

37 "Laudanum," *Quebec Medical Journal/Journal de Médecine de Quebec* 2 (January 1827): 44.

38 Letter to the editor, *Toronto Globe*, 1 December 1870, emphasis in original.

39 "Death from Laudanum at the Montreal General Hospital," *British American Journal of Medical and Physical Science* 2 (January 1847): 250–53.

40 George R. Grassett, "On Poisoning by Opium," *British American Journal of Medical and Physical Science* 2 (April 1847): 313.

41 A. Grant, "Notes on Three Cases of Poisoning," *Medical Chronicle* 6 (October 1858): 197.

42 This procedure was relatively standard across all medical textbooks.

43 Grassett, "On Poisoning by Opium."

44 S.C. Sewell, "Case of Poisoning by Tr. of Opium," *British American Journal of Medical and Physical Science* 1 (June 1845): 61.

45 John Stewart, "Observations on a Case of Poisoning by Tincture of Opium," *British American Journal of Medical and Physical Science* 1 (August 1845): 115–16.

46 Jacalyn Duffin, "'In View of the Body of Job Broom': A Glimpse of the Medical Knowledge and Practice of John Rolph," *Canadian Bulletin of Medical History/Bulletin canadien d'histoire de la médecine* 7, 1 (1990): 9–30.

47 "Coroner's Inquest on the Body of Job Broom," editorial, *Medical Chronicle* 3 (September 1855): 149–55.

48 Several Toronto newspapers followed the inquiry closely. The *Globe* provided detailed transcriptions of the Broom and the Blackie trials, as well as commentary and correspondence. It also noted Dickson's eventual exoneration. See *Toronto Globe*, 28 and 31 July 1855 and 9, 15, 16, 18, 21, and 22 August 1855.

49 Duffin, "'In View of the Body,'" 16, emphasis in original.

50 Although usually associated with cessation of drinking, delirium tremens also occurred after prolonged drinking sprees.

51 Duffin, "'In View of the Body,'" 16.

52 Testimony of Dr. Rolph, *Toronto Globe*, 16 August 1855.

53 Ibid. See also Robert Christison, *A Treatise on Poisons in Relation to Medical Jurisprudence, Physiology, and the Practice of Physic*, 4th ed. (Edinburgh, UK: Adam and Charles Black, 1845).

54 "The Blackie Inquest! Medical Treatment!" testimony of William Aikins, *Toronto Globe*, 16 August 1855, emphasis added.

55 See, for example, discussions of treatment for delirium tremens in Dr. Corrigan, "Delirium Tremens," *British American Journal of Medical and Physical Science* 2 (November 1846): 183–84; Edward Stanley, "On Delirium Tremens," *Medical Chronicle* 3 (September 1855): 143–46; James Crawford, "Case of Delirium Tremens from the Use of Opium," *Medical Chronicle* 3 (October 1855): 161–63; and Anonymous, "Delirium Tremens: Treatment of," *Canada Medical Record* 7 (September 1878): 269.

56 "The Blackie Inquest! Verdict Rendered!" testimony of Dr. Russell, *Toronto Globe,* 21 August 1855.
57 "The Blackie Inquest! Medical Treatment!" testimony of Dr. Widmer, *Toronto Globe,* 18 August 1855.
58 "The Blackie Inquest! Verdict Rendered!" testimony of Dr. Nicol, *Toronto Globe,* 21 August 1855.
59 See "Doctors Differing," *Toronto Globe,* 17 August 1855.
60 On perceptions of the physician's character, see S.E.D. Shortt, "Physicians, Science and Status: Issues in the Professionalization of Anglo-American Medicine in the Nineteenth Century," *Medical History* 27, 1 (1983): 51. On the acceptability of treatment, see S.E.D. Shortt, "'Before the Age of Miracles': The Rise, Fall, and Rebirth of General Practice in Canada, 1890–1940," in *Health Disease and Medicine: Essays in Canadian History,* ed. Charles Roland (Toronto: Hannah Institute for the History of Medicine, 1984), 130; and John Harley Warner, *The Therapeutic Perspective: Medical Practice, Knowledge, and Identity in America, 1820–1885* (Cambridge, MA: Harvard University Press, 1986), 11–36. Those who suggest that diagnosis and prognosis were at least as important as treatment include Paul Starr, *The Social Transformation of American Medicine: The Rise of a Sovereign Profession and the Making of a Vast Industry* (New York: Basic Books, 1984), 14; and Charles E. Rosenberg, "Introduction," in *The Structure of American Medical Practice,* by George Rosen, ed. Charles E. Rosenberg (Philadelphia: University of Pennsylvania Press, 1983), 7–10. In this sense, Dickson's uncertainty and Philbrick's swift and decisive action may have contributed to onlookers' perception of their credibility.
61 Pereira, *Elements,* vol. 2, 1749.
62 Ibid., vol. 2, 1747.
63 Ibid., vol. 1, 136.
64 Wood, *Treatise on the Practice,* 2nd ed., vol. 2, 771.
65 Ibid., 4th ed., Vol. 1, 548 (digestive system), 468 (rheumatism), 494 (gout).
66 Austin Flint, *A Treatise on the Principles and Practice of Medicine* (Philadelphia: Henry C. Lea, 1866), 188.
67 Ibid., 386.
68 William Osler, *The Principles and Practice of Medicine,* 6th ed. (New York and London: D. Appleton, 1907), 1095.
69 G. Fielding Blandford, *Insanity and Its Treatment: Lectures on the Treatment, Medical and Legal, of Insane Patients,* First Edition (Edinburgh: Oliver and Boyd, 1871), 232.
70 A. Church and F. Peterson, *Nervous and Mental Diseases,* 2nd ed. (Philadelphia: W.B. Saunders, 1900), 710.
71 With apologies to René Laennec and Jackie Duffin.
72 N.D. Jewson, "The Disappearance of the Sick-Man from Medical Cosmology, 1770–1870," *Sociology* 10, 2 (1976): 225–44.
73 Warner, *Therapeutic Perspective.*
74 See Norman Howard Jones, "A Critical Study of the Origins and Early Development of Hypodermic Medication," *Journal of the History of Medicine* 2 (1947): 201–42; John S. Haller Jr., "Hypodermic Medication: Early History," *New York State Journal of Medicine* 81, 11 (October 1981): 1671–79.
75 See Jacalyn Duffin, *To See with a Better Eye: A Life of R.T.H. Laennec* (Princeton: Princeton University Press, 1998).
76 "Hypodermic Medication," extract from the *National Medical Review,* in *Canada Lancet* 12 (September 1879): 4.
77 See Berridge, *Opium and the People,* ch. 12; Timothy Hickman, *The Secret Leprosy of Modern Days: Narcotic Addiction and the Cultural Crisis in the United States, 1870–1920* (Boston and Amherst: University of Massachusetts Press, 2007), 36–42; David Musto, *The American Disease: Origins of Narcotic Control,* 3rd ed. (Oxford and New York: Oxford University Press, 1999), 73–77; David Courtwright, *Dark Paradise: A History of Opiate Addiction in America* (Cambridge, MA, and London: Harvard University Press, 1982), 42–50; and Morgan, *Drugs in America,* 22–24.

Chapter 3: Canada's First Drug Laws

1 *Statutes of Canada* (1859), Cap. XCVIII.

2 Mason's occupation is not clear. Some writers referred to him as "Whiskey Detective Mason," whereas others called him the "notorious police informer." Neither epithet seems to have referred to an official occupation but rather to his preoccupation with seeking out violators of the liquor-licensing bill and prosecuting them for profit. On Mason's reputation, see "Illegal Sale of Poison," *Canadian Pharmaceutical Journal* 4 (December 1870): 179; and "The Sale of Poisons," *Canadian Pharmaceutical Journal* 4 (December 1870): 180.

3 "An Act Respecting Tavern and Shop Licenses," *Statutes of the Province of Ontario* (1868–69), Cap. XXXII, ss. 27 and 31.

4 "An Act Respecting the Sale of Strychnine and Other Poisons," *Statutes of the Province of Canada* (1859), Cap. XCVIII.

5 "Illegal Sale of Poison," *Canadian Pharmaceutical Journal* 4 (December 1870): 179–80.

6 "The Sale of Poisons," *Toronto Globe,* 29 November 1870.

7 "Poison Vending," *Canada Lancet* 3 (January 1871): 190–91.

8 "Sale of Poisons Case," *Canadian Pharmaceutical Journal* 4 (January 1871): 7. The pharmacists' lawyer argued that the evidence taken in the case "was in some points defective," and the court agreed to try another case as a test. In this one, Mason did not do so well. As the *Canadian Pharmaceutical Journal* noted several months later, Gale and Mason had a falling out, and Gale abandoned Mason in the courts. Since Gale was Mason's principal witness, the case against the pharmacists fell apart. See "The Sale of Poison Case," *Canadian Pharmaceutical Journal* 4 (April 1871): 40.

9 In Nova Scotia, New Brunswick, and Prince Edward Island, the law restricted to pharmacists (and physicians) the ability to compound and sell poisons, but it put no restrictions on the conditions around the sale. Such conditions appeared in subsequent amendments.

10 Peter Bartrip, "A 'Pennurth of Arsenic for Rat Poison': The Arsenic Act, 1851 and the Prevention of Secret Poisoning," *Medical History* 36, 1 (1992): 53–69; S.W.F. Holloway, "The Apothecaries' Act 1815: A Reinterpretation – Part 1," *Medical History* 10 (1966): 107–29; "The Apothecaries' Act 1815: A Reinterpretation – Part 2," *Medical History* 10 (1966): 221–36. Virginia Berridge, *Opium and the People: Opiate Use and Drug Control Policy in Nineteenth and Early Twentieth Century England* (London: Free Association Books, 1999), 113–22.

11 Glenn Sonnedecker, ed., *Kremers and Urdang's History of Pharmacy,* 4th ed. (Madison, WI: American Institute of the History of Pharmacy, 1986), 214–19.

12 Ibid., 216–17.

13 David Courtwright, *Dark Paradise: A History of Opiate Addiction in America* (Cambridge, MA/ London: Harvard University Press, 1982), 52–53.

14 Isaac Campos, *Home Grown: Marijuana and the Origins of Mexico's War on Drugs* (Chapel Hill: University of North Carolina Press, 2012), esp. 182–85.

15 Desmond Manderson, *From Mr. Sin to Mr. Big: A History of Australian Drug Laws* (Melbourne: Oxford University Press, 1993), 84.

16 Jeremy A. Greene and Elizabeth Siegel Watkins, "Introduction: The Prescription in Perspective," in *Prescribed: Writing, Filling, Using, and Abusing the Prescription in Modern America,* ed. Jeremy A. Greene and Elizabeth Siegel Watkins (Baltimore, MD: Johns Hopkins University Press, 2012), 4.

17 R.D. Gidney and W.P.J. Millar, *Professional Gentlemen: The Professions in Nineteenth-Century Ontario* (Toronto: University of Toronto Press, 1994), 203–11; Thomas Haskell, "Professionalism versus Capitalism: R.H. Tawney, Emile Durkheim, and C.S. Peirce on the Disinterestedness of Professional Communities," in *The Authority of Experts: Studies in History and Theory,* ed. Thomas Haskell (Bloomington: Indiana University Press, 1984), 180–225; David A. Hollinger, "Inquiry and Uplift: Late Nineteenth-Century American Academics and the Moral Efficacy of Scientific Practice," in *The Authority of Experts: Studies in History and Theory,* ed. Thomas Haskell (Bloomington: Indiana University Press, 1984), 142–56.

18 See R.J. Clark, "Professional Aspirations and the Limits of Occupational Autonomy: The Case of Pharmacy in Nineteenth-Century Ontario," *Canadian Bulletin of Medical History/ Bulletin canadien d'histoire de la médecine* 8, 1 (1991): 43–63.

19 I discuss the Apothecaries Act in much more detail in Dan Malleck, "Refining Poison, Defining Power: Medical Authority and the Creation of Canadian Drug Prohibition Laws, 1800–1908" (PhD diss., Queen's University, 1999). But far better than that, see S.W.F. Holloway, "The Orthodox Fringe: The Origins of the Pharmaceutical Society of Great Britain," in *Medical Fringe and Medical Orthodoxy, 1750–1850*, ed. W.F. Bynum and Roy Porter (London: Croom Helm, 1987), 129–57; Roy Porter and Dorothy Porter, "The Rise of the English Drugs Industry: The Role of Thomas Corbyn," *Medical History* 33, 3 (1989): 277–95; and Holloway, "Apothecaries' Act 1815."

20 For more on the early years of Quebec pharmacy, see Johanne Collin and Denis Béliveau, *Histoire de la Pharmacie au Québec* (Montreal: Musée de la pharmacie du Québec, 1994); Johanne Collin, "Genèse d'une profession: Les pharmaciens au Québec au XIXe siècle," *Canadian Bulletin of Medical History/ Bulletin canadien d'histoire de la médecine* 14, 2 (1997): 253–57. Although the provinces of Lower and Upper Canada were united in 1841, many of the laws remained specific to each province, a concession to the cultural and political differences in the provinces. So legislation respecting issues like legal or medical professional licensure were normally passed for either of the two provinces. Indeed, although legally Lower Canada had become Canada East, most of the laws retained the former name in the title.

21 Stanley William Jackson, *The First Pharmacy Act of Ontario* (Toronto: Ontario College of Pharmacy, 1967), 2; *Consolidated Statutes of Canada* (1848), s. 16.

22 Archibald Hall, *Letters on Medical Education (Originally published in the Montreal Gazette) Addressed to the Members of the Provincial Legislature of Canada* (Montreal: Armour and Ramsay; Kingston: Ramsay, Armour, 1842), 24–27.

23 A. Von Iffland, "Education of Apothecaries and Druggists," *Medical Chronicle* 4 (February 1857): 333.

24 Ibid.

25 Ibid., 334.

26 See "Petition of A. Savage and Others, Apothecaries, Chemists and Druggists, of Canada East, for an Act of Incorporation," (15 February 1849) in *Journals of the Legislative Assembly of the Province of Canada* Vol. 8 (1849): 84 (petition received); 85 (issue referred).

27 Ibid.

28 Clark, "Professional Aspirations."

29 "An Apothecary's Bill for Lower Canada," *British American Journal* 1 (January 1860): 46.

30 "An Act to Amend Chapter Seventy-One of the Consolidated Statutes for Lower Canada, Respecting the Medical Profession and the Sale of Drugs," *Statutes of Canada*, 27–28 Vic., ch. 51, s. 1, 269–70; "College of Physicians and Surgeons for Lower Canada," *Canada Medical Journal* 1 (February 1865): 395–96.

31 Von Iffland, "Education of Apothecaries," 333.

32 "Bills before Parliament, III. An Act to Regulate the Education of Apothecaries, Chemists and Druggists and the Sale of Poisons," *British American Journal* 1 (May 1860): 239.

33 "College of Physicians and Surgeons for Lower Canada," *Canada Medical Journal* 1 (February 1865): 395–96; Gidney and Millar, *Professional Gentlemen*.

34 Ronald Hamowy, *Canadian Medicine: A Study of Restricted Entry* (Toronto: Fraser Institute, 1984), 20–22, 300n62.

35 Gidney and Millar, *Professional Gentlemen*, 22–25, 415n85. See also Gert H. Brieger, "Classics and Character: Medicine and Gentility," *Bulletin of Medical History* 65, 1 (1991): 88–109; and Rebecca J. Tannenbaum, "Earnestness, Temperance, Industry: The Definitions and Uses of Professional Character among Nineteenth-Century American Physicians," *Journal of the History of Medicine and Allied Sciences* 49, 2 (April 1994): 251–83.

36 "The Druggists' Bill," *Toronto Globe*, 28 January 1871.

37 "A Little Bill," editorial, *Halifax Citizen*, 25 April 1874.

38 "Montreal Chemists' Association," *Montreal Witness*, 30 December 1869.

39 "The Quebec College of Pharmacy," *Montreal Witness*, 27 October 1869. On John Dougall's reforming zeal in theory, see Paul Rutherford, *A Victorian Authority: The Daily Press in Late Nineteenth-Century Canada* (Toronto: University of Toronto Press, 1982), 48–51; for Dougall's

reforming zeal in practice, see Peter DeLottinville, "Joe Beef of Montreal: Working-Class Culture and the Tavern, 1869–1889," *Labour/Le Travail* 8–9 (1981–82): 9–40.
40 "A Little Bill," editorial, *Halifax Citizen*, 25 April 1874.
41 Medicus, untitled letter, *Halifax Reporter and Times*, 28 April 1874. This "Medicus" was not Archibald Hall, who died in 1868.
42 Ibid., emphasis in original.
43 "The Doctor's Bill," editorial, *Montreal Witness*, 27 October 1869.
44 Ibid.
45 Ibid.
46 See Haskell, "Professionalism versus Capitalism."
47 Medicus, untitled letter, *Halifax Reporter and Times*, 28 April 1874.
48 "The Sale of Poisons," *Toronto Globe*, 29 November 1870.
49 "The Sale of Poisons," letter to the editor, *Toronto Globe*, 5 December 1870.
50 "The Sale of Poisons," *Toronto Globe*, 29 November 1870.
51 See A. Hall, "Remarks on the Late Case of Accidental Poisoning in Quebec," *Canada Medical Journal* 1 (February 1865): 353–58, 391–93.
52 "Legislature of Ontario," *Toronto Telegram*, 26 November 1869.
53 "Legislature of Ontario - After Recess," *Toronto Globe*, 26 November 1869.
54 "Poison Vending" editorial *Canada Lancet* 3 (January 1871): 190–91.
55 "Legislative Council," *Halifax Reporter and Times*, 15 March 1876.
56 "An Apothecaries Bill for Lower Canada," *British American Journal* 1 (January 1860): 46–47.
57 "Doctors and druggists," *Montreal Evening Star*, 23 July 1869, emphasis in original.
58 "The Percentage System," *Canadian Pharmaceutical Journal* 2 (September 1869): 131.
59 Chemicus, "Correspondence: Questionable Trading," *Canadian Pharmaceutical Journal* 3 (September 1869): 132.
60 "The Percentage System," *Canadian Pharmaceutical Journal* 3 (September 1869): 131.
61 Druggist, "Communications: The Percentage System," *Canadian Pharmaceutical Journal* 3 (October 1869): 150–51.
62 "The Doctors and The Druggists," *Montreal Witness*, 1 November 1869.
63 "Competition for Prescriptions," editorial, *Canada Medical Journal* 6 (November 1869): 235.
64 "Bonuses to Doctors," letter to the editor, *Montreal Witness*, 6 December 1869.
65 "Doctors' Percentages," letter to the editor, *Montreal Witness*, 14 December 1869.
66 "Montreal Chemists' Association," *Montreal Gazette*, 7 September 1869.
67 "Montreal Chemists' Association," *Montreal Gazette*, 6 December 1870.
68 "The Proposed College of Pharmacy," *Montreal Evening Star*, 22 October 1869.
69 "The Pharmacy Bill," *Montreal Evening Star*, 7 December 1869.
70 "The Quebec College of Pharmacy," *Montreal Witness*, 27 October 1869.
71 Edward Blake, quoted in the account of the legislature debates in "Legislature of Ontario," *Toronto Globe*, 12 January 1871.
72 Editorial, *Toronto Telegraph*, 9 December 1869.
73 See amended Bill 135 (1869–70 session) and the list of modifications to Bill 20 (1871 session), in *Legislative Journals of Ontario*, 1 February 1871, 103.
74 "Account of Legislature – Pharmaceutical Society" and "– Pharmaceutical Society Bill," *Halifax Citizen*, 20 April 1875; "Account of Legislature," *Halifax Citizen*, 24 April 1875.
75 "Legislative Council," *Halifax Reporter and Times*, 15 March 1876.
76 "The Pharmacy Bill," *Montreal Herald*, 3 December 1869.
77 "Proposed College of Pharmacy," *Montreal Evening Star*, 22 October 1869.
78 Collin and Béliveau, *Histoire de la Pharmacie au Québec*, 114.
79 "Legislature – Sale of Poisons," *Toronto Leader*, 27 January 1871.
80 "An Act to Establish the Pharmaceutical Association of British Columbia," *Statutes of British Columbia* (1891), Cap. 33, s. 12.
81 "A Dominion Pharmacy Act," editorial, *Canadian Pharmaceutical Journal* 11 (December 1877): 166.
82 "An Act Respecting the Sale of Strychnine and Other Poisons," *Provincial Statutes of Canada* (1859), Cap. XCVIII (passed in 1849); "An Act to Prohibit the Use of Strychnine and Other

Poisons for the Destruction of Certain Kinds of Wild Animals," *Provincial Statutes of Canada* (1859), Cap. LX, s. 4 (passed in 1849). By the time of confederation, Quebec's physicians had secured a law to regulate the province's pharmacists.

83 For the Northwest Territories, see "An Ordinance Respecting Poisons," Ordinance No. 12 of 1885, which repealed "An Ordinance Respecting Poisons," Ordinance No. 14 of 1878, both in the records of the Saskatchewan Archives Board, micro. 5.15, reel 2.

84 "An Act for the Protection of Game in the Province of Manitoba," *Statutes of Manitoba* (1879), Cap. X, s. 10; "An Ordinance Respecting Poisons," Ordinance No. 12 of 1885, Northwest Territories Ordinances, in the records of the Saskatchewan Archives Board, micro. 5.15, reel 2.

85 "Answer to Enquiries Regarding the Pharmacy Act," *Canadian Pharmaceutical Journal* 4 (March 1871): 30.

86 "The Quebec Pharmacy Act of 1874 [*sic:* 1875]," *Canadian Pharmaceutical Journal* 8 (April 1875): 326–28.

87 "Pharmacy in Nova Scotia," editorial, *Canadian Pharmaceutical Journal* 10 (June 1877): 405–6.

88 "The New Brunswick Pharmacy Act," editorial, *Canadian Pharmaceutical Journal* 17 (May 1884): 147–48.

89 New Brunswick Pharmacy Act (1891) 54 Vic., Cap. 32; "An Act to Amend Chapter 106, Revised Statutes, 1900, 'The Pharmacy Act,'" *Statutes of Nova Scotia* (1906), ch. 50, ss. 4 and 5.

90 The first presidents of the Manitoba, BC, and NWT pharmaceutical associations were trained or started their practice in either Ontario or Great Britain.

91 "An Act to Incorporate the New Brunswick Pharmaceutical Society, and to Regulate the Sale of Drugs and Medicines," *Statutes of New Brunswick* (1884), Cap. XX, s. 10; "An Act to Incorporate the Prince Edward Island Pharmaceutical Association," *Statutes of Prince Edward Island* (1905), Cap. XXI, s. 10.

92 "An Act to Establish the Pharmaceutical Association of British Columbia," *Statutes of British Columbia* (1891), Cap. 33 s. 17.

93 "Quebec Pharmacy Act," *Revised Statutes of Quebec* (1875), s. 4, para., 4033.

94 "An Act to Incorporate the Nova Scotia Pharmaceutical Society and to Regulate the Sale of Drugs and Medicines," *Statutes of Nova Scotia* (1876), ch. 11, s. 11.

95 "An Act to Establish a Pharmaceutical Association in the Province of British Columbia," (1891) part 26.

96 "Inexpediency of Physicians Dispensing Drugs," editorial, *Canadian Pharmaceutical Journal* 5, 11 (March 1878): 267. On the process leading up to the bill's withdrawal, see debates as reprinted in *Canadian Pharmaceutical Journal* 5, 11 (March 1878): 272–74.

97 "Petition to the Legislative Assembly of the Pharmaceutical Asso. for Act to Amend Act of Incorporation," 31 May 1883, Provincial Archives of Manitoba. The petition was received on 1 June 1883. See *Journals of the Legislative Assembly of Manitoba* (1883), 31.

98 "The Pharmacy Act, 1884," *Canadian Pharmaceutical Journal* 17, 9 (April 1884): 126. Note that the 1878 Ontario amendments attempted to do this. See "An Act to Amend 'The Pharmacy Act of 1871,'" *Canadian Pharmaceutical Journal* 1877–78): 205–8.

99 "Important Decision Respecting the Sale 11 (of Medicines by Druggists," *Canadian Pharmaceutical Journal* 19 (November 1885): 48.

100 "A Magistrate's Interpretation of the Medical Act – The Druggist Has a Right to Recommend His Drugs," *Canadian Druggist* 2 (January 1890): 17.

101 See "Editorial," *Canadian Pharmaceutical Journal* 6 (June 1873): 405–6, 412. Shuttleworth discussed the case in an editorial, in which he revealed that although the registrar may not have directed Mason to act on behalf of the college, he had provided the "detective" with a list of all members "who were keeping an open shop in violation of the Act." This action was not approved by the council, Shuttleworth explained, but was the result of the exasperation of the registrar over the delinquency of many druggists.

Chapter 4: Chinese Opium Smoking and Threats to the Nation

1 Julia Lovell, *The Opium War* (London: Picador, 2011); David Anthony Bello, *Opium and the Limits of Empire: Drug Prohibition in the Chinese Interior, 1729–1850* (Cambridge, MA, and London: Harvard University Press, 2005); Peter Ward Fay, *The Opium War, 1840–1842:*

Barbarians in the Celestial Empire in the Early Part of the Nineteenth Century and the War by Which They Forced Her Gates Ajar, new ed. (Chapel Hill: University of North Carolina Press, 1997).

2 See Geoffrey Harding, *Opiate Addiction, Morality and Medicine: From Moral Illness to Pathological Disease* (Houndmills, Basingstoke, Hampshire, UK: Macmillan, 1988). Virginia Berridge covers this discussion in Chapter 14, "Britain's 'Opium Harvest': The Anti-Opium Movement" in *Opium and the People: Opiate Use and Drug Control Policy in Nineteenth and Early Twentieth Century England* (London: Free Association Books, 1999): 173–94.

3 Frank Dikötter, Lars Laamann, and Zhou Xun, *Narcotic Culture: A History of Drugs in China* (Chicago: University of Chicago Press, 2004); Frank Dikötter, Lars Laamann and Zhou Xun, "China, British Imperialism, and the Myth of the 'Opium Plague,'" in *Drugs and Empires: Essays in Modern Imperialism and Intoxication, c. 1500–1930*, ed. James H. Mills and Patricia Barton (New York and Basingstoke, UK: Palgrave Macmillan, 2007), 19–38.

4 Canadian missionaries had become an important part of evangelical Christianity by the end of the century. See Rosemary Gagan, *A Sensitive Independence: Canadian Methodist Women Missionaries in Canada and the Orient, 1881–1925* (Ottawa: Carleton University Press, 1992); and Alvyn Austin, *Saving China: Canadian Missionaries in the Middle Kingdom* (Toronto: University of Toronto Press, 1986).

5 "Missionary Register – Java – The Chinese," *Canadian Baptist Magazine and Missionary Register* 1 (February 1838): 213.

6 "Effects of Opium," *Colonial Pearl* 3 (15 November 1839): 365.

7 "Protestant Missions in the East," *The Catholic*, 28 June 1843, 330.

8 Charles E. Rosenberg, *Explaining Epidemics and Other Studies in the History of Medicine* (Cambridge, UK: Cambridge University Press, 1992).

9 "Effects of Opium." On sthenic and asthenic diseases, see Roy Porter, "The Eighteenth Century," in *The Western Medical Tradition: 800 BC to AD 1800*, by Lawrence I. Conrad, Michael Neve, Vivian Nutton, Roy Porter, and Andrew Wear (Cambridge, UK: Cambridge University Press, 1995), esp. 378–79.

10 "Effects of Opium."

11 Ibid.

12 Jonathan Pereira, *Elements of Materia Medica*, 2 vols. (London: Longman, Brown, Green, and Longmans, 1842), vol. 2, 1749.

13 "The Chinese," *The Favourite*, February 1874, 87.

14 "Opium and Life Insurance," *Canadian Journal of Commerce* 38 (2 March 1894): 443–44.

15 On taverns in early Upper Canada, see Julia Roberts, *In Mixed Company: Taverns and Public Life in Upper Canada* (Vancouver: UBC Press, 2009); on early temperance movements, see Jan Noel, *Canada Dry: Temperance Crusades before Confederation* (Toronto: University of Toronto Press, 1995).

16 An Old Resident in China, "Opium Trade and Missions," letter to the editor, *Gospel Tribune*, 2 December 1855, 213.

17 W. Travis Hanes III and Frank Sanello, *Opium Wars: The Addiction of One Empire and the Corruption of Another* (Naperville, IL: Sourcebooks, 2002). The Beijing Convention of 1860 granted a number of rights to Westerners, including the right to evangelize.

18 Quoted in ibid., 79.

19 An Old Resident in China, "Opium Trade and Missions," 213.

20 Andrew Porter, *Religion versus Empire? British Protestant Missionaries and Overseas Expansion, 1700–1914* (Manchester, UK: Manchester University Press, 2004), 206; "Taiping Rebellion," *Wikipedia*, http://en.wikipedia.org/wiki/Taiping_Rebellion.

21 "Chinese Movement," *Church Times*, 22 October 1853, 339.

22 Dr. Medhurst, "Religious Character of the New Chinese Revolution," letter to the editor, *The Presbyterian* 7 (April 1854): 59.

23 "Missionary and Religious Intelligence," *The Presbyterian* 7 (February 1854): 28.

24 "Increasing Success," *Gospel Tribune* 5 (2 May 1855): 20.

25 "English Presbyterian Missions," *Home and Foreign Record* 9 (November 1869): 13.

26 "Missionary Department: Results of Mission Work in China," *Earnest Christianity* 3 (1875): 184.

27 Mr. Masters, Wesleyan Missionary, "The Opium Iniquity," *Maritime Presbyterian Journal* 10 (January 1890): 32.

28 "What Can His Religion Be Like?" *Northern Messenger,* 23 September 1887, 4.

29 Kathleen L. Lodwick, *Crusaders against Opium: Protestant Missionaries in China, 1874–1917* (Lexington: University of Kentucky Press, 1995), 29.

30 "Great Britain," *True Witness and Catholic Chronicle* 19 (25 December 1868): 3.

31 John Burnham, *Bad Habits: Drinking, Smoking, Taking Drugs, Gambling, Sexual Misbehavior, and Swearing in American History* (New York: New York University Press, 1993).

32 J.D. Edgar, "Celestial America," *Canadian Monthly and National Review* 6 (November 1874): 392.

33 "Chinese Opium Smokers," *Canadian Illustrated News,* 24 August 1878, 114.

34 "Effects of Opium-Smoking," *Manitoba Daily Free Press,* 19 December 1879; "Effects of Opium-Smoking," *Canadian Illustrated News,* 20 December 1879, 395. These are the same article.

35 Ibid.

36 "A Royal Commission," editorial, *Victoria Daily Colonist,* 16 May 1895.

37 "Kipling on Opium," editorial, *Manitoba Daily Free Press,* 17 January 1901.

38 Dikötter, Laamann, and Xun, *Narcotic Culture.*

39 Statistics Canada, "BC Table I: Statement of the Population, 1870 – British Columbia," table, in *1870: Census of British Columbia,* database, accessed 12 November 2012.

40 The Act to Regulate the Chinese Population in British Columbia was proclaimed on 16 February 1884. See *Journals of the Legislature of British Columbia* (1883–84), 77.

41 "Appendix: Report of the Select Committee on Chinese Restriction," *Journals of the Legislature of British Columbia* 48 Vic. (1885), xxxix.

42 *Journals of the Legislature of British Columbia* (25 February 1885), 46.

43 Ibid.

44 Patricia A. Roy, *A White Man's Province: British Columbia Politicians and Chinese and Japanese Immigrants, 1858–1914* (Vancouver: UBC Press, 1989); W. Peter Ward, *White Canada Forever: Popular Attitudes and Public Policy toward Orientals in British Columbia,* 2nd ed. (Montreal and Kingston: McGill-Queen's University Press, 1978). See also Kay J. Anderson, *Vancouver's Chinatown: Racial Discourse in Canada, 1875-1980* (Montreal and Kingston: McGill-Queen's University Press, 1991).

45 *Journals of the Legislature of British Columbia* (6 February 1884), 53.

46 "Appendix 4: Evidence of the Select Committee on Chinese Immigration," *Journals of the House of Commons* (1879), 37.

47 Ibid., 57.

48 Ward, *White Canada Forever,* 44–45.

49 Roy, *White Man's Province;* Ward, *White Canada Forever,* 34.

50 John Jessop, "Report of the BC Immigration Agent," *Sessional Papers of the Dominion of Canada,* no. 10 (1886), 127.

51 "Appendix 47: J.W. Trutch to Minister of Agriculture, 10 January 1883," *Sessional Papers of the Dominion of Canada,* no. 14 (1883), 311.

52 *Sessional Papers of the Dominion of Canada,* no. 14 (1884); *Sessional Papers of the Dominion of Canada,* no. 8 (1885); *Sessional Papers of the Dominion of Canada,* no. 10 (1886).

53 *Sessional Papers of the Dominion of Canada,* no. 12 (1887), 116.

54 Ward, *White Canada Forever,* 38.

55 Royal Commission on Chinese Immigration, *Report of the Royal Commission on Chinese Immigration* (Ottawa: Printed by Order of the Commission, 1885), 241.

56 David R. Roediger, *The Wages of Whiteness: Race and the Making of the American Working Class* (London and New York: Verso, 1999).

57 Royal Commission on Chinese Immigration, *Report,* 150–51.

58 "Honorable Commissioner Gray's Report," in ibid., LV.

59 Ibid., LX.

60 Ibid., LIX.

61 "The Chinese Evil," *Halifax Morning Chronicle,* 25 February 1885.

62 "Moral Residents," *Halifax Morning Chronicle,* 17 March 1885.

63 On Canadian missionary movements, see Austin, *Saving China;* and Gagan, *Sensitive Independence.* Note, however, that in both of these books, opium is a minor consideration.

64 On the World's Woman's Christian Temperance Union, see Ian Tyrrell, *Woman's World, Woman's Empire: The Woman's Christian Temperance Union in International Perspective, 1880–1930* (Chapel Hill: University of North Carolina Press, 1991). On the date of its founding, see E.H. Cherrington, *Standard Encyclopedia of the Alcohol Problem* (Westerville, OH: American Issue Publishing, 1930), 2898.

65 "Opium Smoking: A California Father's Awful Discovery," *Manitoba Daily Free Press,* 21 June 1879; "Opium Smoking: A California Father's Awful Discovery – The Patrons of the Opium Dens," *True Witness and Catholic Chronicle,* 16 July 1879.

66 "The Opium Curse," *Canadian Presbyterian,* 22 August 1883, 545.

67 Untitled article, *Manitoba Daily Free Press,* 30 March 1881.

68 Untitled article, *Toronto Globe,* 13 April 1881.

69 "Opium Smoking," *Toronto Globe,* 3 March 1883.

70 "A Toronto Girl's Fate," *Manitoba Daily Free Press,* 27 November 1888.

71 Untitled article, *Manitoba Daily Free Press,* 1 November 1889.

72 "Wing Sing Weds Kate: A Marriage in Colonial Style," *Manitoba Daily Free Press,* 30 June 1885.

73 "Recent Fiction," *The Week* 4 (23 June 1887): 486.

74 Homer B. Sprague, "The Place of Literature in the College Course," *Canadian Education Monthly and School Magazine* 10 (March 1888): 92.

75 "From the World's Fair," *Toronto Globe,* 11 November 1893.

76 "Record Crowd for Citizens Day," *Manitoba Daily Free Press,* 23 July 1903.

77 "Ten Heads Taken Off: An Extensive and Successful Conspiracy Unearthed," *Manitoba Daily Free Press,* 21 June 1893.

78 "Murderous Outrage," *Manitoba Daily Free Press,* 19 August 1898.

79 "A Diabolical Chinaman," *Victoria Daily Colonist,* 19 August 1898.

80 "Chinese Gaming in Toronto," *Manitoba Daily Free Press,* 12 January 1903.

81 "A Tragedy in an Opium Den," *Lethbridge Herald,* 8 July 1908. On the same day, the *Manitoba Daily Free Press* also told the story, with a considerably smaller title font.

82 "Overcoats in Demand," *Manitoba Daily Free Press,* 1 February 1908.

83 "Opium Smoking," *Manitoba Daily Free Press,* 23 July 1881.

84 "Current Events and Opinions," *The Week* 1 (24 January 1884): 115.

85 "What Can His Religion Be Like?," *Northern Messenger,* 23 September 1887, 4.

86 "World's Missionary Conference," *Missionary Review of the World,* August 1888, 586.

87 "Trinity of Monstrous Evils Denounced," *Missionary Review of the World* Vol. 11 (Old series) Vol. 1 (New series) (September 1888): 675–84; quote at 676.

88 "Mission Notes: Opium Hindering the Gospel – A Sad Story," *Canadian Independent,* 15 February 1887, 54.

89 "Mission Notes: Opium Smoking in China," *Canadian Independent,* 15 February 1887, 55.

90 Untitled article, *Presbyterian Review,* 26 December 1895, 589.

Chapter 5: Medicine, Addiction, and Ideas of Nation

1 On the multiple meanings of addiction, see Timothy Hickman, "The Double Meaning of Addiction: Habitual Narcotic Use and the Logic of Professionalizing Medical Authority in the United States, 1900–1920," in *Altering American Consciousness: The History of Alcohol and Drug Use in the United States, 1800–2000,* ed. Sarah W. Tracy and Caroline Jean Acker (Boston and Amherst: University of Massachusetts Press, 2004), 182–202.

2 Harry G. Levine, "The Discovery of Addiction: Changing Conceptions of Habitual Drunkenness in America," *Journal of Studies on Alcohol* 39, 1 (1978): 143–74.

3 David Musto, *The American Disease: Origins of Narcotic Control,* 3rd ed. (Oxford and New York: Oxford University Press, 1999).

4 Virginia Berridge, "Morality and Medical Science: Concepts of Narcotic Addiction in Britain, 1820–1926," *Annals of Science* 36, 1 (1979): 67–85; Virginia Berridge, *Opium and the People: Opiate Use and Drug Control Policy in Nineteenth and Early Twentieth Century England* (London: Free Association Books, 1999); Geoffrey Harding, "Constructing Addiction as a Moral

Failing," *Sociology of Health and Illness* 8, 1 (1986): 76–85; Geoffrey Harding, *Opiate Addiction, Morality and Medicine: From Moral Illness to Pathological Disease* (Houndmills, Basingstoke, Hampshire, UK: Macmillan, 1988).

5   Timothy Hickman, "Drugs and Race in American Culture: Orientalism in the Turn-of-the-Century Discourse of Narcotic Addiction," *American Studies* 41, 1 (Spring 2000): 71–91; Timothy Hickman, *The Secret Leprosy of Modern Days: Narcotic Addiction and the Cultural Crisis in the United States, 1870–1920* (Boston and Amherst: University of Massachusetts Press, 2007); Hickman, "Double Meaning."

6   Howard Padwa, *Social Poison: The Culture and Politics of Opiate Control in Britain and France, 1821–1926* (Baltimore, MD: Johns Hopkins University Press, 2012).

7   Caroline Jean Acker, *Creating the American Junkie: Addiction Research in the Classic Era of Narcotic Control* (Baltimore, MD: Johns Hopkins University Press, 2002); Nancy D. Campbell, *Discovering Addiction: The Science and Politics of Substance Abuse Research* (Ann Arbor: University of Michigan Press, 2007).

8   James Kneale and Shaun French, "The Relations of Inebriety to Insurance: Geographies of Medicine, Insurance and Alcohol in Britain, 1840–1911," in *Intoxication and Society: Problematic Pleasures of Drugs and Alcohol,* ed. Jonathan Herring, Ciaran Regan, Darin Weinberg, and Phil Withington (London: Palgrave Macmillan, 2013), 87–109; Timothy Alborn, *Regulated Lives: Life Assurance and British Society, 1840–1920* (Toronto: University of Toronto Press, 2009), 225.

9   Hasso Spode reminds us that the English-speaking physicians were not the first to medicalize habituation. That credit, Spode argues, belongs to V. Brühl-Cramer. See Hasso Spode, "Transubstantiations of the Mystery: Two Remarks on the Shifts in the Knowledge about Addiction," *Social History of Alcohol and Drugs: An Interdisciplinary Journal* 20, 1 (2005): 125–28. Spode was responding to David Courtwright's focus on Anglo-American concepts of disease when discussing governing ideas of addiction. See David Courtwright, "Mr. ATOD's Wild Ride: What Do Alcohol, Tobacco, and Other Drugs Have in Common?" *Social History of Alcohol and Drugs: An Interdisciplinary Journal* 20, 1 (2005): 105–40.

10   Alcohol and drug historians, generally a very friendly and agreeable lot, have been discussing the primacy of Rush and Trotter (and others) for decades. See the reaction to Harry Gene Levine in Roy Porter, "The Drinking Man's Disease: The 'Pre-History' of Alcoholism in Georgian Britain," *British Journal of Addiction* 80, 4 (1985): 385–96; the reaction to Porter in Jessica Warner, "'Resolv'd to Drink No More': Addiction as a Preindustrial Concept," *Journal of Studies on Alcohol* 55, 6 (1994): 685–91; the reaction to Warner in Peter Ferentzy, "From Sin to Disease: Differences and Similarities between Past and Current Conceptions of Chronic Drunkenness," *Contemporary Drug Problems* 28, 3 (2001): 362–90; and the reaction to the whole thing in James Nicholl, "Vinum Britannicum: The 'Drink Question' in Early Modern England," *Social History of Alcohol and Drugs* 22, 2 (Spring 2008): 190–208. For a broader discussion, I recommend David Courtwright's article "Mr. ATOD's Wild Ride" and the responses in *Social History of Alcohol and Drugs: An Interdisciplinary Journal* 20, 1 (2005) by James Mills, "Morality, Society and the Science of Intoxication: A Response to David Courtwright's 'Mr. ATOD's Wild Ride: What Do Alcohol, Tobacco, and Other Drugs Have in Common?'" (133–37); Ian Tyrrell, "Alcohol, Tobacco, and Other Drugs: A Response to David Courtwright" (129–32); and especially Spode, "Transubstantiations of the Mystery."

11   For more on Trotter, see Porter, "Drinking Man's Disease"; and James Nicholls, *The Politics of Alcohol: A History of the Drink Question in England* (Manchester, UK: Manchester University Press, 2009).

12   Thomas Trotter, *An Essay, Medical, Philosophical, and Chemical, on Drunkenness, and Its Effects on the Human Body,* 4th ed. (London: Longman, Hurst, Kees and Orme, 1810), 43.

13   Ibid., 46.

14   Ibid., 20.

15   The classic discussion of Rush's work is Levine, "Discovery of Addiction."

16   Benjamin Rush, *An Inquiry into the Effects of Ardent Spirits on the Human Body* (Boston: James Loring, 1823), 13.

17   Ibid., 24.

18 Robert MacNish, "Advice to determined drunkards," Chapter 14 of *Anatomy of Drunkenness* First American ed. from Second London ed. (Philadelphia: Carey, Lea and Carey, 1828), 169–72.
19 Ibid., 66.
20 Ibid., 67.
21 Ibid., 51.
22 Berridge, "Morality and Medical Science," 70–71; Harding, "Constructing Addiction," 77–78.
23 Jonathan Pereira, *Elements of Materia Medica*, 2 vols. (London: Longman, Brown, Green, and Longmans, 1842), Vol. 2, 1747.
24 William G. Smith, "An Inaugural Dissertation on Opium" (1832), in *Origins Of Medical Attitudes toward Drug Addiction in America: Eight Studies, 1791–1858*, ed. Gerald Grob (New York: Arno, 1981), 21.
25 *Journals of the Legislative Assembly of Upper Canada* (1849), Appendix ZZZ. I am grateful to Martina Hardwick for this reference. Gugy was probably Bartholomew Conrad Augustus Gugy (1796–1876).
26 Edwin Chadwick, evidence, in "Report from the Select Committee on Inquiry into Drunkenness, with Minutes of Evidence, and Appendix" (1834), *House of Commons Parliamentary Papers,* http://parlipapers.chadwyck.co.uk/marketing/index.jsp. See also Elizabeth Lomax, "The Uses and Abuses of Opiates in Nineteenth-Century England," *Bulletin of Medical History* 47, 2 (March–April 1973), 167.
27 Anonymous, "Opium Eating," *Canadian Monthly* 13 (March 1878): 248.
28 George Ross, "'Case of Poisoning by Opium, Successfully Treated by the Hypodermic Injection of Atropia,' under the Care of Francis W. Campbell," *Canada Medical Journal* 6 (August 1869): 62–65.
29 Joseph Parrish, "The Philosophy of Intemperance," in "Proceedings of the First Annual Meeting of the American Association for the Cure of Inebriates" (1870), in *Proceedings of the American Association for the Cure of Inebriates,* ed. Gerald Grob (New York: Arno, 1981), 35. On Parrish and the American Association for the Study and Cure of Inebriety, see Dan Malleck, "American Association for the Study and Cure of Inebriety," in *Alcohol and Temperance in Modern History: A Global Encyclopedia,* vol. 1, ed. Jack S. Blocker, David M. Fahey, and Ian R. Tyrrell (Santa Barbara, CA: ABC Clio, 2003), 38–39.
30 John Burnham, *Bad Habits: Drinking, Smoking, Taking Drugs, Gambling, Sexual Misbehavior, and Swearing in American History* (New York: New York University Press, 1993).
31 D. McGillivray, "Excessive Use of Morphia, A DRACHM of the Sulphate Taken at One Dose with Impunity," *Canada Medical Journal* 5 (February 1869): 352–54.
32 Ibid.
33 Musto, *American Disease,* 72–75.
34 Mariana Valverde discusses the "addictive personality" in "'Slavery from Within': The Invention of Alcoholism and the Question of Free Will," *Social History* 22, 3 (Autumn 1997): 251–68.
35 H. Wayne Morgan, *Drugs in America: A Social History, 1800–1980* (Syracuse, NY: Syracuse University Press, 1981); David Courtwright, *Dark Paradise: A History of Opiate Addiction in America* (Cambridge, MA, and London: Harvard University Press, 1982), 54–55; Musto, *American Disease,* 1–2, 301n2.
36 On Allbutt, see Berridge, *Opium and the People*; Terry Parssinen and Karen Kerner, "The Development of the Disease Model of Drug Addiction in Britain, 1870–1926," *Medical History* 24, 3 (1980): 275–96, esp. 278.
37 See Parssinen and Kerner, "Development of the Disease Model," 278–79.
38 Eduard Levinstein, *Morbid Craving for Morphia* (London: Smith and Elder, 1878), 2.
39 Ibid., 3.
40 "Delirium Tremens from Morphine," *Canada Lancet* 9 (October 1876): 63; "Du Morphinisme," *L'Union medicale du Canada* 5 (May 1876): 209–10.
41 "De L'abus des injecnions [*sic*] sous-cutanees de morphine," *L'Union medicale du Canada* 5 (Mai 1876): 210–11.
42 Norman Kerr, *Inebriety or Narcomania: Its Etiology, Pathology, Treatment and Jurisprudence* (London: Lewis, 1894), 106.

43   He may also have alluded to the Victorian medical conception of vital power, which offered a gendered notion of proper channelling of energy. Bruce Haley discusses how doctors used a modified form of temperament physiology. Replacing Galenic temperament distinctions (i.e., phlegmatic, bilious, etc.) with temperaments based upon general categories like gender and body size, physicians offered physiologies that explained disease as an abnormal channelling of energy. See Bruce Haley, *The Healthy Body and Victorian Culture* (Cambridge, MA: Harvard University Press, 1978), 43.

44   Kerr, *Inebriety or Narcomania*, 106–7.

45   Joseph Parrish, "Opium Poisoning," in *Proceedings of the Sixth Annual Meeting of the American Association for the Study and Cure of Inebriety* (1875) ed. Gerald Grob (New York: Arno Press Reprint, 1981), 10–11.

46   Kerr, *Inebriety or Narcomania*, 32.

47   American Association for the Study and Cure of Inebriety (AASCI), *The Disease of Inbriety from Alcohol, Opium, and Other Narcotic Drugs: Its Etiology, Pathology, Treatment and Medico-legal Relations*, ed. T.D. Crothers (New York: E.B. Treat, 1893), 317.

48   "Medical Items: Poisons," *Canada Medical and Surgical Journal* 8 (April 1880): 429.

49   Francis Anstie, *Stimulants and Narcotics: Their Mutual Relations* (London: Macmillan, 1864), 79.

50   Edward Hitchcock, *An Essay on Alcoholic and Narcotic Substances* (Amherst, MA: J.S. and C. Adams, 1830), 4. Reprinted in *Nineteenth-Century Medical Attitudes toward Alcoholic Addiction: Six Studies, 1814–1867* ed. Gerald Grob (New York: Arno Press, 1981).

51   Rev. Cushman quoted in "Sunday Reading: Temptations of Young Men," *Montreal Transcript*, 9 January 1847.

52   James Bovell, *A Plea for Inebriate Asylums Commended to the Consideration of the Legislators of the Province of Canada* (Toronto: Lovell and Gibson, 1862), 30.

53   Ibid., 32.

54   As A.B. McKillop has shown, part of the role of science prior to the Darwinist ontological challenge was to learn more about God's design through an empirical examination of the natural world. See A.B. McKillop, *A Disciplined Intelligence: Critical Inquiry and Canadian Thought in the Victoria Era* (Montreal and Kingston: McGill-Queen's University Press, 1979). See also Valverde, "'Slavery from Within,'" 260; Carl Berger, *Science, God and Nature in Victorian Canada* (Toronto: University of Toronto Press, 1983).

55   S.E.D. Shortt, "Physicians, Science and Status: Issues in the Professionalization of Anglo-American Medicine in the Nineteenth Century," *Medical History* 27, 1 (1983): 51–68; Wendy Mitchinson, *The Nature of Their Bodies: Women and Their Doctors in Victorian Canada* (Toronto: University of Toronto Press, 1991), 42–43.

56   See Leonard Blumberg, "The American Association for the Study and Cure of Inebriety," *Alcoholism, Clinical and Experimental Research* 2, 3 (July 1978): 235–40.

57   "Minutes," *Proceedings of the First Annual Meeting of the American Association for the Cure of Inebriates* (1870), 3.

58   Ibid., 8.

59   Alonzo Calkins, *Opium and the Opium Appetite, with Notices of Alcoholic Beverages, Cannabis Indica, Tobacco and Coca, and Tea and Coffee, in their Hygienic Aspects and Pathologic Relations* (Philadelphia: J.B. Lippincott, 1871).

60   Both the SSI and the AASCI intended to challenge scientifically the moralism of earlier temperance movements. See Virginia Berridge, "Society for the Study of Addiction, 1884–1988," *British Journal of Addiction* 85, 8 (August 1990): 991; and Blumberg, "American Association," 237.

61   Parrish, "Philosophy of Intemperance," 30, emphasis in original.

62   However, the ranks of the AASCI were not closed on this issue. Early meetings saw dissent mar the discussions of moral versus medical explanations. Yet, in its primary publication, the AASCI asserted a somatic origin of the weakened will. This assertion may have owed to the influence of Crothers, who was the principal author of the book. See AASCI, *Disease of Inebriety*.

63   This concept was reiterated by Lewis D. Mason, "The Aetiology and Therapeutics of Alcohol Inebriety," reprinted from *Brooklyn Medical Journal*, in *Canada Lancet* 26 (October 1893): 38.

64 Parrish, "Philosophy of Intemperance," 31.
65 Ibid., 32.
66 Parrish, "Opium Poisoning," 10.
67 Ibid., 11.
68 John Harley Warner, "The Principle of Specificity," in *The Therapeutic Perspective: Medical Practice, Knowledge, and Identity in America, 1820–1885* (Cambridge, MA: Harvard University Press, 1986), esp. 80.
69 Parrish, "Opium Poisoning," 11.
70 Ibid., 20.
71 Although the exact makeup of the membership of these organizations is unclear, at least one Canadian practitioner joined the SSI in its first year. Dr. Simon Fitch of Halifax, Nova Scotia, was listed as a member of its council. See reproduction pages of the SSI's first meeting, in Virginia Berridge, "Society for the Study of Addiction," 994–95.
72 Stephen Lett, "Treatment of the Opium Neurosis," *Journal of the American Medical Association* 17, 22 (28 November 1891): 828, emphasis in original.
73 Cheryl Krasnick Warsh, "The Aristocratic Vice," in *Moments of Unreason: The Practice of Psychiatry at the Homewood Retreat, 1883–1923*, 155–70 (Montreal and Kingston: McGill-Queen's University Press, 1989).
74 On Keeley's remedies, see Cheryl Krasnick Warsh, "Adventures in Maritime Quackery: The Leslie E. Keeley Gold Cure Institute of Fredericton, N.B.," *Acadiensis* 17, 2 (Spring 1988): 109–30; Dan Malleck, "Keeley, Leslie Enraught," in *American National Biography*, online ed., http://www.anb.org/articles/12/12-00473.html; and H. Wayne Morgan, "'No, Thank You, I've Been to Dwight': Reflections on the Keeley Cure for Alcoholism," *Illinois Historical Journal* 82, 3 (Autumn 1989): 147–66.
75 Montreal Medico-Chirurgical Society, "The Treatment of Inebriety as a Disease," *Montreal Medical Journal* 8 (March 1896): 736–37. See also Dr. Manchester, "The Treatment of Inebriety by the General Practitioner," *Western Canada Medical Journal* 2 (December 1908): 577–87, in which Manchester endorsed Edwards's treatment.
76 Montreal Medico-Chirurgical Society, "Treatment of Inebriety," 737.
77 "diathesis, *n.*," *OED Online*.
78 See W.F. Bynum, "Darwin and the Doctors: Evolution, Diathesis, and Germs in 19th-Century Britain," *Gesnerus* 40, 1–2 (1983): 46.
79 Paraphrased by A. Jaffe, "Reform in American Medical Science: The Inebriety Movement and the Origins of the Psychological Disease Theory of Addiction, 1870–1920," *British Journal of Addiction* 73, 2 (1978): 140.
80 Ibid.
81 H.J. Brown, *An Opium Cure: Based upon Science, Skill and Matured Experience* (New York: Fred H Brown, 1872), 7, emphasis in original.
82 Stephen Lett, "The Prognosis of Drug Habits, with Some Reference to Treatment," *Canada Lancet* 34, 1 (September 1900): 2. On Lett, see Warsh, "Aristocratic Vice."
83 Anonymous, "Opium Eating," 248–49.
84 J.B. Mattison, "The Treatment of Opium Addiction," *Canada Medical Record* 15 (January 1885): 73.
85 Parrish, "Opium Poisoning," 9, emphasis in original.
86 This is the "elastic" nature of diathesis discussed by Bynum, "Darwin and the Doctors," 46.
87 T.D. Crothers, *The Drug Habits and Their Treatment: A Clinical Summary of Some of the General Facts Recorded in Practice* (Chicago: G.P. Engelhard, 1902), 18.
88 AASCI, *Disease of Inebriety*, 319–20.
89 Ibid., 323–24.
90 Kerr, *Inebriety or Narcomania*, 100.
91 Dolores Peters, "British Medical Response to Opiate Addiction in the Nineteenth Century," *Journal of the History of Medicine* 36, 4 (1981): 478–79.
92 As A. Jaffe noted, "Though experts had long agreed that drugs altered bodily functions, there was little offered in the way of explanations and identification of the mechanisms involved in this alteration process." See Jaffe, "Reform in American Medical Science," 145.

93   Kerr, *Inebriety or Narcomania*, 101. Similarly, in the AASCI's *Disease of Inebriety*, 317–18, physical mechanisms are implied, but the proof of these assertions is demonstrated in sociological and hereditarian factors.

94   Robert Harris, "Report of the Franklin Reformatory Home for Inebriates, 913–915 Locust Street, Philadelphia," *Proceedings of the Annual Meeting of the American Association for the Study and Cure of Inebriates* (1875), 80–83, emphasis in original.

95   Blumberg explains how the AASCI attempted to make room for ideas like those of Harris. He and his institution, however, soon broke away from the AASCI, a movement that may have had more to do with institutional rivalry within Philadelphia than with ideological differences. See Blumberg, "American Association," 236.

96   Charles L. Dana, "The Nature and Frequency of Inebriety, with Remarks on Its Treatment," reprinted from *Canada Medical Record*, in *Canada Lancet* 24 (June 1892): 302.

97   Burnham, *Bad Habits*.

98   Henry Howard, "Address Delivered at the Opening of the Summer Session Clinic for Diseases of the Nervous System, McGill University, April 14, 1885," *Canada Medical and Surgical Journal* 13 (May 1885): 577–95. Here Howard may be referring to the work of individuals like Benjamin Carpenter, who argued that the will may be partly a result of identifiable physical actions, such as unconscious reflexes, but Carpenter and others did not accept the idea that all aspects of the wilful and moral being could be physical phenomena. See Bruce Haley, "Mens Sana in Corpore Sano: Victorian Psychophysiology," in *Healthy Body and Victorian Culture*, 23–45.

99   Henry Howard, "Man's Moral Responsibility from a Scientific Standpoint," *Canada Lancet* 8 (February 1876): 164.

100 Howard, "Address," 579–80.

101 Howard, "Man's Moral Responsibility," 164.

102 Howard, "Address," 583.

103 Ibid., 595.

104 Ibid., 587–88.

105 Berger, *Science, God and Nature*, 47; Mitchinson, *Nature of Their Bodies*, 42–43. The decline of religion has been debated for some time in the field of religious history; for Canada, the most notable discussions are in Ramsay Cook, *The Regenerators: Social Criticism in Late Victorian English Canada* (Toronto: University of Toronto Press, 1985); Michael Gauvreau, *The Evangelical Century: College and Creed in English Canada from the Great Revival to the Great Depression* (Montreal and Kingston: McGill-Queen's University Press, 1991); David B. Marshall, *Secularizing the Faith: Canadian Protestant Clergy and the Crisis of Belief, 1850–1940* (Toronto: University of Toronto Press, 1992), esp. 53–59; and McKillop, *Disciplined Intelligence*.

106 See Jim Baumohl, "Inebriate Institutions in North America, 1840–1920," in *Drink in Canada: Historical Essays*, ed. Cheryl Krasnick Warsh (Montreal and Kingston: McGill-Queen's University Press, 1993), 92–114; Jim Beaumohl and Robin Room, "Inebriety, Doctors, and the State: Alcoholism Treatment Institutions before 1940," in *Recent Developments in Alcoholism*, vol. 5, series editor Marc Galanter, 135–74 (New York and London: Plenum, 1987).

107 Musto, *American Disease*, 74.

108 Levinstein, *Morbid Craving*, 14.

109 Editorial, *Canada Medical and Surgical Journal* 16 (December 1887): 319.

110 Edward Mann, "The Nature and Treatment of the Morphia Habit," *Montreal Medical Journal* 24 (July 1894): 2–3.

111 J.B. Mattison, "Therapeutics of Opium Addiction," *Canada Lancet* 15 (May 1883): 263.

112 Lett, "Prognosis of Drug Habits," 1–4.

113 Eduard Levinstein, "The Abuse of Hypodermic Injections of Morphia (Morphiomania)," reprinted from *Bulletin General de Therapeutique*, trans J. Williams, in *Canada Lancet* 9 (January 1877): 138–42; Anonymous, "The Abuse of Hypodermic Injection of Morphia," *Canada Medical and Surgical Journal* 5 (August 1876): 67–68.

114 James Stewart, "Report on Pharmacology and Therapeutics: On the Use of Cocaine in the Opium Habit," *Canada Medical and Surgical Journal* 14 (April 1886): 539.

115 Morandon de Montyel, "Contribution to the Study of Morphiomania," *Canada Lancet* 18 (April 1886): 242.

116 Lett, "Treatment of the Opium Neurosis," 828.
117 E.C. Mann, "The Disease of Inebriety: Spreeing and Tippling," *Canada Lancet* 27 (June 1895): 306.
118 Parrish, "Opium Poisoning" Proceedings of the Sixth Annual Meeting of the AASCI (1875), 16.
119 J.W. Grosvenor, "What Shall We Do with Our Alcoholic Inebriates?" *Canada Lancet* 28 (May 1896): 301.
120 "Legislation for Inebriates," editorial, *Canada Lancet* 30 (June 1898): 533.
121 John Stewart, "Presidential Address," *Canada Lancet* 41 (October 1905): 104.
122 Ibid., 101.
123 Alfred Schofield, "The Relation of Mind and Body," *Western Canada Medical Journal* 1 (December 1907): 551.
124 J.B. Mattison, "The Prevention of Morphinism," *Canada Lancet* 24 (October 1891): 34.
125 T.K. Holmes, "Address Delivered before the Canadian Medical Association," *Canada Medical and Surgical Journal* 15 (September 1886): 75.
126 "Infant Mortality," editorial, *Western Canada Medical Journal* (1 August 1907): 369.
127 Stewart, "Presidential Address," 101.
128 Ibid., 102.
129 On the WCTU in Canada, see Nancy M. Sheehan, "The WCTU on the Prairies, 1886–1930: An Alberta-Saskatchewan Comparison," *Prairie Forum* 6, 1 (1981): 17–33; Wendy Mitchinson, "The WCTU: 'For God and Home and Native Land' – A Study in Nineteenth-Century Feminism," in *A Not Unreasonable Claim: Women and Reform in Canada, 1880s–1920s*, ed. Linda Kealey (Toronto: Women's Press, 1979), 151–67; Dan Malleck, "Priorities of Development in Four Local Woman's Christian Temperance Unions in Ontario, 1877–1895," in *The Changing Face of Drink*, ed. Jack Blocker and Cheryl Krasnick Warsh (Toronto: Histoire Sociale/Social History, 1997), 189–208; and Sharon Ann Cook, *"Through Sunshine and Shadow": The Woman's Christian Temperance Union, Evangelicalism and Reform in Ontario, 1874–1930* (Montreal and Kingston: McGill-Queen's University Press, 1995).
130 Physicians' relationship to the temperance movement, beyond what we have already seen, was tenuous. See J. Zimmerman, "When the Doctors Disagree: Scientific Temperance and Scientific Authority, 1891–1906," *Journal of the History of Medicine and Allied Sciences* 48, 2 (1993): 171–97; Andrew McClary, "The WCTU Discovers Science: The Women's [*sic*] Christian Temperance Union, Plus Teachers, Doctors and Scientific Temperance," *Michigan History* 68, 1 (January 1984): 16–23; and Philip J. Pauly, "The Struggle for Ignorance about Alcohol: American Physiologists, Wilbur Olin Atwater, and the Woman's Christian Temperance Union," *Bulletin of the History of Science* 64, 3 (1990): 366–92.
131 Ontario WCTU, *Report of the Annual Convention of the Ontario Woman's Christian Temperance Union* (Toronto: William Briggs and Sons, 1895), 144. No record of the request appears in the records of the Ontario Medical Council or the Ontario Medical Association. The health and heredity superintendent, Maria G. Craig, urged the members to approach medical students about the concern over inordinate prescription of dangerous drugs. See Maria G. Craig, "Health and Heredity," *Woman's Journal*, 15 January 1899, 2.
132 Dominion WCTU, *Report of the Annual Convention of the Dominion Woman's Christian Temperance Union* (Toronto: William Briggs and Sons, 1892), 112–13, in Provincial Archives of Ontario, MU8398.1–8.
133 Saloma, "The Opium Habit," *Woman's Journal*, May 1892, 1–2.
134 Geoffrey Harding, *Opiate Addiction, Morality and Medicine: From Moral Illness to Pathological Disease* (Houndmills, Basingstoke, Hampshire, UK: Macmillan, 1988), 36–37.

Chapter 6: Madness and Addiction in the Asylums of English Canada

1 For a discussion of the various ways that scientific research can affect perceptions, see John V. Pickstone, *Ways of Knowing: A New History of Science, Technology and Medicine* (Chicago: University of Chicago Press, 2000).
2 Quebec has been omitted because its asylums were operated under a different governance (many being smaller church-run asylums) and also due to the challenges of analyzing the language of addiction in French. Manitoba has been omitted because after an eight-month

process of winding through the bureaucracy and legalese of three separate government departments, I learned that the records listed on the finding aids were not part of the collection to which I'd finally gained access. So I decided to abandon that province's lunatics to the silence that the overly restrictive government access policies had imposed upon them. Although Canada did see several inebriate asylums open during the last part of the century, since their mandate was to treat pre-identified habituation, tracing the development of the idea of habituation within those asylums' records – if records even exist – would not achieve the purpose of this chapter. Nevertheless, I do include records from the Homewood Retreat because, although it included addicts in its population, it was an asylum that treated other mental illnesses. Moreover, Stephen Lett was an internationally known addiction expert, and his diagnoses are worth considering, especially, as we will see, since some patients in public asylums moved from Homewood to the public institutions.

3　Within the historical literature on asylums, a distinct thread of social stability remains constant. Asylums were created for a variety of reasons, a key one was to contain or treat the insane and thereby ensure social stability, if not progress. For an overview of the challenges to the social-control theory, see Thomas E. Brown, "Dance of the Dialectic? Some Reflections (Polemic or Otherwise) on the Present State of Nineteenth Century Asylum Studies," *Canadian Bulletin of Medical History* 11, 2 (1994): 267–95. See also James E. Moran, *Committed to the State Asylum: Insanity and Society in Nineteenth-Century Quebec and Ontario* (Montreal and Kingston: McGill-Queen's University Press, 2000); Geoffrey Reaume, "999 Queen Street West: Portrait of Life at the Toronto Hospital for the Insane, 1870–1940" (PhD diss., University of Toronto, 1997); Barry Edginton, "The Well-Ordered Body: The Quest for Sanity through Nineteenth-Century Asylum Architecture," *Canadian Bulletin of Medical History* 11, 2 (1994): 375–86; Andrew Scull, "From Madness to Mental Illness: Medical Men as Moral Entrepreneurs," in *The Most Solitary of Afflictions: Madness and Society in Britain, 1700–1900*, 175–231 (New Haven, CT, and London: Yale University Press, 1993); Wendy Mitchinson, "The Toronto and Gladesville Asylums: Humane Alternatives for the Insane in Canada and Australia?" *Bulletin of the History of Medicine* 63, 1 (1989): 52–72; Cheryl Krasnick Warsh, *Moments of Unreason: The Practice of Psychiatry at the Homewood Retreat, 1883–1923* (Montreal and Kingston: McGill-Queen's University Press, 1989); Anne Digby, *Madness, Morality and Medicine: A Study of the York Retreat, 1876–1914* (Cambridge, UK: Cambridge University Press, 1985); S.E.D. Shortt, *Victorian Lunacy: Richard M. Bucke and the Practice of Late Nineteenth-Century Psychiatry* (Cambridge, UK: Cambridge University Press, 1986); and Nancy Tomes, *A Generous Confidence: Thomas Story Kirkbride and the Art of Asylum-Keeping, 1840–1883* (Cambridge, UK: Cambridge University Press, 1984).

4　Moran, *Committed to the State Asylum*, ch. 2.

5　When discussing specific cases from asylums, in order to protect patient privacy, I generally provide given name and initial of surname unless the names are so unique to enable them to be identified easily. In cases where archives have not permitted me to use any actual names, I provide pseudonyms. All patient file numbers are genuine.

6　Henry Maudsley, *Physiology and Pathology of Mind* (London: Macmillan, 1867), 229.

7　G. Fielding Blandford, *Insanity and Its Treatment: Lectures on the Treatment, Medical and Legal, of Insane Patients*, 3rd ed. (Edinburgh: Oliver and Boyd, 1884), 69.

8　Ibid., 160.

9　G. Fielding Blandford, *Insanity and Its Treatment, Lectures on the Treatment, Medical and Legal, of Insane Patients*, 4th ed. (Edinburgh: Oliver and Boyd, 1892), 494.

10　Moran, *Committed to the State Asylum*, 78–79.

11　Halifax Hospital for the Insane, Case books respectively vol. 15, patient no. 93 (admitted 22 June 1860), and vol. 17, patient no. 238 (admitted 13 January 1863). Found in, Case books, RG 25 Series NS, Nova Scotia Hospital fonds, Nova Scotia Archives (hereafter NSH/NSA).

12　These descriptors are from the Halifax Hospital for the Insane, Case books, specifically the "Statement" signed by medical professionals. In this case, it was in the records of patient no. 441 (admitted 29 June 1867) but all were the same. Case books, RG 25 Series NS, NSH/NSA.

13 Moran, *Committed to the State Asylum;* Reaume, "999 Queen Street West"; Cheryl Krasnick Warsh, "The Medical World of the Asylum: Diagnostics and Therapeutics," in *Moments of Unreason,* 37–62; Mitchinson, "Toronto and Gladesville Asylums"; Wendy Mitchinson, "Reasons for Committal to a Mid-Nineteenth-Century Ontario Insane Asylum: The Case of Toronto," in *Essays in the History of Canadian Medicine,* ed. Wendy Mitchinson and Janice Dickin McGinnis (Toronto: McClelland and Stewart, 1988), 88–109; Shortt, *Victorian Lunacy,* 49–56; Barry Willer and Gary Miller, "Classification, Cause and Symptoms of Mental Illness," *Canadian Psychiatric Association Journal* 22, 5 (August 1977): 231–35.

14 G.H. Manchester, "Report of Medical Superintendent of the Public Hospital for the Insane, New Westminster, BC," in "Annual Report on the Public Hospital for the Insane of the Province of British Columbia for the year 1902," in *Sessional Papers of the Province of British Columbia* (1903), E7.

15 Moran, *Committed to the State Asylum,* 79.

16 T. Millman, "Admission of Lunatics into Asylums," *Canada Lancet* 13 (October 1880): 33–38.

17 See Provincial Lunatic Asylum, *By-laws Established by the Board of Directors of the Provincial Lunatic Asylum, Toronto, C.W.* (Toronto: Carter and Thomas, 1852); and Provincial Lunatic Asylum, *By-laws of the Provincial Lunatic Asylum, Toronto, C.W.* (Toronto: Rowsell and Ellis, 1862).

18 Delirium tremens could also be a diagnosis attached to an extreme physical reaction that an individual might have to taking too much alcohol. It was a complicating factor in the death of John Blackie.

19 An example is the case of Richard B., who entered the asylum on 7 September 1846 and stayed for seven hours. See clinical case book RG 10-269, Queen Street Mental Health Centre fonds, Archives of Ontario (hereafter QSMHC/AO).

20 Patient no. 904 (unclear, could be 906); Clinical case book, RG 10-269, QSMHC/AO.

21 Howard J. Shaffer, "The Discovery of Addiction: Levine and the Philosophical Foundations of Drug Abuse Treatment," *Journal of Substance Abuse Treatment* 2, 1 (1985): 42.

22 *Casebook,* 19 February 1863, 234; RS 140-B2, Saint John Lunatic Asylum fonds, Provincial Archives of New Brunswick (hereafter SJLA/PANB).

23 Casebook, 21 June 1862, 211; RS 140-B3, SJLA/PANB.

24 Casebook, 3 February 1876, 115; RS 140-B4, SJLA/PANB.

25 Case file for patient file no. 1039; Patients' clinical casebooks; RG 10-279, London Psychiatric Hospital, Archives of Ontario (hereafter LPH/AO).

26 Case file for patient no. 1012; Patients' clinical casebooks; RG 10-279, LPH/AO.

27 Case file for patient no. 1265; Patients' clinical casebooks; RG 10-279, LPH/AO.

28 Case records for patients no. 4833 and no. 4925; Patients' clinical case files, RG 10-270, QSMHC/AO.

29 Case file, patient no. 806, Casebook, vol. 9; GR 1754, British Columbia Provincial Mental Hospital fonds, British Columbia Archives (hereafter BCPMH/BCA).

30 "Report of the Inspector of Prisons, Asylums and Hospitals," *Sessional Papers of Ontario* (1885), 8. The inspector provided this qualification annually when discussing the table of "Causes of Insanity." This cryptic phrase likely referred to more commonly identified behaviour, like masturbation or alcoholism, but what is important in this quotation is the fact that families kept some conditions secret.

31 Terry Parssinen, *Secret Passions, Secret Remedies: Narcotic Drugs in British Society, 1820–1930* (Manchester, UK: Manchester University Press, 1983), 5.

32 *Journals of the Legislative Assembly of Upper Canada* (1849), Appendix ZZZ.

33 Michael J. Clarke, "'Morbid Introspection,' Unsoundness of Mind, and British Psychological Medicine, c.1830-c.1900," in *Anatomy of Madness,* vol. 3, *The Asylum and Its Psychiatry,* ed. W.F. Bynum, Roy Porter, and Michael Shepherd (London: Routledge, 1988), 71–101.

34 On drug use and industrial society, see Wolfgang Schivelbusch, *Tastes of Paradise: A Social History of Spices, Stimulants, and Intoxicants,* trans. David Jacobson (New York: Pantheon, 1992); on drug addiction as challenging bourgeois sensibilities, see Virginia Berridge, *Opium and the People: Opiate Use and Drug Control Policy in Nineteenth and Early Twentieth Century England* (London: Free Association Books, 1999), chs. 4, 9, and 18.

35 *Fortieth Annual Report of the Medical Superintendent of the Nova Scotia Asylum for Insane, 1896–97*, Table IX, p 23; Appendix 3 of *Journal and Proceedings of the House of Assembly of the Province of Nova Scotia, Session 1898* (Halifax: Queen's Printer, 1898).

36 Statistics were determined by an analysis of the data provided in the annual reports of the BC and the Nova Scotia Asylums. The BC reports did not always provide causes, but in the reports that did, between 1883–93 and 1902–07, intemperance in alcohol was a cause in a fairly regular 10 percent of cases.

37 "Report of the Superintendent of the Provincial Lunatic Asylum," *Journals of the House of Assembly of the Province of New Brunswick* (Fredericton: Queen's Printer, 1903), Table 10, 36–39.

38 See tables listing causes of insanity in annual "Report on the Asylum for the Insane, New Westminster," *Sessional Papers of the Province of British Columbia* (1884–94).

39 Charles E. Rosenberg, "Body and Mind in Nineteenth Century Medicine: Some Clinical Origins of the Neurosis Construct," *Bulletin of the History of Medicine* 63, 2 (1989): 185–97.

40 Records for patient no. 517; Patients' clinical case files, RG 10-270, QSMHC/AO.

41 Records for patient no. 3039; Patients' clinical case files, RG 10-270, QSMHC/AO.

42 Case file for patient no. 883, Case books vol. 1; RG 25 Series NS, NSH/NSA.

43 Casebook, 18 July 1871, 553; RS 140-B3, SJLA/PANB.

44 Casebook, 10 August 1876, 16–1; RS 140-B4, SJLA/PANB.

45 See, for example, Oscar Wilde, *The Picture of Dorian Gray* (London: Oxford University Press, 1974); Charles Dickens, *The Mystery of Edwin Drood* (Oxford: Clarendon, 1972); and Wilkie Collins, *The Moonstone* (London: Chatto, 1907).

46 Case file for patient no. 235, Case books vol. 17; RG 25 Series NS, NSH/NSA.

47 Case file for patient no. 5810; Patients' clinical case files, RG 10-270, QSMHC/AO.

48 Case file for patient no. 5810, emphasis added; Patients' clinical case files RG 10-270, QSMHC/AO.

49 Case file for patient no. 5810; Patients' clinical case files, RG 10-270, QSMHC/AO. The role of morphine in Catherine's condition remains unclear since she died four days after her arrival.

50 His age is not clear; it may have been thirty-one or thirty-seven.

51 The asylum practice was to release patients on probation first. John was formally discharged soon afterward. See case file for patient no. 7773, 403, Patients' clinical case files, RG 10-270, QSMHC/AO.

52 Case file, patient no. 1134, Casebook, vol. 10; GR 1754, BCPMH/BCA.

53 Case file for patient no. 4341; Patients' clinical case files, RG 10-270, QSMHC/AO.

54 Patients' clinical casebooks, vol. 1, 56; RG 10-279, LPH/AO. Early records for this asylum were listed by page number not by patient reference number.

55 Case file for patient no. 1354, Case books vol. 19; RG 25 Series NS, NSH/NSA.

56 Case file for patient no. 2132, Case books vol. 26; RG 25 Series NS, NSH/NSA.

57 Daniel Clark, "Annual Report of the Medical Superintendent of the Asylum for the Insane, Toronto," *Papers of the Legislative Assembly of Ontario* (1898), 39. This sentiment was also expressed by T. Millman, who, while an assistant physician at the London Asylum wrote an article instructing physicians on how to fill in asylum admission forms properly. See Millman, "Admission of Lunatics."

58 See Warsh, *Moments of Unreason*, 38–39.

59 S.A. Armstrong, "Regulation Respecting the Classification of Insanity to Be Adopted in All Hospitals for the Insane of the Province of Ontario," in *Report of the Inspectors of Hospitals for the Insane* (1908), xii–xiii.

60 Warsh, *Moments of Unreason*, 39. On the incongruities between complex asylum diagnostics and facile therapeutics, see Barry Willer and Garry Miller, "Prognosis and Outcome of Mental Illness, 1890–1900, in Ontario," *Canadian Psychiatric Association Journal* 22, 5 (1977): 235–38; and Delores Peters, "British Medical Response to Opiate Addiction in the Nineteenth Century," *Journal of the History of Medicine* 36, 4 (1981): 456.

61 Files for (respectively) patients no. 4049, 4063, and 4087. Patients' clinical casebooks; RG 10-292 Kingston Psychiatric Hospital fonds, Archives of Ontario (hereafter KPH/AO).

62 Case file for patient no. 8532; Patients' clinical case files, RG 10-270, QSMHC/AO.

63 Case file for patient no. 7202, 12 March 1892; RG 10-279, LPH/AO.

64 Case file for patient no. 3203; Patients' clinical casebooks; RG 10-292, KPH/AO.

65 Casebook, vol. 5 page 355; GR 1754, BCPMH/BCA (early books did not list patient numbers).

66 Case file, patient no. 1005, Casebook, vol. 8; GR 1754, BCPMH/BCA.

67 Case file, patient no. 1075, Casebook, vol. 9; GR 1754, BCPMH/BCA.

68 Case file, patient no. 1090, Casebook, vol. 9; GR 1754, BCPMH/BCA.

69 Case file, patient no. 1209, Casebook, vol. 10; GR 1754, BCPMH/BCA.

70 Case file, patient no. 1424, Casebook, vol. 10; GR 1754, BCPMH/BCA.

71 Daniel Clark, *Mental Diseases: A synopsis of twelve lectures delivered at the Hospital for the Insane, Toronto, to the graduating medical classes* (Toronto, Briggs, 1895), 37–38.

72 See Case file for patients no. 8442, 8360, and 8536; Patients' clinical case files, RG 10-270, QSMHC/AO.

73 Case file for patient no. 3952; Patients' clinical casebooks; RG 10-279, LPH/AO.

74 Richard M. Bucke, "Affadavit," in "In the High Court of Justice" (n.d.), in patient file for patient no. 8077; Patients' clinical case files, RG 10-270, QSMHC/AO."

75 Daniel Clark to R. Christie, Inspector of Asylums, 19 November 1896, 1–2; in patient file for patient no. 8077; Patients' clinical case files, RG 10-270, QSMHC/AO."

76 Ibid., 2.

77 Ibid., 3.

78 The High Court decided that the Toronto General Trusts Company (TGTC) would have control of the estate of Edward's family. Since the specific reasons for the trial are not clear, it is difficult to comment upon this decision. However, it appears that Edward was the eldest brother, so the TGTC case was an attempt, at the request of the rest of the family, to put a third party in charge of the funds from Andrew C. Sr.'s estate in order to protect them from misappropriations like those of Edward. In that respect, this court decision was a victory for both sides.

79 Clark, *Mental Diseases*, 37–38, emphasis added.

80 Shortt, *Victorian Lunacy*, 100–9; Rainer Baehre, "The Bucke Era: The Custodial Asylum, Incurability, and Devolution, 1876–1902," in "The Ill-Regulated Mind: A Study in the Making of Psychiatry in Ontario, 1830–1921," 288–372 (PhD diss., York University, 1985).

81 On atavism and Bucke's ideas, see Shortt, *Victorian Lunacy*, 100–1.

82 On class-based moral and social panic, see especially Mariana Valverde, *The Age of Light, Soap and Water: Moral Reform in English Canada, 1885–1925* (Toronto: McClelland and Stewart, 1991); Angus McLaren, *Our Own Master Race: Eugenics in Canada, 1885–1945* (Toronto: McClelland and Stewart, 1990).

83 On the stable middle-class family as an ideal, see Leonore Davidoff and Catherine Hall, *Family Fortunes: Men and Women of the English Middle Class, 1780–1850* (London: Routledge, 1992). On the family of addicts, see Cheryl Krasnick Warsh, "The First Mrs. Rochester: Family Motivations for Commitment and the Dynamics of Social Redundancy," in *Moments of Unreason*, 63–81. Caroline Jean Acker tells a different story in "Portrait of an Addicted Family: Dynamics of Opiate Addiction in the Early Twentieth Century," in *Altering American Consciousness: The History of Alcohol and Drug Use in the United States, 1800–2000*, ed. Sarah W. Tracy and Caroline Jean Acker (Boston and Amherst: University of Massachusetts Press, 2004), 165–81.

84 For a general discussion of the asylum as a repository of socially redundant women, see, for example, Warsh, "First Mrs. Rochester." On the demographics of addicts, see Cheryl Krasnick Warsh, "The Aristocratic Vice," in *Moments of Unreason*, 155–71. David Courtwright scrutinizes a demographic shift from addicted respectable middle-class individuals to recreational use among the "underclass." See David Courtwright, *Dark Paradise: A History of Opiate Addiction in America* (Cambridge, MA: Harvard University Press, 1982), 113–47. An earlier attempt to explore the demographics of opium addicts is William H. Swatos Jr., "Opiate Addiction in the Late Nineteenth Century: A Study of the Social Problem, Using Medical Journals of the Period," *International Journal of the Addictions* 7, 4 (1972): 739–53. Virginia Berridge also discusses upper-class drug use in *Opium and the People*, specifically chs. 5, 9, and 13.

85   Case file for patient no. 7688; Patients' clinical case files, RG 10-270, QSMHC/AO.
86   Case file for patient no. 6461; Patients' clinical case files, RG 10-270, QSMHC/AO.
87   See Warsh, "First Mrs. Rochester."
88   Mrs. R. to Dr. Clark, 24 March 1897, in Case file for patient no. 8026; Patients' clinical case files, RG 10-270, QSMHC/AO.
89   F.L.R. to T.E. nd, ca. 27 Sept 1897, in *ibid.*
90   Clark to F.L.R., 27 Sept 1897, in *ibid.*
91   Mrs. R. to Clark, 28 Sept 1897, in *ibid.*
92   T.E. to Clark, 4 November, 1900, in *ibid.*
93   Clark to T.E., 7 November, 1900, in *ibid.*
94   Warsh, *Moments of Unreason,* 158–59.
95   Casebook, 2 April 1881, and 6 November 1881, 287; RS 140-B4, SJLA/PANB. The record of Dr. T.E.'s stay was crossed out in the casebook. However, since the casebook listed the entry and departure dates, I am assuming that he did remain at the asylum for this brief period. The reason the record was crossed out is unclear, but it seems unlikely that a full case would exist for someone who never stayed at the institution.
96   Casebook, 18 January 1884, 128, and 4 February 1884, 129; RS 140-B6, SJLA/PANB.
97   Patient file for patient no. 6186 (first admitted 13 August 1887); Patients' clinical case files, RG 10-270, QSMHC/AO.
98   The details are in Case file, patient no. 936, Casebook, vol. 9; GR 1754, BCPMH/BCA.

Chapter 7: Proprietary Medicines and the Nation's Health

1   In Canada the topic has seen minor treatment, relative to the work on patent medicines in the United States. The most notable text is Glenn F. Murray, "The Road to Regulation: Patent Medicines in Canada in Historical Perspective," in *Illicit Drugs in Canada: A Risky Business,* ed. Judith C. Blackwell and Patricia G. Erikson (Toronto: Nelson Canada, 1988), 72–87. Shirley Small, "Canadian Narcotics Legislation, 1908–1923: A Conflict Model Interpretation," *Canadian Review of Sociology and Anthropology* 6, 1 (1968): 32, dedicates one short paragraph to the passing of the Proprietary or Patent Medicine Act. Melvyn Green, "A History of Canadian Narcotics Control: The Formative Years," *University of Toronto Faculty of Law Review* 37 (1979): 42–79, and Neil Boyd, "The Origins of Canadian Narcotics Legislation: The Process of Criminalization in Historical Context," *Dalhousie Law Journal* 8 (1983): 102–36, both give it one paragraph. More substantial treatments have not been directly related to addiction concerns. See R.G. Guest, "The Development of Patent Medicine Legislation," *Applied Therapeutics* 8 (September 1966): 786–89; Guildo Rousseau, "La Santé par correspondance: Un mode de mise en marché des médicament brevetés au debut du siècle," *Histoire Sociale/Social History* 28, 55 (1995): 1–25; and L.I. Pugsley, "The Administration and Development of Federal Statutes on Food and Drug Legislation," *Medical Services Journal, Canada* 23 (March 1967): 387–449. For more detailed considerations of patent medicines and addiction in the United States, see H. Wayne Morgan, *Drugs in America: A Social History, 1800–1980* (Syracuse, NY: Syracuse University Press, 1981), 100–4; David Musto, *The American Disease: Origins of Narcotic Control* (New Haven, CT, and London: Yale University Press, 1973), esp. 1–23; and David Courtwright, *Dark Paradise: A History of Opiate Addiction in America* (Cambridge, MA: Harvard University Press, 1982), 56–59. On the patent medicine trade in the United States in general, see James Harvey Young, *The Toadstool Millionaires: A Social History of Patent Medicines in America before Federal Regulation* (Princeton, NJ: Princeton University Press, 1961); and John Parascandola, "Patent Medicines in Nineteenth-Century America," *Caduceus* 1 (Spring 1985): 1–41.

2   See Murray, "Road to Regulation"; Jim Cameron, "Patent Medicines," in *Good for What Ails You: Self-Help Remedies from 19th Century Canada* (Burnstown, ON: General Store, 1995), 149–52; and Rousseau, "La Santé par correspondance." On the tactics of patent medicine manufacturers, see Janice Dickin McGinnis, "*Carlill v Carbolic Smoke Ball Company:* Influenza, Quackery and the Unilateral Contract," *Canadian Bulletin of Medical History/Bulletin canadien d'histoire de la médecine* 5, 2 (1988): 121–41.

3   On the campaign of the *Ladies' Home Journal,* see Edward William Bok, *The Americanization of Edward Bok: The Autobiography of a Dutch Boy Fifty Years After* (New York: Scribner and

Sons, 1921), ch. 30, http://www.bartleby.com/197/. See also Samuel Hopkins Adams, "The Great American Fraud," http://www.gutenberg.org/ebooks/44325.

4 "The Patent Medicine Bill," editorial, *Canadian Pharmaceutical Journal* 40 (March 1907): 359. See also "The Patent Medicine Curse," *Dominion Medical Monthly* 22 (May 1904): 293; and "Retraction," *Canadian Pharmaceutical Journal* 37 (July 1904): 568.

5 R.G. Guest and L.I. Pugsley both make the connection. See Guest, "Development of Patent Medicine Legislation," 786–87; and Pugsley, "Administration and Development," 400–1. Glenn F. Murray is more reserved about whether Adams's articles influenced Canadian legislation. See Murray, "Road to Regulation," 80. On Adams's series in the American context, see Musto, *American Disease*, 10–11; James Harvey Young, "The Great American Fraud," in *Toadstool Millionaires*, 205–25. The editor of the *Canadian Pharmaceutical Journal* noted that the increasing public concern over patent medicines may have been the result of "a vigorous campaign ... by Collier's Weekly' and The Ladies' Home Journal.'"

6 John Harley Warner, *The Therapeutic Perspective: Medical Practice, Knowledge, and Identity in America, 1820–1885* (Cambridge, MA: Harvard University Press, 1986), 17–36; Charles E. Rosenberg, "The Therapeutic Revolution: Medicine, Meaning and Social Change in Nineteenth Century America," in *The Therapeutic Revolution: Essays in the Social History of American Medicine*, ed. Morris Vogel and Charles E. Rosenberg (Philadelphia: University of Pennsylvania Press, 1979), 18–21. For a discussion of therapeutic "pessimism," see S.E.D. Shortt, *Victorian Lunacy: Richard M. Bucke and the Practice of Late Nineteenth-Century Psychiatry* (Cambridge, UK: Cambridge University Press, 1986), 127, 138.

7 "The Wholesalers' Combine," *British Columbia Pharmaceutical Record* 1 October 1905): 1.

8 The invoices of products delivered to Naysmith Pharmacy were pasted into large scrapbooks, some of which survive, in tatters, in R4008-0-9-E (formerly MG 28-III89), Library and Archives Canada (LAC). Until the current government decides that these invoices are not useful to the simplistic national narrative that it wishes to construct, they may be found there.

9 John Hunter, "Nostrums and Proprietary Medicines," *Canada Lancet* 39 (August 1906): 1059-60.

10 See Nasmyth Pharmacy invoices, in *Nasmyth Invoice Book, Part 10, 1880–1886*, MG 28-III89, vol. 1, LAC.

11 J. Worth Estes, *Dictionary of Protopharmacology: Therapeutic Practices, 1700–1850* (Canton, MA: Science History Publications, 1990), 70.

12 Ibid., 112–13. Sydenham's laudanum is discussed in "What Is Laudanum?" editorial, *Canadian Pharmaceutical Journal* 20 (January 1881): 81–82.

13 See Alethea Hayter, *Opium and the Romantic Imagination: Addiction and Creativity in DeQuincey, Coleridge, Baudelaire and Others*, 2nd ed. (New York: Crucible, 1988); M.H. Abrams, *The Milk of Paradise: The Effects of Opium Visions on the Works of DeQuincey, Crabbe, Francis Thompson and Coleridge* (New York: Octagon, 1971); Sheperd Siegel, "Wilkie Collins: Victorian Novelist as Psychopharmacologist," *Journal of the History of Medicine and Allied Sciences* 38, 2 (April 1983): 161-75; Virginia Berridge, *Opium and the People: Opiate Use and Drug Control Policy in Nineteenth and Early Twentieth Century England* (London: Free Association Books, 1999), ch. 5.

14 Near the end of the century, prescriptions in pharmacists' books increasingly requested specific forms of proprietary medicines. See *Cairncross and Lawrence Company Books,* University of Western Ontario (UWO) Regional Room; *Mitchell's Pharmacy,* UWO Regional Room; Nasmyth Pharmacy invoices, in *Nasmyth Invoice Book, Part 10, 1880–1886,* MG 28-III89, vol. 1, LAC. On the expansion of the pharmaceutical industry, see John Parascandola, "Pharmacologists in Government and Industry," in *The Development of American Pharmacology: John J. Abel and the Shaping of a Discipline,* 91–125 (Baltimore, MD, and London: Johns Hopkins University Press, 1992).

15 Untitled editorial, *Montreal Medical Journal* 32 (October 1903): 749.

16 "Adulterated Drugs," *Canadian Druggist* 11 (February 1899): 27; this refers to the report of the Public Analyst from London who investigated tincture of opium and citrate of iron and quinine. Sessional Paper 7b, "Report of the Inland Revenue Department: Part III – Adulteration of Food," Appendix O, *Bulletin No. 60,* 49–55 in *Sessional Papers of the Dominion of Canada* Vol 6 (1899).

17 "Proprietary Preparations," editorial, *Montreal Medical Journal* 32 (May 1903): 361; Bulletin 34 was in Sessional Paper 7a, "Report of the Inland Revenue Department: Part II – Adulteration of Food," Appendix K, Bulletin No. 34, 108–22 in *Sessional Papers of the Dominion of Canada* Vol 5 (1894).

18 Sessional Paper 14, "Report of the Inland Revenue Department: Part III – Adulteration of Food," Appendix O, Bulletin No. 77, 115–25 in *Sessional Papers of the Dominion of Canada* 6 (1901).

19 "Proprietary Preparations," editorial, *Montreal Medical Journal* 32 (May 1903): 361.

20 Untitled editorial, *Montreal Medical Journal* 32 (October 1903): 749.

21 J.T. Fotheringham, "The Physician and Proprietary Medicine," *Canadian Pharmaceutical Journal* 31 (November 1897): 177.

22 "Montreal Notes," *Canadian Druggist* 11 (April 1899): 86.

23 "Prescribed Repetition and Its Dangers," editorial, *Dominion Medical Monthly* 20 (May 1903): 290.

24 "Druggists' Ethics," *Canadian Pharmaceutical Journal* 37 (June 1904): 497.

25 "Druggists and Physicians," *Canadian Druggist* 7 (January 1895): 10.

26 "The Druggist and the Physician," editorial, *Canadian Druggist* 15 (May 1903): 254.

27 Advertisement, *Canadian Pharmaceutical Journal* 34 (1900–01): 336.

28 Untitled editorial, *Dominion Medical Monthly* 26 (June 1906): 304–6.

29 Edmund Moore, "Status of the Medical Profession," *Maritime Medical News* 2 (April 1890): 69; D. MacKintosh, "The Mutual Relations of the Profession and the Public," *Maritime Medical News* 12 (July 1900): 222.

30 R. MacNeill, "Patent and Secret Nostrums," *Maritime Medical News* 11 (April 1899): 119.

31 "Secret Proprietary Medicines," editorial, *Canada Lancet* 18 (July 1886): 343–44.

32 Fotheringham, "Physician and Proprietary Medicine," 179.

33 Hunter, "Nostrums and Proprietary Medicines," 1061.

34 This was discussed after a presentation by R.W. Bruce Smith, the provincial inspector of hospitals and public charities, to the Ontario Medical Association on 28 May 1907. See R.W. Bruce Smith, "Mental Sanitation with Suggestions for the Care of the Degenerate, and Means for Preventing the Propagation of the Species," *Canada Lancet* 40 (July 1907): 977.

35 Several historians have considered the issue of patent medicines as violating professional sovereignty, but the general class-centred discourse about patent medicines has been overlooked. See Morgan, *Drugs in America*, 102; Musto, *American Disease*, 14–15; and Terry Parssinen, *Secret Passions, Secret Remedies: Narcotic Drugs in British Society, 1820–1930* (Manchester, UK: Manchester University Press, 1983), 31–35. The discussion by Berridge, *Opium and the People*, 123–31, includes the "'professional scare' about expanding chlorodyne use" (130).

36 "Stimulants and Narcotics in Proprietary Medicines," *Canada Lancet* 35 (September 1902): 55. The title page of this issue says it is August, 1902, but it is September, since it is issue #1 of a new volume, and the *Canada Lancet*'s volumes ran September–August.

37 Quoted in "Proposal to place Patent Medicines under Dominion Government Control," editorial, *Canadian Pharmaceutical Journal* 27 (October 1893): 31.

38 J. Morrison, evidence, *Journals of the Legislative Assembly of Quebec* (1899), Appendix B, 415.

39 In his biography of Edward Shuttleworth, Ernest Stieb states that Shuttleworth was the editor of the *Canadian Pharmaceutical Journal* until he sold it to G.E. Gibbard in 1900. See Ernest Stieb, "Edward Buckingham Shuttleworth, 1842–1934," *Pharmacy in History* 12, 3 (1970): 91–116. However, the masthead of the journal suggests otherwise. Shuttleworth was listed as the editor until February 1895, and then no editor was listed until July 1896. In December 1896, the journal introduced the change in management, with J.E. Morrison, formerly the editor of the *Montreal Pharmaceutical Journal*, taking over as editor. From August 1896 to October 1901, Morrison was listed as the editor (he noted this affiliation at his testimony to Quebec's Select Committee on Patent Medicines in 1899), with Gibbard listed as business manager. Gibbard became the editor, according to the masthead, in November 1901. My thanks to Laura Elms at the Pharmacy Library, University of Toronto, for her assistance in finding this information.

40 "A Clever Swindle," *Canadian Pharmaceutical Journal* 33 (May 1900): 446.
41 MacKintosh, "Mutual Relations," 222. Another link with race is suggested by Michael McCulloch, "'Dr. Tumblety, the Indian Herb Doctor': Politics, Professionalism and Abortion in Mid-Nineteenth-Century Montreal," *Canadian Bulletin of Medical History/Bulletin canadien d'histoire de la médecine* 10, 1 (1993): 49–66.
42 MacKintosh, "Mutual Relations," 222.
43 "The Patent Medicine Problem," editorial, *Maritime Medical News* 10 (February 1898): 56.
44 C.J. Fagan, "Patent Medicine," *Canada Lancet* 40 (January 1905): 414.
45 Joseph Constant, "President's Address," *Canadian Druggist* 7 (July 1895): 146.
46 Medicus, "'Where Are We At? And Where We Are At; We – Doctor and Druggist,'" letter to the editor, *Canadian Pharmaceutical Journal* 34 (April 1901): 403–4.
47 "Proprietors Banquet," *Canadian Pharmaceutical Journal* 34 (August 1900): 19.
48 On the rise of department stores, see Donica Belisle, *Retail Nation: Department Stores and the Making of Modern Canada* (Vancouver: UBC Press, 2011).
49 HGE, "Unfair Competition," letter to the editor, *Canadian Pharmaceutical Journal* 21 (August 1887): 8.
50 "Montreal Notes," *Canadian Druggist* 11 (March 1899): 61.
51 "Protecting the Druggist," *Canadian Druggist* 4 (June 1892): 22.
52 "Prosecution under the Pharmacy Act," *Canadian Druggist* 4 (July 1892): 8.
53 "Conviction against the T. Eaton Company," *Canadian Druggist* 4 (October 1892): 1.
54 J.N. Woodward, untitled letter to the editor, *Canadian Druggist* 8 (January 1896): 7.
55 See, for example, "Formulae of Secret Medicines," *Canadian Pharmaceutical Journal* 11 (June 1878): 319–24, which continued in the next issue (July 1878) at pages 385–92. This publication of recipes of proprietary remedies became an ongoing feature of the journal.
56 On patent medicine advertising, see Morgan, *Drugs in America*, 102–4; Parascandola, "Patent Medicines in Nineteenth-Century America," 5–16; Young, *Toadstool Millionaires*, 111–24, 165–202; Musto, *American Disease*, 14–15; David L. Cowen and William Helfand, *Pharmacy: An Illustrated History* (New York: Henry Abrams, 1990), 184–86.
57 "Proprietary Medicines," editorial, *Montreal Medical Journal* 22 (May 1894): 866.
58 Ibid., 867.
59 "A Retraction," *Canadian Pharmaceutical Journal* 37 (July 1904): 568.
60 "Proprietary Preparations," editorial, *Montreal Medical Journal* 22 (May 1903): 362.
61 Fagan, "Patent Medicine," 412–13.
62 "Registration of Poisons," *Canadian Druggist* 2 (May 1890): 1.
63 Untitled editorial, *Montreal Pharmaceutical Journal* 2 (1891): 131.
64 "Sale of Proprietary Medicines Containing Poisons," *Canadian Druggist* 5 (March 1893): 1.
65 W.G. Evans, "Correspondence: An Explanation," *Canadian Druggist* 10 (February 1898): 32. The Canadian pharmaceutical press debated Evans's motives. According to the *Canadian Pharmaceutical Journal (CPhJ)*, the Wholesale Druggists Association had not violated any stated promise, contradicting the *Montreal Pharmaceutical Journal* (called the "manufacturers' organ" by the *CPhJ*, which had implied that wholesalers were acting as a "combine" against retailers. See "The Disbanding of the Wholesale Druggist Association," *Canadian Pharmaceutical Journal* 31 (March 1898): 357–58.
66 "W.D. and the P.M.D Association," *Canadian Druggist* 10 (February 1898): 34.
67 "Canadian Wholesale Druggists Association," *Canadian Druggist* 15 (June 1903): 326.
68 "Indian Catarrh Cure," *Canadian Pharmaceutical Journal* 34 (August 1900): 43. The ad itself, on page 41, stated that the cure "contains no cocaine or other opiate."
69 See the advertisement, for example, in *Canadian Pharmaceutical Journal* 37 (December 1903): 233.
70 "Patent Medicines," editorial, *Canadian Pharmaceutical Journal* 39 (March 1906): 358–59.
71 "Proprietary Medicines," editorial, *Canada Lancet* 36 (May 1906): 841–43.
72 Morgan, *Drugs in America*, 65–66; Musto, *American Disease*, 3; Courtwright, *Dark Paradise*, 56–58; Berridge, *Opium and the People*, 163, 221.
73 "Proprietary Medicines," editorial, *Canada Lancet* 36 (May 1906): 841.
74 "Editorial," editorial, *Queen's Medical Quarterly* 9 (October 1904): 161.

75 "Medical Advertising," editorial, *Montreal Medical Journal* 22 (May 1903): 363.
76 Untitled editorial, *Dominion Medical Monthly* 26 (June 1906): 306.
77 "Who Is to Blame?" *Canadian Pharmaceutical Journal* 33 (June 1900): 494.
78 "Drug Habits," *Canadian Pharmaceutical Journal* 37 (September 1903): 63.
79 "The Sale of Narcotics," *Canadian Pharmaceutical Journal* 38 (May 1905): 450.
80 "Unwise Sales," *Canadian Druggist* 11 (July 1899): 153.
81 "Extracts: The Patent-Medicine Curse" (from *Merck's Report*), *Canadian Pharmaceutical Journal* 31 (May 1898): 478.
82 "The Sale of Narcotics," *Canadian Pharmaceutical Journal* 37 (May 1903): 451.
83 "Drug Habits," *Canadian Pharmaceutical Journal* 37 (September 1903): 63.
84 H.R.G., "Correspondence: Repeating Prescriptions," *Canada Medical and Surgical Journal* 8 (December 1879): 211.
85 "Repeating Prescriptions," *Canada Medical and Surgical Journal* 8 (February 1880): 329.
86 Alfred Hy. Mason, "Pharmaceutical Ethics," *Canadian Pharmaceutical Journal* 20 (September 1886): 26.
87 Glenn Murray argues that a "cocaine scare" was equally as influential in driving legislative initiatives as was concern over opium use. See Glenn F. Murray, "Cocaine Use in the Era of Social Reform: The Natural History of a Social Problem in Canada, 1880–1911," *Canadian Journal of Law and Society* 2 (1987): 29.
88 The most comprehensive historical study of cocaine to date may be Joseph Spillaine, *Cocaine: From Medical Marvel to Modern Menace in the United States, 1884–1920* (Baltimore, MD: Johns Hopkins University Press, 2000). On cocaine in Canada, see Murray, "Cocaine Use." Other discussions of cocaine include Robert C. Peterson, "History of Cocaine," in *Cocaine: 1977*, ed. R.C. Peterson and R.C. Stillman, 17–34, NIDA Research Monograph No. 13 (May 1977); Musto, *American Disease*, 7; and Morgan, *Drugs in America*, 18.
89 E.R. Palmer, "The Opium Habit: A Possible Antidote," *Canada Medical Record* 9 (May 1881): 180–81.
90 Morgan, *Drugs in America*, 15–19; Courtwright, *Dark Paradise*, 96–99.
91 James Stewart, "Report on Pharmacology and Therapeutics," *Canada Medical and Surgical Journal* 14 (April 1886): 538.
92 Unsigned editorial, "The Untoward Effects of Cocaine," *Canada Medical and Surgical Journal* 16 (September 1887): 89.
93 "The Exaggerated Dangers of Cocaine," *Canada Lancet* 20 (September 1887): 20.
94 Charles M. Pratt, "Cocaine," *Maritime Medical Journal* 18 (August 1906): 308; W.S. Muir, "An Address on Materia Medica and Therapeutics, Part 2," *Maritime Medical Journal* 3 (February 1891): 27.
95 C. Richard Shaughnessy, "The Cocaine Habit," *Maritime Medical News* 15 (March 1903): 86.
96 "Abuse of coca," editorial, *Canadian Pharmaceutical Journal* 19 (January 1886): 80.
97 W.F. Waugh, "Cocaine," *Canadian Pharmaceutical Journal* 32 (September 1898): 80.
98 Charles H. Heebner, "Regulation of Sale of Habit-Forming Drugs," *Canadian Pharmaceutical Journal* 40 (August 1906): 23.
99 "Cocaine Selling in Quebec," *Canadian Pharmaceutical Journal* 44 (December 1910): 212–14.
100 Heebner, "Regulation of Sale," 23.
101 "Cocaine Restriction," *Canadian Pharmaceutical Journal* 37 (April 1904): 404–5.
102 "The Sale of Cocaine," *Canadian Pharmaceutical Journal* 41 (March 1908): 357.
103 "Editorial Notes," *Canadian Pharmaceutical Journal* 32 (October 1898): 114.
104 "Operations of a Dope Fiend," *Canadian Pharmaceutical Journal* 41 (April 1908): 418; "That Cocaine Fiend," *Canadian Pharmaceutical Journal* 41 (May 1908): 450.
105 "Cocaine Debauchery," *Dominion Medical Monthly* 8 (March 1897): 249.
106 "Editorial Notes," *Canadian Pharmaceutical Journal* 33 (December 1900): 208.
107 E.G. Eberle, "Narcotics and the Habitués," *Canadian Pharmaceutical Journal* 36 (July 1903): 556.
108 Cheryl Krasnick Warsh, "The Aristocratic Vice," in *Moments of Unreason: The Practice of Psychiatry at the Homewood Retreat, 1883–1923* (Montreal and Kingston: McGill-Queen's University Press, 1989), 162–65.

109 "The Cocaine Habit," editorial, *Canada Lancet* 28 (August 1896): 500.
110 Heebner, "Regulation of Sale." Probably the most well-known medical cocaine addict was William Halsted, one of the founders of the Johns Hopkins University. See J.M. Schneck, "Cocaine Addiction and Dr. William S. Halsted," letter to the editor, *Journal of Clinical Psychiatry* 49 (December 1988): 503–4; and his response in J.M. Schneck, "Cocaine Addiction and Dr. William S. Halsted," *Journal of Clinical Psychiatry* 50 (September 1989): 358; A.J. Wright, "More on Cocaine Addiction and Dr. William S. Halsted," letter to the editor, *Journal of Clinical Psychiatry* 50 (September 1988): 358.
111 "Bill 34" (reprinted), *Legislature of Manitoba Bills* (1908), Provincial Archives of Manitoba.
112 *Statutes of Manitoba* (1908), ch. 153; *Statutes of British Columbia* (1908), ch. 178; "An Act to Amend the Pharmacy Act," *Canada Lancet* 41 (May 1908): 804–5; "Bill An Act to Regulate the Sale of Cocaine, Morphine and Their Compounds," *Canadian Pharmaceutical Journal* 44 (March 1911): 373–74; "An Act Respecting Chemists and Druggists" (assented 16 December 1910), *Statutes of Alberta* (1910), ch. 38; "The Pharmacy Act" (assented 23 March 1911), *Statutes of Saskatchewan* (1910–11), ch. 32.

Chapter 8: Regulating Proprietary Medicine

1 Virginia Berridge, *Opium and the People*, 123–31.
2 David Musto, *The American Disease: Origins of Narcotic Control*, 3rd ed. (Oxford and New York: Oxford University Press, 1999), 10–18; David Courtwright, *Dark Paradise: A History of Opiate Addiction in America* (Cambridge, MA, and London: Harvard University Press, 1982), 56–58.
3 See Dan Malleck, "Pure Food and Professional Druggists: Food and Drug Laws in Canada, 1870s–1908," *Pharmacy in History* 48, 3 (2006): 103–15.
4 "The Sale of Quack Medicines," editorial, *Canadian Medical Times* 1 (27 September 1873): 100.
5 "Secret Proprietary Medicines," editorial, *Canada Lancet* 8 (July 1886): 343–44.
6 Other provincial legislatures, such as those in British Columbia, Manitoba, and New Brunswick, had also attempted to deal with the sale of patent medicines, a fact that the minister of inland revenue interpreted in 1908 as suggesting "widespread public opinion that legislation of some kind is necessary." See *Debates of the House of Commons*, 15 June 1908, 10551. I am using Quebec and Ontario as comparative case studies.
7 See Malleck, "Pure Food."
8 "Quebec Pharmacy Act, 1885," *Canadian Pharmaceutical Journal* 19 (August 1885): 7-11.
9 *Statutes of Quebec* (1890), Cap. XLVI, 88–94.
10 "Proposed Legislation to Restrict the Sale of Patent Medicines in Quebec," *Canadian Pharmaceutical Journal* 25 (March 1892): 114.
11 "Patent Medicines and the Pharmacy Act," *Canadian Pharmaceutical Journal* 25 (March 1892): 113–14.
12 Untitled editorial, *Canadian Pharmaceutical Journal* 26 (June 1893): 161–62. On Elliot, see Ernst Stieb, "Elliot, Robert Watt," in *Dictionary of Canadian Biography*, vol. 13, online ed., http://www.biographi.ca/en/bio/elliot_robert_watt_13E.html.
13 Paris Green was also called Schwienfurt Green and was the subject of a number of investigations about its poisonous nature. Prior to the Pharmacy Act of 1871, commentators had registered their concerns over the availability of Paris Green, which apparently had occasionally been used for suicides and homicides.
14 "Bill 137," *Province of Ontario Bills* (1894).
15 "Exemption of Patent or Proprietary Medicines from the Operation of the Ontario Pharmacy Act," *Canadian Pharmaceutical Journal* 28 (May 1895): 143–44.
16 "Exemption of Patent or Proprietary Medicines from the Operation of the Ontario Pharmacy Act," *Canadian Pharmaceutical Journal* 28 (May 1895), 144 (emphasis in original).
17 "The Press and the Quebec Pharmacy Act," *Canadian Pharmaceutical Journal* 32 (February 1899): 306–7.
18 "Bill 78," *Journals of the Legislature of Quebec* (1897–1898), 7, 14, 22, and 30 December 1897, and 7, 12, 13, and 14 January 1898; *Journals of the Legislature of Quebec* (1899).

19 "The Patent Medicine Bill, Bill No. 45," *British Columbia Pharmaceutical Record* 1 (March 1906): 153–54.

20 Untitled editorial, *British Columbia Pharmaceutical Record* 1 (March 1906): 155.

21 Letter from Bodwell & Lawson, Barristers and Solicitors, to R. McBride, 28 February 1906, Premier's Office Fonds, GR 441, box 27, file 89/06, Provincial Archives of British Columbia.

22 "Vancouver Medical Association on Patent Medicines," *Canada Lancet* 39 (April 1906): 749–50.

23 "The Patent Medicine Bill," *Canada Lancet* 39 (June 1906): 909.

24 "A Bill to Kill Patent Medicines," editorial, *Acadian Recorder,* 16 April 1906.

25 "Kill This Bill," editorial, *Halifax Morning Chronicle,* 17 April 1906.

26 "Proposal to Place Patent Medicines under Dominion Government Control," reprinted from *Toronto News,* in *Canadian Pharmaceutical Journal* 27 (October 1893): 31.

27 On the passing of legislation related to pure food and drugs, see L.I. Pugsley, "The Administration and Development of Federal Statutes on Foods and Drugs in Canada," *Medical Services Journal, Canada* 23, 3 (March 1967): 387–449.

28 "Bill 254" (presented by Mr. German), *Legislature of Ontario, Bills* (1900). This bill also placed extremely high fines on the illegal sale of patent medicines. It did not pass beyond the first reading, and was not reintroduced.

29 "Patent Medicine Legislation," editorial, *Dominion Medical Monthly* 16 (February 1902): 91–92.

30 "Physicians Taking Action," *Canadian Pharmaceutical Journal* 32 (November 1898): 162–63. The results of these requests are not clear. However, that the Quebec government continued to legislate and investigate the issue suggests that it refused to entertain this entreaty.

31 Ibid.

32 See, for example, "Stimulants and Narcotics in Proprietary Medicines," editorial, *Canada Lancet* 34 (August 1902): 55; "Secret Proprietary Medicines," editorial, *Canada Lancet* 18 (July 1886): 343; and "The Growth of Quackery," editorial, *Canada Lancet* 36 (August 1904): 1147.

33 W.H. Moorehouse, "Presidential Address," *Canada Lancet* 36 (September 1903): 10.

34 "Vancouver Medical Association on Patent Medicines," *Canada Lancet* 41 (April 1906): 750.

35 "Probable Legislation Regulating Patent Medicines," *Canadian Pharmaceutical Journal* 39 (March 1906): 354–55. This argument was repeated often. See "Proposal to Place Patent Medicines under Dominion Government Control," *Canadian Pharmaceutical Journal* 27 (October 1893): 31; "Patent Medicines," *Canadian Pharmaceutical Journal* 39 (March 1906): 358–59; and A.E. DuBerger, "Return to an Order of the House of Commons, Dated April 23, 1906, for a Copy of the Report of A.E. DuBerger, on the Drug and Proprietary Medicine Trade of Canada," *Sessional Papers of the Dominion of Canada,* no. 125 (1906), 22–23.

36 Some of the details of the formation of the 1908 legislation are in Glenn F. Murray, "The Road to Regulation: Patent Medicines in Canada in Historical Perspective," in *Illicit Drugs in Canada: A Risky Business,* ed. Judith C. Blackwell and Patricia G. Erikson (Toronto: Nelson Canada, 1988), 72–87.

37 DuBerger, "Return to an Order."

38 As several historians have noted, the articles in *Collier's Weekly* attracted the attention of many Canadians. This is the perspective of both R.G. Guest, "The Development of Patent Medicine Legislation," *Applied Therapeutics* 8 (September 1966): 786–89, who does not note Sullivan's earlier activities, and Murray, "Road to Regulation," who does. According to Murray, ibid., 79, Stockton said that he had the public interest in mind.

39 *Debates of the House of Commons,* 21 February 1907, 3464. Unfortunately, the records of this committee were destroyed in the Parliament Buildings fire of 1916.

40 *Debates of the House of Commons,* 11 March 1907, 4441.

41 "Up, Druggists!" *BC Pharmaceutical Record* 2 (October 1906): 67–68.

42 "Will Somebody Please Wake Up the Drug Trade?" *BC Pharmaceutical Record* 2 (November, 1906), 91.

43 "Canadian Pharmaceutical Association," *BC Pharmaceutical Record* 3 (October 1907): 67–68.

44 "The Patent Medicine Bill," *Canadian Pharmaceutical Journal* 41 (April 1908): 399.

45 *Debates of the House of Commons,* 15 June 1908, 10553.
46 *Debates of the Senate,* 17 July 1908, 1670.
47 Ibid., 1667.
48 Ibid.
49 Ibid., 1669.
50 Ibid., 1672.
51 Murray, "Road to Regulation," 82.
52 "Some Important Acts of Parliament," *Canadian Pharmaceutical Journal* 42 (August 1908): 23.
53 "The Ways of the Patent Medicine Man," *Canada Lancet* 43 (September 1909): 5–6.
54 "The Unsatisfactory Canadian Patent Medicine Act," *Journal of the American Medical Association* 53 (25 September 1909), 1034.
55 "The Unsatisfactory Canadian Patent Medicine Act," *Canadian Practitioner and Review* 34 (December 1909): xxx. Apparently, this page was appended with three others to the end of the last issue of this volume and was therefore numbered out of sequence.
56 "'The Unsatisfactory Canadian Patent Medicine Act,'" editorial, *Canadian Journal of Medicine and Surgery* 28 (November 1909): 320–21.
57 J.C. McWalter, "The Quack Medicine Traffic," *British Medical Journal* 2, 2542 (18 September 1909): 793.

Chapter 9: New Drug Laws and the Creation of Illegality

1   "The Morphine Habit," *Manitoba Daily Free Press,* 25 January 1881.
2   "The Opium Habit: Noble Victims of the Fatal Vice in England," *Manitoba Daily Free Press,* 3 April 1883.
3   "Morphinomania," editorial, *Toronto Globe,* 24 September 1887.
4   "Trafficing [sic] in Opium Here: Operations of Chinese Smugglers Unearthed by City Policy – Demi-Monde Customers – The Vice Prevalent," *Manitoba Daily Free Press,* 19 April 1901.
5   "Confessions of an Opium Smuggler," *Manitoba Daily Free Press,* 23 October 1903. Newspapers reported on this story across the country. See "Confessions of Smuggler," *Portage La Prairie News,* 28 October 1903; "Smuggling Opium," *Brandon Daily Sun,* 23 October 1903; "A Smuggler Gang Found at the Soo," *Toronto Daily Star,* 23 October 1903; "Chinese Smuggling Industry Is Exposed," *Ottawa Evening Journal,* 23 October 1903.
6   "A Novel Method," *Manitoba Daily Free Press,* 22 May 1895.
7   "The United States: San Francisco," *Manitoba Daily Free Press,* 20 June 1887.
8   "They Have Caught On: Government Officials Discover That There Is a Good Deal of Smuggling Going on in Manitoba," *Brandon Sun Weekly,* 10 October 1888.
9   "The Opium Trade: It Has Developed Enormously in Canada," *Manitoba Daily Free Press,* 14 September 1893.
10 "Notes from the Capital/Growth of Opium Smoking," *Toronto Globe,* 5 November 1891.
11 "Opium Smuggling," *Toronto Globe,* 27 February 1888.
12 "The Drug Habit," *Toronto Globe,* 10 November 1903.
13 Mary Markwell, "Prairie Pot Pourri: The Opiate – Its Dangers," *Manitoba Daily Free Press,* 25 July 1908.
14 David Courtwright, *Dark Paradise: A History of Opiate Addiction in America* (Cambridge, MA, and London: Harvard University Press, 1982), ch. 1.
15 Louise Foxcroft, *The Making of Addiction: The "Use and Abuse" of Opium in Nineteenth-Century Britain* (Aldershot, UK: Ashgate, 2007), 3.
16 "The Opium Habit: A Remarkable Number of Men Who Have Been Victims of This Pernicious Habit," *Manitoba Daily Free Press,* 17 June 1890.
17 "A Whole Town Enslaved by the Cocaine Habit," *Toronto Globe,* 19 January 1897.
18 "Drug Store News: Way in Which the Gordon-Mitchell Drug Co Are Conducting Their Stores," *Manitoba Daily Free Press,* 4 May 1907.
19 "Beware the Seductive Pie," editorial, *Toronto Globe,* 20 February 1908.
20 Diaries of William Lyon Mackenzie King, 18 March 1894, Library and Archives, Canada, http://www.bac-lac.gc.ca/eng/discover/politics-government/prime-ministers/william-lyon -mackenzie-king/Pages/diaries-william-lyon-mackenzie-king.aspx (hereafter King Diaries).

21 Ibid., 22 June 1895.
22 Admissions Registers, patient no. 7772. Toronto Lunatic Asylum Admissions Register, RG 10-271, Queen Street Mental Health Centre fonds, Archives of Ontario.
23 King Diaries, 5 October 1895.
24 "Petition of Nova Scotia Conference of the Methodist Church," dated 8 August 1905, "General Correspondence," R174-26-2-E file 2130, Department of the Secretary of State of Canada fonds, Library and Archives, Canada.
25 Charles L. Ingles, Hon. Clerical Secretary, and W.S. Battin, Hon. Lay Secretary, to Hon. R.W. Scott, Secretary of State for the Dominion of Canada, c. 20 June 1905, "General Correspondence," R174-26-2-E file 1724, Department of the Secretary of State of Canada fonds, Library and Archives, Canada.
26 See G.G. Huxtable of the Dominion Alliance for the Total Suppression of the Liquor Traffic to Wilfrid Laurier, 18 November 1907, Laurier Papers, mf-C855, 132312-14, Library and Archives Canada (LAC).
27 S.D. Chown to W.L. Mackenzie King, 24 November 1908, *Records of the Evangelism and Moral Reform Service*, box 2, file 33B, United Church Archives. Also in W.L.M. King Papers, MG 26, J1, vol. 8, 7292, LAC.
28 "Clerk, Morals Committee: That the Dominion Government Be Asked to Prohibit the Manufacture and Sale of Opium," in "General Correspondence," R174-26-2-E file 1544, Department of the Secretary of State of Canada fonds, LAC.
29 "The City Fathers Have Long Session," *Victoria Daily Colonist*, 4 June 1907; "Hall Presents League's Desire," *Victoria Daily Colonist*, 22 October 1907.
30 "Against Opium," *Victoria Daily Colonist*, 7 June 1908.
31 Editorial, *Victoria Daily Colonist*, 10 June 1908.
32 Editorial, *Victoria Daily Colonist*, 5 July 1908.
33 Chown to Sir Wilfrid Laurier, 26 May 1908, W.L.M. King Papers, MG 26, J1, vol. 8, 7294, LAC.
34 Ibid., 7297.
35 Mona-Margaret Pon, "Ng Mon Hing," in *Dictionary of Canadian Biography*, vol. 15, online ed., http://www.biographi.ca/en/bio/ng_mon_hing_15E.html.
36 Ibid.
37 Peter Hing to W.L.M. King, 24 November 1908, W.L.M. King Papers, MG 26, J1, vol. 8, 8010, LAC.
38 "Seek to Check Opium Manufacture," *Victoria Daily Colonist*, 3 July 1908; on the Victoria League, see "Agitation against the Use of Opium," *Victoria Daily Colonist*, 18 June 1908.
39 Peter Hing to W.L.M. King, 24 November 1908, W.L.M. King Papers, MG 26, J1, vol. 11, 10691, LAC.
40 Peter Hing to Charles J. Doherty, 3 May 1909, W.L.M. King Papers, MG 26, J1, vol. 11, 10693-95, LAC.
41 W.L.M. King, *Report by W.L. Mackenzie King, CMG Deputy Minister of Labour on the Need for the Suppression of the Opium Traffic in Canada* (Ottawa: S.E. Dawson, 1908), 13.
42 *Debates of the House of Commons*, 10 July 1908, 12550; Untitled editorial, Vic*toria Daily Colonist*, 18 July 1908. Such a motion was the first step in passing legislation, and upon its approval a bill was presented.
43 *Debates of the House of Commons*, 10 July 1908, 12550.
44 *Debates of the House of Commons*, 13 July 1908, 12851.
45 *Debates of the House of Commons*, 18 July 1908, 13523.
46 "Notes and Comments," *Toronto Globe*, 6 July 1908.
47 "Women's Realm: Here and There," *Victoria Daily Colonist*, 16 July 1908.
48 "Preservation of Canadian Church," *Manitoba Daily Free Press*, 1 October 1908.
49 "A Hindrance to Temperance Work," *Toronto Globe*, 15 June 1909.
50 "Canada's Traffic in Opium" editorial, *Canadian White Ribbon Tidings* 4 (15 September 1908), 1244.
51 "House Passes Anti-Opium Bill," *Victoria Daily Colonist*, 14 July 1908; "Three Months Grace for Opium Dealers," *Victoria Daily Colonist*, 16 July 1908; "Parliament to Close Monday," *Victoria Daily Colonist*, 18 July 1908.

52 "Protection of Youth," *Victoria Daily Colonist,* 4 June 1907.
53 *Debates of the House of Commons,* 26 January 1911, 2519.
54 P.J. Giffen, Shirley Endicott, and Sylvia Lambert, *Panic and Indifference: The Politics of Canada's Drug Laws* (Ottawa: Canadian Centre on Substance Abuse, 1991), 77.
55 "May Revive Practice of Smuggling Opium," *Victoria Daily Colonist,* 9 December 1908.
56 "Opium Smugglers Were Captured," *Victoria Daily Colonist,* 10 September 1909.
57 "Smuggling Ring in Victoria," *Victoria Daily Colonist,* 12 June 1909.
58 "Opium Smuggling," *Victoria Daily Colonist,* 14 September 1909; "Chinese Smugglers," *Victoria Daily Colonist,* 16 September 1909.
59 "Opium Smuggling," *Manitoba Daily Free Press,* 1 January 1910.
60 "Opium Found in Vancouver Harbour," *Victoria Daily Colonist,* 8 March 1910.
61 "Smuggle Opium," *Manitoba Free Press,* 15 May 1911.
62 "American Victims of Opium Habit," *Lethbridge Herald,* 2 August 1910.
63 "Smuggling of Opium," *Montreal Gazette,* 20 November 1909.
64 "To the Jury Today," *Montreal Gazette,* 22 September 1908.
65 "Montreal Murders," *Toronto Globe,* 5 November 1908.
66 "Opium in Penitentiary," *Toronto Globe,* 26 November 1908; "Opium Smuggled to Convicts," *Montreal Gazette,* 26 November 1908.
67 "Caught Gambling," *Chilliwack Progress,* 3 May 1911.
68 Francis Phillips, "Gossip from Gotham," *Ottawa Journal,* 3 September 1910.
69 "Lee Chu Was Missing," *Montreal Gazette,* 17 February 1909.
70 "Opium Den Keeper Is Heavily Fined," *Ottawa Journal,* 29 July 1909.
71 "Opium Selling by Chinaman," *Winnipeg Tribune,* 6 February 1911.
72 "Sale of Poisonous Drugs," *Montreal Gazette,* 25 November 1908.
73 "Gov't Will Deal with Cocaine Evil," *Montreal Gazette,* 26 November 1910; "To Regulate Sale of Cocaine," *Montreal Gazette,* 9 February 1911.
74 "Proposed Bill Respecting Habit-Forming Drugs," *BC Pharmaceutical Record* 6 (February 1911): 183–85.
75 "Habit-Forming Drugs," *BC Pharmaceutical Record* 6 (March 1911): 195–97.
76 David Musto, *The American Disease: Origins of Narcotic Control,* 3rd ed. (Oxford and New York: Oxford University Press, 1999), 30–36.
77 "Beginnings of International Drug Control," *UN Chronicle* 35, 1 (1998): 8–9.
78 See "King to Represent Canada in Congress," *Manitoba Daily Free Press,* 6 November 1908.
79 "Albert Henry George Grey, 4th Earl Grey (1851–1917)," in *Behind the Diary: A King's Who's Who Biographies,* Earl Grey Papers, MG 27-IIB2, LAC, http://www.collectionscanada.gc.ca/king/023011-1050.22-e.html.
80 J.G. Shearer to King, 23 November 1908, in W.L.M. King Papers, MG 26, J1, vol. 10, 9317–18, LAC; Henry Moyle to King, 11 December 1908, W.L.M. King Papers, MG 26, J1, vol. 9, 8959, LAC.
81 Eby to King, 4 December 1908, W.L.M. King Papers, MG 26, J1, vol. 8, 7542–43.
82 King to Eby, 7 December 1908, W.L.M. King Papers, MG 26, J1, vol. 8, 7544–45.
83 Musto, *American Disease,* 30–31.
84 "Report of the International Opium Commission, Shanghai, China," (Shanghai: *North China Daily News and Herald* Ltd. 1909)," 19; Musto, *American Disease,* 30–31.
85 Virginia Berridge, *Opium and the People: Opiate Use and Drug Control Policy in Nineteenth and Early Twentieth Century England* (London: Free Association Books, 1999), 246–57.
86 Desmond Mandersion, *From Mr. Sin to Mr. Big: A History of Australian Drug Laws* (Oxford: Oxford University Press, 1993), 54–58.
87 King to Laurier, 17 February 1909, Laurier Papers, mf-C873, 151924, LAC.
88 "Report of the International Opium Commission," 20.
89 "Report on Opium and Morphia in Canada," Laurier Papers, mf-C873, 151931-3, LAC.
90 "Report of the International Opium Commission," 84.
91 See Wright to King, 4 January 1911, W.L.M. King Papers, MG 26, J1, vol. 19, 17228–29, LAC.
92 Wright to King, 5 December 1910, W.L.M. King Papers, MG 26, J1, vol. 16, 14734, LAC.
93 *Debates of the House of Commons,* 25 November 1910, 260–61.
94 *Debates of the House of Commons,* 17 January 1911, 1803.

95   King to Wright, 30 January 1911, W.L.M. King Papers, MG 26, J1, vol. 19, item 17233, LAC.
96   *Debates of the House of Commons,* 26 January 1911, 2521.
97   The text of Martin's speech, printed in the *Canadian Druggist,* calls the consequences "hateful," not "harmful." See "Canadian Pharmaceutical Association Annual Meeting," *Canadian Druggist* 22 (October 1910): 610.
98   *Debates of the House of Commons,* 26 January 1911, 2530.
99   Ibid., 2533–34.
100 Ibid., 2534
101 Ibid., 2535.
102 Ibid., 2549.
103 Ibid., 2550.
104 Ibid., 2550.
105 The change that allowed substances to be added by a mere order-in-council was not made until 1938, and by then the law was considerably different. See Giffen, Endicott, and Lambert, *Panic and Indifference,* 91. However, it is worth noting that other substances were added to the schedules prior to 1938, notably cannabis, by an order-in-council, using a tricky legislative sleight of hand that legalized such moves under the Department of Health Act. See Giffen et al., 165–66.
106 *Debates of the House of Commons,* 26 January 1911, 2552–53.
107 Giffen, et al., *Panic and Indifference,* 164.

Conclusion: Baneful Influences

1   "The International Opium Convention Signed at the Hague, January 23, 1912," *League of Nations Treaty Series,* 29 (1922), http://www.worldlii.org/int/other/LNTSer/1922/29.html. On Canada's post-1911 challenges, see P.J. Giffen, Shirley Endicott, and Sylvia Lambert, *Panic and Indifference: The Politics of Canada's Drug Laws* (Ottawa: Canadian Centre on Substance Abuse, 1991).
2   Catherine Carstairs, *Jailed for Possession: Illegal Drug Use, Regulation, and Power in Canada, 1920–1961* (Toronto: University of Toronto Press, 2006), 7, calls it the Opium and Drug Branch; Giffen, Endicott, and Lambert, *Panic and Indifference,* 104, call it the Opium and Narcotic Drugs Branch. The latter seems to be the case.
3   Carstairs, *Jailed for Possession,* 7. The Royal Canadian Mounted Police was an amalgamation of the Dominion Police and the North-West Mounted Police, formed in 1920.
4   Giffen, Endicott, and Lambert, *Panic and Indifference,* 104–10.
5   On Anslinger's influence, see David Musto, *The American Disease: Origins of Narcotic Control,* 3rd ed. (Oxford and New York: Oxford University Press, 1999).
6   As I noted earlier in this book, the range of post-drug-prohibition research is much more diverse and nuanced than the studies of the creation of the drug laws. For a compelling discussion of the impact of criminalization and the cultures that it engendered, see especially Carstairs, *Jailed for Possession;* for an analysis of the legal and social impact of the laws, see Giffen, Endicott, and Lambert, *Panic and Indifference;* for an exploration of the challenges and failures of attempts to modify marijuana laws, see Marcel Martel, *Not This Time: Canadians, Public Policy, and the Marijuana Question, 1961–1975* (Toronto: University of Toronto Press, 2006); and for what remains a nuanced discussion of the legal ramifications of Canada's drug policy, see Neil Boyd, "The Origins of Canadian Narcotics Legislation: The Process of Criminalization in Historical Context,'" *Dalhousie Law Journal* 8 (1983): 102–36.
7   Two valuable works on the cultural construction of knowledge, especially as it relates to scientific discovery, are Bruno Latour, *Science in Action: How to Follow Scientists and Engineers through Society* (Cambridge, MA: Harvard University Press, 1987); and John V. Pickstone, *Ways of Knowing: A New History of Science, Technology and Medicine* (Chicago: University of Chicago Press, 2000). On addiction specifically, see Nancy D. Campbell, *Discovering Addiction: The Science and Politics of Substance Abuse Research* (Ann Arbor: University of Michigan Press, 2007); Caroline Jean Acker, *Creating the American Junkie: Addiction Research in the Classic Era of Narcotic Control* (Baltimore, MD: Johns Hopkins University Press, 2002); and Timothy Hickman, *The Secret Leprosy of Modern Days: Narcotic Addiction and the Cultural Crisis in the United States, 1870–1920* (Boston and Amherst: University of Massachusetts Press, 2007).

8 See Suzanne Morton, *At Odds: Gambling and Canadians, 1919–1969* (Toronto: University of Toronto Press, 2003), which does include pre-1919 issues; Craig Heron, *Booze: A Distilled History* (Toronto: Between the Lines, 2003); Dan Malleck, *Try to Control Yourself: The Regulation of Public Drinking in Post-Prohibition Ontario, 1927–44* (Vancouver: UBC Press, 2012); Carolyn Strange and Tina Loo, *Making Good: Law and Moral Regulation in Canada, 1867–1939* (Toronto: University of Toronto Press, 1997).

Bibliography

Abrams, M.H. *The Milk of Paradise: The Effects of Opium Visions on the Works of DeQuincey, Crabbe, Francis Thompson and Coleridge.* New York: Octagon, 1971.

Acker, Caroline Jean. *Creating the American Junkie: Addiction Research in the Classic Era of Narcotic Control.* Baltimore, MD: Johns Hopkins University Press, 2002.

–. "Portrait of an Addicted Family: Dynamics of Opiate Addiction in the Early Twentieth Century." In *Altering American Consciousness: The History of Alcohol and Drug Use in the United States, 1800–2000,* ed. Sarah W. Tracy and Caroline Jean Acker, 165–81. Boston and Amherst: University of Massachusetts Press, 2004.

Alborn, Timothy. *Regulated Lives: Life Assurance and British Society, 1840–1920.* Toronto: University of Toronto Press, 2009.

Allen, Richard. *The Social Passion: Religion and Social Reform in Canada, 1914–28.* Toronto: University of Toronto Press, 1971.

Anderson, Benedict. *Imagined Communities: Reflections on the Origin and Spread of Nationalism.* Rev. ed. London: Verso, 1991.

Anderson, Kay J. *Vancouver's Chinatown: Racial Discourse in Canada, 1875–1980.* Montreal and Kingston: McGill-Queen's University Press, 1991.

Austin, Alvyn. *Saving China: Canadian Missionaries in the Middle Kingdom.* Toronto: University of Toronto Press, 1986.

Baehre, Rainer. "The Ill-Regulated Mind: A Study in the Making of Psychiatry in Ontario, 1830–1921." PhD diss., York University, 1985.

Bartrip, Peter. "A 'Pennurth of Arsenic for Rat Poison': The Arsenic Act, 1851 and the Prevention of Secret Poisoning." *Medical History* 36, 1 (1992): 53–69. doi: 10.1017/S00257273 00054624.

Baskerville, Peter, and Eric W. Sager. *Unwilling Idlers: The Urban Unemployed and Their Families in Late Victorian Canada.* Toronto: University of Toronto Press, 1998.

Baumohl, Jim. "Inebriate Institutions in North America, 1840–1920." In *Drink in Canada: Historical Essays,* ed. Cheryl Krasnick Warsh, 92–114. Montreal and Kingston: McGill-Queen's University Press, 1993.

Beaumohl, Jim, and Robin Room. "Inebriety, Doctors, and the State: Alcoholism Treatment Institutions before 1940." In *Recent Developments in Alcoholism,* vol. 5, Series editor Marc Galanter, 135–74. New York and London: Plenum, 1987. doi: 10.1007/978-1-4899 -1684-6_6.

"Beginnings of International Drug Control." *UN Chronicle* 35, 1 (1998): 8–9.

Belisle, Donica. *Retail Nation: Department Stores and the Making of Modern Canada.* Vancouver: UBC Press, 2011.

Bello, David Anthony. *Opium and the Limits of Empire: Drug Prohibition in the Chinese Interior, 1729–1850.* Cambridge, MA, and London: Harvard University Press, 2005.

Berger, Carl. *Science, God and Nature in Victorian Canada.* Toronto: University of Toronto Press, 1983.

Berridge, Virginia. "Morality and Medical Science: Concepts of Narcotic Addiction in Britain, 1820–1926." *Annals of Science* 36, 1979): 67–85.

–. *Opium and the People: Opiate Use and Drug Control Policy in Nineteenth and Early Twentieth Century England.* Rev. ed. London: Free Association Books, 1999.

–. "Society for the Study of Addiction, 1884–1988." *British Journal of Addiction* 85 (August 1990): 983–1087. doi: 10.1111/j.1360-0443.1990.tb02605.x.

Blumberg, Leonard. "The American Association for the Study and Cure of Inebriety." *Alcoholism, Clinical and Experimental Research* 2 (July 1978): 235–40. doi: 10.1111/j.1530-0277.1978.tb05805.x.

Boyd, Neil. "The Origins of Canadian Narcotics Legislation: The Process of Criminalization in Historical Context." *Dalhousie Law Journal* (1983): 102–36.

Brieger, Gert H. "Classics and Character: Medicine and Gentility." *Bulletin of Medical History* 65, 1 (1991): 88–109.

Brown, Thomas E. "Dance of the Dialectic? Some Reflections (Polemic or Otherwise) on the Present State of Nineteenth Century Asylum Studies." *Canadian Bulletin of Medical History/Bulletin canadien d'histoire de la médecine* 11, 2 (1994): 267–95.

Burnham, John. *Bad Habits: Drinking, Smoking, Taking Drugs, Gambling, Sexual Misbehavior, and Swearing in American History.* New York: New York University Press, 1993.

Busby, Vicki. "'Doctors Can't Cure It': Traditional Medical Practices in Nineteenth-Century Upper Canada: Survival Strategies in a Developing Society, 1783–1920." MA thesis, Queen's University, 1993.

Bynum, W.F. "Darwin and the Doctors: Evolution, Diathesis, and Germs in 19th-Century Britain." *Gesnerus* 40, 1-2 (1983): 43–53.

Cameron, Jim. *Good for What Ails You: Self-Help Remedies from 19th Century Canada.* Burnstown, ON: General Store, 1995.

Campbell, Nancy D. *Discovering Addiction: The Science and Politics of Substance Abuse Research.* Ann Arbor: University of Michigan Press, 2007.

Campos, Isaac. *Home Grown: Marijuana and the Origins of Mexico's War on Drugs.* Chapel Hill: University of North Carolina Press, 2012. doi:10.5149/9780807882689_campos.

Carstairs, Catherine. *Jailed for Possession: Illegal Drug Use, Regulation, and Power in Canada, 1920–1961.* Toronto: University of Toronto Press, 2006.

–. "The Racist Roots of Canada's Drug Laws." *The Beaver* 84, 1 (February-March 2004): 11–12.

Cherrington, E.H. *Standard Encyclopedia of the Alcohol Problem.* Westerville, OH: American Issue Publishing, 1930.

Clark, R.J. "Professional Aspirations and the Limits of Occupational Autonomy: The Case of Pharmacy in Nineteenth-Century Ontario." *Canadian Bulletin of Medical History/Bulletin canadien d'histoire de la médecine* 8, 1 (1991): 43–63.

Clarke, Michael J. "'Morbid Introspection,' Unsoundness of Mind, and British Psychological Medicine, c.1830–c.1900." In *Anatomy of Madness*, vol. 3, *The Asylum and Its Psychiatry*, ed. W.F. Bynum, Roy Porter, and Michael Shepherd, 71–101. London: Routledge, 1988.

Collin, Johanne. "Genèse d'une profession: Les pharmaciens au Québec au XIXe siècle." *Canadian Bulletin of Medical History/Bulletin canadien d'histoire de la médecine* 14, 2 (1997): 253–57.

Collin, Johanne, and Denis Béliveau. *Histoire de la Pharmacie au Québec.* Montreal: Musée de la pharmacie du Québec, 1994.

Collins, Wilkie. *The Moonstone.* London: Chatto, 1907.

Comack, A. Elizabeth. "The Origins of Canadian Drug Legislation: Labelling versus Class Analysis." In *The New Criminologies in Canada: State, Crime and Control,* ed. Thomas Fleming, 65–86. Toronto: Oxford University Press, 1985.

Connor, J.T.H. "Minority Medicine in Ontario, 1795–1903: A Study of Medical Pluralism and Its Decline." PhD diss., University of Waterloo, 1989.

Conrad, Lawrence I., Michael Neve, Vivian Nutton, Roy Porter, and Andrew Wear. *The Western Medical Tradition: 800 BC to AD 1800*. Cambridge, UK: Cambridge University Press, 1995.

Cook, Ramsay. *The Regenerators: Social Criticism in Late Victorian English Canada*. Toronto: University of Toronto Press, 1985.

Cook, Sharon Ann. *"Through Sunshine and Shadow": The Woman's Christian Temperance Union, Evangelicalism and Reform in Ontario, 1874–1930*. Montreal and Kingston: McGill-Queen's University Press, 1995.

Corrigan, Philip, and Derek Sayer. *The Great Arch: English State Formation as a Cultural Revolution*. Oxford: Basil Blackwell, 1985.

Courtwright, David. *Dark Paradise: A History of Opiate Addiction in America*. Cambridge, MA, and London: Harvard University Press, 1982.

–. "Mr. ATOD's Wild Ride: What Do Alcohol, Tobacco, and Other Drugs Have in Common?" *Social History of Alcohol and Drugs: An Interdisciplinary Journal* 20, 1 (2005): 105–24.

Cowen, David L. "George Bacon Wood." In *American National Biography*. Online ed. http://www.anb.org/articles/12/12-00997.html.

Cowen, David L., and William Helfand. *Pharmacy: An Illustrated History*. New York: Henry Abrams, 1990.

Crellin, John K. *Home Medicine: The Newfoundland Experience*. Montreal and Kingston: McGill-Queen's University Press, 1994.

Davidoff, Leonore, and Catherine Hall. *Family Fortunes: Men and Women of the English Middle Class, 1780–1850*. London: Routledge, 1992.

Dean, Mitchell. *Governmentality: Power and Rule in Modern Society*. London: Sage, 1999.

DeLottinville, Peter. "Joe Beef of Montreal: Working-Class Culture and the Tavern, 1869–1889." *Labour/Le Travail* 8–9 (1981–82): 9–40. doi:10.2307/25140071.

Dickens, Charles. *The Mystery of Edwin Drood*. Oxford: Clarendon, 1972.

Digby, Anne. *Madness, Morality and Medicine: A Study of the York Retreat, 1876–1914*. Cambridge, UK: Cambridge University Press, 1985.

Dikötter, Frank, Lars Laamann, and Zhou Xun. "China, British Imperialism, and the Myth of the 'Opium Plague.'" In *Drugs and Empires: Essays in Modern Imperialism and Intoxication, c. 1500–1930*, ed. James H. Mills and Patricia Barton, 19–38. New York and Basingstoke, UK: Palgrave Macmillan, 2007.

–. *Narcotic Culture: A History of Drugs in China*. Chicago: University of Chicago Press, 2004.

Driver, Elizabeth. *Culinary Landmarks: A Bibliography of Canadian Cookbooks, 1825–1949*. Toronto: University of Toronto Press, 2008.

Duffin, Jacalyn. *History of Medicine: A Scandalously Short Introduction*. Toronto: University of Toronto Press, 1999.

–. *Langstaff: A Nineteenth Century Medical Life*. Toronto: University of Toronto Press, 1993.

–. *To See with a Better Eye: A Life of R.T.H. Laennec*. (Princeton: Princeton University Press, 1998).

–. "'In View of the Body of Job Broom': A Glimpse of the Medical Knowledge and Practice of John Rolph." *Canadian Bulletin of Medical History/Bulletin canadien d'histoire de la médecine* 7, 1 (1990): 9–30.

Edginton, Barry, "The Well-Ordered Body: The Quest for Sanity through Nineteenth-Century Asylum Architecture." *Canadian Bulletin of Medical History/Bulletin canadien d'histoire de la médecine* 11, 2 (1994): 375–86.

Estes, J. Worth. *Dictionary of Protopharmacology: Therapeutic Practices, 1700–1850*. Canton, MA: Science History Publications, 1990.

Fay, Peter Ward. *The Opium War, 1840–1842: Barbarians in the Celestial Empire in the Early Part of the Nineteenth Century and the War by Which They Forced Her Gates Ajar*. New ed. Chapel Hill: University of North Carolina Press, 1997.

Ferentzy, Peter. "From Sin to Disease: Differences and Similarities between Past and Current Conceptions of Chronic Drunkenness." *Contemporary Drug Problems* 28, 3 (2001): 362–90.

Foxcroft, Louise. *The Making of Addiction: The "Use and Abuse" of Opium in Nineteenth-Century Britain*. Aldershot, UK: Ashgate, 2007.

Gagan, Rosemary, *A Sensitive Independence: Canadian Methodist Women Missionaries in Canada and the Orient, 1881–1925*. Ottawa: Carleton University Press, 1992.

Gauvreau, Michael. *The Evangelical Century: College and Creed in English Canada from the Great Revival to the Great Depression*. Montreal and Kingston: McGill-Queen's University Press, 1991.

Gidney, R.D., and W.P.J. Millar. *Professional Gentlemen: The Professions in Nineteenth-Century Ontario*. Toronto: University of Toronto Press, 1994.

Giffen, P.J., Shirley Endicott, and Sylvia Lambert. *Panic and Indifference: The Politics of Canada's Drug Laws*. Ottawa: Canadian Centre on Substance Abuse, 1991.

Green, Melvyn. "A History of Canadian Narcotics Control: The Formative Years." *University of Toronto Faculty of Law Review* 42 (1979): 42–79.

Greene, Jeremy A., and Elizabeth Siegel Watkins., eds. *Prescribed: Writing, Filling, Using, and Abusing the Prescription in Modern America*. Baltimore, MD: Johns Hopkins University Press, 2012.

Grob, Gerald, ed. *Origins of Medical Attitudes toward Drug Addiction in America*. New York: Arno, 1981.

Grzybowski, Andrzej, and Krzysztof Pietrzak. "Pioneers in Neurology: Napoleon Cybulski (1854-1919)." *Journal of Neurology* 260 (February 2013): 695–96. doi: 10.1007/s00415 -012-6658-4.

Guest, R.G. "The Development of Patent Medicine Legislation." *Applied Therapeutics* 8, 9 (September 1966): 786–89.

Haley, Bruce. *The Healthy Body and Victorian Culture*. Cambridge, MA: Harvard University Press, 1979.

Haller, John S. Jr. "Hypodermic Medication: Early History." *New York State Journal of Medicine* 81, 11 (October 1981): 1671–79.

Hamowy, Ronald. *Canadian Medicine: A Study of Restricted Entry*. Toronto: Fraser Institute, 1984.

Hanes, W. Travis, III, and Frank Sanello. *Opium Wars: The Addiction of One Empire and the Corruption of Another*. Naperville, IL: Sourcebooks, 2002.

Harding, Geoffrey. "Constructing Addiction as a Moral Failing." *Sociology of Health and Illness* 8 (1986): 76–85.

–. *Opiate Addiction, Morality and Medicine: From Moral Illness to Pathological Disease*. Houndmills, Basingstoke, Hampshire, UK: Macmillan, 1988.

Haskell, Thomas. "Professionalism versus Capitalism: R.H. Tawney, Emile Durkheim, and C.S. Peirce on the Disinterestedness of Professional Communities." In *The Authority of Experts: Studies in History and Theory*, ed. Thomas Haskell, 180–225. Bloomington: Indiana University Press, 1984.

Hayter, Alethea. *Opium and the Romantic Imagination: Addiction and Creativity in DeQuincey, Coleridge, Baudelaire and Others*. 2nd ed. New York: Crucible, 1988.

Heron, Craig. *Booze: A Distilled History*. Toronto: Between the Lines, 2003.

Hickman, Timothy. "The Double Meaning of Addiction: Habitual Narcotic Use and the Logic of Professionalizing Medical Authority in the United States, 1900–1920." In *Altering American Consciousness: The History of Alcohol and Drug Use in the United States, 1800–2000*, ed. Sarah W. Tracy and Caroline Jean Acker, 182–202. Boston and Amherst: University of Massachusetts Press, 2004.

–. "Drugs and Race in American Culture: Orientalism in the Turn-of-the-Century Discourse of Narcotic Addiction." *American Studies* 41, 1 (Spring 2000): 71–91.

–. *The Secret Leprosy of Modern Days: Narcotic Addiction and the Cultural Crisis in the United States, 1870–1920*. Boston and Amherst: University of Massachusetts Press, 2007.

Hollinger, David A. "Inquiry and Uplift: Late Nineteenth-Century American Academics and the Moral Efficacy of Scientific Practice." In *The Authority of Experts: Studies in History and Theory*, ed. Thomas Haskell, 142–56. Bloomington: Indiana University Press, 1984.

Holloway, S.W.F. "The Apothecaries' Act 1815: A Reinterpretation." *Medical History* 10, 2 (1966): 107–29. doi: 10.1017/S0025727300010917.

–. "The Apothecaries' Act 1815: A Reinterpretation – Part 2," *Medical History* 10 (1966): 221–36.

–. "The Orthodox Fringe: The Origins of the Pharmaceutical Society of Great Britain." In *Medical Fringe and Medical Orthodoxy, 1750–1850,* ed. W.F. Bynum and Roy Porter, 129–57. London: Croom Helm, 1987.

Jackson, Stanley William. *The First Pharmacy Act of Ontario.* Toronto: Ontario College of Pharmacy, 1967.

Jaffe, A. "Reform in American Medical Science: The Inebriety Movement and the Origins of the Psychological Disease Theory of Addiction, 1870–1920." *British Journal of Addiction* 73, 2 (1978): 139–47. doi: 10.1111/j.1360-0443.1978.tb00134.x.

Jewson, N.D. "The Disappearance of the Sick-Man from Medical Cosmology, 1770–1870." *Sociology* 10, 2 (1976): 225–44.

Jones, A.W. "Early Drug Discovery and the Rise of Pharmaceutical Chemistry." *Drug Test Analysis* 3, 6 (2011): 337–44. doi: 10.1002/dta.301.

Jones, Norman Howard. "A Critical Study of the Origins and Early Development of Hypodermic Medication." *Journal of the History of Medicine* 2, 2 (1947): 201–42.

Kneale, James, and Shaun French. "The Relations of Inebriety to Insurance: Geographies of Medicine, Insurance and Alcohol in Britain, 1840–1911." In *Intoxication and Society: Problematic Pleasures of Drugs and Alcohol,* ed. Jonathan Herring, Ciaran Regan, Darin Weinberg, and Phil Withington, 87–109. London: Palgrave Macmillan, 2013.

Latour, Bruno. *Science in Action: How to Follow Scientists and Engineers through Society.* Cambridge, MA: Harvard University Press, 1987.

Levine, Harry G. "The Discovery of Addiction: Changing Conceptions of Habitual Drunkenness in America." *Journal of Studies on Alcohol* 39, 1 (1978): 143–74.

Lodwick, Kathleen L. *Crusaders against Opium: Protestant Missionaries in China, 1874–1917.* Lexington: University of Kentucky Press, 1995.

Lomax, Elizabeth. "The Uses and Abuses of Opiates in Nineteenth-Century England." *Bulletin of the History of Medicine* 47, 2 (1973): 167–76.

Loo, Tina, and Carolyn Strange. *Making Good: Law and Moral Regulation in Canada, 1867–1939.* Toronto: University of Toronto Press, 1997.

Lovell, Julia. *The Opium War.* London: Picador, 2011.

Malleck, Dan. "American Association for the Study and Cure of Inebriety." In *Alcohol and Temperance in Modern History: A Global Encyclopedia,* vol. 1, ed. Jack S. Blocker, David M. Fahey, and Ian R. Tyrrell, 38–39. Santa Barbara CA: ABC Clio, 2003.

–. "Keeley, Leslie Enraught." In *American National Biography.* Online ed. http://www.anb.org/articles/12/12-00473.html.

–. "Priorities of Development in Four Local Woman's Christian Temperance Unions in Ontario, 1877–1895." In *The Changing Face of Drink,* ed. Jack Blocker and Cheryl Krasnick Warsh, 189–208. Toronto: Histoire Sociale/Social History, 1997.

–. "Pure Food and Professional Druggists: Food and Drug Laws in Canada, 1870s–1908." *Pharmacy in History* 48, 3 (2006): 103–15.

–. "Refining Poison, Defining Power: Medical Authority and the Creation of Canadian Drug Prohibition Laws, 1800–1908." PhD diss., Queen's University, 1999.

–. *Try to Control Yourself: The Regulation of Public Drinking in Post-Prohibition Ontario, 1927–44.* Vancouver: UBC Press, 2012.

Manderson, Desmond. *From Mr. Sin to Mr. Big: A History of Australian Drug Laws.* Melbourne: Oxford University Press, 1993.

Marshall, David B. *Secularizing the Faith: Canadian Protestant Clergy and the Crisis of Belief, 1850–1940.* Toronto: University of Toronto Press, 1992.

Martel, Marcel. *Not This Time: Canadians, Public Policy, and the Marijuana Question, 1961–1975.* Toronto: University of Toronto Press, 2006.

McClary, Andrew. "The WCTU Discovers Science: The Women's [sic] Christian Temperance Union, Plus Teachers, Doctors and Scientific Temperance." *Michigan History* 68, 1 (January 1984): 16–23.

McCulloch, Michael. "'Dr. Tumblety, the Indian Herb Doctor': Politics, Professionalism and Abortion in Mid-Nineteenth-Century Montreal." *Canadian Bulletin of Medical History/ Bulletin canadien d'histoire de la médecine* 10, 1 (1993): 49–66.

McGinnis, Janice Dickin. "*Carlill v Carbolic Smoke Ball Company:* Influenza, Quackery and the Unilateral Contract." *Canadian Bulletin of Medical History/Bulletin canadien d'histoire de la médecine* 5, 1 (1988): 121–41.

McKillop, A.B. *A Disciplined Intelligence: Critical Inquiry and Canadian Thought in the Victoria Era.* Kingston and Montreal: McGill-Queen's University Press, 1979.

McLaren, Angus. *Our Own Master Race: Eugenics in Canada, 1885–1945.* Toronto: McClelland and Stewart, 1990.

Mills, James. "Morality, Society and the Science of Intoxication: A Response to David Courtwright's 'Mr ATOD's Wild Ride: What Do Alcohol, Tobacco, and Other Drugs Have in Common?'" *Social History of Alcohol and Drugs: An Interdisciplinary Journal* 20, 1 (2005): 133–37.

Mitchinson, Wendy. *The Nature of Their Bodies: Women and Their Doctors in Victorian Canada.* Toronto: University of Toronto Press, 1991.

–. "Reasons for Committal to a Mid-Nineteenth-Century Ontario Insane Asylum: The Case of Toronto." In *Essays in the History of Canadian Medicine,* ed. Wendy Mitchinson and Janice Dickin McGinnis, 88–109. Toronto: McClelland and Stewart, 1988.

–. "The Toronto and Gladesville Asylums: Humane Alternatives for the Insane in Canada and Australia?" *Bulletin of the History of Medicine* 63, 1 (1989): 52–72.

–. "The WCTU: 'For God and Home and Native Land' – A Study in Nineteenth-Century Feminism." In *A Not Unreasonable Claim: Women and Reform in Canada, 1880s–1920s,* ed. Linda Kealey, 151–67. Toronto: Women's Press, 1979.

Moran, James E. *Committed to the State Asylum: Insanity and Society in Nineteenth-Century Quebec and Ontario.* Montreal and Kingston: McGill-Queen's University Press, 2000.

Morgan, H. Wayne. *Drugs in America: A Social History, 1800–1980.* Syracuse, NY: Syracuse University Press, 1981.

–. "'No, Thank You, I've Been to Dwight': Reflections on the Keeley Cure for Alcoholism." *Illinois Historical Journal* 82, 3 (Autumn 1989): 147–66.

Morton, Suzanne. *At Odds: Gambling and Canadians, 1919–1969.* Toronto: University of Toronto Press, 2003.

Murray, Glenn F. "Cocaine Use in the Era of Social Reform: The Natural History of a Social Problem in Canada, 1880–1911." *Canadian Journal of Law and Society* 2 (1987): 29–43. doi: 10.1017/S0829320100001149.

–. "The Road to Regulation: Patent Medicines in Canada in Historical Perspective." In *Illicit Drugs in Canada: A Risky Business,* ed. Judith C. Blackwell and Patricia G. Erikson, 72–87. Toronto: Nelson Canada, 1988.

Musto, David. *The American Disease: Origins of Narcotic Control.* 3rd ed. Oxford and New York: Oxford University Press, 1999.

Nicholls, James. *The Politics of Alcohol: A History of the Drink Question in England.* Manchester, UK: Manchester University Press, 2009. doi: 10.7228/manchester/9780719077050.001. 0001.

–. "Vinum Britannicum: The 'Drink Question' in Early Modern England." *Social History of Alcohol and Drugs* 22, 2 (Spring 2008): 190–208.

Noel, Jan. *Canada Dry: Temperance Crusades before Confederation.* Toronto: University of Toronto Press, 1995.

Padwa, Howard. *Social Poison: The Culture and Politics of Opiate Control in Britain and France, 1821–1926.* Baltimore, MD: Johns Hopkins University Press, 2012.

Parascandola, John. *The Development of American Pharmacology: John J. Abel and the Shaping of a Discipline.* Baltimore, MD, and London: Johns Hopkins University Press, 1992.

–. "Patent Medicines in Nineteenth-Century America." *Caduceus* 1 (Spring 1985): 1–41.

Parssinen, Terry. *Secret Passions, Secret Remedies: Narcotic Drugs in British Society, 1820–1930.* Manchester, UK: Manchester University Press, 1983.

Parssinen, Terry, and Karen Kerner. "The Development of the Disease Model of Drug Addiction in Britain, 1870-1926." *Medical History* 24, 3 (1980): 275–96. doi: 10.1017/S0025727300040321.

Pauly, Philip J. "The Struggle for Ignorance about Alcohol: American Physiologists, Wilbur Olin Atwater, and The Woman's Christian Temperance Union." *Bulletin of the History of Science* 64, 3 (1990): 366–92.

Peters, Dolores. "British Medical Response to Opiate Addiction in the Nineteenth Century." *Journal of the History of Medicine* 36, 4 (1981): 455–88.

Peterson, Robert C. "History of Cocaine." In *Cocaine: 1977*, ed. R.C. Peterson and R.C. Stillman, 17–34. NIDA Research Monograph No. 13, May 1977.

Pickstone, John V. *Ways of Knowing: A New History of Science, Technology and Medicine.* Chicago: University of Chicago Press, 2000.

Pon, Mona-Margaret. "Ng Mon Hing." In *Dictionary of Canadian Biography,* vol. 15. Online ed. http://www.biographi.ca/en/bio/ng_mon_hing_15E.html.

Porter, Andrew. *Religion versus Empire? British Protestant Missionaries and Overseas Expansion, 1700–1914.* Manchester, UK: Manchester University Press, 2004.

Porter, Roy. "The Drinking Man's Disease: The 'Pre-History' of Alcoholism in Georgian Britain." *British Journal of Addiction* 80, 4 (1985): 385–96. doi: 10.1111/j.1360-0443.1985.tb03010.x.

–. "The Eighteenth Century." In *The Western Medical Tradition: 800 BC to AD 1800,* by Lawrence I. Conrad, Michael Neve, Vivian Nutton, Roy Porter, and Andrew Wear, 371–476. Cambridge, UK: Cambridge University Press, 1995.

Porter, Roy, and Dorothy Porter. "The Rise of the English Drugs Industry: The Role of Thomas Corbyn." *Medical History* 33, 3 (1989): 277–95. doi: 10.1017/S0025727300049565.

Pugsley, L.I. "The Administration and Development of Federal Statutes on Food and Drug Legislation." *Medical Services Journal, Canada* 23 (March 1967): 387–449.

Reaume, Geoffrey. "999 Queen Street West: Portrait of Life at the Toronto Hospital for the Insane, 1870–1940." PhD diss., University of Toronto, 1997.

Roberts, Barbara. *From Whence They Came: Deportation from Canada, 1900–1935.* Ottawa: University of Ottawa Press, 1988.

Roberts, Julia. *In Mixed Company: Taverns and Public Life in Upper Canada.* Vancouver: UBC Press, 2009.

Robertson, Marion. *Old Settlers' Remedies.* Barrington, NS: Cape Sable Historical Society, 1960.

Roediger, David R. *The Wages of Whiteness: Race and the Making of the American Working Class.* London and New York: Verso, 1999.

Rosenberg, Charles E. "Body and Mind in Nineteenth Century Medicine: Some Clinical Origins of the Neurosis Construct." *Bulletin of the History of Medicine* 63, 2(1989): 185–97.

–. *Explaining Epidemics and Other Studies in the History of Medicine.* Cambridge, UK: Cambridge University Press, 1992. doi: 10.1017/CBO9780511666865.

–. "Introduction." In *The Structure of American Medical Practice,* by George Rosen, ed. Charles E. Rosenberg, 7–10. Philadelphia: University of Pennsylvania Press, 1983.

–. "The Therapeutic Revolution: Medicine, Meaning and Social Change in Nineteenth Century America." In *The Therapeutic Revolution: Essays in the Social History of American Medicine,* ed. Morris Vogel and Charles Rosenberg, 485–506. Philadelphia: University of Pennsylvania Press, 1979.

Rousseau, Guildo. ""La Santé par correspondance: Un mode de mise en marché des médicament brevetés au debut du siècle." *Histoire Sociale/Social History* 28, 55 (1995): 1–25.

Roy, Patricia A. *A White Man's Province: British Columbia Politicians and Chinese and Japanese Immigrants, 1858–1914.* Vancouver: UBC Press, 1989.

Rutherford, Paul. *A Victorian Authority: The Daily Press in Late Nineteenth-Century Canada.* Toronto: University of Toronto Press, 1982.

Schivelbusch, Wolfgang. *Tastes of Paradise: A Social History of Spices, Stimulants, and Intoxicants.* Trans. David Jacobson. New York: Pantheon, 1992.

Schneck, J.M. "Cocaine Addiction and Dr. William S. Halsted." Letter to the editor. *Journal of Clinical Psychiatry* 49, 12 (December 1988): 503–4.

–. "Cocaine Addiction and Dr. William S. Halsted." *Journal of Clinical Psychiatry* 50, 9 (September 1989): 358.

Scull, Andrew. *The Most Solitary of Afflictions: Madness and Society in Britain, 1700–1900.* New Haven, CT, and London: Yale University Press, 1993.

Shaffer, Howard J. "The Discovery of Addiction: Levine and the Philosophical Foundations of Drug Abuse Treatment." *Journal of Substance Abuse Treatment* 2, 1 (1985): 41–57. doi: 10.1016/0740-5472(85)90021-2.

Sheehan, Nancy M. "The WCTU on the Prairies, 1886–1930: An Alberta-Saskatchewan Comparison." *Prairie Forum* 6, 1 (1981): 17–33.

Shortt, S.E.D. "'Before the Age of Miracles': The Rise, Fall, and Rebirth of General Practice in Canada, 1890–1940." In *Health Disease and Medicine: Essays in Canadian History,* ed. Charles Roland, 123–52. Toronto: Hannah Institute for the History of Medicine, 1984.

–. "Physicians, Science and Status: Issues in the Professionalization of Anglo-American Medicine in the Nineteenth Century." *Medical History* 27, 1 (1983): 51–68. doi: 10.1017/S0025727300042265.

–. *Victorian Lunacy: Richard M. Bucke and the Practice of Late Nineteenth-Century Psychiatry.* Cambridge, UK: Cambridge University Press, 1986.

Siegel, Sheperd. "Wilkie Collins: Victorian Novelist as Psychopharmacologist." *Journal of the History of Medicine and Allied Sciences* 38, 2 (April 1983): 161–75. doi: 10.1093/jhmas/38.2.161.

Small, Shirley. "Canadian Narcotics Legislation, 1908–1923: A Conflict Model Interpretation." *Canadian Review of Sociology and Anthropology* 6, 1 (1968): 36–46.

Smart, Reginald G. *Forbidden Highs: The Nature, Treatment, and Prevention of Illicit Drug Abuse.* Toronto: Addiction Research Foundation, 1983.

Solomon, R., and T. Madison. "The Evolution of Non-Medical Opiate Use in Canada, Part 1, 1870–1929." *Drug Forum* 5, 3 (1976): 239–49.

Sonnedecker, Glenn, ed. *Kremers and Urdang's History of Pharmacy.* 4th ed. Madison, WI: American Institute of the History of Pharmacy, 1986.

Spode, Hasso. "Transubstantiations of the Mystery: Two Remarks on the Shifts in the Knowledge about Addiction." *Social History of Alcohol and Drugs: An Interdisciplinary Journal* 20, 1 (Fall 2005): 125–28.

Starr, Paul. *The Social Transformation of American Medicine: The Rise of a Sovereign Profession and the Making of a Vast Industry.* New York: Basic Books, 1984.

Stieb, Ernest. "Edward Buckingham Shuttleworth, 1842–1934." *Pharmacy in History* 12, 3 (1970): 91–116.

–. "Elliot, Robert Watt." In *Dictionary of Canadian Biography,* vol. 13. Online ed. http://www.biographi.ca/en/bio/elliot_robert_watt_13E.html.

Strange, Carolyn. *Toronto's Girl Problem: The Perils and Pleasures of the City.* Toronto: University of Toronto Press, 1995.

Strange, Carolyn, and Tina Loo. *Making Good: Law and Moral Regulation in Canada, 1867–1939.* Toronto: University of Toronto Press, 1997.

Swann, John P. "Horatio C. Wood." In *American National Biography.* Online ed. http://www.anb.org/articles/12/12-00998.html.

Swatos, William H., Jr. "Opiate Addiction in the Late Nineteenth Century: A Study of the Social Problem, Using Medical Journals of the Period." *International Journal of the Addictions* 7, 4 (1972): 739–53.

Sweet, Victoria. "Hildegard of Bingen and the Greening of Medieval Medicine." *Bulletin of the History of Medicine* 73, 3 (1999): 381–403. doi: 10.1353/bhm.1999.0140.

Tannenbaum, Rebecca J. "Earnestness, Temperance, Industry: The Definitions and Uses of Professional Character among Nineteenth-Century American Physicians." *Journal of the History of Medicine and Allied Sciences* 49, 2 (April 1994): 251–83. doi: 10.1093/jhmas/49.2.251.

Taylor, K.W., and H. Michell. *Statistical Contributions to Canadian Economic History.* Vol. 2. Toronto: Macmillan, 1931.

Tomes, Nancy. *A Generous Confidence: Thomas Story Kirkbride and the Art of Asylum-Keeping, 1840–1883.* Cambridge, UK: Cambridge University Press, 1984.

Trasov, G.E. "History of the Opium and Narcotic Drug Legislation in Canada." *Criminal Law Quarterly* 4 (1962): 274–82.

Tyrrell, Ian. "Alcohol, Tobacco, and Other Drugs: A Response to David Courtwright." *Social History of Alcohol and Drugs: An Interdisciplinary Journal* 20, 1 (Fall 2005): 129–32.

–. *Woman's World, Woman's Empire: The Woman's Christian Temperance Union in International Perspective, 1880–1930*. Chapel Hill: University of North Carolina Press, 1991.

Valenza, Robin. *Literature, Language, and the Rise of the Intellectual Disciplines in Britain, 1680–1820*. Cambridge, UK: Cambridge University Press, 2009. doi: 10.1017/CBO 9780511635601.

Valverde, Mariana. *The Age of Light, Soap and Water: Moral Reform in English Canada, 1885–1925*. Toronto: McClelland and Stewart, 1991.

–. "'Slavery from Within': The Invention of Alcoholism and the Question of Free Will." *Social History* 22, 3 (Autumn 1997): 251–68. doi: 10.1080/03071029708568008.

Vaupel, E. "Arthur Eichengrün: Tribute to a Forgotten Chemist, Entrepreneur, and German Jew." *Angewandte Chemie International Edition* 44, 22 (2005): 3344–55. doi: 10.1002/anie. 200462959.

Ward, W. Peter. *White Canada Forever: Popular Attitudes and Public Policy toward Orientals in British Columbia*. 2nd ed. Montreal and Kingston: McGill-Queen's University Press, 1978.

Warner, Jessica. "'Resolv'd to Drink No More': Addiction as a Preindustrial Concept." *Journal of Studies on Alcohol* 55, 6 (1994): 685–91.

Warner, John Harley. *The Therapeutic Perspective: Medical Practice, Knowledge, and Identity in America, 1820–1885*. Cambridge, MA: Harvard University Press, 1986.

Warsh, Cheryl Krasnick. "Adventures in Maritime Quackery: The Leslie E. Keeley Gold Cure Institute of Fredericton, N.B." *Acadiensis* 17, 2 (Spring 1988): 109–30.

–. *Moments of Unreason: The Practice of Psychiatry at the Homewood Retreat, 1883–1923*. Montreal and Kingston: McGill-Queen's University Press, 1989.

Weiner, Dora. *The Citizen-Patient in Revolutionary and Imperial Paris*. Baltimore, MD: Johns Hopkins University Press, 2001.

Wilde, Oscar. *The Picture of Dorian Gray*. London: Oxford University Press, 1974.

Willer, Barry, and Gary Miller. "Classification, Cause and Symptoms of Mental Illness." *Canadian Psychiatric Association Journal* 22, 5 (August 1977): 231–35.

–. "Prognosis and Outcome of Mental Illness, 1890–1900, in Ontario." *Canadian Psychiatric Association Journal* 22, 5 (1977): 235–38.

Wright, A.J. "More on Cocaine Addiction and Dr. William S. Halsted." Letter to the editor. *Journal of Clinical Psychiatry* 50, 9 (September 1988): 358.

Young, James Harvey. *The Toadstool Millionaires: A Social History of Patent Medicines in America before Federal Regulation*. Princeton, NJ: Princeton University Press, 1961.

Zimmerman, J. "When the Doctors Disagree: Scientific Temperance and Scientific Authority, 1891–1906." *Journal of the History of Medicine and Allied Sciences* 48, 2 (1993): 171–97. doi: 10.1093/jhmas/48.2.171.

Index

Note: "(f)" following a page number indicates a figure; "(t)" following a page number indicates a table

Acadian Recorder, 203
Acker, David, 4
Adams, Samuel Hopkins, 169, 194-95, 200, 208
addiction: to alcohol, 11, 45, 111-19, 139, 145, 147(t), 272n36; and anti-drug panic, 189-93; and behavioural changes, 148-49, 155-58; causation, 120, 122-30, 138, 186-89, 266n62, 268n93; to cocaine, 189-93; as deviance, 158-62; effect on medical treatment, 48-49; and family upheaval, 159-62, 273n78; iatrogenic, 134-35, 148, 158, 187-88, 216; as a medical condition, 154-55; and mental illness, 138, 139, 140-55, 147(t), 157, 162; and outsider status, 135-36; perceptions of, 138-40; poverty and, 87; predisposition to, 116, 124-27; reification of, 135; scientific investigations into, 121-22, 124; of social elites, 155-58, 158-62; treatment of, 130-32, 144-45, 162-63, 163-64; of women, 4, 152-53, 159, 161-62, 216, 252n10. *See also* addiction, to opium/opiates
addiction, to opium/opiates: *vs.* addiction to alcohol, 111-19; criminalization of, 219; effects of, 137-38, 145, 216-17, 221, 222; hypodermic syringe and, 51, 117; iatrogenic, 4, 39, 47-49, 108, 116, 220; and laudanum, 46; and mental illness, 139-40, 145-50, 147(t), 150-55; morphinism, 149; perceptions of, 47-49, 114-16, 117, 119, 121, 137-40; and possibility of reform, 190; and secrecy, 144, 271n18; self-medication and, 18; of social elites, 125; and social problems, 139; as threat

to nation, 108; treatment for, 49, 130-31, 163-64; of women, 101,103-4,105, 232
addicts, 144-45, 271n18; database of, 246
adrenaline, 26-27
Adulteration Act (1884), 204, 207
Aikins, William, 43-44, 45, 46
Alberta Pharmacy Act (1892,1910), 61(t); poison schedule, 193
alcohol: campaigns against, 228-29 (*see also* missionaries; Woman's Christian Temperance Union [WCTU]); as cause of mental illness, 147(t); in Chase's remedies, 25-26, 26(t); and drug abuse, 114; *vs.* narcotics, 111; in patent medicines, 186, 200-1; regulated, 195, 210
alcoholism. *See* addiction, to alcohol
alienists. *See* physicians, asylum
Allbutt, Clifford, 117, 130
American Association for the Cure of Inebriety (AACI). *See* American Association for the Study and Cure of Inebriety (AASCI)
American Association for the Study and Cure of Inebriety (AASCI), 114, 119, 121-23, 126, 133, 266n60, 266n62, 268n93, 268n95
American Temperance Association, 121
Anderson, Benedict, 8
Anglican Synods, 223, 227
Anslinger, Harry J., 246
Anstie, Francis, 120
anti-Chinese sentiment: and Chinese-exclusion legislation, 8-9, 96-97, 99; opium and, 84-85, 96, 231-32 (*see also*

Printed and bound in Canada by Friesens

Set in Stone by Artegraphica Design Co. Ltd.

Copy editor: Robert Lewis

Proofreader and indexer: Dianne Tiefensee